Robert E. Guy

The Synods in English

Being the Text of the four Synods of Westminster

Robert E. Guy

The Synods in English
Being the Text of the four Synods of Westminster

ISBN/EAN: 9783337188955

Printed in Europe, USA, Canada, Australia, Japan

Cover: Foto ©ninafisch / pixelio.de

More available books at **www.hansebooks.com**

THE
SYNODS IN ENGLISH:

BEING THE TEXT

OF THE

FOUR SYNODS OF WESTMINSTER,

TRANSLATED INTO ENGLISH,

AND ARRANGED UNDER HEADINGS; WITH NUMEROUS
DOCUMENTS AND REFERENCES.

BY THE

REV. ROBERT ~~HEIGHTWSER~~.

THE RIGHT REVEREND BISHOP HEDLEY, O.S.B.

WITH A PREFACE BY THE SAME.

·

STRATFORD-ON-AVON: ST. GREGORY'S PRESS, WARWICK ROAD.

MDCCCLXXXVI.

CONTENTS.

		PAGE
I.	Preliminary Documents	1
II	Provincial Synods	12
III.	Diocesan Synods	38
IV.	Bishops	41
V.	Chapters, Canons, etc.	98
VI.	Priests	130
VII.	Singers and Ecclesiastical Music	185
VIII.	Regulars	196
IX.	Colleges and Seminaries	218
X.	The Laity	243
XI.	The Four Synodal Addresses	290
XII.	Appendix	309

PREFACE.

The name of this book speaks for itself. The translator's purpose has been not merely to give, in English, the complete text of the Four Synods of Westminster, but to make that text more profitable to the clergy by arranging it under ten or twelve distinctive headings, which cover the whole of the matter of the Decrees.

Every mission-house in the country ought to be furnished with the original text of the Provincial Synods, for therein is contained that most authentic and binding Church Law, which, next to the Canon Law and the Pontifical Constitutions, is the chief rule of the English clergy. But the present version has been undertaken in the hope and belief that it will make the original, if not better understood, at least more accessible and more impressive. To read a text in a translation is like seeing an object in a mirror: we have a different medium, and new relations to surrounding objects. Thus, a translation brings out shades of meaning hitherto latent; it awakens associations of imagination before unstirred; it places antique phrases side by side with modern modes of speech; and it brightens and sharpens the thought and idea by taking it out of a dead language and putting it into a living one.

It can hardly be denied that the text of our English Synods does not receive from the clergy that amount of study and attention which it ought to have. Bishops know well, from their experience of visitations, that even the practical and disciplinary portions of the Decrees are too frequently unknown; whilst, as regards the admirable and edifying paragraphs of spiritual admonition scattered up and down the various chapters, it is not too much to say that few ever recur to them at all. Yet the pages, especially of the Fourth Synod, which regard the priest's personal sanctification, his household, and his mission, contain what may truly be called a complete picture of priestly duty, which will bear reading again and again. Words like these are better than any book of spiritual reading, for they are the words of the actual and present pastors of the English Church;

they have the express approval of the Holy See; and they are adapted in a most special manner to the circumstances of the times in which we live. A priest who neglects them necessarily loses what a man loses who neglects the word of God which is spoken to him. A priest who reads and ponders them has before his eyes the ideal, not of a primitive missionary or a mediæval monk, not of a French, Italian, or Spanish priest, but of a pastor whose lot is cast in the great towns or the country villages of England in this nineteenth century. Here he finds placed before him the spirit and essence of those universal laws of clergy life which have accumulated during the centuries of the Church's warfare; but here also he is taught how to encounter and to solve on true Evangelical principles and in the genuine spirit of our Lord Himself, the questions and problems of modern life which meet him at every turn; the question of the education of the poor, of the education of the rich; the question of the maintenance of priest and church and school; the problem of spiritual intercourse with non-catholics; and the problem of announcing God's word, in season and out of season, to those within the fold and those without.

It is hoped that this English translation of the Synodical Decrees will lead to a considerably increased use of these Four Synods of the English Church, for the purposes of information and of observance. A constant reference to an undisputed law is the only means of attaining either the true ecclesiastical spirit, perfect ecclesiastical practice, or that unity of views and of outward action which is so fair a feature of a National Church. It would astonish some of us to find how much of positive law there is in our Provincial Synods. Numberless points on which individual priests, with their diversities of taste and of bringing up, are inclined to be a law to themselves, and (to say the truth) sometimes truly are, we see plainly decided by the Episcopate in these pages. And when the law is not so strictly laid down, still the mind and feeling of the chief pastorate are in many instances very clearly expressed, and a reverent study of their words will lead to unity, devotion, and peace. The very text of these Synods, when we come to consider the matter, is a precious legacy from departed rulers or a gift from honoured names still in our midst. It may not be possible to point out what bishop or theologian wrote this paragraph or that. But Cardinal Wiseman, Bishop Grant, and the present Bishop of Birmingham in the earlier Synods, and His Eminence Cardinal Manning in the Fourth, have left an impress upon the Decrees which it is not difficult to follow in phrase and paragraph even to those who were not present at the meetings themselves. This is especially, or perhaps I should say more visibly, true of the Four Synodical Pastoral Letters, which it has been considered useful to reprint in this volume. The first three are unmistakably the work of the first Cardinal Archbishop of the restored hierarchy. We can trace in them that weight of phrase, that slightly old-fashioned but perfectly genuine eloquence, and that warm and simple piety, which characterise all the writings of the large-hearted Cardinal Wiseman. There is no less strong evidence that the Fourth Letter is from the pen of his successor. The words of men like these, adopted as they have been by the whole of the Bishops of England, and (as regards the Decrees) confirmed by the Supreme Pontiff, are naturally precious to the heart of every priest whose ministry lies in the country which they have served so well. These prelates, and the other bishops and priests who laboured with them, weighed and pondered every word they wrote. The form of the phrases, sentences, paragraphs, as now finally left to us, is the outcome of much thought and discussion and prayer. It is no wonder, then, that any one who reads these pages with a genuine desire to find guidance and light, discovers a depth and precision of meaning and an aptness of word and epithet, which lift these canonical injunctions very far out of the list of ordinary ecclesiastical reading.

It is hoped that the reader will approve of the distribution of the matter under headings. This has made it necessary, as I need hardly observe, to bring together extracts from different Synods. But the advantages of the plan seem to be numerous. It saves much searching; it gives the whole existent legislation on any particular point in one view, and presents, at the same time, the chronological development of that legislation. If the text of the Synods is to be really used by the clergy as a handy manual of professional duty, some such arrangement as this seems absolutely required.

The merely technical details of the Synodical meetings, with the lists of officers, etc., have been omitted. But it has been thought useful to give what may be called the "Order of the Day" as laid down in each Synod, and the method of procedure, because on both these points the clergy should be well-informed. Procedure is always the visible embodiment of law.

An interesting feature in the volume is the translation for the first time into English of long and elaborate "Instructions," chiefly from the Sacred Congregation of Propaganda, on matters connected with missionary life in these countries; for example, on Mixed Marriages, on Duplication, on Education, etc. Still larger documents, such as the Brief *Romanos Pontifices*, which settles the relations between the Regulars and the Bishops, had already been translated; but they have here been carefully revised and reprinted.

It will be observed that many of the Roman documents here translated have attached to them the formal superscriptions and directions which are borne by the originals. At the risk of repetition and of what may appear to be superfluous formality, it was thought better to retain these, in order that readers might gather from these examples some idea of that style of the Roman *curia* which has to be used in communications with the Holy See.

In all translations the difficulty frequently recurs of deciding whether a sentence or a phrase should be turned into a free version, or kept more closely to the original even at the expense of stiffness and harshness. This difficulty is necessarily very great in a work like the present. Some will find it too literal and will complain of its being taken out of one language without being put into any other, whilst others will regret that the translator has not made the presence of technical and theological terms more plainly felt. I do not think that, taking into consideration the whole of a very exacting task, either of these complaints can fairly be made. The translator, whilst conscious that his work has many defects, trusts that he has given, in fair English, a faithful version of the Latin and Italian documents he has had to deal with; and I have great satisfaction in recommending the book to all English-speaking priests and the public generally.

✠ J. C. HEDLEY, O.S.B.

FEAST OF ST. FRANCIS DE SALES,
January 29th, 1886.

"Church Students should likewise be taught the principles of Common and of Canon Law, *the decrees and instructions of the Provincial Councils of Westminster,* as well as Sacred Hermeneutics and Church History."—IV. SYNOD ix. 13.

PROVINCIAL COUNCILS OF WESTMINSTER.

CHAPTER THE FIRST.

PRELIMINARY DOCUMENTS.

The following letters have reference to the re-establishment of the Hierarchy and to subsequent changes in Sees.

I. Westminster, p. 152.

APOSTOLIC LETTER OF OUR MOST HOLY LORD, BY WHICH THE EPISCOPAL HIERARCHY IN ENGLAND IS RESTORED.

PIUS IX., CHIEF PONTIFF.

For all time to come.

The power of governing the Universal Church given by Our Lord Jesus Christ to the Roman Pontiff in the person of Saint Peter has in all ages kept alive that wondrous solicitude of the Apostolic See, by which it studies the good of the Catholic religion in all parts of the world and zealously takes measures for its increase. And this corresponds with the plan of its Divine Founder, Who, by appointing it a head, provided with wondrous wisdom for the Church's safety until the end of time. The noble realm of England experienced with other nations the benefit of this solicitude, as its history testifies to the Christian religion being introduced in the very beginning of the Church and afterwards extremely flourishing therein; but that, towards the middle of the fifth century, when the Angles and Saxons had been introduced into the island, not only were all public institutions seriously disorganised but religion also. But it is clear at the same time, that Our most holy predecessor Gregory the Great sent thither, first of all, the monk Augustine with his companions, and afterwards several others of the episcopal dignity, together with many priests and monks; brought over the Anglo-Saxons to embrace the Christian religion; and by his own perseverance secured that in Britain, which had begun to be called also England, the Catholic religion should be again completely restored and extended. But, to recur to more modern times, We think that throughout the whole history of the Anglican schism which was set on foot in the sixteenth century, nothing is more clear than the care bestowed and never intermitted by the Roman Pontiffs Our predecessors to succour and by every means possible assist the Catholic religion endangered as it was, and brought to the last extremity in this realm. And to this end were, amongst other means, those provisions and arrangements of the Sovereign Pontiffs, or at least by their command and with their approval, that in England there should not be wanting those who would attend to Catholic interests there; and that young Catholics of good parts should cross to the continent for their education and especially for being carefully instructed in ecclesiastical learning, who, when afterwards ordained and sent back to their country, might sedulously devote themselves to the aid of the people by means of preaching and the Sacraments, and to the defence and propagation of the true Faith. But perhaps those things are better known which have reference to the endeavours of Our predecessors that the English Catholics, whom so cruel and wild a storm had stripped of the presence and pastoral care of their Bishops, should again have leaders dignified with the episcopal character. Now the Apostolic letter of Gregory XV, which begins "Ecclesia Romana," dated March 23rd, 1623, shews that the Supreme Pontiff as soon as was possible consecrated William Bishop to be Bishop of Chalcedon, and put him with ample faculties and the usual powers of Ordinaries to rule over the Catholics of England and Scotland; and subsequently, Urban VIII, on the death of Bishop, repeated his Apostolic letter of February 4th, 1625, of the same tenor, to Richard Smith, giving to Smith the bishopric of Chalcedon and the same faculties that had been granted to Bishop. Later on, when James II. had begun to reign in England, better times seemed to have come to the Catholic religion. But this opportunity Innocent XI immediately made use of, and appointed John Leyburn, Bishop of Adrumetum, Vicar-Apostolic of the whole kingdom of England, in 1685. And after this, by another Apostolic letter of January 30th, 1688, which begins "Super Cathedram"—he associated with Leyburn three more Bishops having titles of churches *in partibus infidelium*, as Vicars-Apostolic: and hence, with the assistance of the Apostolic Nuncio in England, Ferdinand Archbishop of Amasan, that Pontiff divided the whole of England into four districts, to wit, the London, Western, Midland and Northern, and over these the Vicars-Apostolic began to rule with suitable faculties and with the usual powers of Ordinaries. And to these, by his great authority and his most lucid answers, Benedict XIV., in his Constitution beginning with the words "Apostolicum Ministerium," as well as other Pontiffs amongst Our predecessors, together with Our Congregation for the Propagation of the Faith, were guides and helpers in their due and proper management of so weighty a charge. This division of the whole of England into four Vicariates-Apostolic continued until the time of Gregory XVI., who by his Apostolic letter of July 3rd, 1840, beginning "Muneris Apostolici," taking particularly into account the increase which the Catholic religion had undergone in the realm, made a fresh ecclesiastical division of the country, doubled the number of Vicariates-Apostolic, and consigned for its government in things spiritual the whole of England to the Vicars-Apostolic of the London, the Western, the Midland, the Welsh, the Lancashire, the Yorkshire, and the Northern Districts. These matters which We have here touched upon, to the omission of many others, are plain evidence that Our predecessors have earnestly applied themselves to strive and to work for the restoration and benefit, as far as lay in their power, of the Church in England after her terrible fall.

Having therefore before Our eyes such a bright example from Our predecessors, wishful in the discharge of Our Supreme Apostolate to emulate it, and Our judgment seconding Our affection for that beloved portion of the Lord's vineyard, We from the very commencement of Our Pontificate determined to carry on the work so well begun, and to apply Ourselves most earnestly that the Church's scope in that realm might be daily enlarged. Wherefore, on careful consideration of the complete present state of Catholic affairs in England, weighing in Our mind the very great and increasing number of Catholics there, and beholding former obstacles, which stood exceedingly in the way of the propagation of the Catholic Faith, day by day removed, We deemed that the time had come for the form of Ecclesiastical government in England to be restored to that position, in which it exists in those countries where there is no reason for the government being by the extraordinary means of Vicars-Apostolic. We felt that the circumstances of the times and of the case had brought it about, that there was no longer necessity for the Catholics of England being ruled by Vicars-Apostolic, but rather that such a change had taken place as to warrant a return to the ordinary Episcopal mode of government. In addition, the Vicars-Apostolic themselves had in the meantime unanimously asked this of Us, a great number as well of the clergy as of members of the laity well-known for their virtue and position had petitioned for it from Us, and by far the greater number of Catholics in England were longing for it. Turning over all these matters in Our mind, We omitted not to implore the help of the Great Almighty God, that, in the settlement of so important a matter, We might come to understand and duly accomplish what would most redound to the Church's good. We moreover invoked the aid of the Most Blessed Virgin Mary, Mother of God, and of those Saints who had adorned England by their sanctity, that they would vouchsafe to help Us with God by their patronage to the end that this matter might be happily accomplished. Finally, We consigned the entire case to Our venerable brothers, the Cardinals of the Holy Roman Church of Our Congregation for the Propagation of the Faith, for their careful and serious consideration. But their opinion was in complete accord with Our own wish, and We willingly determined upon approving of it and of carrying it into effect. Therefore, having weighed the whole matter Ourselves, We, at Our own instance, with full knowledge, and in the plenitude of Our Apostolic power, constitute and decree that in the realm of England there be re-established according to the common laws of the Church the Hierarchy of ordinary Bishops, taking their appellations from the Sees, which by this Our letter We erect in each District of the Vicariates-Apostolic.

And to commence with the London District, there will be two Sees therein, to wit, Westminster, which We raise to the rank of the Metropolitan or Archiepiscopal dignity, and Southwark, which, as with the others to be set down farther on, We assign to the same as Suffragans. And the Diocese of Westminster shall have that portion of the said District which lies north of the river Thames and comprises the counties of Middlesex, Essex, and Hertford: but Southwark, the remainder on the south side of the river; that is, the counties of Berkshire, Hampshire, Surrey, Sussex and Kent, together with the Isles of Wight, Jersey, Guernsey, and the others in their vicinity.¹

In the Northern District there shall be one Episcopal See, taking its name from the city of Hexham, and this Diocese shall be co-terminous with the District.

The District of York shall also form one Diocese, and its Bishop shall have his See in the city of Beverley.²

In the Lancashire District there shall be two Bishops, one of whom shall take his title from the See of Liverpool, and have for his Diocese, with the Isle of Man, the hundreds of Lonsdale, Amounderness, and West Derby; but the other, who will have for his See the city of Salford, will receive as his Diocese the hundreds of Salford, Blackburn, and Leyland.³ As to the county of Chester, although it belongs to this District, We shall now transfer it to another Diocese.

In the District of Wales there will be two Episcopal Sees, to wit, Shrewsbury and the united churches of Newport and Menevia. Shrewsbury will comprise the northern portion of the District, that is, the counties of Anglesea, Caernarvon, Denbigh, Flint, Merioneth, and Montgomery, and to these we add the county of Chester from the Lancashire District, and the county of Shropshire from the Midland. But to the Bishop of Menevia and Newport, we assign for his Diocese the counties of the southern portion of the District, that is, the shires of Brecon, Cardigan, Caermarthen, Glamorgan, Pembroke, and Radnor, as well as the English counties of Hereford and Monmouth.

In the Western District We appoint two Episcopal Sees, Clifton and Plymouth, to the former of which We assign for Diocese the counties of Gloucester, Somerset and Wilts; to the latter, the counties of Devon, Dorset and Cornwall.

The Midland District from which We have taken the county of Shropshire, will have two Episcopal Sees, Nottingham and Birmingham, to the former of which for Diocese We assign the counties of Nottingham, Derby and Leicester, as well as the counties of Lincoln and Rutland, which We detach from the Eastern District; to the latter, Staffordshire, Warwickshire, Worcestershire and Oxfordshire.

Finally, in the Eastern District, there shall be but one Episcopal See, which shall take its title from the city of Northampton, and which shall have for its Diocese the District as marked out up to the present time, with the exception of the counties of Rutland and Lincoln, which We have already assigned to the aforesaid Diocese of Nottingham.

Thus, therefore, in the most prosperous realm of England, there will be one Ecclesiastical Province, composed of one Archbishop or Metropolitan and twelve Suffragan Bishops, by whose zeal and pastoral solicitude, We trust that Catholic interests there will, by God's grace, be daily enriched with large additions. Wherefore, We wish that it be now reserved to Us and to the Roman Pontiff Our successors, to make division of the same Province, and to add to the number of Dioceses according as circumstances shall require; and, speaking generally, according as it may seem expedient in the Lord, freely to make new arrangements in regard of the same.

In the meanwhile, We command the above named Archbishop and

---

1. See p. 9.   2. See p. 8.   3. See p. 8.

Bishops to transmit at the stated times their returns, concerning the condition of their churches, to our Congregation of Propaganda, and not to leave off keeping it well informed as to all matters which they judge likely to be of spiritual benefit to their flock. For We shall continue to make use of the services of this same Congregation in matters connected with the English churches. But, as regards the sacred government of the clergy and laity and in all matters relating to the pastoral office, the Archbishop and Bishops of England will now enjoy all rights and powers which the other Catholic Archbishops and Bishops of other countries, by the common law of the sacred Canons and Apostolical Constitutions, use and have power to use, and will be bound likewise by the same obligations which by the same common discipline of the Catholic Church bind other Archbishops and Bishops. But, whatsoever things were in vogue, whether in the ancient state of the churches of England, or in its subsequent missionary condition by reason of special constitutions, privileges, or peculiar customs, as circumstances are now changed, they will carry with them for the future neither rights nor obligations. And, therefore, that no doubt may remain, We in the plenititude of Our Apostolic authority, take away from such special constitutions and privileges, whatever be their nature, and from such customs however immemorial, and deprive them of all power of in any way binding or establishing a right. Hence the Archbishops and Bishops of England will be free to decree whatsoever pertains to the fulfilment of the common law, or by the general discipline of the church comes under the authority of the Bishops. But, on Our part, We shall certainly not fail to aid them by Our Apostolic authority, and most readily shall We attend to their requests in reference to those matters which may appear conducive to the greater glory of the Divine Name, and to the salvation of souls. For in the restoration of the ordinary Hierarchy of Bishops, and in decreeing by this Our letter the observance of the common law of the church, We have had an eye mainly to this, that We might provide for the prosperity and increase of the Catholic religion throughout the realm of England; yet at the same time it was before Us that We were yielding to the desires as well of Our venerable brethren carrying on the business of the Church in that kingdom by the Vicarious authority of the Apostolic See, as of a vast number of Our beloved children amongst the clergy and laity, from whom We had received most earnest petitions for this end. Frequently had their forefathers prayed for this same thing from Our predecessors, who had begun to send Vicars-Apostolic to England at a time when Catholic Bishops in possession by ordinary law of their own churches in the kingdom could not remain there; and hence their plan of again and again subsequently increasing the number of Vicars and of the Vicariates, had by no means for its object that Catholic interests in the realm of England should always remain under an extraordinary kind of control, but rather that making provision according to circumstances for their enlargement, they might at the same time prepare the way for the final restoration of the ordinary Hierarchy. Therefore We, to Whom by God's best gift it has been granted to perfect so great a work, wish it hereby declared that it was far from Our mind and counsels that the Prelates of England, when endowed with the titles and rights of ordinary Bishops, should in any way whatsoever be deprived of the advantages they heretofore enjoyed under the title of Vicars-Apostolic. For reason does not permit that what at the desire of the English Catholics has been decreed by Us for the good of religion in their midst should turn to their detriment. Accordingly, We rest surely in the well-founded hope that those same beloved children of Ours in Christ who have never failed amongst so many vicissitudes to aid by their alms and largesse the Catholic cause in the realm of England, and the Prelates who exercised Vicarious authority therein, will act with still greater generosity towards the Bishops who are now bound by a still faster bond to the English churches, so that they may be in nowise wanting in the temporal means that have to be devoted to the splendour of the churches and of the divine worship, to the support of the clergy and the poor, and to other ecclesiastical uses.

In conclusion, We upraise Our eyes to "the hills whence comes help" to Us from the Great and Good God, and with every kind of prayer and petition with thanksgiving, We humbly beg that whatsoever has been decreed by Us for the Church's good, He will strengthen by the power of His divine assistance, and that to those whose duty it chiefly is to carry Our decrees into execution He will impart the aid of His grace, that they may feed the flock of God in their midst, and evermore earnestly apply themselves to extend the greater glory of His name. And to secure still greater abundance of heavenly grace for this end, We again invoke as Our intercessors with God, the Most Holy Mother of God, the Blessed Apostles Peter and Paul, with the other heavenly patrons of England, and specially St. Gregory the Great, that, as it has been granted to Us, however unworthy, to re-establish Episcopal Sees in England, just as he in his time did to the great advantage of the Church, this restoration of Episcopal Dioceses effected by Us in that kingdom may also turn to the benefit of the Catholic religion.

Decreeing that this Our Apostolic letter shall at no time be branded with the mark of surreption and fraud, or with any kind of defect owing to Our intention, or impugned, but be ever valid and binding, and that its prescriptions shall bear full force in all points, and must be observed inviolably. Notwithstanding Apostolical sanctions and those, whether general or special, issued in synodal, provincial and universal Councils; as well as rights of the old Sees of England, of the missions, and of the Vicariates-Apostolic afterwards established therein, and of any churches or places of devotion; or privileges confirmed even by oath, and ratified by the Apostolic or any other authority; and all things else whatsoever to the contrary. For all these, so far as they are in opposition to the aforesaid decrees, We expressly annul, even though for their annulment special mention would have to be made or any other more minute form adhered to.

We likewise decree that whatsoever any one may knowingly or unknowingly, by whatsoever authority, advance otherwise than the above, be null and void. And it is Our will that to the printed copies of this letter, when signed by a public notary and countersigned by any ecclesiastical dignitary, the same credence be given as would be to the notification of Our will at sight of this document.

Given at Rome, at St. Peter's, under the Seal of the Fisherman, September 29th, 1850, in the fifth year of Our Pontificate.

A. CARDINAL LAMBRUSCHINI.

I. Westminster, Appendix, p. 160.

REPLY OF OUR MOST HOLY LORD, POPE PIUS IX., TO THE MOST EMINENT AND REV. THE ARCHBISHOP AND THEIR RIGHT REV. LORDSHIPS THE BISHOPS OF ENGLAND, ON THEIR THANKING HIM FOR THE RESTORATION OF THE HIERARCHY OF ENGLAND.

To our beloved son Nicholas Wiseman, Cardinal Priest of the Holy Roman Church by the title of St. Pudentiana, Archbishop of Westminster, and to Our Venerable Brethren the Bishops of England, his Suffragans.

PIUS IX., SUPREME PONTIFF.

Beloved son and venerable brethren, health and Apostolical Benediction.

A subject of the greatest pleasure to Us was your most courteous letter of November the twentieth last,[1] in which you, beloved son, and you, venerable brethren, made known to Us that you and Our beloved children, the Catholics of the noble realm of England, were filled with joy at the recent restoration by Us, in accordance with the common law of the Church, of the ordinary Hierarchy of Bishops in this same kingdom. And We trust with you that this same restoration so long desired by you and the same Catholics may, by God's assistance, avail to the greater glory of His name and to the salvation of souls. And We are confident that towards so good an end you, in your well-known devotion, virtue, wisdom and prudence, will with even still greater readiness devote all your solicitude and thought. Nor do We doubt that it is your wish to again and again excite and enkindle the spirit of religion in your clergy, that ecclesiastics adorned with every virtue, as is so becoming in those engaged in the divine ministry, and zealously giving their labour, may like good soldiers of Jesus Christ, more eagerly exercise their priestly zeal under your guidance, and with all industry, care and striving may carry on the salutary business of the talents, which is to gain souls for Christ. Nor indeed, is it necessary for you, beloved son, and venerable brethren, to be taught by Us that amid straits and difficulties however grievous, all Our hope and trust must be placed in the help of Him, Who fails not to aid, to comfort and to console by His heavenly power those who are labouring for His Church and fighting the good fight. We certainly do not omit in every prayer and petition with thanksgiving, humbly and fervently to implore Our most merciful Father and God of all consolation, that He will ever graciously pour forth upon you an abundance of all heavenly gifts, and that He will bless your pastoral labours and cares, to the end that His Holy Church may daily increase in your midst, and be blessed and honoured with new and still more splendid triumphs. And as an auspice of this protection from on high as well as a pledge of Our most earnest good will in your regard, We most affectionately impart from the very depths of Our heart to you, beloved son and venerable brothers, to all your clergy, and to the faithful laity entrusted to your watchfulness, Our Apostolic Benediction.

Given at Rome, at St. Peter's, December 22nd, 1850, being the fifth year of Our Pontificate.

PIUS IX., SUPREME PONTIFF.

---

1. I have not been able to procure a copy of this letter.—[ED.]

II. Westminster. Appendix II., p. 69.

APOSTOLIC LETTER ADDING THE HUNDRED OF LEYLAND TO THE CHURCH OF LIVERPOOL.

PIUS IX., SUPREME PONTIFF.

For all time to come.

When We restored the ecclesiastical Hierarchy in the kingdom of England and appointed several Episcopal Churches as Suffragan to the Archiepiscopal See of Westminster, by an Apostolic Letter upon this matter in the form of Brief, of September 29th, 1850, in laying down the limits of the Episcopal church of Salford, We assigned the hundred of Leyland to the said church of Salford. But as it has become known to Us upon most weighty testimony that it would have been better had that portion been joined to the church of Liverpool, We, by the advice of Our venerable brothers, the Cardinals of the Holy Roman Church appointed for the Propagation of the Faith, have concluded that it should be taken from the church of Salford and added to the See of Liverpool. Therefore, at Our own instance, with full knowledge, and on mature deliberation, We, in the plenitude of Our Apostolic authority do by this present letter take away and separate the said Hundred of Leyland from the territory of the church of Salford, and add it for ever to the church of Liverpool, and likewise consign it for ever to the government of the Bishop of Liverpool. Notwithstanding Our rule and that of the Apostolic Chancery relating to not taking away a right obtained, as well as Our letter in the form of Brief of September 29th, of the previous year, and other Apostolic letters, and general or special constitutions and ordinations issued in universal, provincial and synodal councils, and other things whatsoever to the contrary.

Given at Rome, at St. Peter's, under the Seal of the Fisherman, June 27th, 1851, in the sixth year of Our Pontificate.

For my Lord Cardinal Lambruschini.

A. PICCHIONI, Substitute.

LETTER APOSTOLIC IN THE FORM OF A BRIEF, BY VIRTUE OF WHICH THE DIOCESE OF BEVERLEY IS DIVIDED INTO TWO NEW AND DISTINCT DIOCESES CALLED LEEDS AND MIDDLESBROUGH.[1]

LEO PP. XIII.

FOR A PERPETUAL REMEMBRANCE OF THE MATTER.

Whatsoever things We, looking out, as from a watchtower from this sublime Chair of Most blessed Peter, see to be most likely to turn out well, prosperously, and happily for the interests of the Catholic Faith; these same things do We, with due deliberation, endeavour to bring about by the exercise of Our Apostolic authority. When, therefore, Our

---

1. As translated in the *Tablet*, March 1st, 1883.

Ven. Brother, Robert Cornthwaite, Bishop of Beverley, in England, had reported to Us that his Diocese was far too extensive, and that, in consequence, to provide more safely and more abundantly for the spiritual good of the faithful, it would be well and most advantageous if the said diocese were divided into two Sees, and each of them intrusted to the care of its own Ordinary, when the opportune moment arrived, We placed the matter in the hands of Our Venerable Brethren, the Cardinals of the Holy Roman Church, who preside over affairs that concern the Propagation of the Faith. And in order that the said division might result most surely in the eternal welfare of souls, We directed the said Bishop of Beverley himself to mark out the respective boundaries of the new diocese and to communicate to Us whatever else he might judge expedient in the Lord. When, therefore, with great care and his accustomed zeal in the Pastoral Office, he had fulfilled with the greatest nicety the duty assigned to him, We, on the advice of the same Our Venerable Brethren, and by virtue of Our Apostolic authority, decreed those things which are written below.

By virtue of these presents, We divide the diocese of Beverley, which is so extremely extensive, into two distinct dioceses: and to one of them, which lies to the North, We assign a name taken from the City of Middlesbrough; to the other a name taken from the City of Leeds. Furthermore it is Our pleasure that the Bishop of the first shall have his See in the City of Middlesbrough, and the Bishop of the second in the City of Leeds; and that the first diocese shall consist of the North and East districts, called "Ridings," together with that part of the county and city of York which lies on the north bank of the river Ouse; and the second shall embrace the district called the West Riding, together with the part of the county and city of York which is south of the said river Ouse. At the same time, to make provision for the temporal needs of the new See of Middlesbrough, it is Our desire that there should be made over to it whatever belongs to that part of the actual Diocese of Beverley which we have assigned to the new See of Middlesbrough; furthermore, a third part of all the funds that were common; and still further, one half of the actual Episcopal Mensa of Beverley, according to the agreement made with the clergy, when collections were set on foot for the diocese as then constituted.

Finally, We decree, &c.

Apostolic Letter Dividing the See of Southwark into Southwark and Portsmouth.

LEO. XIII., SUPREME PONTIFF.

For all time to come.

Our beloved Son, Henry Edward Manning, Cardinal Priest of the Holy Roman Church, by Apostolical dispensation Archbishop of Westminster, and the other Prelates of England, in their solicitude for the well-being and convenience of the faithful, have directed their attention to the extensive nature of the Diocese of Southwark, and on several occasions have proposed that this Apostolic See should divide the said Diocese into two portions. But when last year the Diocese of Southwark was deprived of its Pastor by the death of James Danell, of happy memory, it was intimated to Our same Venerable Brother, the Archbishop of Westminster, through the Council of Our Venerable Brethren, the Cardinals of the Holy Roman Church for the Propagation of the Christian name, that at length the Holy See would willingly accept the proposition in reference to the aforesaid division. Hence the division of the Diocese of Southwark was by renewed petitions sought by the same Archbishop and his Suffragan Bishops. Wherefore, We at once entered upon the question with Our aforesaid Brethren of the Propagation of the Faith, and all things being duly considered and weighed, We deemed that the said Diocese should be divided into two parts. We, therefore, with the advice of the same Venerable Brethren of Ours, by Our Apostolic authority do completely separate and withdraw from the Diocese of Southwark the two counties of Berkshire and Hampshire, together with the islands in the British Sea, commonly called the *British Channel*, belonging to England, and do establish and appoint a new Diocese, which shall consist of the aforesaid two counties and islands. Of this new Diocese We will that the Bishop shall have his See in the City of Portus Magnus, commonly called *Portsmouth*, and We name it from the same City, so that this new Diocese shall be called the Diocese of Portsmouth. Moreover, We order that the Cathedral Church of the Diocese of Portsmouth and of its Chapter that has to be appointed, shall be the church which is now in progress to the honour of St. John the Evangelist, in the City itself of Portsmouth. But the elder Church of Southwark will retain its old name, its old See, and its old Cathedral to the honour of St. George, with its Chapter, that will have again to be reconstituted; and Surrey, Kent and Sussex will continue under its jurisdiction. For the future, We prescribe that the boundary lines between the Dioceses of Southwark and Portsmouth shall be the same as those between the counties of Surrey and Sussex and Berkshire and Hampshire. Finally, with the advice of the same Venerable Brethren of Ours, We by Our Apostolical authority have consigned the question of the division of the funds of the Dioceses of Southwark and Portsmouth to Our Venerable Brother the Archbishop of Westminster and two of the Seniors of his Suffragans, with this understanding, however, that this division and allotment shall be completed before either Bishop is appointed to his See. These things We will determine, prescribe, and publish, decreeing that this Our Letter is and shall be good, valid, and efficacious, and that it acquires and obtains its plenary and complete power, and holds good most fully for future times for those to whom it refers or may refer, and that thus in its provisions it must be judged and defined by all judges ordinary and delegated, even Auditors of causes of the Apostolic Palace, Nuncios of the Apostolic See, and Cardinals of the Holy Roman Church, even though Legates *à latere*, every kind of power and authority being taken from each of them of otherwise judging and interpreting; and that should anything different be attempted by anyone, by whatsoever authority, in ignorance or with knowledge, it is null and void. Notwithstanding Our own and the Apostolic Chancery's rule concerning not taking away an acquired right, as well as that of Our Predecessor of happy memory, Benedict XIV., upon the division of properties, and other Apostolic Constitutions and Ordinances, and other things whatsoever to the contrary.

Given at Rome, at St. Peter's, under the Fisherman's ring, May 14th, 1882, the fifth year of Our Pontificate.

TH. CARD. MERTEL.

I, the undersigned, bear witness that this document agrees in every respect with the original, which is kept in the Archiepiscopal Archives of Westminster.

Westminster, July 14th, 1882.

By command of my most Eminent and Reverend Lord the Cardinal Archbishop of Westminster.

JAMES J. GUIRON, Secretary.

CHAPTER THE SECOND.

PROVINCIAL SYNODS OR COUNCILS.

Synopsis of "Provincial Councils" by the Abbé D. Bouix, with Illustrative References to our own Provincial Councils.

As Father Bouix observes in the introduction to his Provincial Councils, whilst Benedict XIV.'s treatise wholly exhausts the subject of Diocesan Synods, there is no work—or rather there was no work previous to his—which treats fully of Provincial Synods.

A brief synopsis, therefore, of the points in that work which have reference to practical rather than controversial matter, may well precede in this volume an epitome of Benedict XIV.'s treatise upon Diocesan Synods. Sufficient alone will be given here, in regard to both works, to enable those engaged in preparing for either a Provincial or Diocesan Synod to form an idea of the nature of the subjects discussed at length therein.

1.—Scope and subject of Provincial Councils, p. 20.

2.—Though not infallible, still divinely assisted, p. 30.

3.—Should be held every three years. No reason, even in France, why the law of the Council of Trent should be considered obsolete, p. 38.

4.—A Papal Legate can summon a Provincial Council, p. 72.

5.—Ordinarily, to the Metropolitan it belongs to summon it, p. 85; and to publish its decrees, in his own name[1] if he pleases, p. 89; also, to interpret doubtful points subsequently, p. 90.

6.—He can order[2] Bishops to attend; but when once the Council is opened, his powers are in many ways limited, unless a majority of the Bishops uphold him. See the especial points enumerated, pp. 93 and 96.

7.—In default of the Metropolitan, it belongs to the next oldest (not by age, but consecration) Bishop to summon the Provincial Council, and not to the Metropolitan's Vicar-General, p. 99.

8.—An Archbishop without Suffragans cannot summon one (e.g., of Abbots, &c.); nor can he be chosen as Metropolitan by exempt Bishops in fulfilment of the mandate of the Council of Trent, p. 102.

9.—Some twenty chapters follow upon what prelates and others have the right to attend Provincial Synods, what kind of voice each shall have, and the laws of precedence amongst them.

The following extracts show what has been the practice in our own Synods:

---

1. St. Charles Borromeo does this in his Second Provincial Synod of Milan, although he had decreed the Acts of the First Synod " by the counsel and consent " of the other Bishops.

2. See Edict of IV. Westminster, p. 32.

I.—PROVINCIAL COUNCIL OF WESTMINSTER.

Preparatory Meeting held July 9th, 1852.

As the Roman Ceremonial prescribes that precedence amongst the Bishops should be determined by the date of their promotion, and the Apostolic Letters containing the promotion of several of them were of the same date, it was decided that these Bishops should, at meetings of this kind, hold rank according to the day of consecration, and if that were the same in any instance precedence should be allowed to the elder in years. (I. West. p. 7.)

The case came on of the Procurators of the Bishops of Liverpool and Nottingham, who were absent through ill-health, and the Bishops considered that, as by a decree of the Sacred Congregation of Cardinals Interpreters of the Council of Trent, it is left to the Synod to grant or refuse a decisive voice, and as there are to be two Procurators present at this first Synod, in priestly orders, to only eleven Bishops, these determined that they should have a deliberative voice alone.

The names were read out of the Bishops' Theologians and the deputies from Chapters, and when the Archbishop had noticed that in some instances the same Theologians were brought by Bishops as had been deputed by some Chapters, and that considerable inconvenience might arise, as well from the small number of Theologians present, as for other reasons, the matter was fully discussed; and in the end the Fathers determined that in this Synod only could such double representation be allowed, with a protest on the part of the Procurator against this passing into a precedent.

The names of the Superiors of Religious Orders who were to be admitted were read out. A reply was sent to the Abbot of St. Bernard's, of the Cistercian Order, who was absent through ill-health, that he could not send a Procurator. The question arose as to allowing Procurators of Chapters a decisive voice in discussions concerning their Chapters, but no decision was come to.

In the Acts of the First Session of Wednesday, July 7th, we find the following records:—

That Procurators for the Bishops of Liverpool and Nottingham were admitted with a deliberative voice, the latter, however, upon the promise to get his papers couched in due form. (1. West. p. 13.)

The question was discussed amongst the Bishops as to admitting a Procurator for the Chapter of Liverpool. The difficulty arose from this, that, as it was given out, the Bishop in 1851, by virtue of an Apostolic Letter of November, 1850, and previously to the receipt of the new instructions from the Sacred Congregation, and likewise before the Holy See had given a Cathedral to the Chapter of the Diocese of Liverpool, had established a Chapter of one dignitary and twelve canons[1]; and this appointment seemed uncanonical. It was the unanimous opinion of the Fathers that these difficulties should be settled by the Holy See, and that the only business of the Synod was to see whether the letter of appointment to be presented by the Procurator of the Chapter was properly drawn up and signed.

---

1. It was subsequently ascertained that, in accordance with the terms of the Decree of the Sacred Congregation, only ten Canons were appointed.

Another question was then discussed in reference to the Procurator of the Chapter of Hexham. And when, by the admission of the Bishop himself, it was clear that the Chapter was established without the canons having received charge by due installation of their Cathedral church or made any profession of faith; six Bishops were of the opinion that the Procurator of the Chapter of Hexham could be admitted, but four thought that he should not be admitted except as a Theologian. All, however, considered that the Bishop of Hexham should make a special application upon the subject to the Synod. Subsequently the Promoter added to his general protest the following special points. (1. West. p. 14.)

"I likewise protest against any prejudice being raised against this ters not yet established of Nottingham, of Newport and Menevia, and of Synod by reason of the absence of . . . . . deputies of the Chap- Hexham established in the way just explained. And since the Chapters of Southwark and Beverley were summoned, but their Procurators have not yet arrived, I beg that a protest relative to their absence be admitted, and that they themselves should lay the grounds of their excuse before the Bishops of Beverley and Birmingham deputed for this purpose; and that in the case of the Procurator for Beverley, the Bishop of Northampton should act in place of the Bishop of Beverley."

"And since the Bishops of Southwark and Northampton have brought as Theologians the same persons that their Chapters had respectively chosen to represent them, and since many inconveniences might arise from their twofold position of this kind, I beg that they may be admitted only under caution and protest, lest their presence might pass into a precedent."

And subsequently it is recorded that:

On the same day came the Rev. Joseph Render, the deputy for the Chapter of Beverley, who had been detained at York through a disturbance amongst the people.

The admission of the deputies for the Chapters of Southwark and Beverley was deferred, owing to a flaw in the letters of delegation furnished by the Chapters.

And on Friday, the 9th, there were brought in the deputies of the Chapters of Southwark and Beverley, and after a brief examination of the cause of their delay, they were admitted.

Another point was also raised and settled:

The Rev. Mr. Crooke, Procurator for the Bishop of Liverpool, asked the Fathers as to whether, during the course of the Council, he could inform his Bishop as to its acts and decrees; and the Fathers, seeing that the Bishop had given a general mandate to his delegate, and that he could not oblige him to give his deliberate vote according to the notion of the one who had sent him, but only in accordance with what the Procurator himself might conscientiously and to the best of his judgment deem to be right in the Lord; moreover, and especially in view of the vow laid down by the Sacred Congregation of Propaganda as to secrecy, considering that the letters sent by the Procurator might fall into other hands, replied, that the said Procurator, inasmuch as the same law of secrecy was laid down in the name of the Synod, could tell his Bishop *vivâ-voce* what decrees had been passed when the Synod was over, but not before.

SECOND PROVINCIAL COUNCIL.

Preparatory Meeting held July 9th, 1855.

The Fathers determined that the two Coadjutors, namely, the Archbishop of Trebizond and the Bishop of Gerra, had no right to a decisive voice without the unanimous consent of the Fathers. Without binding any future Synods, all and each accorded a decisive voice to the two Coadjutors, but a deliberative voice only to the invited Bishops. But the next day two Vicar-Capitulars begged to be allowed in future to walk after the Bishops, without any prejudice to their already recognised right of precedence.

The Procurators of Chapters were introduced in the usual way. (By a declaration of the Sacred Congregation of Propaganda, August 16th, 1856, it is clear that the Chapter of Clifton acted rightly in deputing a Procurator in addition to the Vicar-Capitular, inasmuch as he, so long as the See was vacant, took the Bishop's place.)

THIRD PROVINCIAL COUNCIL.

THE COADJUTOR BISHOP.

On July 12th, 1859, at a quarter-past nine a.m., a meeting of Bishops was held, and, in conjunction with his Eminence the Archbishop, made arrangements for the General Congregation which was to follow immediately. . . . . . As it was the Bishops' opinion that the Archbishop of Trebizond, Coadjutor with right of succession to his Eminence the Archbishop, had no right to a decisive voice, he was admitted by the Fathers with a consultative voice. And although the question was discussed as to whether, upon the reply of the Sacred Congregation of Rites, in the Aquileia case, September 30th, 1596 *(in Gardellini vii., p. 46),* the right to sit above Bishops not raised to the Archiepiscopal dignity belonged to the same Coadjutor Archbishop, who adduced this reply: the Bishops considered that the Sacred Congregation of Propaganda had fixed this place below the Bishops enjoying jurisdiction in its review of the Acts of the Second Provincial Council.

Among the minutes of the First Session, held July 13th, we read:

At three o'clock in the afternoon a meeting of the Bishops was held, and the letter of his Eminence the Prefect of the Sacred Congregation of Propaganda, of June 30th, 1859, which had come to hand the previous day, was read; and from this it was clear that the opinion of the Fathers in reference to not allowing the Coadjutor with right of succession a decisive voice was in conformity with the judgment of the Sacred Congregation.

This letter (given in III. West. App., p. 80) is as follows:

LETTER OF HIS EMINENCE THE LORD CARDINAL PREFECT OF THE SACRED CONGREGATION OF PROPAGANDA, JUNE 30TH, 1859, TO HIS EMINENCE THE ARCHBISHOP OF WESTMINSTER.

I have the pleasure of acquainting you with what Propaganda has lately done with regard to the right of Coadjutor Bishops with future succession when present at Synods. The question as to the right of

Coadjutor Bishops to sit in Synod with a deliberative voice was discussed in January of this year, when the Acts and Decrees of the Third Provincial Synod of Tuam were under consideration. The Consultor, who had given his opinion upon the Synod of Tuam, quoted for the affirmative view a decision of the Sacred Congregation of Rites, to be met with in Gardellini, T i., p. 24, third edition. But their Eminences, the Fathers, on the contrary, considered that it did not meet the case. For, from the words of the Decree, *Coadjutors with future succession should sit at Provincial Synods according to the date of their promotion*, it can only be concluded that Coadjutor Bishops must take their seats in Synod according to the time of their promotion, but nothing can be deduced from the above words as to their having a right to a deliberative voice. And this all the more so, seeing that it would follow that one and the same church would have two votes. But this is not all. For the Provincial Synod of Quebec, having yielded to the Coadjutor Bishops of the Province that they should sit in Council with a decisive voice, the following question was proposed at the General Meeting in May, 1852, "Is there any objection to be made with regard to the Acts of the Council of Quebec?" And their Eminences the Fathers replied—*Affirmatively and with an understanding*. The understanding being that a letter should be written, which should state that it is not proper to give Coadjutors a decisive voice, and that, for greater security, the Holy Father's sanction for the Acts has been asked for.

Report of the First General Congregation. The Procurators of the Chapters were introduced, and showed their papers as deputies. (p. 11.) And farther on: (p. 16.)

A meeting of the Bishops was held in the Vesting-room, and the Rev. Daniel Rock, S.T.D., Canon, presented in their presence his letter of deputation as Procurator for the Chapter of Southwark, in place of the Rev. Canon Tierney, who had been obliged by ill-health to retire from the Synod. The Bishops of Beverley and Birmingham, the Judges of Excuses, reported that they had gone into the question as to whether a Canon ordinarily dwelling in another Diocese, but who goes to the Cathedral for Divine Office on the days prescribed by the Statutes of the Chapter, fails in regard to the law of residence, and hence becomes incapable of acting as deputy for a Procurator; and that, seeing that the Holy See had reduced the obligation of residence to the duty of going to the Divine Office on stated days, they considered that there was no objection whatsoever to his exercising the office of Procurator. Thereupon the Rev. D. Rock was admitted, &c.

At the Third Sacred Congregation there were present with consultative voice, granted by the Fathers, the Most Rev. Archbishop Spaccapietra of Trinidad, and the Right Rev. Bishop Forçade of Guadaloupe, in India. (p. 18.)

FOURTH PROVINCIAL SYNOD.

Tuesday, July 22nd, 1873.

First General Congregation.

. . . . Each Procurator of a Chapter was called upon by the Secretary to produce his papers and did so, with the exception of the Procurator of the Chapter of Nottingham, who was not present. But the Secretary of the Chapter informed the Metropolitan that the Chapter did not wish to make use of their privilege of being represented at the Synod by a Procurator. After showing their papers the Procurators retired.

Then came the Right Reverend Father Abbot Alcock, O.S.B., and in his capacity of Mitred Abbot and Pro-Visitor of the Anglo-Belgian Province of the Casinese Congregation, asserted his right to be present at the Synod. Having heard the case, the Fathers of the Synod, however, ruled that he had no right by reason of his abbatial dignity, because this was merely personal and not pertaining inseparably to the Monastery which he governed; and, besides, it was by no means clear that the Anglo-Belgian Province had been canonically established, inasmuch as no authentic document to this effect had been laid before the Metropolitan, the Ordinary of the Diocese in which the Right Rev. Abbot resided, or the Fathers of the Council. Hence they did not allow his right. However, saving the rights of the Synod and of the Right Reverend Abbot, they would willingly allow him the privilege of being present at the Council as a Synodal Theologian. But as to the rights, they promised to inquire into them afterwards. In the same way, although a Province of the Capuchin Fathers had not yet been formed in England, the Very Reverend Father Emidius, O.S.F.C. was most cordially invited.

Then the Procurator of the Chapter of Liverpool came forward and maintained that precedence over the other Chapters was due to his by reason of priority of erection. The question was referred to the Judges of Complaints and Excuses.

Meanwhile they decided that the order of sitting followed in the previous Councils of Westminster should be adhered to.

Then two Procurators of Chapters protested in their own names and those of the others against a special invitation not having been sent to each Chapter, signed by the Metropolitan, as in preceding Synods. After the protest had been made and accepted, the other Procurators came in, and the Archbishop gave an account as to the omission. He was of opinion that a special summons should be issued to each Chapter, and this accordingly he had considered sufficiently provided for by his Secretary, who had sent a letter, together with copies of the letters of Indiction and Edict, to each Chapter. However, he promised to submit the question to the Sacred Congregation.

The Fathers of the Synod, in deference to the wish of the Sacred Congregation of Propaganda, invited the Most Illustrious and Reverend the Archbishop of Nazianzus to the deliberations of the Council with a consultative voice.

10.—The whole of the Third Part of Bouix, from p. 208 to p. 398, is taken up with the discussion, so necessary for France at the time he wrote (1849), of the attitude of Provincial Councils towards the Holy See. What our own four Provincial Synods have thought and done in this matter is clear enough. In the first place, all four are published with the Sovereign Pontiff's approval, embodied in an official letter from the Sacred Congregation of Propaganda. (See below.) Secondly, in the third and fourth Synods the Fathers are bound to secrecy as to decrees, &c., "until the confirmation of the Decrees by the Holy See" (III. West. p. 11, IV. West. p. 9); and the same is asserted by the first Synod in the Pastoral Address of the Fathers: "You are not ignorant that the Acts of a Provincial Council have no authority, and therefore cannot be made public, nor can its decrees be enforced, until they have been submitted to the correction and judgment of the Holy Apostolic See, and so have received its confirmation." Thirdly, a like spirit of perfect submission is manifest in the address to the Holy Father of each Synod (I. West. p. 104, II. West. p 33, III. West. p. 3, IV. West.. p. 6). Lastly, the following declaration is signed, together with the Acts of the Synod, by all the Bishops, &c. : "We submit all and each of the statutes, decrees, and acts of this Synod with due obedience and reverence to the authority, correction, and emendation of the Holy Roman Church, the Mother and Mistress of all churches, and to the judgment of the Roman Pontiff, Christ's Vicar, to be emended, corrected, or altered." (I. West. p. 102.)

OFFICIAL APPROBATION OF THE ACTS AND DECREES OF THE FIRST PROVINCIAL COUNCIL OF WESTMINSTER.

Hardly had the Bishops of England time to make due arrangements forthwith for the government of their newly-appointed churches, before His Most Eminent and Right Reverend Lordship Nicholas, under the title of St. Pudentiana, Cardinal of the Holy Roman Church, Wiseman, Archbishop of Westminster, in accordance with the decrees of the Sacred Council of Trent, undertook to convene a Provincial Synod. This was held at St. Mary's College, Oscott, and concluded in three sessions on July the 7th, 13th, and 17th, 1852. And its acts, decrees, and other Synodal decisions were then forwarded to the Sacred Congregation for revision and confirmation. Accordingly, after a careful examination of them had been made at a general meeting of the Sacred Congregation, March 8th, 1853, it was proposed by His Most Eminent and Right Reverend Lordship Lewis, of the Holy Roman Church Cardinal, Altieri, that they should be passed, and, after due consideration of all points, the Most Eminent and Reverend Fathers judged that all that had been done was well worthy of commendation, especially by reason of the particular care with which, as with one and the same mind, the Bishops, with the help of their assistants, had striven to promote the good of religion and the salvation of souls. So, with certain modifications, in accordance with special instructions, they considered that the Decrees should be approved of, as well as the Statutes for Chapters of Canons, and the arrangements as to missionary rectors, taking chiefly into account that the observance of the Canon Law cannot yet be established upon all points.

This decision of the Sacred Congregation was laid before our Most Holy Lord Pope Pius IX. by the undersigned Secretary at an audience on March 13th, and His Holiness graciously approved thereof upon all points, all things whatsoever to the contrary notwithstanding.

Given at Rome, at the Office of the S.C. of P.F., May 14th, 1853.

J. PH. CARDINAL FRANSONI, Prefect.
AL. BARNABÒ, Secretary.

Place ✠ of the Seal.

The following are the Addresses of the assembled Fathers to the Supreme Pontiff, with the Holy Father's replies to the same (referred to p. 18):—

I. Westminster, p. 104.

LETTER OF THE FATHERS TO OUR MOST HOLY LORD POPE PIUS IX.

MOST HOLY FATHER,

Although when first the Ecclesiastical Hierarchy was granted us by your Holiness we did not omit to make known to you by letter our gratitude, yet now that we are assembled together at our first Provincial Council, we have considered it to be the chief duty of our undertaking again to approach your Holiness's sacred feet, and to lay before you, with the full affection of our souls, what experience of so great a blessing has made us feel in regard to it.

And although, together with the acts of this Synod, a fuller account of our doings will be sent to your Holiness, yet it was our wish, sanctioned by a special decree, that previously to the dissolution of the Council, a letter signed by all the Bishops should testify to your Holiness the love and gratitude with which we regard your Holiness's great favours conferred upon us.

And if hitherto these have been most abundant and remarkable, now do we see them wonderfully increased by benefits heaped upon benefits, whether we look at the establishment of the Cathedral Chapters, the plan for recommendations to the Episcopacy, or to the new system of almost parochial government; all of which your Holiness has with such wisdom and such kindness vouchsafed to grant. For in all of these we see the pledge of your trust and paternal love, not only as regards ourselves, but also the worthy clergy of England, who most faithfully share with us our labours and our difficulties.

But what shall we say of the all but innumerable advantages which we not unjustly trust will follow from this our Provincial Council for the whole people confided to us? Not easily from any other source than a restored Hierarchy could these ever have come. And truly, indeed, we can with difficulty find words to express with what peace and calmness of mind, with what charity and fraternal love, all matters have been deliberated upon, discussed, and, without any party spirit, yea, as we trust, without any human feeling, been defined and decreed. Nor among the numbers of clergy, secular and regular, summoned by us from all parts and assembled here to work together with us, was there any dissension or unpleasantness to be checked; all rather were impelled by the one desire of honouring God and edifying the Church, and performed the duties assigned to them with earnest and cheerful minds. But when the decrees proposed by us are submitted to the supreme judgment of your Holiness for emendation, correction, and confirmation by your Apostolic authority, it will be plainly evident how it lay to our hearts to shew ourselves in accord and conformity with the Holy Roman Church, not only in matters pertaining to faith, but even in those of the least importance.

Wherefore, kissing the feet of your Holiness, we with the utmost devotion beg your Apostolic benediction upon ourselves and upon the flocks entrusted to us.

St. Mary's, Oscott, July 17th, 1852.

Your Holiness's most humble and devoted servant and creation,
NICHOLAS, CARDINAL WISEMAN.

Most humble and obedient and devoted sons and servants,

✠ JOHN, Bishop of Beverley.
✠ WILLIAM, Bishop of Northampton.
✠ THOMAS JOSEPH, O.S.B., Bishop of Newport and Menevia.
✠ WILLIAM BERNARD, Bishop of Birmingham.
✠ WILLIAM, Bishop of Hexham.
✠ THOMAS, Bishop of Southwark.
✠ WILLIAM, Bishop of Salford.
✠ GEORGE, Bishop of Plymouth.
✠ THOMAS, Bishop of Clifton.
✠ JAMES, Bishop of Shrewsbury.

I, JOHN CROOKE, Procurator of the Bishop of Liverpool, have signed in his name.

I, FRANCIS CHEADLE, Procurator of the Bishop of Nottingham, have signed in his name.

REPLY OF OUR MOST HOLY LORD.

To Our Beloved Son, Nicholas Wiseman, Cardinal Priest of the Holy Roman Church, under the Title of St. Pudentiana, and to the Venerable Bishops of England

PIUS IX., CHIEF PONTIFF.

Beloved Son and Venerable Brothers, health and Apostolical benediction. A great joy and delight to Us was the letter which you, beloved Son and Venerable Brothers, have sent to Us, dated and signed by you on the 17th of July, previously to the dissolution of the Provincial Council lately held by you, in order that thereby you might more fully give expression to your sense of gratitude for the restoration by Us in your realm of England, in accordance with the common law of the Church, of ordinary episcopal government. For in this letter there is wonderful evidence of your religion, your devotion, and your singular faith, love and reverence towards Us and this Chair of Peter; of the great pastoral care and solicitude also with which you are filled for the increase of God's glory, and for procuring by every means the salvation of your beloved sheep. And although these manifestations of the sincerity of your religious spirit are neither new to Us nor unexpected by Us, they have greatly pleased Us, since We are well aware of the goodness and zeal for the Catholic cause which underlie them. And it was very delightful to Us to learn from this same letter that the whole of your clergy have in complete unity aided you in your Provincial Council, and have manifested abundant signs of devotion, and that in framing the Acts of the same Council you have considered nothing more important, nothing more at heart, than to hold firmly to the teaching of the Roman Church, the Mother and Mistress of all Churches, and with the utmost zeal to make decrees best adapted for the defence of the Catholic faith, for increasing the splendour of divine worship, for promoting ecclesiastical discipline, and for procuring the spiritual salvation of your people. And be well persuaded that We shall most willingly receive the Acts of the same Council which you properly desire to submit to the judgment of this Holy See and to Our own. And We doubt not, beloved Son and Venerable Brothers, that, relying upon the divine assistance and fulfilling with still greater readiness your ministry, watchful in all things, and working like good soldiers of Jesus Christ, you will ever direct all your cares, your thoughts, your aims, and your plans to this end, that the Catholic Church and her saving doctrine may daily receive increase; that ecclesiastics, ever mindful of their vocation and dignity, may strive to shine day by day more brightly by their gravity, holiness of life, and knowledge especially of sacred sciences, that they may set an example to Christian people of every kind of virtue, and under your guidance skilfully, wisely, and religiously perform the duties of their ministry, as well as labour most earnestly for the eternal salvation of men; that the faithful entrusted to you, nourished more and more by the words of faith and strengthened by the gifts of grace, may grow in the knowledge of God and tread with ready steps the paths of the Lord; that miserable wanderers may throw off their blindness of mind and disperse darkening mists of error, open their eyes to the light of truth, and return to the one fold of Christ. And amid the terrible straits and perplexities which, in times like the present in particular, cannot be separated from the episcopal charge, never despair; but, strengthened in the Lord and in the power of His might, go on fighting the good fight of faith, keeping before your eyes that unchanging crown of glory promised to those who persevere by the eternal Prince of Pastors; and recalling to mind that they who instruct many to justice shall shine like stars for all eternity. And be assured that nothing will be more pleasing to Us, nothing more desirable, than to do all that We can, that We may know to be conducive to the greater good of yourselves and your churches. But meanwhile, We omit not in every prayer and petition, with thanksgiving, humbly and earnestly to beg of our most clement and merciful Father and God of all consolation that He will ever benignly pour forth upon you the richest gifts of His goodness, and bless your pastoral cares and labours, so that His Holy Church may be increased and adorned in your country by still greater and more noble triumphs. And as an augury of this protection and a pledge of Our exceeding good-will towards you, receive the Apostolic benediction, which from the depth of Our heart We most affectionately bestow upon each of you, beloved Son and Venerable Brothers, upon all your clergy, and upon the faithful laity entrusted to your care.

Given at Rome, at St. Peter's, August 26th, 1852, in the seventh year of Our Pontificate.

PIUS IX., POPE.

I. Westminster, Appendix III., p. 162.

LETTER OF THE MOST EMINENT AND REVEREND LORD ARCHBISHOP OF WESTMINSTER TO OUR MOST HOLY LORD, UPON THE DESPATCH OF THE ACTS AND DECREES OF THE SYNOD TO ROME.

MOST HOLY FATHER,

A few days ago, upon an opportunity presenting itself, I took care that the Acts and Decrees of our Provincial Synod of Westminster should be sent to the Most Eminent Prefect of the Sacred Congregation of Propaganda, that he might lay them with due respect and submission at your Holiness's feet. For whatsoever they contain, the Fathers therein assembled felt deeply should be submitted to the judgment and correction of the Holy Apostolic See, to the end that everything might receive its efficacy from the power and sanction of its authority. For nothing lay more to their hearts than in everything to cling to, be in agreement with, and by the strictest bonds of obedience and unity to be bound to the Chair of Peter, that is, to your Holiness. Receive, therefore, Most Holy Father, these first fruits of our restored Ecclesiastical Hierarchy, which we owe to your Holiness, and may they be to you some small token of our filial love and gratitude. And if any portion is found not unworthy of your Holiness's supreme approval, in however small a degree, we shall not repine at the task we have undertaken, nor shall we consider that our labours have been in vain.

I have also, Most Holy Father, added, at the wish of the Bishops, some petitions asking for various concessions and favours, the which I most humbly commend to your Holiness's good-will and paternal kindness.

With joy in the Lord, I announce to your Holiness that everything went on in the Synod not only calmly and peacefully, but with the utmost charity and love; or rather, I will say, that by God's grace all met together prepared to further mutual edification and general progress in ecclesiastical devotion. On the part of all there was earnestness in deliberations, prudence in arriving at determinations, preciseness in speech, devotion in religious exercises. The observance of the rites and ceremonies was most exact, the celebration of the sacred functions becoming and solemn. The rules laid down by the Fathers were kept faithfully, one and all shared the same frugal meals, the mode of life was the same for each. Delightful indeed was it to witness so many gathered together from all parts of the kingdom, and heretofore unknown to each other, now like brethren dwelling together, and as though actuated by one soul and one heart, assiduously and without the shadow of party spirit, applying themselves to the same work. Justly, therefore, had thanks to be offered to God for such wonderful gifts from His goodness, and this by the order of the Fathers was publicly and properly done throughout all the dioceses of England on the Feast of the Assumption into heaven of the Mother of God.

It only remains for me to kiss your Holiness's sacred feet, and earnestly to beg that the Apostolical Benediction may be copiously poured forth upon me and my Suffragans.

Your Holiness's most humble, devoted, and attached
Servant and Creation,

NICHOLAS, CARDINAL WISEMAN.

THE REPLY TO THE FOREGOING LETTER.

To Our Beloved Son, Nicholas Wiseman, Cardinal Priest of the Holy Roman Church, under the Title of St. Pudentiana, Archbishop of Westminster.

PIUS IX., CHIEF PONTIFF.

BELOVED SON,

Health and Apostolical Benediction. The greatest joy was afforded Us by your most exemplary letter, in which you made known to Us that the first Provincial Synod of Westminster since the re-establishment by Us of your Ecclesiastical Hierarchy has been held by you and by your Venerable Brethren the Bishops of England, and that the Acts of the Synod have been sent to the Cardinal Prefect of our Sacred Congregation of Propaganda, in order that they may be examined and approved of in the usual way. For from this same letter We have with no small pleasure again seen how great is the devotion, the love, and the veneration of yourself and the said Bishops towards Us and this Chair of Peter. But it was most pleasing to Us to observe that nothing lay more to your heart and to the hearts of these Bishops than with united minds, bound together by the bond of mutual charity, and with the utmost solicitude, earnestness, and prudence to do all you could to decree chiefly those things which each of you considered most likely to conduce to the promotion of God's glory amongst you, to the defence of the cause of His Holy Church, and to the furtherance of the sanctity of the clergy and the salvation of souls. Hence did it come about that, by God's grace, your Synod was peacefully, becomingly, prosperously, and happily begun and finished. You, therefore, and the Venerable Brethren your Suffragan Bishops, do We earnestly congratulate in the Lord for this, and with Our whole soul bestow upon you the praises you so well deserve. But as regards the Acts of the same Synod, and the several petitions of which you speak, Our aforesaid Congregation, organised for propagating the Faith, will not fail to send you a suitable reply. But meanwhile We encourage both you and these same Bishops in reliance upon divine assistance to go on fulfilling your episcopal ministry with even greater readiness, to apply yourselves to that salutary traffic with talents—which is the gaining of souls for Christ—and to leave nothing undone to make our most holy religion grow and flourish daily more and more in your kingdom, and poor wanderers throw off their mental blindness, dispel the darkness of error, behold the light of truth, and return to the paths of salvation and justice. Finally, We would have you to be well aware of the special regard We have in the Lord for you and for the other Bishops of England. And in testimony of this, Our most earnest good-will, as well as an auspice of all heavenly gifts, We most affectionately impart from Our inmost heart Our Apostolical Benediction to you, beloved Son, and to these same Bishops, as well as to the clergy and faithful laity of all your churches.

Given at Rome, at St. Peter's, December 2nd, 1882, in the seventh year of Our Pontificate.

PIUS IX., CHIEF PONTIFF.

II. Westminster, p. 33.

LETTER OF THE FATHERS TO OUR MOST HOLY LORD, POPE PIUS IX.

MOST HOLY FATHER,

We, the Metropolitan and Bishops of the Province of Westminster, in England, with pleasure and with joy lay the Acts and Decrees of our second Provincial Synod at your Holiness's feet, which we most humbly kiss.

For we may rejoice in the Lord that, once again in Synod assembled, we have been able peacefully to make such decrees as we may hope will conduce exceedingly to the spiritual progress of our clergy and people. We may rejoice that the clergy here assembled have shown themselves most ready to further our wishes and to work with us, with the utmost earnestness and affection, in everything in any way affecting the glory of God and the honour of the Church. In fine, we may not unworthily rejoice, when we see that what was planted at our first Council, and has for three years been watered by us, has, God giving the increase, fixed its roots deeply amongst us; and hence may we augur well of the Synod just concluded. But we approach your Holiness with a sense of the greatest gratitude for your goodness ever manifested towards us, which now encourages us to beg for farther favours, and we arranged a special decree, inserted among the Acts of this Synod, that with due solemnity our thanks should be conveyed to your Holiness for the glorious definition of the Immaculate Conception of the Blessed Virgin Mary, as well as for the liberality with which you vouchsafed, in your paternal affection and hospitality, to welcome several of us during our visit to the Eternal City. We have deputed the Reverend William Clifford, Canon and Vicar-Capitular of the now widowed Church of Plymouth, who was present throughout the Synod, to lay at the feet of your Holiness the aforesaid Acts and Decrees, as we trust, for your approbation, after the necessary corrections and emendations have been made. It therefore remains for us to prostrate ourselves at your Holiness's feet and most earnestly beg your Apostolical Benediction upon ourselves and upon the flocks entrusted to us.

St. Mary's College, in Synod assembled, July 15th, 1855.

Your Holiness's most humble, attached, and obedient
Servant and Creation,

NICHOLAS, CARDINAL WISEMAN

Most humble, obedient, and devoted Servants and Sons,

✠ JOHN, Bishop of Beverley.
✠ GEORGE, Bishop of Liverpool.
✠ WILLIAM, Bishop of Northampton.
✠ THOMAS JOSEPH, O.S.B., Bishop of Newport and Menevia.
✠ WILLIAM BERNARD, O.S.B., Bishop of Birmingham.
✠ WILLIAM, Bishop of Hexham.
✠ THOMAS, Bishop of Southwark.
✠ JAMES, Bishop of Shrewsbury.
✠ RICHARD, Bishop of Nottingham.
THOMAS BRINDLE, Vicar-Capitular of Clifton.
WILLIAM CLIFFORD, Vicar-Capitular of Plymouth.
✠ GEORGE, Archbishop of Trebizond, Coadjutor of Westminster.
✠ ALEXANDER, Bishop of Gerra, Coadjutor Bishop of Liverpool.

The special Decree referred to in this letter is as follows:—

II. Westminster, p. 22.

I.—The Beginning of the Synod.

II.—The Immaculate Conception of the Most Blessed Virgin Mary, dogmatically defined by our Most Holy Lord.

Truly under the happiest of auspices should we consider that this our Synod has been convened and has been begun. For it follows so closely upon the dogmatic definition of the Immaculate Conception of the Mother of God, that justly to Her protection may we entrust all that has been said and done by us. Hence, if we have already taken care that public thanksgiving should be made to Almighty God, all the more have we considered that here together in more solemn form these thanks should be renewed, so that at the very commencement of our work we might upraise our hands and eyes to the God of all consolation, give Him thanks for so great a blessing, and beg that in His clemency He will, for most sweet Mary's sake, free and preserve the Church and the whole world from the evils that threaten it. And specially does it seem likewise befitting that we should express our gratitude to our Most Holy Lord Pius the Ninth, in that, yielding to impulses from above, and guided by the rays of a heavenly illumination, he has happily issued this magnificent definition and spread his own joy over the whole of the world. Nor was this enough. But it was his wish that as many of us as possible should rejoice together with him; and all of us who visited the Eternal City he most graciously welcomed, and set an example to the whole Church of that episcopal virtue described by St. Paul, by treating us with the most unbounded hospitality.

Hence it came to pass that Bishops of our body became associated with very many of the most illustrious Bishops of the world, and stood by the

Chief Pontiff, as it were, witnesses of that most auspicious definition. Hence, too, there was amongst our flocks a more lively kind of appreciation of so great a blessing and a keener participation in the universal joy.

Receiving, therefore, ourselves this definition with humble and most grateful souls, we hereby unanimously proclaim it to the clergy and people committed to us, and most affectionately commend it to their devotion. Let them hearken to the decision of their Father's voice and be glad thereat. Let them congratulate their Mother herself as they behold and wisely make their own this addition to her dignity, this greater abundance of honour, this more sublime prerogative of mercy, this new reason for an increase of devotion, of purity and innocence, this complement, as it were, and most perfect crown of all her original beauty. May fervent devotion, firm trust, and filial love towards Mary, free from all sin, grow day by day in the souls of us all. In our lives may the glory that comes chiefly from charity shine forth, the bright splendour of humility, burning love of God, earnest love of our neighbour, that we may display ourselves as a spectacle of these virtues with which as with a wreath of consummate glory our heavenly Father has crowned Mary.

And may her most sweet name be invoked by us at this outset of our work, as a sign and pledge of that divine grace by which, cherished and aided, the duty committed to us having been successfully undertaken may be brought to a still more successful conclusion.

Reply of Our Most Holy Lord.

PIUS IX., CHIEF PONTIFF.

Beloved Son, and Venerable Brethren Our beloved Sons, health and Apostolical Benediction. Most pleasing was it to Us to receive your letter, written as it was with a deep feeling towards Us of devotion, affection, and reverence, dated the 15th of July last, and just delivered to Us by Our beloved Son, William Clifford, Canon and Vicar-Capitular of the vacant Church of Plymouth, whom you have sent to lay before Us and the judgment of the Holy See, together with this letter, the Acts of the second Provincial Synod recently held by you. We received this beloved Son with all due affection of Our paternal heart, and with the utmost pleasure heard what he told to Us of your affairs. But We have commanded Our Congregation of Propaganda to go carefully through the Acts of the said Synod, as is their wont, and then to lay the whole matter plainly before Us, in order that in due time a fitting reply may be made to you. But meanwhile We chiefly congratulate you upon having again met together in the name of the Lord, and after interchange of counsels having decreed those things which you judge may be conducive to the greater good of your faithful. And it was especially pleasing to Us to gather from your letter that your clergy, wisely mindful of their vocation, were obedient to you, cheerfully seconded your wishes, and with all solicitude, care, and earnestness aided you upon all matters that regarded the greater glory of God, the good and honour of Holy Church, and the salvation of souls. Nor, indeed, is it with less pleasure that we recognise the abundant fruits reaped, by God's assistance, from what was decided by you and approved by Us in the first Provincial Council. And seeing that we were by no means unaware of the special devotion it is your glory to pay to Mary, the Most Holy Mother of God, neither new nor unexpected came to Us the expression of the joy that filled you by reason of the dogmatic definition promulgated by Us of the Immaculate Conception of the same most glorious Virgin. Yet, indeed, not slight was the consolation which this manifestation of your deep devotion conveyed to Us. But whilst We rejoice exceedingly in the Lord at these things, We give encouragement to your souls, beloved Son, and Venerable Brothers and beloved Sons, to rely upon the divine assistance and go on fulfilling your ministry with still greater zeal, and carrying on all those things by means of which the Catholic Church and her saving doctrine in your midst may be daily more and more extended; that the faithful daily nourished more and more with the words of our most holy faith and strengthened by the gifts of grace, may grow in the knowledge of God, and may walk with still greater readiness in the paths of the Lord; and that those who are miserably astray may banish darkness from their minds and look upon the light of truth, and return to the one fold of Christ. In fine, be assured of the singular good-will with which We embrace you. As a pledge of this and an augury of all heavenly gifts, We wish that Our Apostolical Benediction may be with you, and this from Our inmost heart We willingly impart to yourselves, beloved Son and Venerable Brothers and beloved Sons, to all the clergy of your churches, and to the faithful laity.

Given at Rome, at St. Peter's, December 29th, 1855, in the tenth year of Our Pontificate.

PIUS IX.

To Our beloved Son, Nicholas Wiseman, Cardinal of the Holy Roman Church, Archbishop of Westminster, and to Our Venerable Brethren, &c., &c. *Here follow the names of all the signatories to the Bishops' letter.*

III. *Westminster, p. 3.*

LETTER OF THE FATHERS TO OUR MOST HOLY LORD.

MOST HOLY FATHER,

Kissing your Holiness's sacred feet, we lay at them all that we, the Archbishop and Bishops of England, have by our united desires thought it proper to decree in this our third Provincial Synod. And we shall receive them back when approved of and confirmed, or even amended by your Holiness, in the exercise of your supreme jurisdiction, faithfully to be put into execution.

In this Synod we made it our first object that we should strive earnestly more and more and day by day to turn to better account the immense blessings which the Ecclesiastical Hierarchy has conferred upon us. Now the Holy Synod of Trent held that nothing was more important than that each Bishop should have his Seminary for the education of his clergy, wherein he might cherish as in his own bosom his still tender children, and with his paternal hand guide and support them as they grow up.

In addition, not one of the Pontiffs who have ruled the Church of the whole world from the Apostolic See has so laboured for the promotion of the education of the clergy, not one has with such extraordinary and wonderful care brought it to a state of perfection as your Holiness. For besides what you have most completely accomplished in other cities, chiefly in your own, amongst so many eminent witnesses of your munificence shine forth, like unto two splendid constellations, those ornaments of your good city, honoured with the Blessed Virgin's name, the College and Seminary which have sprung from the wondrous solicitude of your paternal heart. But neither time nor change will ever rob our hearts of the feeling and gratitude that to the College founded for England the holy and venerable name of Pius has been given.

Following such footsteps in our humble way, this work, this labour we have with ready minds chiefly imposed upon ourselves of establishing also as speedily as possible in each of our dioceses a Seminary for its exclusive use. Many obstacles have to be surmounted by us, many inconveniences to be borne with; but since we rely not upon our own poor strength, but upon the power of a compassionate God, we willingly devote ourselves bravely to put up with anything, provided our eyes may see this salutary work and that we may receive this new blessing from our Lord.

Prostrate before your Holiness, we most humbly and devotedly beg that pledge and sign of his blessing—the Apostolical Benediction—which we crave that your Holiness will abundantly bestow upon us, and upon the people entrusted to us.

In Synod at St. Mary's, Oscott, July 24th, 1859.

Your Holiness's most humble and devoted Servant and Creation,

NICHOLAS, CARDINAL WISEMAN.

Most humble, obedient, and devoted Sons and Servants,

✠ JOHN, Bishop of Beverley.
✠ THOMAS JOSEPH, O.S.B., Bishop of Newport and Menevia.
✠ WILLIAM BERNARD, O.S.B., Bishop of Birmingham.
✠ WILLIAM, Bishop of Hexham.
✠ THOMAS, Bishop of Southwark.
✠ JAMES, Bishop of Shrewsbury.
✠ RICHARD, Bishop of Nottingham.
✠ ALEXANDER, Bishop of Liverpool.
✠ WILLIAM, Bishop of Plymouth.
✠ WILLIAM, Bishop of Clifton.
✠ FRANCIS, Bishop of Northampton.
✠ GEORGE, Archbishop of Trebizond, Coadjutor of the Most Eminent Cardinal Archbishop of Westminster.

IV. Westminster, p. 6.

Letter of the Fathers of the IV. Council of Westminster to Our Most Holy Lord Pope Pius IX.

Most Holy Father,

We most humbly approached your Holiness's feet and implored your Apostolical Benediction, as we were beginning this our Synod; we gratefully turn again to You, now that we are happily bringing it to a termination.

The second Council of Westminster, held in 1855, was commenced under truly fortunate and happy auspices, for the universal Church was then exulting with joy at the recent promulgation by You, Most Holy Father, of the Dogmatic Constitution concerning the Conception without original sin of the Most Blessed Mary, Mother of God. We have held this our fourth Synod under auspices less joyous, perhaps, yet glorious and replete with blessings, as well by reason of the contests of invincible truth against error, as of the victories gained by the Church over the world. On the one side we see the Church everywhere insolently troubled, Your good city sacrilegiously taken from You, and Yourself, Most Holy Father, Christ's Vicar, fallen into the hands of wicked and scoffing men; but on the other, the authority of the Nineteenth Œcumenical Council condemning the errors of the present day, and the infallible magistracy of Peter's successor proclaimed indeed by Your supreme authority, but welcomed with one voice and one soul by the whole world.

Most sincere thanks, therefore, do we offer You, Most Holy Father, for having in Your thoughtful wisdom, and when it was beyond reach almost of our hopes, vouchsafed to convene the Vatican Council in these rueful times. For in the course of ages all and each of the Articles of Catholic Faith have been controverted, and long since despised and rejected by the haughty ones of this world. The perverse minds of men have consequently reverted to the truths of the natural order; and, lo! that Gnosticism, which foully depreciates or insolently abandons the idea of the Creator, or even the existence of God, has again been revived. Against the apostles of this form of apostacy we have to fight for the light of reason that is implanted in us; the struggle is now for the foundations of the knowledge of God and of the soul. Things have come to this, that, abandoning all principles of certainty, whether divine or human, the votaries of a false science, as they call it, not recognising in themselves the image of God, giving out that men are merely animals and without spirit, regard as fables the creation by God, the laws of morality, and the dictates of conscience, as well as the very soul itself; and thus overthrow society from its very foundations, and prevent the affairs of men from recovering from the confusion and ruin and being restored to order. This our Synod has, therefore, from its heart rendered thanks to You, Most Holy Father, for having by the Dogmatic Constitutions on Catholic Faith and the Church of Christ, with the full assent of the sacred Œcumenical Council of the Vatican, vouchsafed to rank and define amongst the articles of faith, and to propose as dogmas to be believed by all with Divine and Catholic faith, the foundation truths of the natural order, as well as the infallible magistracy which You possess.

Finally, returning to your Holiness's feet, we again beg the Apostolical Benediction upon ourselves and upon all that has been done in this Synod. Working together in perfect peace and never-failing charity, for two and twenty days, we have at length happily brought all things to a conclusion. Never, in our former Councils, have fraternal charity, zeal for souls, or sacerdotal spirit shone forth with greater lustre. Never have the vigour of life in the development of the Catholic Church in England, nor her fruitfulness in spiritual gifts, nor her richness in every good work more clearly manifested themselves. The vineyard which You, Most Holy Father, planted, is increasing and fructifying. May it increase and fructify still, until from sea to sea the shade of saving truth may cover the whole of England.

Bless, therefore, Most Holy Father, our counsels, correct our mistakes, confirm what has been rightly done, that this our meeting may not be to us unto humiliation, but to the glory of God and to the edification, prosperity, and peace of the Church in our beloved England.

We most humbly beg Your Apostolical Benediction.

Your most humble and devoted Servants and Sons,

✠ HENRY EDWARD, Archbishop of Westminster.
✠ THOMAS JOSEPH, O.S.B., Bishop of Newport and Menevia.
✠ WILLIAM BERNARD, O.S.B., Bishop of Birmingham.
✠ JAMES, Bishop of Shrewsbury.
✠ RICHARD, Bishop of Nottingham.
✠ WILLIAM, Bishop of Plymouth.
✠ WILLIAM, Bishop of Clifton.
✠ FRANCIS, Bishop of Northampton.
✠ ROBERT, Bishop of Beverley.
✠ JAMES, Bishop of Hexham and Newcastle.
✠ JAMES, Bishop of Southwark.
✠ HERBERT, Bishop of Salford.
✠ BERNARD, Bishop of Liverpool.

In Synod, at St. Edmund's College, August 12th, 1873.

11.—Two documents, one called the Indiction, addressed to all who should attend a coming Provincial Synod, the other—the Edict—addressed to the body of the faithful, should be issued by the Metropolitan (p. 399).

The following are given in full among the Acts of our Synods.

I. Westminster, p. 5.

INDICTION OF THE PROVINCIAL SYNOD OF WESTMINSTER.

Nicholas, by the divine mercy Cardinal Priest of the Holy Roman Church, under the title of Saint Pudentiana, Wiseman, Archbishop of Westminster. To their Most Illustrious and Right Reverend Lordships the Suffragan Bishops of the Metropolitan See of Westminster, Health in the Lord.

Seeing that it is now a year and more since the Ecclesiastical Hierarchy was most graciously granted by the Holy See to the pious desires of the English Catholics; and that it was most wisely enacted by the Holy Council of Trent that "Metropolitans should not omit to convene Synods in their provinces"; and, moreover, that the express and ever to be revered will of the Holy Apostolic See has been signified to us in reference to this matter;

We, by the present letter, summon and convene in the Lord a Provincial Synod of the Suffragan Bishops of the See of Westminster, to meet at St. Mary's College, Oscott, a place which seems easy of access to all, and otherwise most convenient, on July 5th, and, with the divine assistance, the following days, until it shall be happily dissolved.

Wherefore, Most Illustrious and Right Reverend Brethren, we earnestly exhort you to appoint—each in his own diocese—prayers to be devoutly made to Almighty God, especially during the on-coming time of Lent, that the divine wisdom which cometh down from the Father of lights may illumine the minds of us all, and that the Holy Spirit may warm the inmost recesses of our hearts with His fruitful grace, and that thus whatever He loveth we may love, and that what is well pleasing to Him to be determined we may be able to determine. For we have, in this first Synod, to discuss matters of the greatest moment, touching the state and discipline of the Catholic Church of England—to wit, the splendour of divine worship, the proper administration of the Sacraments, our own duties and those of the whole body of the clergy, the Catholic education of children, the encouragement of devotion amongst the faithful, and, in a word, the fidelity of all to the true and orthodox faith, and their progress in the practice of piety.

We, therefore, Most Illustrious and Right Reverend Brethren, in the discharge of the duty—far too lofty a one for our merits—committed to us, summon you all and each to the said Synod by this present letter, that you may assemble together on the aforesaid day at the aforesaid place, in order to treat in common upon questions of this kind. We also ask that this summons to the Synod should be made known by you to all those, if any there are, in your dioceses who have, or maintain that they have, any right to be present at the Synod, in order that they may lay before us in good time the title they possess or think they possess.

God grant that, by the intercession of the Most Blessed and Immaculate Virgin Mary, Mother of God, of the Blessed Apostles Peter and Paul, and of the patrons of England—to wit, the most glorious Martyrs George and Thomas—this Synod, convened amongst us in the true and Catholic faith, the first for so many years, may redound to His honour and glory, to the exaltation of Holy Mother Church, to the good of souls redeemed by the blood of Christ, and to an increase of piety and heavenly wisdom in us all.

Given at Westminster, the Feast of the Purification of the B.V.M., February 2nd, 1852.

NICHOLAS, CARDINAL WISEMAN,
Archbishop of Westminster.

IV. Westminster, p. 2.

The Indiction.

Henry Edward, by the grace of God and the favour of the Apostolic See, Archbishop of Westminster, to their Most Illustrious and Right Reverend Lordships the Suffragan Bishops of the See of Westminster, Health in the Lord.

Thirteen years have now elapsed since the Third Council of the Province of Westminster was held, and you have most wisely judged, Venerable Brethren, that the time has come when we should set ourselves to celebrate the Fourth Provincial Council during this year.

Very many and most grave circumstances of our times, which affect the Catholic Church in other countries and in this realm, most urgently call upon the rulers of churches to mature their plans. And, since the duty of summoning the Synod falls upon us, we indict and convene the Fourth Provincial Synod of Westminster by this present letter, to be held at our College of St. Edmund, and begun upon the twentieth of July in the present year, unless you, Venerable Brethren, should come to a different arrangement, after consulting as to the place and time at our next Easter meeting.

Wherefore, with fraternal affection, we beg of your Right Reverend Lordships to inform all those ecclesiastics who by the arrangements of Pontifical law have any position in a Provincial Synod, with respect to this summons and command; and invite and arouse betimes in the Lord the clergy and faithful to pour forth their prayers, that, under the guidance of the Holy Spirit, the deliberations of the Fourth Provincial Synod of Westminster may be brought to a happy and a holy conclusion.

Given at Westminster, on the Feast of St. Mathias the Apostle, February 24th, 1873.

✠ HENRY EDWARD, Archbishop of Westminster.

WILLIAM A. JOHNSON, Secretary.

Place ✠ of Seal.

IV. Westminster, p. 4.

The Edict.

In the name of the Holy and Undivided Trinity, Father, and Son, and Holy Ghost. Amen.

Henry Edward, by the grace of God and the favour of the Apostolic See, Archbishop of Westminster, to all the faithful of our Province, Health in the Lord.

So great and so weighty and so holy should be the anxiety of those whom the heavenly Spirit has willed should be and be called Pastors, that no will, no diligence, no love, in fine, should be wanting upon their parts in reference to those things which pertain not only to the preservation but to the extension of the most holy worship of God, of the authority and dignity of the Church, and the discipline of both clergy and laity. Since, therefore, for the correction of morals, and for the return to and progress in Christian piety, the Fathers of Trent, under the guidance of the Holy Ghost, the Author of righteous counsels, determined to renew that old decree of other Councils, that every three years a Provincial Synod should be celebrated; and since for grave and manifold reasons thirteen years have now elapsed since we held a Westminster Synod of the kind, we, in the holy solicitude which is due from us towards the members of the faith entrusted to us, have desired again to summon the Suffragan Brethren of our Province, by a letter written to each of them, to the Church of the College of St. Edmund for a Council, and to fix a day for the commencement of the same, namely, the 22nd of next July. But that the Indiction of this our Council may be spread abroad, and become known unto all and each of those who by right, custom, or privilege should be present at it; and, lest anyone might plead the excuse that he knew nothing of it, or say that he was rejected or overlooked, to all and each of these, as well as to any others who may consider upon whatever grounds that they should be present, we by this Edict, publicly promulgated, signify, indict, and proclaim the same; and we likewise order all and each of those who should be present to repair thither to the Council on the day appointed, under the penalties determined by canonical sanctions.

We likewise advise, and through the love of our Lord Jesus Christ we exhort all the faithful of our Province, by constant prayer and other duties of Christian piety, to implore help for us as we are transacting business of such importance, in order that, aided by His assistance, and keeping before our mind's eye the model of a most strict and holy discipline, we may decree whatever may tend or be essential to its restoration, for God's glory, as well as for the salvation of those who rely upon our faith and care.

And for testimony of all these things, we wish this Edict to be drawn up and printed by our authority, and fortified with our seal, and then to be published to the people, with the signature of our Secretary, by being affixed to the doors of the Cathedral Churches of our Province.

Given at Westminster, July 10th, 1873.

✠ HENRY EDWARD, Archbishop of Westminster.
WILLIAM A. JOHNSON, Secretary.

Place ✠ of Seal.

12.—Usual to indict the next Provincial Council before breaking up the one sitting (p. 405); and, indeed, to fix stated times and the places for all future Councils.

I. *Westminster, p. 30.*

The Promoter: "Most Eminent and Reverend Lord Metropolitan, it has been arranged that the next Provincial Synod should be indicted in Session. I therefore humbly beg that the Second Provincial Synod should be proclaimed and indicted to all for July the tenth, that is, the Tuesday after the Sixth Sunday after Pentecost, eighteen hundred and fifty-five,"

His Eminence the Archbishop having listened to what the Fathers had to say upon the point, made the following decree:—
Nicholas, &c.

Having heard the opinions of the Bishops of the Province present at the end of the last Session of our First Provincial Synod, we decree that the Second Synod shall be held, if it so pleases God, on the tenth and following days of July—that is, beginning with Tuesday of the sixth week after Pentecost, eighteen hundred and fifty-five.

In testimony of which we have ordered this proclamation to be made in this Session, July 17th, 1852.

N., CARDINAL WISEMAN.

Place ✠ of Seal.

By command of my Most Eminent and Reverend Lord the Archbishop.

F., CANON SEARLE, Secretary.

See also II. West., p. 16; III. West., p. 18; and IV. West., p. 23.

13.—A Provincial Council should be held every three years *at least* (p. 412).

14.—The place to be fixed by the Metropolitan, but should usually be his Cathedral. Should he die previously to the Synod, his successor cannot make any change (p. 414, &c).

15.—As to the penalties for not summoning, coming at all to, or leaving the Synod, incurred by Metropolitans, Suffragans, and others, and causes excusing from attendance (pp. 416 and 429).

16.—As to the Decree, "De non Præjudicando," discussed p. 430, it is given in full in I. West., p. 44, and IV. West., p. 32, and is as follows:

As it might happen, especially in a first Synod such as this, that some mistake might be made as to the order in which each person should sit or speak, or as to the title, honour, or precedence due to any one, or the place to be assigned to him, therefore, to avoid any question or claim in the future, we declare that no one shall acquire or lose any right through such mistake, but that each one's rights continue just the same as if nothing in reference to them had happened in this Synod. Nor, should anyone have been summoned or admitted to the Synod without any right, will any privilege accrue to him subsequently.

17.—For the private Congregation, which has become almost customary, though not binding, in modern times, see p. 432.

At our Synods there were always one or two preparatory meetings, properly so called, but what is styled therein the First General Congregation arranged all that Bouix ascribes as the peculiar function of the *private* Congregation, such as claims to be present and of precedence, and the formulæ of the Decrees *Upon Opening the Synod, Mode of Living during the Synod, Faith, &c.*

I. Westminster, p. 42.

UPON OPENING THE SYNOD.

In the name of the Most Holy and Undivided Trinity, Father, Son, and Holy Ghost. Amen.

We, Nicholas, by the divine mercy, under the title of St. Pudentiana,

Cardinal Priest of the Holy Roman Church, Wiseman, Archbishop of Westminster, to the praise and glory of God Almighty, and of our Saviour Jesus Christ, to the honour of the Most Blessed and Immaculate Virgin Mary, Mother of God, of the Blessed Apostles Peter and Paul, of the Holy Martyrs George and Thomas, and of all the Saints, to the edification of the Church of God, for the correction of abuses, and for the increase of piety and zeal for souls in both clergy and laity.

We determine and decree, with the counsel and assent of their Most Illustrious and Right Reverend Lordships the Bishops of England, that on this day, which is the sixth of the month of July of this year, A.D. 1852, a commencement shall, by the help of God, be made, and now has been made, of this Provincial Synod of England, at St. Mary's College, Oscott, the which Synod we had convened and indicted for this day and place, by our letter of the second of February last. God grant that whatsoever is begun and completed by us may redound to His honour, to the good of the Church, and to the salvation of souls, and be a great means of increase to the same.

On the Mode of Life to be Practised at the Synod.

As neither he that planteth nor he that watereth is anything, but He alone Who giveth the increase, God (2 Cor. iii. 7), and as from Him is all our sufficiency, and without Him we can of ourselves not even meditate any good, all our dependence must be placed upon Him, that the Holy Spirit may illumine our hearts, and bring our counsels to a happy end. Wherefore we enjoin upon all present at this Synod so to live during it as to aim at pleasing God, praying without ceasing that our Lord's plentiful grace may descend upon us. Let all, therefore, in the morning spend some time in meditation, and either offer to God the unbloody Victim, or refresh themselves day by day with this heavenly Food. In the corridors and rooms let there not be heard uproar, nor the noise of many talkers, nor the footsteps of persons walking. Even at time of recreation let reserve be apparent in gait, in countenance, and in conversation; so that should anyone speak he may utter the words of God (1 Peter iv. 11); nor, since they are to receive a holier law from our Lord, let them, like the Israelites in the desert, be caught in frivolity, and deservedly suffer chastisement from Him.

Let there be a common table for all who are assisting at the Synod, simple and frugal, which should be seasoned with the reading of Holy Scripture and the canons of the Holy Synod of Trent, as with the flavour of a spiritual salt.

In the evening, let all betake themselves at the hour appointed to their examination of conscience and usual prayers. And let Benediction of the Most Holy Sacrament be given as often as the Fathers wish.

Finally, at all the Congregations, let freedom of speech be granted to all; yet so as the bounds of due respect and deference be not exceeded. But let everything be done in charity, the bond of which should indissolubly unite the hearts of us all in the peace of Christ. Nor let anyone occupy the time of the Synod by lengthy observations; but whatever is to be said, let it be stated briefly and simply, beginning with the youngest and going on to the older members.

The Officials of the Synod.

That everything may go on orderly, and the Acts of this Synod be duly and lawfully drawn up, we elect the following, &c., &c. The offices named are the Promoter, the Secretaries, the Masters of Ceremonies, the Curator, and the Notary.

Appointment of Judges for Personal Questions.

And to prevent the Synod's spending time, listening to questions that concern the rights or acts of individuals, and so being kept from matters of more importance, we appoint as Judges of Questions of this description their Most Illustrious and Right Reverend Lordships the Bishops of Beverley and Birmingham; and it will be their duty to make full inquiry into and report to us concerning the excuses of those who are absent, and the reasons of the departure of any who may leave before the Synod is dissolved.

On not Leaving.

We strictly enjoin all and each of those who have come to this Synod, and in virtue of holy obedience and under the penalties legally enacted, not to leave before the end of the Synod and the signing of the Decrees, unless for reasons laid before them the Fathers have thought fit to give permission to anyone to depart.

For the Decrees on Not Prejudicing and Faith see pp. 34 and 106.

I. Westminster, p. 16.

And when all had agreed to these (Decrees), with the understanding that the clause concerning the daily reception of Holy Communion by those who did not say Mass should be interpreted in an exhortative rather than a binding sense, the Most Eminent Archbishop said: "The Decrees just read are consented to by the Fathers; with their consent, therefore, we decree them as read."

18.—These decrees, customary as they are, Bouix considers not obligatory (p. 443).

19.—Manner of conducting the business of the Council (p. 436).

20.—The usual Profession of Faith (p. 444.) See the records of our own Synods (p. 47).

21.—Terms and titles which should not be made use of (pp. 452 to 462).

22.—In case there is difference of opinion between the Metropolitan and his Suffragans, the weight of authority inclines to the opinion that the Metropolitan should yield (p. 465).

23.—The Council's power over Bishops and Metropolitan (pp. 467, 504).

24.—As to the Council's power in matters of faith, Bouix is satisfied with Cardinal Bellarmine's decision (de Conciliis, c. 10).

    1.—It can judge special cases of manifest heresy in individuals, and can excommunicate them.

    2.—It can pronounce upon a matter of heresy itself which is plain, and in reference to which there is nearly the unanimous opinion of Theologians.

    3.—It can even define a doubtful point of doctrine, if delegated by the Holy See, or if its decision is sent to the Sovereign Pontiff and confirmed by him (p. 515).

25.—In matters of discipline a Provincial Council must not deal with points of general application, or which touch upon what are styled "majora"—or subjects of high import; but its scope is "to see to the purity of faith being maintained in the Province and to the encouragement of piety—by measures adapted to the particular circumstances of time and place" (p. 519).

26.—"Care is very necessary lest, without intending it, the Council should touch upon the rights of the Holy See" (p. 520.) Recommendations of Pontiffs and Canonists upon this head (pp. 520, 536).

27.—Bishops bound to hold a Diocesan Synod within six months of the Provincial Council, and to publish its Decrees therein (p. 537). See I West. p. 88.

28.—The remainder of the work is occupied with the Ceremonial question.

CHAPTER THE THIRD.

SYNOPSIS OF THE TREATISE ON DIOCESAN SYNODS BY BENEDICT XIV.

The only preliminary remark that need be made in reference to the subjoined synopsis is, that the aim has been to give a list, not of the several questions raised by Benedict XIV., such as are met with in the ordinary Indices to his work, but of the conclusions he comes to after careful and very lengthy examination.

BOOK I.

1.—A Diocesan Synod belongs to the power of jurisdiction; and not exclusively to diocesan law, nor to the law of jurisdiction, being of a mixed nature (iv. 1 and 4).

2.—The Bishop may hold his Diocesan Synod in any part of the diocese (v.).

3.—A Diocesan Synod should be held annually (vi.). The Sacred Council of Trent also says: "Diocesan Synods also shall be held every year."—Session xxiv. on Reformation, c. 2. And Benedict XIV. reprobates the opinions of those Canonists who would soften in practice the rigour of this Decree (vi. 5).

BOOK II.

4.—The Vicar-General can assemble a Diocesan Synod by special mandate from the Bishop, but not without (viii. 4).

5.—The Vicar-Capitular can hold a Diocesan Synod (ix. 7).

6.—Vicars-Apostolic, who are appointed to govern a church on the death or translation of its Bishop, have the same power as Vicar-Capitulars; as to other matters, all depends upon the powers given them by the Holy See on their appointment (x. 10).

BOOK III.

7.—Regulars belonging to a Congregation are not bound to attend Diocesan Synods; others are, and these as well, if they have the care of souls (i. 8, 9, 10).

8.—Those who have to be present (iv., &c., &c.), and the order of sitting (x.).

9.—Penalties for non-attendance (xii.).

BOOK IV.

10.—This Book is devoted to the various officials at the Synod and appointed during the Synod—*e.g.*, the Diocesan Examiners. (See I. Westminster, p. 57).

BOOK V.

11.—Amongst the observances of a Diocesan Synod, the Bishop is recommended to make his profession of faith, or rather to subscribe to such profession on its being read aloud for once and all by the Secretary of the Synod, as all others present have to do (i. and ii.).

12.—Settlement of reserved cases at the Synod ; and how far such reservation affects the faculties of regulars (iv. and v.).

13.—The Cathedraticum (vi, &c. See also III. West., p. 53).

14.—The Diocesan Tax for Masses (viii. &c).

Book VI.

15.—Synodal Constitutions, matter and style of (i. and ii.) Examples of important Synodal regulations as to marriages in heretical countries (v., vi., and vii.).

Book VII.

16.—This Book is taken up with the points which Diocesan Synods should be careful to exclude from any constitutions made therein ; as is also the ninth Book.

Book VIII.

17.—The eighth Book gives many matters treated of in Diocesan Synods in reference to the Sacraments of Extreme Unction, Holy Orders, and Matrimony.

Book IX.

18.—The ninth—more questions, mainly in reference to the Holy See, to be avoided ; the rights of regulars to be respected.

Book X.

19.—Diocesan Synods should very reluctantly impose censures, especially those known as *latæ sententiæ* (i., ii.) ; although such a censure may be decreed against an inconsiderable fault, owing to special circumstances (iii.).

20.—Usury or interest (iv., v.).

21.—Stock Exchange speculations on the part of the clergy to be put down by the Synod (vi.).

22, 23.—Diocesan investments (viii.). Fees and fines (ix. and x.).

Book XI.

24.—Novelties to be avoided in the Decrees (i., ii., &c.). Special kinds of novelty ; modern ecclesiastical law not to be set aside under pretence of restoring ancient discipline ; what female relatives may live with a priest ; Synodal Decree of Milan as to precautions for preservation of purity amongst the children of a household.

25.—Questions as to fasting and abstinence to be avoided by a Diocesan Synod (v.).

26.—Also, certain questions as to convents and canons (vi.) ; as well as concerning eunuchs singing in church, suckling infants, the Cæsarean operation &c. (vii.).

27.—Synods not to be set down as unduly severe which prescribe the cassock, &c., for clerics (vii.) ; forbid wigs (ix.) ; disallow attendance at games, hunts, dances, and theatres (x.) ; prescribe the constant study of the old Penitential Canons (xi.) ; check the use of vain adornments of women when they approach the Sacraments of the Holy Eucharist and Penance.

28.—Examples of immoderate severity are cited (xiii.), such as forbidding the smoking or chewing of tobacco or taking snuff before Holy Communion, and making use of the help and patronage of the secular power to obtain a benefice ; the latter under pain of excommunication, *ipso facto*.

29.—Likewise, compelling all adults to hear a sermon every Sunday and holiday in the parish church (xiv.).

Book XII.

30.—The twelfth Book exhausts the question as to Synodal Decrees which are in opposition to common law and Apostolic sanctions.

Book XIII.

31.—The thirteenth, and last, treats of many important practical matters relating to Diocesan Synods. Amongst these are the following:

1.—The extent to which the Placet or non-Placet of the clergy can affect the Bishop's Synodal Statutes. He must consult his Chapter as to these; but is not bound to follow its opinion.

2.—The Bishop alone signs Synodal Decrees.

3.—Diocesan Synodal Decrees need not be submitted to the Holy See for revision or approbation.

4.—Ordinarily speaking, Synodal Decrees are fully promulgated by being read out at the Synod, and are binding upon each person the moment they become known to him. The question as to how far they bind regulars and some others is treated of.

5.—Synodal Decrees may be annulled by their author or his successor, by general non-acceptance, or by custom. As to individuals, they may be dispensed by the Bishop.

6, 7, 8, 9, 10, 11.—The Bishop's visit to the threshold of the Apostles and the Status Animarum he has to present to the Holy See. (See H. West., App. iii., p. 70.)

13 to 25.—Requests, suggestions, &c., to be made on such occasions by Bishops.

CHAPTER THE FOURTH.

BISHOPS.

I. GENERAL DUTIES OF BISHOPS.

1. *Westminster, xxix., p. 87.*

Since "judgment should begin with the house of God" (I. Peter iv. 17), and a Bishop should be "made a pattern of the flock from the heart" (Ib. v. 3), and excel his people and clergy less by the splendour of his sacred robes and the height of his ecclesiastical rank than by eminence in virtue and purity of life; therefore, those points which touch ourselves must not be passed over in silence, but, fearful of becoming reprobate whilst preaching to others, we make the following decrees in reference to our own duty:

1.—Mention was made above[1] of the accurate knowledge of the flock committed to him that a priest should acquire. With much more force does this apply to Bishops. For they, like watchmen placed on the walls of Jerusalem, should unweariedly keep a look out upon every side. They should, therefore, obtain an exact account of every portion of their diocese, to the end that they may become thoroughly acquainted with it.

2.—But this should not satisfy them without going through the whole of it themselves. And this could be easily done, if each Bishop were to divide his diocese into three parts and take one part each year. He would then, in the space of three years, examine into the whole of it, and give the Sacrament of Confirmation in every church in it.

3.—Yet it is of the last importance that he should not omit the regular episcopal visitation.[2] Now this visitation must not be made anyhow, nor according to any old custom, but, as far as is possible, in the way set down in the Roman Pontifical. The Bishop must go through and inspect the church, the priest's house, the schools, and the cemetery, and carefully examine their surroundings and contents—to wit, the church furniture, altars, tabernacle, and whatever else pertains to the divine worship or to the administration of the Sacraments. And if he perceives that there is need of any improvement he must issue his decrees to this effect, and take care that his Vicar-General or the Rural Dean sees that they are carried out. Bishops must also remember that the duty lies upon them of conforming to the Apostolical Constitutions by going from time to time to Rome and laying before the Holy See the state of their dioceses,[3] and visiting the threshold of the Holy Apostles.

---

1. I. West. xxvii. n. 2.   2. See Rescript, p. 73.   3. See p. 50.

IV., West. x. p. 49.

Every four years, according to a Constitution of Sixtus V.—*Romanus Pontifex, s. 4*—the Bishops of England are bound to lay before the Supreme Pontiff as accurate an account as is possible of the flocks committed to their charge.

4.—When a new church is to be built, a plan of the whole, with the fullest details, must be submitted to the Bishop. And this not so much that he may give his opinion upon its beauty or appearance, as that he may know whether or not everything about it is in conformity with the rubrics and ecclesiastical law, and whether or not everything connected with the structure is adapted to aid the piety of the faithful. He should, therefore, look to the altars being of adequate size and suitable for exposition of the most Blessed Sacrament (in places where this is customary); to the altar steps being properly arranged, and to the seats for those ministering at the altar being made in accordance with the rubrics; and to the faithful being able easily to see the altar and the sacred rites performed at it. Nor should he allow the architect to go on with the building until he has complied with the rubrics, decrees, and customs approved of by the Church, in all these particulars.

5.—As soon as this Provincial Synod is finished and its decrees have been approved of or amended by the Holy See, each Bishop will convoke his Diocesan Synod, and promulgate the decrees of this Provincial Synod, as well as do and decree all that herein or otherwise is prescribed to be done and decreed in such a Synod. He shall hold a Diocesan Synod, if possible, every year.

6.—No Bishop shall ordain a cleric born in the diocese of another without a testimonial or dimissorial letter from his own Bishop. And this rule should be kept in the case of converts who wish to enter upon the sacred ministry.

7.—When a priest wishes to leave the diocese to which he belongs, he should have a letter of "ex-corporation" from his Ordinary: and no Bishop should aggregate to his diocese any priest who has not such a letter.

A Decree of Propaganda is then referred to, which is as follows:

I. West., Appendix xxiii., p. 149.

That the Bishops of England may pontificate out of their own dioceses. April 21st, 1852.

If most grievous have been the evils in every place that have arisen from the neglect of Bishops as to the duty of residence, this is especially the case in those countries where, owing to the mingling of the faithful with infidels and heretics, they are exposed to greater dangers. The Bishops and Vicars-Apostolic of such places, so far as these are under the jurisdiction of the Sacred Congregation of Propaganda, have on several occasions been forbidden to pontificate beyond the bounds of their episcopate or vicariate, even with the consent of the Ordinaries. But since there can be no doubt about the care the Bishops of England take to keep the law of residence, and seeing that they have asked that the scope of this rule might be relaxed in their regard, the Sacred Congregation of Propaganda, considering that it not unfrequently happens to be necessary or very convenient that they should pontificate in other English dioceses than their own, and at times also in the neighbouring countries of Ireland and Scotland, agreed at a general meeting on April 5th, 1852, that the Holy Father should be petitioned to relax the above-mentioned rule in favour of the Bishops of England for the three kingdoms, so that they might, with the consent of the Ordinaries, pontificate in any part of them. This decision was referred by the undersigned Secretary to our Most Holy Lord Pope Pius IX., in an audience upon the sixth day of the same month and year, and his Holiness graciously approved of it, and granted the necessary faculties for carrying it out, all things whatsoever to the contrary notwithstanding.

J. PH. CARD. FRANSONI, Prefect.

AL. BARNABÒ, Secretary.

Place ✠ of the Seal.

The following letter IV. Westminster, Appendix iv. p. 136, has reference to the directions (No. 7) given above.

COMMENDATORY LETTERS TO BE REQUIRED. LETTER FROM THE SACRED CONGREGATION OF PROPAGANDA.

MOST ILLUSTRIOUS AND REVEREND LORD,

Most wisely and safely was it ordained in olden times that clerics should not be hastily received by Bishops, especially wandering and unknown priests; but that undoubted testimony as to the goodness of their past lives and habits, as well as of their service in the ministry, should be required of them. And inasmuch as clerics of this kind, with no trustworthy recommendations, are always subjects of suspicion, and are often found to have been guilty of crimes or in other ways irregular, fugitives from justice or banished from their own country: it is necessary, in order to forestall the malice of some men and to keep clear of frauds, that careful inquiry should be made concerning them before they are allowed to say Mass or administer the Sacraments. Hence, with the utmost wisdom was it decreed by the Council of Trent, Session xxiii., c. 16., on Reformation, that "No strange cleric, without a commendatory letter from his Ordinary, should be allowed to say Mass or to administer the Sacraments." And this Constitution of the Fathers of Trent the Apostolic See has ever striven to have carefully kept throughout the whole world unto the present day. Wherefore, in the Councils held of late, notably in that of Baltimore, wise precautions have been decreed in this matter.

With great concern, therefore, has the Sacred Congregation of Propaganda heard more than once, that it happens at times at churches of missions that priests and clerics without such aforementioned commendatory letters are received without difficulty into dioceses, yea, and allowed even to pass from church to church without them. Whence it happens that some priests are subjects rather of scandal than of example to the faithful; and are for destruction rather than edification.

Hence, lest in the future the road to similar evils may be open, the Sacred Congregation lays its special command upon all Bishops dwelling in missionary parts, as well as upon Vicars- and Prefects-Apostolic, that without any hesitation they require commendatory letters from their own Bishops from strange clerics and priests. And those who have them not are in no way to be received.

It was this that had to be notified to your Highness; and I pray God to preserve you unto great length of days.

April 20th, 1873.

  Your most faithful servant in Christ,
   AL. CARD. BARNABÒ,
    For the Reverend Father the Secretary.
  ACHILL. CAN. RINALDINI, Official of the Sacred Congregation.

The fourth Synod has also a decree upon Episcopal Visitations:—

IV. West., xiv., p. 64.

Since the duty of visitation is so intimately connected with the pastoral office that, by the law of the Sacred Canons and the Decrees of Councils (Provincial Synod of Milan, part iii., Decree on Visitation), it cannot and must not be overlooked, it was justly determined in the first Synod of Westminster (xxix. p. 87) that Bishops should not fail to make their episcopal visitation at stated times. And in this visitation they are first of all to find out whether or not all the decrees made at our Provincial Synods in reference to the mode of life and good name of the clergy, the administration of the Sacraments and the care of the flock, as well as to the material state of churches and ecclesiastical goods, are observed to the very letter. In the first Synod of Westminster it was decreed (Decree xxvii. on Regulars) that all missionary and public churches, whether served by seculars or by regulars, are subject to the Bishop's visitation. This, however, as regards the churches of regulars, is to be understood according to the Sacred Canons, and particularly the Constitution of Benedict XIV., *Firmandis* (Appendix xi., note 1.) In order, therefore, that this visitation may the more easily and successfully be carried out, and that everything to be done in it may be more sure of being managed with mutual good-will and for the common zeal of the Church of God, we consider that a plan should be laid down upon the lines of our former Synods and the prescriptions of the Holy See, and ratified at this Synod.

Then follow regulations which have mainly reference to priests and regulars, and which will be found in their proper place below. The two last, however, directly refer to Bishops.

IV. Westminster, xiv.

2.—In all churches which are served whether by secular or by regular missioners the bench rent should be subject to the Bishop's approbation; and in all other public churches it should be fixed in accordance with the statutes of the diocese. Moreover, it is for the Bishop to judge as to the space to be left free for the use of the poor.

3.—The schools of Missions, saving the lawful privileges of regulars (Appendix xi., note 2), are subject to episcopal visitation, both as regards the fabric and the accounts, and the discipline and management; as well as their relations with the civil power. But where the fabric does not belong to the mission, it is exempt from visitation.

II. Westminster, viii. 11., p. 27.

The poor or free ground not to be altered without the Bishop's leave (p. 137.)

II. GENERAL DUTIES OF BISHOPS CONTINUED.

The general duties of Bishops are also referred to in the fourth Provincial Synod:—

IV. Westminster vii., p. 33.

1.—The good shepherd knows his sheep and his sheep know him (John x. 4, 11). When, therefore, the holy Council of Trent wished to restore discipline to the Church and to reform the morals of both clergy and laity, it began with the episcopacy, and reminded the chief pastors of the Church in most solemn words that upon the virtue of superiors rests the salvation of subjects (Session VI. on Reformation, c. 1). Accordingly, all those who have been chosen and appointed by the Holy Spirit to rule over the Church of God should bear in mind that they have not been raised to the highest grade of the priesthood for their own glory, ease, or pride, but to govern and excel the clergy in all sanctity, chastity, and piety, and to shew forth in themselves the living models of full perfection in the pastoral and sacerdotal spirit.

2.—They are set by the Lord upon a watch tower, not only that they may be able to see from on every side their sheep, but likewise that they may be seen by the flock as examples of virtue. Bishops, therefore, receive the fulness of a royal priesthood for the edification and perfection of the Church. To them alone has been committed the chief duty of choosing, educating, and ordaining those levites and priests, through whom the living and compact body of the Church, firmly knit, increases and is perfected to the measure of the age of Christ. Truly, therefore, is the dignity of the episcopate to be dreaded. For a Bishop must not only be perfect, but established in the state of already acquired perfection, that from him, as from an abundant source, the full perfection of the pastoral and sacerdotal life may descend upon the whole of the clergy. "The religious state does not pre-suppose perfection, but leads up to perfection; but the dignity of the pontificate pre-supposes perfection." (S. Thomæ Opusc: De Perfectione Vitæ Spiritualis, c. xix.). Wherefore, a Bishop is bound beyond others to be perfect; that is, to be indued with the most ardent love of God and of his neighbour, with humility, with obedience; to be inseparably one in filial devotion with the Holy and Apostolic See, and ready to give his life for his brethren, which is the chief sign of perfection. Finally, as the living image of our Lord Jesus Christ, Who is the divine model of the mixed life, and therefore of every kind of perfection, a Bishop must shew forth in himself all the perfections of the active and contemplative life united.

3.—As this our Synod, therefore, witnesseth, we with the utmost respect and veneration receive the Holy and Apostolic decrees concerning the dignity of Bishops, as well as the prescripts of the Œcumenical Councils, especially of the Council of Trent, concerning the fulfilment of the office of good shepherds, the restoration of ecclesiastical discipline, and the education of our clergy in learning and piety; we will ourselves observe them to the very letter, and will strive, as far as in us lies, to make them be observed by others.

4.—May our Lord, the Bishop and Shepherd of our souls, grant that our weakness may be aided by the Holy Spirit, that we may firmly and faithfully fulfil every part of our duty to the end of our lives, and that when the Lord shall come, we may be able with joy to render an account of the stewardship committed to us.

The passage referred to in the Council of Trent is as follows (Waterworth's Translation, p. 49):—

"The same sacred and holy Synod, the same Legates of the Apostolic See presiding—wishing to apply *(lit, to gird)* itself to restore ecclesiastical discipline, which is exceedingly relaxed, and to amend the depraved manners of the clergy and Christian people, has thought fit to begin with those who preside over the greater churches; for the integrity of those who govern is the safety (salus) of the governed. Trusting, therefore, that by the mercy of our Lord and God, and the provident vigilance of His own Vicar on earth, it will surely for the future happen that those who are most worthy, and whose previous life, in every stage thereof, from their infancy to their riper years, having been laudably passed in the exercises of ecclesiastical discipline, bears testimony in their favour, will be assumed unto the government of churches in accordance with the venerable ordinances of the Fathers, for that it is a burthen whose weight would be formidable even unto angels: (the Synod) admonishes all those who, under whatsoever name and title, are set over any patriarchal, primatial, metropolitan, and cathedral churches, and hereby accounts all such admonished, that, *taking heed to themselves*, and to the whole flock, *wherein the Holy Ghost has placed them to rule the Church of God which He hath purchased with His own Blood* (Acts xx. 28), they be vigilant, as the Apostle enjoins, *that they labour in all things, and fulfil their ministry* (2 Timothy iv. 5): but let them know, that fulfil it they cannot, if like hirelings they abandon the flocks committed to them, and apply not themselves to the keeping of their own sheep, *whose blood will be required at their hands* (Ezech. xxxiii. 6) by the Supreme Judge; seeing that it is most certain that, if the wolf have devoured the sheep, the shepherd's excuse will not be admitted, that he knew not thereof."

IV. *Westminster x. 1, p. 46.*

The Holy and Œcumenical Vatican Council, in its definition of the primacy of the Roman Pontiff, clearly teaches us the pastoral duty of Bishops in these words;—" To Peter alone did Jesus after His resurrection give the jurisdiction of chief shepherd and ruler over His whole flock, when he said, *Feed my lambs, feed my sheep* (Conc. Vat., Constit. Dogmat. Prima, de Ecclesia Christi, cap. 1)." "Bishops," continues the Holy Synod, "who, chosen by the Holy Spirit, have succeeded the Apostles, like true shepherds feed and govern, each his own, the flocks committed to them" (ib. cap. 3), having to render a severe account to the Divine Shepherd of the sheep under their care.

A practical decree as to the residence of Bishops was issued by his Eminence Cardinal Wiseman in the first Session of the second Provincial Synod, July 11th, 1855:—

II. *Westminster, p. 14.*

As to the absence of Bishops who have failed in keeping residence to the extent of over three months, whether continuously or at several times, contrary to the prescription of the Council of Trent, we decree that it must be inquired into.[1]

III. PROFESSION OF FAITH, &c.

I. *Westminister ix. p. 49.*

In accordance with the Decrees of the Council of Trent and the Constitutions of the Supreme Pontiffs (Session xxiv., c. 1 and 12, on Reformation; and the Bull of Pius IV.—*In Sacrosancta*), we order that those who are appointed to the positions enumerated below shall promptly and within the time prescribed make their profession of faith according to the form given by Pius IV. in the Bull.—*Injunctum Nobis*, A.D. 1564. These are:—

1.—Bishops at the first Provincial Synod they attend; and this we have not omitted.
2.—Vicar-Generals.

---

[1] In all the six Councils of Milan, referred to passim, there is much concerning the duty of episcopal residence.

3.—Canons, on their nomination, at the Chapter; and within a couple of months before the Bishop.
4.—Rectors of churches and others who have the cure of souls.
5.—Professors of Theology and Philosophy in Seminaries and Colleges.

Ib. xxv., n. i., p. 80.

Whoever, therefore, is placed over any congregation should make his profession of faith in presence of the Bishop or his Vicar-General, and promise to teach the same inviolate to the faithful entrusted to him.

At the first Provincial Synod of Westminster the Promoter said:—

"I, Thomas Grant, Bishop of Southwark, beg and suggest that all and each of the Bishops shall not omit to make their profession of faith in this the first Synod they are at, according to the Decree of the Sacred Council of Trent and the Bull of Pius IV.; saving, however, the rights of their Eminences the Cardinals, seeing that by reason of their privileges they are not to be included in this request, or are not bound to make their profession of faith save to the Supreme Pontiff or to the Sacred College.

THOMAS, Bishop of Southwark, Promoter.

His Eminence then issued the following decree:—

"Nicholas, by the divine mercy, under the title of Saint Pudentiana, Cardinal Priest of the Holy Roman Empire, Wiseman, Archbishop of Westminster, &c. Since by the goodness of God and the intercession of the Virgin Mother of God, the first Synod of the Province of Westminster has this day been assembled, we shall make our profession of faith in accordance with the Bull of Pius IV. of happy memory, and the Constitution of the Council of Trent, and we prescribe and enjoin, under the penalties due, that all and each of the Bishops should afterwards make the same profession at this first Session.

"Given on the 7th of July, 1852, at St. Mary's College, Oscott."

N., CARD. WISEMAN.

By command of my Most Eminent and Reverend Lord Archbishop.

L. ✠ S.   F. CANON SEARLE, Secretary.

His Eminence then recited the form of profession called the Creed of Pope Pius IV.—(See I. West., p. 21, and Ritual p. 83,)—after which, seated upon the faldstool, and holding the book of the Gospels, he received the profession of faith of his Suffragans, who approached and placing both their hands upon the book pronounced the following formula:—

"I, N., Bishop of N., accept all and each of the definitions of the Sacred Council of Trent, and likewise promise and profess true obedience to the Supreme Roman Pontiff; I abhor and anathematize all heresies condemned by the Sacred Canons and General Councils, especially by the

same Council of Trent; and profess my faith according to the formula prescribed by Pius IV., which his Most Eminent Lordship, the Metropolitan, has just read, and thus do I accept, promise, profess, anathematize, vow and swear : so help me God, and this Holy Gospel of God."
(From the Acts of the Council of Milan).

First came the Bishops of Beverley, Northampton, and Birmingham; then the others, successively in the same way, made their profession. *(I. West., p. 23).*

At the second Synod (see p. 14), the Bishops who had not yet made their profession of faith according to the Creed of Pius IV., were summoned—to wit, the Bishops of Liverpool, Gerra, and Troy; and as they proceeded duly to make it they were joined by the Archbishop of Trebizond, who, although he had made it at the first Synod, was wishful, for safety's sake, to make it again after his translation from the See of Plymouth to that of Trebizond.

After them the profession was made by the Vicar-Capitulars of the dioceses of Clifton and Plymouth, and by the Reverend Father Abbot of Saint Bernard's.

In the Acts of the third Synod of Westminster, after an enumeration of the Bishops (Liverpool, Clifton, and Plymouth) who had to make their profession of faith as attending a Provincial Synod for the first time, we read as follows :—

III. *Westminster, s. i., p. 13.*

Here it seems best to insert the suggestion of the Sacred Congregation of Propaganda, made in a letter of May 8th, 1860, to his Eminence the Archbishop in the following words :—

"In the Acts of the Synod it is stated that the Bishops who were attending for the first time made their profession of faith according to the Creed of Pope Pius IV. But although it seems sufficient for the strict letter of the law that the Bishops alone should make their profession who have not made it at previous Synods; and since by constant custom it has come to be understood that this should be done by all the Fathers at the Council; therefore, the Sacred Congregation wishes that at future Councils all the Bishops without any distinction should make their profession of faith according to the formula of Pius IV."

Accordingly, in the fourth Synod we find that—

The following Decree as to making the profession of faith was then announced :—

IV. *Westminster, Session i., p. 13.*

Henry Edward, by the grace of God and the favour of the Apostolic See, Archbishop of Westminster, &c.

Since by the goodness of God and the intercession of the Most Blessed Mary, Mother of God, the fourth Synod of the Province of Westminster has this day been assembled, and we are going to make our profession of faith in accordance with Bull of Pius IV., of happy memory, and the Constitutions of the Council of Trent, we order and enjoin upon all and each of the Bishops, under the penalties due, that they afterwards make the same profession at this the first Session.

Given the 23rd of July, 1873, at St. Edmund's College.

✠ HENRY EDWARD,

L. ✠ S.   Archbishop of Westminster.

By command of my Most Illustrious and Reverend Lord, the Archbishop.

JAMES J. GUIRON, Secretary.

The Metropolitan, then turning to the altar, and all the Bishops, made their profession of faith in the following formula of Pius IV.

To enable the Bishops to fulfil the obligations referred to (p. 41,) the subjoined list of questions has been issued by the Sacred Congregation of Propaganda :

II. *Westminster, p. 70.*

1.—State the name, age, and country of the Bishop, and, if a regular, to what religious institute he belongs.
2.—The size and character of the diocese.
3.—The province in which it is situate, or the number of provinces it contains.
4.—If it is an archiepiscopal church, the number and character of its suffragans; but, if an episcopal church, the name of the Archbishop.
5.—Has the Bishop a cathedral and dwelling of his own, and in what city?
6.—Has he any special faculties from the Holy See; and, if so, what are they?
7.—Has he any property of his own; to what amount; and of what kind?
8.—Enumerate the missions of the diocese, and their distance from one another.
9.—When was the visitation of the diocese completed; and was it conducted according to canonical law?
10.—When were provincial or diocesan synods held?
11.—Has there been any unpleasantness with neighbouring Bishops with respect to exercise of jurisdiction?
12.—Has the Bishop a chapter, and how many canons are there?
13.—Are there any prebends, and what are they?
14.—What amount of service do the canons render to the cathedral; and do they likewise discharge the duty of parish priests in portions of the diocese?
15.—Do they reside in their parishes?
16.—Do they mix themselves up with the government of the church and hinder the free exercise of the Bishop's jurisdiction?
17.—Has he a seminary, and where? How many young men are there in it, and what is their course of studies?
18.—Are the regulations of the Council of Trent as to seminaries observed?
19.—Are there parish priests in the diocese, or merely missioners?
20.—Are the parish priests for life, or removable at the Bishop's will; and do they say Mass *pro populo* on feast days?

21.—Are they selected by the Bishop?
22.—How many parishes are there? Is the Blessed Sacrament kept in them, and in what manner?
23.—Have they fixed boundaries and a church of their own; and how many chapels are there in each parochial district?
24.—Are any of the parishes in the hands of religious Orders? Which are they?
25.—Have the parish priests assistants to help them in the cure of souls?
26.—State the number and position of the Catholics dwelling in each place.
27.—Are there Catholic schools, and how many? What number of children are educated in them?
28.—Is Christian doctrine, free from all error, taught therein in the vernacular, and to what extent does an opposite state of things exist?
29.—Are there any non-Catholic schools, and how many? How many Catholics frequent them?
30.—State the number of native priests and of aliens.
31.—Likewise, the country, character, duties to which they apply themselves, and the particular use in the service of the church of the latter?
32.—Have priests of this kind faculties from the Holy See; and at whose expense do they live?
33.—Are there amongst them any students from the Sacred Congregation of Propaganda; their names, and do they discharge their duties satisfactorily?
34.—State also the name, age, and character of any priests who are natives of the diocese and yet not in it; likewise the places where they are located; what they are doing there; and are they in any way bound to the service of their own church.
35.—Are there any clerics of this kind, and how many; how, and upon what title, are they ordained; where do they dwell; and what is required of them before they are promoted to holy orders?
36.—Are there any regular missioners; how many; of what Order and country?
37.—Are certain districts given up to any Order, and by whose authority?
38.—Where do such religious dwell; under what Superiors; and how many houses have they?
39.—Have they duly appointed convents, or simply houses; is enclosure kept in them?
40.—Do they live in community and with regular observance, or alone and in private houses with seculars, and even with women?
41.—How do they dress?
42.—Do they admit natives of the diocese to the habit and to profession, and by whose authority?
43.—Have the regulars any special faculties; and do they lay these before the Bishop before making use of them?
44.—In what respects are they under the Bishop?
45.—In what way are they supported; do they take anything in return for administering the Sacraments; and in what estimation are they held?

46.—In what way do they do good work for the salvation of souls and the increase of religion?

47.—Is there any convent of nuns; of what institute; by whose authority founded; under whose care is it, and who serves it?

48.—Is community life kept therein; and are the nuns bound by solemn vows of poverty, chastity, and obedience, and to keep enclosure?

49.—Are there in the diocese any pious foundations or legacies bequeathed for pious purposes?

50.—Are the proceeds of such bequests properly administered and the canons relating to such matters attended to?

51.—Enumerate all the several abuses which have sprung up even amongst Catholics as to faith, religious rites, morals, the administration of the Sacraments, preaching the Word of God, or of any other kind.

52.—Explain the principal causes of these abuses and how they may be eradicated.

53.—Are marriages properly contracted?

54.—Has Catholicity been on the increase or decrease—say, for the last twenty years; and how is this increase or decrease to be accounted for?

55.—Finally, the Bishop should weigh carefully the spiritual needs of Christianity in his diocese; clearly state them; and propose suitable means for making up for the mistakes of the past and for the furtherance of religion in the future.

IV. DIOCESAN OFFICIALS.

I. Westminster, xiv., p. 56.

1.—It is meet that in every diocese a Vicar-General should be appointed, and that such faculties as the Bishop shall think proper shall be given to him in writing; so that, when the Bishop is absent or hindered, he may be able to attend to the ecclesiastical business of the diocese and assist the Bishop in the government of the church.

2.—In addition to the Vicar-General, the Bishop may also appoint Vicars-Foran, or, as they used to be called in England, and are now commonly called, Rural Deans, giving them certain faculties, in writing, for their use in a specified district.

3.—It will be the duty of the Rural Dean to take the chair at the meetings or conferences upon cases of conscience and liturgy throughout the district assigned to them, to attend to priests who are sick, to look after the administration of church property, to see to sacred edifices being kept in repair, and to lay before the Bishop or Vicar-General such matters as need attention.

4.—It is also befitting that the Bishop should select from his chapter or from the body of his clergy a few men of judgment to help him in the administration of the temporalities of the diocese. He should often advise with these, to the end that pious foundations may be managed in the best way possible and maintained in safety; and that the collections made amongst the faithful may be distributed and applied with wisdom and advantage and without any party spirit.

5.—Every Bishop must appoint synodal examiners for his diocese, and that at his next Diocesan Synod.

6.—At this also, he should select five of his most suitable priests to form a *Commission of Inquiry* (as was decreed above, *c. xiii*). And it seems proper that two of these should be members of the chapter, and the other three taken from the body of the clergy.

7.—Every Bishop should have a keeper of the archives. And his duty it will be to take charge of all papers and documents that have reference to the diocese; and he should take copies of them, in case the originals should fall into other hands. Moreover, he should have a complete list of them all.

The decree referred to is as follows:— *1 Westminster xiii. 3, p. 55.*

The Bishop should, at his Diocesan Synod, select five of his most suitable priests to form a *Commission of Inquiry*; and one of these should be made by the Bishop, President of the Commission.

How the Bishop is to supply vacancies on the Commission, (see p. 159).

As to the appointment by the Bishop of Missionary Rectors and the use to be made of the Commission of Inquiry, see chap. vi. on Missionary Rectors, p. 130.

Also:

IV. West., xv. 3. p. 67.

A *defender of marriages* shall be named at each of the Diocesan Synods, saving the Bishop's right, however, of changing him.

VI.

V. HOLY ORDERS.

I. Westminster, xxi. p. 71.

The chief point of pastoral care is to bring up and appoint to positions in the Church ministers and dispensers of the mysteries of God, who are worthy, faithful, and endowed with every kind of virtue. We, therefore, direct that the following rules should be strictly followed in regard to the education and ordination of clerics:—

1.—Bishops should hold ordinations at the times fixed by Canon Law as far as possible, and either in their cathedrals or in the churches or chapels of seminaries. They should be conducted with the greatest solemnity, and all the rites prescribed in the Roman Pontifical should be fulfilled.

2.—But inasmuch as amongst those to be ordained there are either converts, or the children of converts, or persons who have in other ways incurred irregularity, the Bishop should make careful inquiry, so that, if there should be anyone thus circumstanced, he may be freed from the irregularity before ordination. It seems, therefore, advisable that our Lord his Holiness should be petitioned, that, in seminaries common to several Bishops, the one actually ordaining should have the faculty of absolving from irregularity those even who are not his subjects, with the consent of their Ordinaries. And, indeed, when the doubt arose as to whether the extraordinary faculty of ordaining out of the usual times could be exercised in the case of all the students in seminaries of this kind, the Sacred Congregation of Propaganda issued a decree in April last, which was approved of by his Holiness, and in which the faculty is given to Bishops, in whose dioceses there are such colleges, of ordaining out of the usual times students who are not their subjects, with the consent of their respective Ordinaries.

The following is the decree referred to:— *I. Westminster, Appendix xv., p. 143.*

His most Eminent and Reverend Lordship, Cardinal Nicholas Wiseman, Archbishop of Westminster, and their Right Reverend Lordships the Bishops of England, have intimated that doubts have arisen as to the extraordinary faculty granted to them—No. 1 upon their paper—for giving ordinations out of the times prescribed by Canon Law, inasmuch as in England there are seminaries common to several dioceses in which clerics who are subjects of another diocese are being educated. Their Eminences, therefore, at a general meeting on April 5th, 1852, thought fit to yield to the prayer of this petition—viz., that the Bishops in whose dioceses there are seminaries of this description may make use of the above-mentioned faculty in favour of those even who are not their subjects, with the leave of the respective Ordinaries.

This decision of the Sacred Congregation of Propaganda was by the undersigned Secretary laid before our Most Holy Lord Pope Pius IX., in an audience of the sixth day of the same month and year, and his Holiness graciously approved of it and assented to the petition presented, all things whatsoever to the contrary notwithstanding.

Given, &c.

AL. BARNABÒ, Secretary.

The question as to irregularity was set at rest by the subjoined reply of Propaganda:— *Ib. Appendix xv., p. 143.*

MOST HOLY FATHER,

Since, in Form No. 2, which is usually given to the Bishops of England, it is laid down that no Bishop can make use of the faculties therein granted beyond the bounds of his own diocese; and since it often happens that one Bishop has to hold ordinations for a seminary common to several dioceses, the Archbishop and Bishops of the Provincial Council of England beg that the Bishop actually ordaining, either in the seminary or out of it, may, with the consent of the Ordinary of each of the candidates, absolve them from any irregularity, but that in other respects they should adhere to the tenor of the same paper, No. 2.

In an audience with his Holiness, granted March 13th, 1853, our Most Holy Lord Pius, by divine Providence Pope Pius IX., on my laying the matter before him, as Secretary of the Sacred Congregation of Propaganda, graciously yielded to this petition, in accordance with the opinion of their Eminences, all things whatever to the contrary notwithstanding.

Given at Rome, from the said Sacred Congregation of Propaganda, May the 14th, 1853.

L. ✠ S. AL. BARNABÒ, Secretary.

Two other rescripts follow, which have reference to ordinations:—

I. Westminster, Appendix xvi. and xvii., p. 144.

His Most Eminent and Reverend Lordship, Cardinal of the Holy Roman Church, Nicholas Wiseman, and their Right Reverend Lordships the Bishops of England have come to the conclusion that, taking into consideration the state of their churches, it is hardly feasible for clerics to be promoted to the greater orders upon titles elsewhere admissible. They have, therefore, asked that for a limited number of cases the faculty may be given them of ordaining upon the title of the mission. This petition was referred to a general meeting of the Sacred Congregation of Propaganda, held April 5th, 1852, and their Eminences decided that, subject to the pleasure of his Holiness, a similar faculty to one granted in 1741 to the Bishops of Ireland might be given; to wit, that the Bishops who have the government of English dioceses should be able to promote clerics of their several dioceses, to the number of twelve, upon the title of the mission, provided that those to be thus ordained should previously have promised upon oath to devote their services to the mission, just in the way and under the same form of oath as the students of Papal foundations, the burthen in all cases resting upon the consciences of the Ordinaries.

This decision of the Sacred Congregation was laid before his Holiness our Lord Pope Pius IX., in an audience on the sixth day of the same month and year, by the undersigned Secretary, and his Holiness graciously approved of it, and granted the faculty prayed for, all things whatsoever to the contrary notwithstanding.

J. PH. CARDINAL FRANSONI, Prefect.

L. ✠ S. AL. BARNABÒ, Secretary.

Most Holy Father,

Since, by reason of the poverty of many places, there are hardly grounds for hope that benefices ample enough to constitute a title for ordination will be founded, and since it is not easy to fill up the void under the title of patrimony, the Archbishop of Westminster and the Bishops of England, in Provincial Council, beg that your Holiness will deign to extend farther the indult granted last year, that they may be able to ordain upon the title of the mission.

In an audience with his Holiness, granted March 13th, 1853, our Most Holy Lord Pius, by divine Providence Pope Pius IX., upon the representation of me, the undersigned Secretary of the Sacred Congregation of Propaganda, at the wish of their Eminences of the Sacred

Congregation, graciously granted that the Archbishop and Bishops might each promote twelve candidates upon the title of the mission, observing everything prescribed in the former indult, all things whatsoever to the contrary notwithstanding.

Given at Rome, from the Office of the Sacred Congregation of Propaganda, March 14th, 1853.

L. ✠ S.   AL. BARNABÒ, Secretary.

Bishops are admonished as to the duty of training up clerics and ordaining only those who are worthy. *IV. Westminster, vii. 34; quoted above p. 45.*

To them alone has been committed the chief duty of choosing, educating and ordaining those levites and priests, through whom the living and compact body of the Church, firmly knit, increases and is perfected to the measure of the age of Christ.

Ib. c. ix., n. 6, p. 38.

Bishops, either personally or by means of examiners specially appointed for this purpose, must use every care and precaution in their selection of candidates for the priesthood. And they should use every means in their power, and encourage others, to make and increase provision, in the way of *burses*, for the education of ecclesiastical students.

Ib. p. 39.

Bishops should leave nothing undone, each in his own diocese, to establish diocesan seminaries, in which clerics may be taught theology and philosophy without being mixed up with lay students.

III. Westminster, ii., c. i., p. 44.

Then, indeed, could every Bishop watch over the education of his own subjects, and instil into them his own spirit.

IV. Westminster. ix., n. 7, p. 39.

The Bishop should appoint a Spiritual Director in his seminary.

Ib. n. 13, p. 42.

The books to be used in the seminary to be submitted to the Bishop, and promising students selected by him for completing their studies in Rome.

Ib. n. 18, p. 45.

Finally, since by the teaching of Benedict XIV., the Bishop is bound to know his candidates for ordination, and since upon his conscience falls the burthen of their ordination, therefore will it be his duty as their pastor and father frequently to visit them, that he may know his own and be known by them: besides, he will take care to exact a strict account, at least every year, from the rector of the talent and character, as well as progress in learning and virtue of each of the seminarists.

Benedict XIV. most earnestly admonished all the Bishops of the Catholic Church as follows in regard to the management of their seminaries :—" But it is of necessity that these Colleges should be attended to by you with especial care ; to wit, by frequently visiting them ; by ascertaining the history, talent and progress in studies of each of the young men ; by appointing for their education proper masters, endowed with the ecclesiastical spirit ; by gracing their literary examinations or their ecclesiastical functions from time to time by your presence, and by giving rewards to such as have given proof of their good qualities, and have earned something beyond ordinary praise. You will not repent of having laboured at watering young plants such as these ; but your trouble will one day produce gladsome fruit in the rich abundance of good workmen. Oftentimes have Bishops been wont to grieve that the harvest indeed is great, and the labourers few, but perchance they might also grieve that they themselves had not taken the pains they ought to have done that the labourers should be ready and fit for the harvest work : for good and earnest workmen are not born, but made ; and their being made depends upon the Bishop's activity and care." (*Encyclical letter, Dec. 3rd, A.D., 1740*).

I. Westminster, xxi., 6 p. 28.

Priests ordained upon the title of patrimony subject to the Bishop of the diocese. (See p. 146).

VI. MATRIMONY.

I. Westminster, xxii., 1, p. 73.

Questions as to Banns and their introduction to be referred to the Bishop. (p. 147).

Ib. xxii. 8 and 9, p. 74.

How dispensation are to be granted. (p. 147).

IV. Westminster, xv., p. 66.

ON MATRIMONIAL CAUSES SO FAR AS THEY BELONG TO THE FORUM EXTERNUM.

Notwithstanding all the decrees, general and special, that have been made in our Provincial and Diocesan Synods upon Matrimony, as difficulties often, and at times even great scandals, are liable to arise, owing to the ignorance or rashness of those who have matrimonial causes in hand, we think it fit to make a few declarations and to decree that they shall be faithfully attended to.

1.—By matrimonial *causes* are meant questions as to the validity of marriages ; and these belong solely to the *forum externum*, and depend for judgment concerning them upon the Ordinary. To the Ordinary, therefore, recourse must be had when there is any question as to marriage of travellers and strangers ; any question as to contracting a fresh marriage whilst any doubt exists as to the validity of a previous one ; any question as to any kind of doubt about the death of a former husband or wife, or about the freedom to marry of those who wish to do so. For to the Ordinary does it belong to judge as to whether those who are called travellers are truly such, and to give them permission to marry; it is for him to judge as to whether strangers who have come hither have either domicile or *quasi*-domicile, in the sense in which it is lawfully understood, or, at any rate, by permission of their Ordinary, are sufficiently under his jurisdiction. And in all other matters of doubt, if any such, after careful inquiry, remain, it is the Ordinary's duty alone to weigh these, and, if necessary, after a judicial investigation, to pronounce judgment upon them.

2.—But as regards marriages *already contracted*, we most earnestly admonish and command in the Lord all priests who have the cure of souls, to make it known to all concerned, that they have no authority to decide in such matters, even though they are satisfied as to the proof of the invalidity of any former marriages; but that before presuming to proceed to a fresh marriage they must have recourse to the Ordinary and await his authoritative decision.

3.—Whenever in a matrimonial cause a judical investigation as to the validity or nullity of the marriage is to take place, it must be managed in the way prescribed by law, and a *defender of the marriage* must be appointed. And in order to this, a *defender of marriages* shall be named at each of the Diocesan Synods, saving the Bishop's right, however, of changing him.

4.—In the management of matrimonial cases or causes, priests must be as exact and careful as possible in inquiring into facts and circumstances, in collecting proofs and the necessary documents, and in preparing those who are about to marry that they may receive the grace given in this Sacrament. But whenever for any reason recourse has to be had before the marriage to the Ordinary, the matter should not be laid before him until all things connected with it are completed as far as possible. For it is the Ordinary's duty to give judgment upon a case when it has been carefully drawn up and fully investigated, and to grant permission or dispensation; but by no means, either by himself or by his officials, or by letters, or by examination of the parties, to make an inquiry into the facts, to exact proofs, or to get possession of documents. (As to *Mixed Marriages and Marriages by heretical Ministers*, see Appendix vii. and xiv.).

II. Westminster, App. vii., p. 79.

INSTRUCTION OF THE HOLY OFFICE AS TO MARRIAGE, IN CASES WHERE THERE IS A PRESUMPTION THAT THE BAPTISM OF THE NON-CATHOLIC PARTY IS INVALID.—*Wednesday, December 20th, 1837.* (See *I. Westminster, chap. xxii.*).

Our Most Holy Lord, by divine Providence Pope Gregory XVI., having, at the usual audience of the Reverend Father the Commissary-General of the Holy Office, heard of the doubt submitted by the

Reverend Father the Lord Bishop of New York, as to whether baptism should be administered conditionally in the case of a non-Catholic about the validity of whose previous baptism there was suspicion, when desirous of contracting marriage with a Catholic who had obtained a dispensation from the Apostolic See for this purpose; and having taken the suffrages of their Eminences the general Inquisitors, said:

Let the decree be given which was sent, Wednesday, September 17th, 1830, to the Reverend Father his Lordship the Bishop of Le Pay, and which was as follows:—

"Are Calvanists and Lutherans living in those parts, whose baptism is a matter of doubt and suspicion, to be regarded as infidels, so that between them and Catholics the impediment of difference of religion should be considered diriment?"

To this case the Sacred Congregation on the same day made this reply: (1) as to non-Catholics whose ritual prescribes baptism, but without the requisite use of the essential matter and form, each special case must be examined into; (2) as to those who, in compliance with their ritual, baptize validly, the baptism is to be deemed valid; (3) but if it is well known that the custom of any sect is against any baptism, the marriage is null.

His Holiness ordered that to these decisions it should be added that: in the third case, mentioned in the above decree, that is in the certain nullity of the baptism of the non-Catholic, the same Bishop of New York should make an application upon each special occasion.

ANGELUS ARGENTI, Notary, &c.

Ib. viii., p. 80.

INSTRUCTION OF THE HOLY OFFICE AS TO THE KIND OF PROOF REQUISITE BEFORE A SECOND MARRIAGE IS CONTRACTED. (See I. Westminster, chap. xxii.) *Wednesday, June 12th, 1882.*[1]

The great wars and other convulsions to which our times have been exposed are still the cause of many petitions coming to Rome from women, and some times men, who have no legal document attesting the death of a long absent spouse, and yet ask permission to contract fresh nuptials. Now the Apostolic See, or rather the Supreme and Sacred Congregation of their Eminences, those Cardinals of the Roman Church who were deputed to this work, rests solely for its determination upon ecclesiastical law, according to which the death must not be presumed merely by reason of the lapse of years, but must be proved to have occurred. And hence, in the reply of Lucius III., provision has been made by Canon Law (c. *Dominus etc.*, upon second marriages): "That no one for the future shall presume to enter upon a second marriage until it is clear that his or her former spouse is dead." And the kind of proof that is required may be gathered from the decree— *Cum alias*—of Clement X., made for all future times, Thursday, August

---

[1]. See Benedict XIV's Constitution given in Dr. Smith's Ecclesiastical Law, vol. ii., app. iv., with the following note:—Nearly this whole constitution is taken up in defining the duties of the judge, of the defender of the marriage, the force and effect of sentences in matrimonial causes.

Also, the Instruction of the S. Congregation of the Council, Ib. App. v., of which the author writes:—This Instruction, as its heading intimates, lays down in detail the formalities of trials in matrimonial causes of nullity, and is of the greatest practical importance also in this country. Also, see Ib. App. vi.

21st, 1670, and contained in the Roman Bullarium. In this the Sovereign Pontiff gives an Instruction for the guidance both of the court of his Eminence the Reverend Lord Cardinal-Vicar of the City and of the courts of other Ordinaries, as to the examination of the testimony in favour of a fresh marriage.

First of all, an authentic document as to the death itself should, if possible, be had. For this is prescribed (*Nos. 10 and 11*): "If a witness answers that those who are desirous of marrying have already had wife or husband, but that these are dead, he should be asked as to the place and time of their death, and as to how he (the witness) knew that they were married, and that they are dead. And if his answer should be that they died in some hospital or that he saw them buried in a certain church, or that after a battle they were buried by soldiers, permission to marry must not be given before an authentic confirmation has been received from the rector of the church at which the burial took place; or, if possible, from the commander of the regiment in which the party served as a soldier. If, however, testimony of this description cannot be had, the Sacred Congregation does not mean to put out of the question other kinds of proof, which by common law may be accepted, provided they are sound and ample."

From these last words is derived the rule followed by this Sacred Congregation in cases where direct authentic testimony as to death cannot be had, namely, that it must be supplied by sound and ample proofs of other kinds. Of these notably is that which arises from the account of trustworthy witnesses, concerning whom it is prescribed in the same Instruction: "Relations, as being presumably better informed, rather than strangers, and fellow-citizens rather than others, should be accepted as witnesses in these matters; but neither wanderers nor soldiers, unless for some special reason, and upon mature reflection, should be allowed." And where the person who gives testimony is treated of, it is prescribed that, "together with the witnesses, some other person known to the notary should appear, who may give evidence as to the name and surname of the witness himself, as well as to his ability to give testimony." But, considering the many great difficulties which surround proof of death of this nature, the Sacred Congregation would reject no evidence which tends to enable them to see as to whether a number of concurrent testimonies, which apart could not generate certainty, might not do so when all taken together. Hence presumptions and conjectures, by means of which the evidence of witnesses is strengthened, are admissible, and account may be taken of public talk and rumours. Certain authentic facts, too, which pre-suppose the death are allowed their weight. It also happens that the evidence of well-informed and trustworthy witnesses may have been heard by others at a time which puts it beyond the reach of suspicion; and so, should it be impossible to examine the immediate witnesses themselves, either by reason of their decease, absence, or some other cause, the evidence of those who state what they have heard from them may be taken, should they be of opinion that, all things considered, there is sufficient proof of death for a prudent decision as to it.

Now, seeing that this is a matter of the utmost moment, inasmuch as it is of faith, that matrimony is indissoluble by the divine law, and that there cannot be a second marriage during the lifetime of the other party, the Sacred Congregation weighs each case, and, after taking the opinion of several theologians and experts in canon law, gives final judgment as to the sufficiency of the proof of death, and as to there being no obstacle to the petitioner's contracting fresh nuptials.

IV. *Westminster, App. xiii., p. 151.*

INSTRUCTION TO THE BISHOPS OF ENGLAND UPON MIXED MARRIAGES.

MOST ILLUSTRIOUS AND REVEREND LORD,

Since the issue of the Instruction to all Archbishops, Bishops, and other Ordinaries, concerning *dispensations for the impediment of difference of religion in the case of mixed marriages,* which was signed by his Most Eminent and Reverend Lordship Cardinal Antonelli, certain facts have come to the knowledge of this Sacred Congregation, not only in reference to the increased facility in some places for contracting mixed marriages without just and grave cause, but also to the dispensations which are granted by delegated authority for such marriages, which makes it abundantly clear that that admirable Instruction is in some places misunderstood, and is misconstrued into a sense totally opposed to its letter and spirit in others. For that Instruction expressly recalls the Catholic Church's opinion as to marriages of this kind between Catholics and non-Catholics, when it explicitly declares that the Church "has ever disapproved of them and regarded them as unlawful and dangerous, by reason of the evil participation in things divine, of the constant danger of perversion to the Catholic party, and of the bad education of the offspring." And then it puts the Ordinary in mind of "the most ancient canons as well as more recent decisions of Chief Pontiffs, by which latter, although the severity of the canons has been somewhat relaxed, so that mixed marriages are at times allowed, this is only done for grave reasons and with reluctance, and solely on express condition that all necessary and fitting precautions be previously taken that are called for by the natural and divine law; so that, forsooth, not only it may not be possible for the Catholic party to be perverted, but that the Catholic may understand that it is a matter of duty to strive for the conversion of the non-Catholic, and likewise that the whole of the issue of the mixed marriage, of both sexes, must of necessity be educated in the holiness of the Catholic religion.

And, this being the case, it has been a matter of surprise to this Holy Congregation that anyone should have thought that in the aforesaid Instruction there had been any departure from the principles which the Holy See has ever held and taught concerning mixed marriages. And, lest from any wrong interpretation of that Instruction, copious as it in every sense is, the people committed to you should suffer harm, I earnestly, in the Lord, crave your care that you will endeavour, on a fitting opportunity, to teach and inculcate upon the clergy and faithful under your jurisdiction the true doctrine and practice of the Church in reference to mixed marriages.

Accordingly, as you are well aware, *it by no means suffices* for allowing a mixed marriage, *that the parties are ready to agree to the precautions* alluded to above, *as well as to the other requirements usually noted in the Rescripts of the Apostolic See, but true and grave causes are absolutely requisite*, that the faculty of dispensing with the impediment of difference of communion may be lawfully put in execution. For these precautions are exacted by the natural and divine law, and must be insistted upon, that the intrinsic danger of all mixed marriages may be removed; but, besides, there must of necessity be some grave difficulty, which cannot in any other way be overcome, for the faithful to be allowed to expose themselves to great dangers in regard of faith or morals, even with these timely precautions. And if, in the aforementioned Instruction, the custom of making use of the rite prescribed in the Diocesan Ritual for marriages, always of course, without the celebration of Mass, seems to be tolerated for mixed marriages, this is only granted as something exceptional and on condition that *everything connected with the matter, with the place and the persons has been carefully considered, the burthen resting on the Bishop's conscience of the truth and necessity of every item of the circumstances.* So far is it from truth that by anything therein the principles which the Holy See has at all times proclaimed, are in the least degree departed from.

Wherefore I earnestly appeal to your charity, that to your utmost in the Lord you will endeavour and strive to keep the faithful under your charge from contracting mixed marriages, and so keep clear of the great dangers which ever accompany them. And this you will the more easily accomplish, if you are careful that they are made aware in time of their special duty of hearkening to the Church in this matter, as well as of obeying their superior, who would have to render a very strict account to the eternal Prince of Pastors, if they not merely allowed mixed marriages at times for weighty reasons, but permitted them readily and at the mere will of petitioners.

I pray God to keep you safe and well.

Given at Rome, at the office of the Sacred Congregation of Propaganda, March 25th, 1868.

AL. CARDINAL BARNABÒ, Prefect.

JOHN SIMEONI, Secretary.

To the Most Reverend Lord Archbishop of Westminster.

Ib. xiv, p. 154.

On Marriages Before Non-Catholic Ministers.

My Most Eminent, Reverend, and Honoured Lord,

The abuse which was some months ago brought before the Holy See as existing in England, namely, that in cases of mixed marriage the Catholic party is usually compelled to renew the consent in presence of an heretical minister, was laid before the Supreme Congregation of the Holy Office together with the final observations your Eminence was pleased to make upon the question. Now, the most Eminent Inquisitors, several having examined into the same on Wednesday, the 8th of this month, have passed the resolution, that: "The abuse in question must be abolished, mainly by reason of the scandal arising from it; that the faithful are to be taught betimes, whenever an opportunity offers itself, what a sin they commit and what censures they contract by renewing their consent before an heretical minister in his religious capacity. But, as to special cases, the Instruction of Wednesday, February 17th, of this year, to the Bishops of the Kingdom of Hanover, should be made known to the English Bishops."

Forwarding to your Eminence herewith the aforesaid Instruction, I beg that, with your wonted kindness, you will communicate to your Suffragans as well the above-mentioned resolution of the Holy Office as the Instruction connected with it. And, with the profoundest respect, I reverently kiss your hand.

Rome, Propaganda, June 13th, 1864.

From your Eminence's most humble and devoted servant,

AL. CARDINAL BARNABÒ, Prefect.

A. CAPALTI, Secretary.

To the Most Eminent and Reverend Cardinal Wiseman, Archbishop of Westminster.

Instruction Given to the Bishops of the Kingdom of Hanover, *Wednesday, February 17th, 1864.*

It is well known that in some places a non-Catholic minister occupies the position of a mere civil magistrate, and that persons about to marry are accustomed, and indeed obliged, to present themselves before him for a legal end—namely, that they may be regarded as lawfully married and their offspring deemed legitimate. Now, if non-Catholics are pressing in the matter, or the civil law binding, there is no objection to the Catholic party accompanying the non-Catholic to the non-Catholic minister solely for the purpose of supplying the legal duty, either before or after the marriage is contracted according to the form prescribed by the Council of Trent. For the Sacred Congregation answered *affirmatively* to the question, some time ago laid before it, as to whether a Catholic who is contracting marriage with a non-Catholic, in presence of his parish priest, may lawfully, at the instance of non-Catholics, ratify this marriage in the presence of a non-Catholic minister, provided there be no show or use of heretical rites, and that the action of the heretical minister be, and be considered to be, for the civil and legal satisfaction of the parties.

But, whenever the non-Catholic minister is supposed to be in a sacred character, and discharging, as it were, the duty of a parish priest, it is unlawful for the Catholic party to renew his consent to marriage with a non-Catholic before such a ministry, because it would be made use of as a kind of complement to the religious ceremony, and the Catholic party would be joining in an heretical rite, and hence there would be an implicit yielding to heresy, and altogether unlawful communion with heretics in things divine. Wherefore, although this evil custom has grown so strong that it can hardly be put down by the clergy, every effort of earnestness and zeal must be made to extirpate it. And, indeed, Benedict XIV. clearly teaches that it is unlawful for those who are contracting marriage to present themselves before a non-Catholic minister, if he acts in a sacred capacity; and that those thus contracting are guilty of grievous sin and to be admonished.

Let, therefore, parish priests and missioners be instructed in good time by you to teach the faithful, both at catechetical instructions in the church and in private, the constant doctrine and practice of the Church; so that they may happily keep, as far as possible, from mixed marriages; or, at any rate, may be completely opposed to celebrating marriage before a non-Catholic minister in his *quasi*-sacred capacity, for this is altogether unlawful and sacrilegious. This was the reply given to the Ordinary of Treves on Wednesday, April 21st, 1847.

Parish priests should, moreover, be made aware that they must not remain silent if the question is put to them by the contracting parties, or if they happen to know for certain that they are going before a non-Catholic minister, acting in his sacred capacity, to renew their consent; but they must admonish them as to the very grievous sin they are committing and the censures they are incurring.

But if in any special case the parish priest is not asked by the parties as to whether they may go to the non-Catholic minister, and no mention is made by them of their being about to do so, and yet he should foresee that they actually will go to renew their consent, he may, with a view to the avoidance of great evils, hold his peace, if he judges from the circumstances of the case that any warning will be of no avail, or rather harmful as turning material sin into formal, provided there is no danger of scandal, and that the other conditions required by the Church have been fulfilled and the precautions duly taken, notably the one that concedes full liberty in the exercise of religion to the Catholic party and the education of the offspring in the Catholic religion. But if it is a case of the consent being renewed before the parish priest after marriage has been contracted in the presence of a non-Catholic minister, and this is publicly known, or even made known to the parish priest by the parties themselves, he shall not be present at this marriage unless everything has been done that ought to be, and the Catholic party repenting of the deed has undergone previously due penance and received absolution from the censures contracted.

The Sacred Congregation, therefore, has great confidence in the Lord that you will adhere wisely and unswervingly to these points, and secure that the deposit of inviolable doctrine be kept pure and safe; that the morals of Catholics may be in accordance with their faith; that the evils apprehended may be averted; and that the faithful, strengthened by teaching and example, may walk in the path of justice.

VII. MISCELLANEOUS RESCRIPTS AFFECTING BISHOPS.

I. *Westminster, App. xii., p. 141.*

INSTRUCTION TO THE ARCHBISHOP OF WESTMINSTER AND THE BISHOPS OF ENGLAND AS TO THE FACULTY OF KEEPING THE MOST HOLY EUCHARIST IN THE CHAPELS OF GENTLEMEN.

Near the country seats of Catholic gentlemen there are frequently chapels of a church-like character; and sometimes petitions are sent to the Holy See for the faculty of keeping therein the most Holy Eucharist.

Now, in a matter of such importance, a uniform system was desirable; and, therefore, it seemed meet that the opinion of the Bishops should be asked, and this was done by his Eminence in the Provincial Synod of last year. Having gone thoroughly into the matter, they thought proper to divide these chapels into three classes, according to the distinctive differences that usually occur between them, in order that due provision might be made for every case.

First of all, then, there are chapels of this description which are not far from the church, and are *domestic oratories* in the strict ecclesiastical sense of the term, established for the spiritual benefit of the family; in these, accordingly, the ecclesiastical regulations made for such cases, and the terms of the Indult granting them, must be adhered to; and in other respects the opinion of the Holy See must be asked in each individual case.

Secondly, there are other chapels which are frequented not only by the household and servants, but by the tenants and labourers upon the adjacent land, and which, moreover, may be very convenient for missioners to go to in order to procure the Most Holy Eucharist for the sick, inasmuch as the church is some way off.

And, thirdly, there are those which are farther from the church and established as succursals and affiliations to churches having for the cure of souls.

With respect, therefore, to chapels of the second and third kind, their Eminences have considered that, if the Bishop thinks fit, the most Holy Eucharist may be kept in them; provided, however, that oratories of this class are held by the Bishop to be *public* or *quasi-public:* and, moreover, that daily or at least weekly the holy sacrifice of the Mass be offered up in them; *servatis servandis*, and the whole responsibility resting upon the conscience of the Bishop and of the gentlemen to whom such chapels belong.

As our Most Holy Lord has approved of the decision of their Eminences, and has granted the requisite faculties at the good pleasure of the Holy See, this is made known to his Eminence, in order that the rest of the English Bishops may know in good time what regulations have to be attended to in this matter.

Given at Rome, at the Office of the Sacred Congregation of Propaganda, May 14th, 1853.

J. PH. CARDINAL FRANSONI, Prefect.

L. ✠ S.   AL. BARNABÒ, Secretary.

Ib. App. xxi., p. 148.

The faculty of establishing Confraternities is given to the Bishops:—

At an audience of his Holiness, granted August 31st, 1851, our Most Holy Lord Pius IX., by divine Providence Pope, at the instance of me, the undersigned Secretary of the Sacred Congregation of Propaganda, on the petition of the Reverend Father Lord Thomas Grant, Bishop of Southwark, has granted to the Most Eminent and Reverend the Archbishop of Westminster, as well as to all and to each of their Reverend Lordships, the Suffragan Bishops of the Kingdom of England, the faculty for five years of establishing in the several parts of their respective dioceses the pious practice of the Way of the Cross, and all Confraternities approved of by the Holy See, with the power of enrolling in them the faithful of both sexes, and of blessing the scapulars and insignia peculiar to these same Confraternities, together with the application of all the indulgences and privileges which have been bestowed by the Sovereign Pontiffs upon those who perform the aforesaid work of the Way of the Cross, as well as upon such Confraternities, scapulars, &c.

Given at Rome, at the Office of the Sacred Congregation of Propaganda, on the day and year above noted.

Gratis, without any payment whatsoever under any pretence.

AL. BARNABÒ, Secretary.

L. ✠ S.

II. Westminster, App. xv. Supplement, p. 95.

THE SACRED RESCRIPT CONCERNING THE PIOUS PRACTICE OF THE WAY OF THE CROSS.

MOST HOLY FATHER,

His Eminence the Archbishop of Westminster and his Suffragan Bishops beg that Your Holiness will graciously vouchsafe to grant to each of the Ordinaries for his respective diocese an Indult to enable him to erect the pious stations of the Way of the Cross, and to bless and fix these in the places arranged for them, either himself or by others delegated by the Bishop.

And, inasmuch as the Bishops have not been able to put up the stations themselves, by reason of the distances of the places, and yet the faculty of delegating the duty to priests was not included in the old Indult, the Apostolic sanction is asked for all those stations erected under a mistaken delegation by the Bishops to any priests.

They likewise beg that they may have, each in his own diocese, the faculty of establishing all and each of the Confraternities approved of by the Holy See, with the power of delegating priests in separate churches and chapels to bless and distribute scapulars and other tokens of the same Confraternities.

And they most humbly pray that the faithful may gain all the indulgences and spiritual blessings granted, and in future to be granted, to those performing the aforesaid stations and joining the same Confraternities.

Wherefore, &c.

May 7th, 1857.

Making use of the faculties graciously granted by our Most Holy Lord, by divine Providence Pope, Pius IX., during his absence from the City, his most Eminent and Reverend Lordship, Alexander, of the Holy Roman Church Cardinal Priest, Barnabò, Prefect of the Sacred Congregation of Propaganda, in the presence of me, the undersigned Secretary of the same Sacred Congregation, consented to the sanatio for past concessions, and gave the necessary and proper faculties for five years, according to the request for the future, *provided that there are no religious whose privilege it is, &c.*

Given at Rome, at the Office of the said Sacred Congregation, the day and year above-mentioned.

      CAJETAN, Archbishop of Thebes, Secretary.

L. ✠ S.

I. *Westminster, App. Part iii., p. 167.*

PERMISSION TO SAY MASS FOR THE DEAD ON DOUBLE FEASTS.

MOST HOLY FATHER,

 The Vicars-Apostolic of England, and in their name Nicholas Wiseman, Bishop of Melipotamus, and Coadjutor of the Vicar-Apostolic of the Central District, prostrate at the feet of your Holiness, humbly beg that you will graciously vouchsafe to them an Indult such as already is in force in Scotland—to wit, that in places where, by reason of the want of priests, Mass cannot be sung, low Masses may be said when the corpse is present, even upon double feasts. Wherefore, &c.

 At an audience with his Holiness, granted March 7th, 1847, our Most Holy Lord Pius, by divine Providence Pope Pius IX., at the instance of me, the undersigned Secretary of the Sacred Congregation of Propaganda, having fully considered the points advanced, graciously extended the Indult already granted to the Vicariates-Apostolic of Scotland, to all the Vicariates-Apostolic of England; in other respects the matter and text of the said Indult to be adhered to. All things whatsoever to the contrary notwithstanding.

 Given at Rome, at the Office of the said Sacred Congregation, the day and year as above.

 Gratis, without any payment whatsoever under any pretence.

      JOHN, Archbishop of Thessalonica, Secretary.

L. ✠ S.

Ib. App. Part ii., p. 169.

TABLE OF SUPPRESSED FEASTS, UPON WHICH ALL PRIESTS, AS WELL SECULARS AS REGULARS, IN ENGLAND WHO HAVE THE CURE OF SOULS ARE BOUND TO OFFER UP MASS AND TO APPLY IT *Pro Populo*.[1]

 The Feast of the Annunciation of the Blessed Virgin Mary, and the Monday and Tuesday of Easter week and Whitsun week.

  24th Feb.—St. Matthias, Apostle.
  12th March.—St. Gregory the Great, Apostle of England.
  20th March.—St. Cuthbert (in the County of Durham only).
  23rd March.—St. George, Patron of England.
  1st May.—SS. Philip and James, Apostles.
  3rd May.—Finding of the Holy Cross.
  26th June.—St. Augustine, Apostle of England.
  25th July.—St. James, Apostle.
  26th July.—St. Anne, Mother of the Blessed Virgin Mary.
  10th August.—St. Laurence, Martyr.
  24th August.—St. Bartholomew, Apostle.

---

[1] It has been since decided that the Bishops alone are thus bound in this country. See Synod Diœc. Suth., p. 243. Ed.

21st Sept.—St. Matthew, Apostle.
28th Oct.—SS. Simon and Jude.
30th Nov.—St. Andrew, Apostle.
21st Dec.—St. Thomas, Apostle.
26th Dec.—St. Stephen, First Martyr.
28th Dec.—Holy Innocents, Martyrs.
29th Dec.—St. Thomas of Canterbury, Patron of the Secular Clergy of England.
31st Dec.—St. Silvester, Pope and Confessor.

THE WAY OF THE CROSS, CONFRATERNITIES, AND SCAPULARS.

III. Westminster, App. iii., p. 98.

MOST HOLY FATHER,

Nicholas Cardinal Wiseman, Archbishop of Westminster, and the Bishops of England, prostrate at the feet of your Holiness, beg a renewal of the faculty granted them for five years, May 7th, 1857, of erecting the Stations of the Cross either personally or by their delegates, likewise of establishing *approved of* Confraternities, and of delegating priests to bless and distribute scapulars and tokens of these same Confraternities. His Eminence the Archbishop and the Bishops, the petitioners, humbly beg that the said faculty may be renewed without the clause, *provided that there are no religious whose privilege it is, &c.*

Wherefore, &c.

At an audience with the Most Holy Father, granted March 27th, 1862, our Most Holy Lord Pius IX., by divine Providence Pope, at the instance of me, the undersigned Cardinal Prefect of the Sacred Congregation of Propaganda, graciously assented to the prayer in the form and terms of the old grant, minus, however, the clause, *provided that there are no religious whose privilege it is, &c.*

Given at Rome, at the Office of the Sacred Congregation of Propaganda, the day and year as above.

Gratis, without any payment whatsover under any pretence.

L. ✠ S. AL. C. BARNABÒ, Prefect.

ON THE PURITY OF WINE USED AT MASS.

IV. Westminster, App. viii., p. 141.

MOST ILLUSTRIOUS AND REVEREND LORD,

Great as are the advantages derived from the new inventions of the skill of man, in the present century, yet the use of them begets abuses by no means few in number, and these in reference to matters of the gravest moment. Since, therefore, owing to the progress of chemistry, it has been brought about that many things are compounded and composed in imitation of natural productions, it very often happens, especially in countries where grapes are scarce, that wines are made which in no way consist of the juice of the grape. And on this account, several Bishops of the Church have had recently to issue decrees prohibiting altogether the use of manufactured wine at the altar, in order to make sure, as was but proper, of the integrity of the wine for the divine Sacrifice. And for this purpose, just as in the City itself, his Eminence the Vicar of his Holiness appointed certain places where wine of the grape, known to be such, could be purchased by rectors of churches and other priests; so, in other parts, the Bishops have laid down regulations with the same object, according as they deemed them to be expedient. And thus, even in America, a matter of such moment did not escape the watchfulness of the Bishops; and, therefore, it was notified to this Sacred Congregation that decrees had been made in Provincial Synods against using artificial wine in the Sacrifice of the Mass. But since, in spite of all this, relief as to the obligations of Masses in which artificial wine had been *bonâ fide* made use of, has lately been asked of our Most Holy Lord, it has appeared to his Holiness that the anxiety and decrees of the Bishops in this matter have not fully and in all places been corresponded to. This being the case, the Most Holy Father has ordered that the vigilance of all and each of the Bishops and Vicars-Apostolic dependent upon the Sacred Congregation established for the propagation of the Christian Name, especially in places where the vine is little or in no way cultivated, should be urged in his name to issue prescriptions or address precautions to priests, by means of which all danger of nullity may be entirely removed from the sacrifice of the Altar, which is the highest act of religion.

Whilst not omitting to bring this to the knowledge of your Lordship, according to the wish of our Most Holy Lord, I pray God to keep you well and safe.

Given at Rome, at the Office of the Sacred Congregation of Propaganda, March 10th, 1861.

    Your Highness's most devoted brother,

L. ✠ S.   AL. CARD. BARNABÒ, Prefect.

        CAJ., Archbishop of Thebes, Secretary.

I. Westminster, xviii., p. 66.
Bishops to take precautions as to the purity of Altar Wine (p. 140).

VIII. MISCELLANEOUS REFERENCES.[1]

The following references to the obligations, prerogatives, &c., of Bishops, are given with a view to save space, instead of the passages themselves, some of them of considerable length; they are all contained in some portion or other of the work:

I. Westminster, xiii., p. 55.

The Bishop may establish new missions in any portion even of a missionary rector's district (p. 155).
And also in the districts or parishes of regular missioners (p. 203).

Ib., xvi., p. 60.

The Bishop's permission requisite for Baptism elsewhere than in the church (p. 134).

---

1. See Synodi Diœceseos Suthwarcensis, 1850-1868. p. 243.

Ib. xvii., p. 62.

A list of those confirmed to be given to the Bishop (p. 137).

Ib. xviii., p. 63.

Benediction—with Monstrance—not to be given without the Bishop's permission (p. 138).

Ib. p. 64.

The Bishop's approval necessary for the place where the most Blessed Eucharist is kept, if not in the church (p. 139).

Ib. 67.

The Bishop's permission necessary for duplication (p. 140).

Ib. xix., p. 68.

The Bishop to be consulted in cases where there are not proper confessionals (p. 141).

Ib. xxii., p. 73.

Introduction of practice of publishing banns to be left to the Bishop (p. 147).

Ib. xxiv., c. 2, p. 77.

The Ordinary to absolve those in holy orders who have been present at a scenic representation in a public theatre (p. 150).

IV. Westminster, xi., c. 9, p. 53.

Or in any place used for the time-being as a public theatre (p. 176).

I. Westminster, xxii., c. 7, p. 78.

The Bishop to see that a clergy retreat is given at least every two years (p. 151).

Ib., and IV. Westminster, xi., c. 12, p. 54.

The Bishop's leave requisite for laying aside for a time the Roman collar (p.p. 150, 177).

I. Westminster, xxiv., c, 8. p. 78.

The Bishop to see that conferences are held and to make due arrangements (p. 151).

Ib. c. 9, p. 79.

The Bishop's leave requisite for acceptance of duty of tutor, trustee, &c., by a priest (p. 151).

Ib. xxv., c. 1, p. 80.

The Bishop to receive profession of Faith of Missionary Rectors (p. 152).

Ib. c. 4.

No alienations or notable additions in regard to church property by even Missionary Rectors, without the Bishop being consulted (p. 152).

Ib. c. 5.

The Bishop's consent necessary for acceptance of perpetual obligations. If existing obligations are too burthensome, the matter must be submitted to him (p.p. 152, 153).

IV. Westminster, x. c. 11, p. 50.

No burthens to be added to the Mission in the way of Masses without the Bishop's leave (p. 172).

I. Westminster, xxv., c. 6, p. 80.

Foundations for Masses to be arranged with the Bishop (p. 153).

IV. Westminster, xi., c. 3, 51.

The Bishop's written permission requisite for School-mistress to live in the presbytery (p. 174).

Ib. c. 4.

The Bishop's consent necessary for priest to live in lodgings or with a private family (p. 174).

I. West. xxv., c. 11, p. 82.

The Bishop's leave requisite for a Mission (p. 154).

Ib. c. 12.

Appointment of priests, missionary rectors included—completely in the hands of the Bishop (p. 154).

IV. Westminster, xi., c 6. p. 52.

The Rector of the mission must answer to the Bishop for everything pertaining to it (p. 175).

I. Westminster, xxv. c. 14. p. 83.

Leave of absence for those who have the care of souls to be obtained in writing from the Bishop or Vicar-general, if for more than a few days (p. 154).

II. Westminster, x., p. 31.

The Bishop's permission requisite for absence of a missioner on any Holiday or Sunday (p. 164).

I. Westminster, xxvi., c. p. 83.

College accounts to be submitted annually to the Bishop (ch. ix.).

Ib. xxvii. c. 1, p. 84.

Churches of regulars, subject to episcopal visitation (p. 193).

IV. Westminster, xiv, p. 66.

The Bishop's power of inspecting the accounts of regular missions (p. 195).

I. Westminster, xxvii., c. 2, p. 85

The Bishop to be consulted as to the removal of regular missioners (p. 193).

Ib. c. 3.

Approbation of the Bishop requisite for regular missions (p. 194).

II. Westminster, viii., 6, 7. p. 25.

How the Bishop is to act in cases where regulars have certain rights in a mission (p. 160).

I. Westminster, xxviii., c. 1, p. 86.

The Bishop's permission necessary for foundation of Convents (216)

Ib., c. 5.

Accounts of Convents to be submitted to the Bishop (216).

Ib., Statuta Capitularia iv., c. 17, p. 93.

The Bishop when celebrating may choose his own canonical attendants (p. 111).

Ib., &c., c. 23, p. 94.

The Bishop to choose one of the two Canons to attend to the observance of Rubrics and Ceremonies (p. 112).

Ib., &c., r., c. 24, p. 94.

The Bishop has power over the administration of the spiritualities and temporalities of the Cathedral (p 112).

IV. Westminster, viii., c. 1, p. 35.

The Bishop's permission to be absent from choir or chapter meetings to be obtained by Canons (p. 107).

I. Westminster, c. 27, p. 94.

The Bishop to arrange as to the Canon Theologian's lectures (p. 112).

Ib., &c., c. 28, p. 92.

The Bishop to arrange as to the place and time for the Canon Penitentiary to hear confessions (112).

Ib., &c., c. 29.

The Bishop to arrange the concursus for vacancies (p. 112).

Ib., &c., c. 34, p. 96.

The Bishop free to examine books of attendance of Canons (p. 113).

Ib., vii., c. 35.

The Bishop can summon extraordinary chapter meetings (p. 113).

Ib., ix., c. 50, p. 100.

The Bishop can examine capitular resolutions &c. (p. 116).

IV. Westminster, viii., c. 2, p. 35.

More explicit instructions as to the Bishop's power to examine the capitular books (p. 117).

II. Westminster, viii., c. xi., p. 27.

The Bishop to be consulted as to changes in raising income of missions (p. 161).

Ib., c. xii.

The Bishop to appoint rural dean, or some other, to give inventory to newly appointed missioner (p. 161).

Ib., &c. xvi.

The Bishop in Diocesan Synod to specify amount of Fees for Baptism, &c., &c., (p. 162).

BISHOPS.

Ib., c. xix., p. 30.

The Bishop's express permission necessary before any deeds connected with Church property are signed (p. 163).

Ib., c. xxi.

The Bishop's signature (or the Superior's) should be had by those who go about collecting for any religious object (p. 163).

IV. Westminster, xvi., c. 1 and 2, p. 68.

The Bishop's approbation necessary in all cases of this kind (163).

III. Westminster, xv., c. 1, p. 49.

The Ordinary's privileges and powers over Colleges and the Professors thereof (ch. ix.).

Ib., xvi., p. 51.

Directions to Bishops as to districts that run into a neighbouring diocese (p. 164).

IV. Westminster, xiii., c. 2, p. 62.

The Bishop to encourage the use of the Gregorian Chant (187).

PASTORAL VISITATIONS.

MOST ILLUSTRIOUS AND REVEREND LORD,

"After the explanations given to me by your Lordship in the name of the other English Bishops concerning the practice of receiving offerings from the faithful on occasion of the pastoral visitation, there is no reason why it should not be continued with discretion, that is, if the Bishops do not accept such offerings in cases where they would be too burthensome to the faithful or to the Mission."

With this reply to your Lordship's letter of October 20th,

I pray the Lord to give you length of days and every blessing.

Rome, Propaganda, 30th Nov., 1882.

Your Lordship's most affectionate Brother,

JOHN CARDINAL SIMEONI, Prefect.

✠ D. ARCHBISHOP OF TYRE, Secretary.

SUPPLEMENT TO CHAPTER THE FOURTH.

The following Instructions came under the Editor's notice after the Chapter upon Bishops had been printed. He is indebted for several of them to the new Edition of the Decreta Quatuor Conciliorum Provincialium Westmonasteriensium.

INSTRUCTION OF THE SACRED CONGREGATION OF PROPAGANDA UPON THE TITLE FOR ORDINATION. [Ed. Salford, p. 380.]

I. Since it is in every way unbecoming and quite beneath the dignity of Clerics in Holy Orders to be compelled to procure the necessaries of life by eleemosynary help or sordid gain, care has from the earliest times, as everyone knows, been taken, that provision should be made for the decent and unfailing support of all who were to be raised to Sacred Orders in the Church of God. Indeed, of old no one was ordained without being appointed to a fixed church, to which he was attached for good, that from it he might receive wherewith to live becomingly.[1] But later on, with a view to arrange satisfactorily for the sustenance of the clergy, a title for Ordination took its rise. And the obligation for this was first of all approved of for the ordination of Deacons and Priests, and subsequently by Innocent III. for Subdeacons also.[2] What the Synod of Trent decreed upon this matter is known to all;[3] and when its most salutary prescriptions were, as time went on, in sundry places becoming neglected, Innocent XI., of blessed memory, in an Encyclical letter to all the Bishops, issued by the Sacred Congregation of the Council, May 13th, 1679, most pressingly ordered them to be attended to.

II. There are then two kinds of title—the *Ecclesiastical* and the *Patrimonial*. This latter, which owes its origin to Alexander III.,[4] and which began to be customary towards the end of the thirteenth century, holds good, when the person to be ordained is possessed of property, other than coming from the Church, of such a sure and interest-bearing nature as to be deemed by the Bishop sufficient for his decent support. And to this kind of title belongs that of *Pension*, the which must not only be sufficient for the proper maintenance of the cleric, but be also permanent. These two titles must be regarded as exceptional and allowed as it were by dispensation, should the Bishop deem it necessary or convenient that one so circumstanced should be admitted to ordination.[5]

---

1. Council of Chalcedon, c. vi.   2. Council of Lateran, iii., c. v.
3. Session XXI., on Reform, c. ii.
4. C. 4. de Præb. *Thomassinus* De vet et nov. discipl. *part* 2. *l.* 1. *Cap.* 9. n. 2.
5. Council of Trent, as above, and Benedict XIV. Inst. Eccl. 26. n. 1 and 2.

III. The ecclesiastical title has a twofold division, namely, the title of *Benefice* and the title of *Poverty*, each of which has its subsidiaries and exceptional subdivisions, such as the titles of *Common Life*, *Service of the Church*, the *Mission*, *Sufficiency* and *College*. Now the title of Benefice consists in the permanent right of receiving the proceeds of the property of the Church, by reason of some spiritual office constituted by ecclesiastical authority; and this should be styled the ordinary and chief title for sacred Orders.[1]

IV. The title of *Poverty* belongs to religious profession, by virtue of which, those who have made their solemn vows in an approved Religious Order have all the necessaries of life in common, whether these come from the property possessed by the Order, or from the pious offerings of the faithful. That which is styled *Common Life* pertains to those clerics who, after the manner of Religious, live together a life of discipline but without vows, or with merely simple ones, and hence can leave or be dismissed the religious house and return to the world. For the title of *Poverty* does not belong to these, as is clear from the Constitution, *Romanus Pontifex*[2] of S. Pius V. And only those can be raised to Holy Orders under the title of *Common Life*, whose Congregation or Institute has been specially privileged for this by the Apostolic See.

V. The title of *Service of the Church* which was a common one formerly, as was noted above, but subsequently came to be exceptional, is sometimes allowed in the case of those who have neither ecclesiastical Benefice or pension, nor are possessed of any patrimony of their own, but yet are ordained for the service of some church, and can be supported by such service and the pious offerings of Christ's faithful, without at any time being removed or departing from such church, unless some provision is otherwise made for them. Upon this title it is clear that Sixtus V., of blessed memory, allowed the Patriarch of Venice to confer Sacred Orders upon his clerics.[3]

VI. Finally, passing by the titles of *Sufficiency* and *College* (inasmuch as being of rare occurrence it is enough to merely make mention of them) the title of the *Mission* has grown into use, in the absence of any other legitimate title, in the case of those who are desirous of receiving Holy Orders in order to devote themselves to the Apostolic Missions. And this often happens in Missionary parts, where circumstances are such that the common law of the Church with regard to the requisite title for Holy Orders cannot be observed to the letter. Those who have been ordained by this title receive the necessaries of life from the Apostolic Ministry at the Missions to which they have been appointed.

VII. But it is certain that Ordinaries cannot confer Sacred Orders upon Clerics by the title of the Mission, without a special Indult from the Holy See; for it is a question of exceptional title which has come into vogue in opposition to the common law. And this indult is usually granted to the Superiors of Missions or of Colleges or Congregations that serve Missions, either for a fixed term, or a definite number of cases. But Superiors should remember to make use of it sparingly;

---

1. Fagnanus, in c. 4, de Præbend. n. 24.   2. October 14th, 1568.
3. Campanile, Div. jur. can. rubr. 8 Cap. 4 n. 14, and Gartias De Benef. p. 2, c. 16, n. 96.

for by the title of the Mission certainly not all clerics, without discrimination, who appear however indifferently disposed to a Missionary career, are to be raised to Holy Orders. For if, according to the warning of St. Paul, hands are not to be hastily imposed upon any one, this is especially the case, when it is a question of those who are being raised to the arduous duty of the Apostolic Ministry. Hence this title is only to be made use of in favour of those who, by their disposition and docility, their uprightness, talent, proficiency in sacred studies, morality, and contempt for the things of the world, give promise of being earnest preachers of the Gospel. And in reference to this matter, the burthen rests upon the consciences of those same Superiors.

VIII. Just as the students of pontifical colleges, all those who wish to be received amongst the sacred ministers under the title of the Mission, are bound first of all to take an oath that they will labour perpetually on behalf of the mission to which they are or shall be sent. And with a view to secure their services for the Missions at whose expense they are kept, this oath the Holy See has unfailingly been wont to exact from those who wish to take advantage of this title. To this Instruction [1] is added a Form of the oath already approved of and customary, and the Sacred Congregation strictly enjoins its use by all, in order that uniformity may be kept up in this matter.

IX. It is not essential that one who is to be promoted to Holy Orders by this title should be actually on the Mission, but it is sufficient if he is ready to go on Missions at the time and in the way his Superiors may think fit that he should be sent, and order him to go.

X. Those who are ordained by this title are in virtue of this oath precluded from entering any Religious Order without permission from the Holy See; for it has been reserved to its judgment—after first hearing from the Ordinary to whom he is subject—to decide whether the needs of the Missions to the services of which he has bound himself may allow this. That is, the public must take precedence of private good, just as it has been granted to some Orders that their religious should not be allowed to pass to one more severe without the leave of Superiors.

XI. As in the case of other titles, so this one in question can, in accordance with canon law, be lost, and may be taken away by the Ordinary with the consent, however, of the Sacred Congregation, whose place it is to free those thus ordained from the obligation of their oath. But if, when any title is lost, including that of the Mission, no other is substituted in its place, the Priest is not thereupon suspended, but Ordinaries are bound to insist upon those ordained to obtain some other title, as is provided for by the Sacred Canons. This Sacred Congregation made this declaration at a general meeting, September 1st, 1856.

XII. Likewise, regular Priests who have made solemn vows, and been permitted by the Apostolic indulgence to live in the world, or who have made simple vows and have left their Congregation or Institute, will be under the necessity of furnishing themselves with a canonical title, in order not to be compelled, to the shame of their position, to get a living by begging; and in missionary parts they must at least prove that they have sufficient means to support themselves in a becoming manner.

XIII. Those who have attained ecclesiastical Orders by the title of

---

[1.] See p. 183.

some special Mission undoubtedly lose their title if they give up the duties of a Missioner, and are bound to provide themselves with some other; but if they are deputed to the service of another Mission, there must be a fresh permission from the Holy See for them to avail themselves of the title of this Mission; nor can they avail themselves of the faculty, which the Ordinary of the Mission may hold of ordaining Clerics by the above-mentioned title.

XIV. Let Ordinaries employ upon the Mission priests who have been admitted to Holy Orders by other titles, without departing from the prescriptions of law; for they have no power to compel them to exchange these for the title of the Mission. Moreover, the Sacred Congregation exhorts Ordinaries to introduce as far as possible other legitimate titles for Holy Orders.

XV. Finally, the Sacred Congregation, seeing that it conduces considerably to the increase of Missions, if those who have been brought up as future preachers of the Gospel in colleges or in seminaries, seculars or regulars, or have been raised to Orders by the title of the Mission, from time to time recall to mind the oath by which they have bound themselves to co-operate with God for the salvation of souls; exhorts them to be careful to renew the oath every year on the anniversary of their taking it, and seriously reflect upon the divine goodness in their regard which has made them Ministers of his Word, for the announcement of the wonders of His might and power; upon how imperishable a crown of glory is prepared for them in heaven if they holily fulfil their duty; and, on the other hand, how severe a sentence awaits them should any soul perish—and may this never happen!—by reason of their negligence or sloth. And that they may do this more readily and cheerfully, let them remember that Pius VI., of blessed memory, at an audience of May 7th, 1775, granted a plenary indulgence, applicable to the souls in Purgatory, and available for all time to come, to all, not only on the day of their first taking the aforesaid oath, but also on the said day of their renewing it, provided that on each they omit not to cleanse their conscience by the Sacrament of Penance, and to receive Eucharistic Communion or offer up the Sacrifice of the Mass.

Given at Rome, at the office of the said Sacred Congregation, April 27th, 1871.

INSTRUCTION UPON QUASI-DOMICILE, FOR THE BISHOPS OF ENGLAND AND THE UNITED STATES, WEDNESDAY, JUNE 7TH, 1867.

[Ed. Salford, p. 414.]

There are two requisites for that quasi-domicile which is required in these cases, namely, residence in the place where the marriage takes place, and the intention of remaining there for more than half a year. Hence, if it is legitimately proved that both or either of the parties has the intention of remaining for more than half a year, from the date of the concurrence of the two events, namely, this intention and the actual residence, it must be decided that a quasi-domicile has been acquired, and that the marriage that has taken place with this qualification is valid. But if there is no absolute proof of the aforesaid intention, recurrence must be had to such indications of it as may be forthcoming, and which may furnish a moral certainty. But in a matter of this secret and internal nature it is difficult to get such indications as will render the judge secure: and hence the rule laid down by the Supreme Pontiff Benedict XIV. must be strictly adhered to, namely, that it must be seen whether for a month or more previous to the marriage one or both were living in the place where the marriage took place, and if this is found to have been the case, it may be lawfully presumed that there was the intention of remaining the greater part of a year, and that a domicile had been acquired, and that the marriage was accordingly a valid one. But if this lawful presumption, arising from residence of a month's duration, is disproved by facts to the contrary, by which it is surely and abundantly clear that the aforesaid intention of remaining in no sense existed, then it is manifest that a contrary determination must be arrived at, for presumption must give place to certainty. Moreover, it is clear also that actual residence is powerless to create a quasi-domicile, if the party dwells in the place as a wanderer and traveller, and not really and truly as a resident, as people do who have a genuine and properly so-called domicile in the same place.

INSTRUCTION OF THE SACRED CONGREGATION OF PROPAGANDA ON MATRIMONIAL DISPENSATIONS. [Ed. Salford, p. 415.]

As a dispensation is a relaxation of the common law granted by one who has the power and with full knowledge of the "cause," it is clear that dispensations from matrimonial impediments must not be conceded without a lawful and weighty reason. Moreover, everyone readily understands that the more serious the impediment in the way of the marriage the more serious is the reason for dispensation requisite. Now supplicatory letters not unfrequently come to the Holy See for some dispensation of this kind, based upon no canonical grounds. It likewise sometimes happens that in petitions of this description things are omitted which should of necessity be introduced to preclude the dispensation from being null. It has therefore seemed opportune to go briefly through, in this Instruction, the chief grounds which have been usually deemed sufficient for obtaining matrimonial dispensations in accordance with canonical sanctions, and a prudent consideration for ecclesiastical requirements; and then to point out what must of necessity be expressed in the petition for the dispensation.

And to begin with the grounds for dispensations, it will be worth while at the outset to observe that while one reason is sometimes taken by itself not sufficient, it may be so considered when coupled with another; for those which avail not singly, do so when taken together. (*Aret. B. 5, C. on proof.*) Grounds of this description are the following:

1. *Smallness of the place*, either absolute or relative (as regards the female petitioner alone), seeing that in the place of her birth or even domicile a woman's relationship is so widely spread that she is unable to meet with anyone to be married to of an equal position with her

own, save a relative by blood or by marriage, without leaving her country, which would be a hardship to her.

2. *The advancing age of the woman*, if for instance she is over twenty-four and has not hitherto met with one of her own position to whom she might be married. But this reason does not hold good in the case of a widow wishful to marry again.

3. *Deficiency or absence of dowry*, if, a woman has not actually a dowry large enough to enable her to marry another of her own position, unconnected by blood or marriage, in her own place of abode. And this reason becomes all the more weighty when the woman has no dowry at all, and a relation by blood or by marriage is willing to marry her, or even to make a suitable settlement upon her.

4. *Contentions about inheritance that have already arisen*, or *serious or imminent danger of the same*. If a woman has on hand an important suit in reference to her inheriting wealth of great amount, and there is no one else to undertake a contention of this kind and carry it on at his own expense save the person who is desirous of marrying her, a dispensation is usually granted, for it is of benefit to the community at large that an end should be put to the contention. Closely allied to this is another reason, namely, that *her dowry is in litigation*, and the woman has no other through whose assistance she will be able to recover her property. A reason of this nature, however, suffices only in cases of remote grades of relationship.

5. *Poverty on the part of a widow*, with a numerous family, which some man promises to support. But at times a widow obtains the benefit of a dispensation owing to her youth and the danger of incontinence.

6. The *blessing of peace*; and under this head come not only treaties between realms and princes, but the cessation of serious enmities, disturbances, and ill-will between citizens. This reason is brought forward either to do away with the serious enmities that have sprung up between the blood relations or the connections by marriage of the contracting parties, and which would be completely put an end to by the celebration of the nuptials; or, when serious quarrels have existed between the relatives and connections of the contracting parties, and, although a commencement of amity has been made, yet the celebration of the nuptials would greatly conduce to its completion.

7. Too great, a suspicious, or dangerous *familiarity*, as well as having, almost unavoidably, to dwell together under the same roof.

8. Previous *connection* with a relation by blood or by marriage, or with any other party under an impediment, and *pregnancy, with consequent legitimisation of the offspring*, in order to provide for the well-being of the offspring and the good name of the mother, who would otherwise remain unmarried.

9. *Disgrace coming upon the woman*, arising from a suspicion that through over familiarity with a relative or connection she had been seduced by him, although the suspicion should be false, in a case when, unless she marries, a woman seriously defamed would either remain unmarried or must marry beneath her, or serious loss would ensue.

10. *Revalidating a marriage*, which has been contracted in good faith and publicly in the way prescribed by the Council of Trent, because its dissolution could hardly be brought about without grave public scandal and heavy loss, especially on the woman's part (c. 7 on Consanguinity).

But if the parties have got married in bad faith they by no means deserve the favour of a dispensation, as the Council of Trent decides. (Sess. XXV., c. v., on Reform. Matrimony).

11. *Danger of a mixed marriage, or of its being celebrated before a non-Catholic minister.* When there is danger of those wishful to be married, though connected in even one of the closer degrees, going before a non-Catholic minister for the marriage in defiance of the authority of the Church, by reason of the refusal of a dispensation, there are just grounds for dispensing, for there is imminent danger not only of a most serious scandal to the faithful, but also of apostacy and loss of faith on the part of those so doing and disregarding the impediments to matrimony, especially in countries where heresy flourishes unchecked. This was the teaching of this Sacred Congregation in an Instruction of April 17th, 1820, sent to the Archbishop of Quebec. Likewise, when the Vicar-Apostolic of Bosnia had asked as to whether he could grant a dispensation to such Catholics as had no other grounds than an uncontrolled love, when it is foreseen that if the dispensation is refused they will contract marriage before an unbelieving judge, the Sacred Congregation of the Holy Office on Wednesday, August 14th, 1822, decreed, "The answer to be given to the Petitioner must be that in such a case he may make use of the faculties granted him in Formula II., as he shall deem expedient in the Lord." The same must be said in the case of a Catholic woman who ventures upon marriage with a non-Catholic man.

12. *Danger of incestuous concubinage.* From the above-mentioned Instruction of 1822 it is clear that the remedy of a dispensation must be had recourse to to prevent anyone continuing to live in concubinage, to the public scandal and manifest danger of eternal salvation.

13. *Danger of a civil marriage.* From what has been said it follows that probable danger of those who are petitioning for the dispensation having only a civil marriage, as it is called, if they cannot get one, is a lawful reason for dispensing.

14. *The removal of grave Scandal.*

15. *Putting a stop to open concubinage.*

16. *Merit*, that is in the case of one who has, by resisting the enemies of the Catholic faith, or by generosity towards the Church, or by his learning, virtue, or some other means deserved well of Religion.

Such are the more common and strong grounds which are usually brought forward when matrimonial dispensations are to be petitioned for; and Theologians and Canonists treat of them exhaustively.[1]

But this Instruction now turns to those points which, in addition to the grounds for obtaining the dispensation, must, whether by law, custom, or the practice of the Curia, be expressed in the petition, or the dispensation becomes null, if the truth is kept back or what is untrue is advanced even in ignorance. These are:

1. The *Name and Surname* of the Petitioners must both be written down distinctly and clearly without any abbreviations.

2. *The Diocese of birth or of actual domicile.* When Petitioners have a domicile out of the diocese of their birth they can ask if they please that

---

[1] Amongst others Pyrrhus Corradus should be referred to:—"Praxis dispensationum Apostolicarum," Lib. vii. and viii., as well as Vincentius De Justis—"De Dispensationibus Matrimonialibus," Lib. iii.

the dispensation should be sent to the Ordinary of the diocese in which they are actually residing.

3. The *species* (in its most determinate form) of the impediment, whether it is consanguinity or affinity, arising from lawful or unlawful connection; public morality—(honestas)—arising from espousals or the marriage ceremony; in the case of an impediment by reason of "crime," whether it arose from murder of the party's spouse with the promise of marriage, or from such murder with adultery, or from adultery alone with the promise of marriage; in spiritual relationship, whether it is between a god-parent and the person baptized, or between a god-parent and one of the parents of the person baptized.

4. The *Degree of Consanguinity*, or *affinity*, or morality (honestatis),[1] arising from a marriage ceremony, and whether it is a simple or mixed degree, the more remote as well as the less, together with the line, and whether it is direct and collateral; likewise, whether the Petitioners are related by a double tie of consanguinity, both on the father's and mother's side.

5. *The Number of Impediments*; for instance, is the consanguinity or affinity twofold or manifold, or is there affinity as well as relationship, or any other kind of impediment diriment or impedient.

6. *Various circumstances*, such as whether the marriage is to be or has been contracted; if contracted, it must be stated whether this was done in good faith, at least on one side, or with a knowledge of the impediment; likewise, whether it was after proclamation of banns and in accordance with the prescriptions of the Council of Trent; or, whether with the view of more easily obtaining a dispensation; finally, whether it has been consummated, if in bad faith, at least on one side, or with knowledge of the impediment.

7. *Incestuous connection* between the parties before the execution of the dispensation, whether previous or subsequent to the petition for it,—whether with the intention of more easily obtaining the dispensation, or whether without such an intention; and whether the connection is publicly known, or whether it is secret. If these matters are kept back, the Sacred Congregation of the Holy Office, on Wednesday, August 1st, 1866, declared that dispensations for all the forbidden degrees of consanguinity, affinity, spiritual and legal relationship, as well as of public morality (honestatis), were surreptitious and nowhere and in no way of any avail. But in petitioning for a dispensation from the impediment of affinity of the first or second degree in the collateral line, if the impediment arises not only from a consummated marriage with the deceased partner of either Petitioner, but also from connection previous to marriage, or fornication with the said deceased committed before any marriage had taken place, it is not necessary that mention should be made of illicit intercourse of this nature, as is clear from the reply of the Sacred Penitentiary of March 20th, 1842, given with the approval of Gregory XVI., of blessed memory, to the Bishop of Namur, which the same Tribunal declared to be public in a letter of December 10th, 1874.

These matters should not be lost sight of, not only by those who have recourse to the Holy See to obtain any matrimonial dispensation, but by

---

1. Which constitutes an impediment to the fourth degree. [Ed.]

those who, by Pontifical delegation, can of themselves dispense, in order to make proper use, as is but right, of the faculties they possess.

Given at the Office of the Sacred Congregation of Propaganda, May 9th, 1877.

Residence on the Part of Bishops. [Ed. Salford, p. 421.]

Most Illustrious and Right Reverend Lord,

Since it is of divine precept that Rectors of souls should know their flock and feed it with the Word of God, the Sacraments and good example, they are bound to personal residence in their Dioceses or Churches. And without this they cannot possibly personally fulfil the duty committed to them. Hence at all times has the Church of God never failed to proclaim and insist upon the duty of pastoral residence; and of this her solicitude not only do the ancient canons bear ample testimony, but also the holy Tridentine Synod, Session VI., c. 1, on Reformation, and Session XXIII., on Reformation, c. 1, as well as very recently Benedict XIV., Supreme Pontiff, who in his Constitution "Ad Universæ Christianæ Reipublicæ statum," published September 3rd, 1746, both carefully inculcated and most clearly explained the obligation of residence.

But if everywhere the Pastors of souls are in duty bound to live continually in the midst of their flock, by a still stronger bond are those thus bound who have been charged with the cure of souls in Missionary parts. For since the faithful in the Missions have to experience greater dangers, whilst usually they have fewer aids to virtue, they stand in peculiar and most urgent need of the watchfulness and assistance of their Pastors. It is not therefore to be wondered at if nothing has been more at heart with the Sacred Council for the Propagation of the Christian Name, than by their Decrees to provide that the Bishops and Vicars-Apostolic under their jurisdiction should reside, as far as possible, in their Missions without any interruption. And indeed the Holy See has gone so far as to forbid under the strictest penalties the said Prelates from pontificating in any other Diocese or District, even with the consent of the Ordinary.

But since, notwithstanding all this, it not unfrequently happens that Prelates over Missions, without any reference to the Apostolic See or real necessity or canonical reason, go off on very long journeys, and hence the Missions entrusted to them are liable to suffer no slight harm, the Most Eminent and Right Reverend Fathers of this Sacred Congregation, at a general meeting on January 21st of this year, considered it expedient that the canonical regulations concerning the residence of Pastors, as well as the Decrees which have been published in reference to this obligation for Missionary parts—that no one for the future should quit, even for a time, the Diocese or District over which he is placed—should be recalled to the memory of the aforesaid Prelates. And while I make known to your Lordship the will of their Eminences, I do not omit to enclose the Decrees alluded to above.[1]

---

1. See below.

At the same general meeting the Most Eminent and Reverend Fathers also determined that a list of *Questions*, in reference to the account that has to be sent to the Sacred Congregation of the state of the Dioceses or Misssions under them, should be sent to all the Bishops, Vicars, and Prefects Apostolic of Missions. For seeing that all those who are placed over Missions are bound to submit the said account at stated times to the Holy See, the Sacred Council wishes that they should prepare it for the future upon the plan of the Fifty-five Questions, which are given on an adjoining page,[1] and that they should be particularly careful as to accuracy in reference to what concerns the life, probity, and knowledge of their priests.

Finally, since it is found by experience that many of the youths sent to Rome to be entered as students at the Urban College do not attain the object for which they are educated, through want of an ecclesiastical vocation, of health, or of sufficient talent for the study of the sciences, their Eminences have willed that a prospectus should be sent to all the Superiors of Missions—in order that when they have obtained permission from the Sacred Congregation to send youths to the Urban College they may see what qualifications these should possess, lest, otherwise, it might turn out that the Church would receive no return for the great expense of their education, and the good hopes of the Missions be frustrated. As in duty bound, I make known these matters to your Lordship, and pray that God may long preserve You well and safe.

Given at Rome, at the Office of the Sacred Congregation of Propaganda, April 24th, 1861.

RESIDENCE ON THE PART OF THE PRELATES OF MISSIONARY PARTS.— DECREES AND DECLARATIONS OF THE SACRED CONGREGATION OF PROPAGANDA.

I.

At a General Congregation in presence of His Holiness, March 28th, 1651.

"His Holiness decreed that the Bishops under the jurisdiction of the Sacred Congregation of Propaganda could not pontificate in any other churches but their own, even with the consent of the Ordinaries thereof, under pain of suspension, to be incurred *ipso facto*, and reserved to the same Pontiff, unless fixed by the aforesaid Sacred Congregation in a certain place as Vicars-Apostolic, or sent as Administrators of some Church."

Similar Decrees were issued by the same Sacred Congregation, July 26th, 1662, and July 17th, 1715.

II.

At a particular Congregation of Propaganda, May 7th, 1669.

Seeing that by repeated Decrees of the Sacred Congregation the use of Pontificals beyond the limits of the Dioceses allotted to the Bishops of the same Sacred Congregation is forbidden, the Bishop of Heliopolis has put the question :

---

1. See p. 50.

"Are the said Decrees to be understood as in force in Europe only, or are they extended to other places through which one would have to pass to arrive at his church."

"The Sacred Congregation replied that the prohibitory Decrees concerning the said use of Pontificals were applicable to all parts, even beyond the confines of Europe."

N.B.—The Sacred Congregation having ascertained that the general prohibition contained in the above Decrees was at times in no small degree inconvenient, especially in cases where Bishops are obliged through ill-health to have recourse to some neighbouring Prelate, to do those things for him which pertain to the Episcopal power, at a general meeting, August 2nd, 1819, considered that His Holiness might be petitioned for some relaxation of the same, so that when Bishops or Vicars-Apostolic betake themselves to other Dioceses or Vicariates for some reasonable cause or urgent necessity, they may give each other permission to make use of Pontificals, provided, however, that there is always the consent of the Bishop or Vicar of the place, and that in other respects the precept as to residence remains in full force. *This the Supreme Pontiff, Pius VII., ratified and approved of, at an audience of August 8th of the same year.*

III.

At a General Congregation, July 10th, 1668,

The Most Eminent and Reverend Fathers of the Sacred Council for the Propagation of the Christian Name, having considered the allegations made against the Bishops subject to the same Sacred Council who, to the detriment of their Dioceses, left them for Rome or elsewhere, determined upon the decree—"Let Bishops subject to the Sacred Congregation proceed not even to Rome under any pretext without leave of the Sacred Congregation. They have renewed the Decree of 1626."

INSTRUCTION OF THE SACRED CONGREGATION OF PROPAGANDA UPON THE VISIT TO THE SACRED THRESHOLD (OF THE APOSTLES).

1. Among the chief duties incumbent, according to what has been laid down by the Holy Fathers and Canons, upon Patriarchs, Primates, Archbishops, and Bishops, is to be especially included that of visiting the Sacred Threshold of the Apostles, and when doing so of paying homage and obedience to the Roman Pontiff, and giving an account of how they have fulfilled their pastoral charge, and of everything connected with the condition of their churches, the character and habits of their clergy and people, and the salvation of the souls entrusted to them. And this duty, which is, as it were, the mark of unity and of communion with the Apostolic See, follows naturally from those rights which it is clear, by virtue of the primacy which he by Divine institution possesses over the whole Church, belong to the Roman Pontiff. And no one is unaware of what Sixtus V., of happy memory, prescribed upon this matter in his famous Constitution *Romanus Pontifex*, of December 20th, 1585.

2. But inasmuch as from time to time doubts regarding the way in which Bishops should comply with this duty have arisen, and hence great anxiety in regard to the observance of their oath, by which they pledged themselves to fulfil it, the Sacred Council instituted for the Propagation of the Christian Name have deemed it part of their solicitude to explain clearly the Sixtine Constitution, in order that the plainer the enactments of the law, the more readily may they be complied with by all.

3. And to begin with, it is important to call to mind what is prescribed in § 7 of the said Constitution. "In order duly to fulfil this duty let all patriachs, primates, archbishops and bishops of Italy, or of the Islands of Italy from which the passage to Italy can easily be performed, such as Sicily, Sardinia and Corsica, as well as others of the provinces adjacent to Italy, together with those of Dalmatia and Greece, which are near the coast of Italy and Sicily, undertake the journey and by God's help accomplish it every *three years*; those of Germany, France, Spain, Belgium, Bohemia, Hungary, England, Scotland, Ireland, and all others in Europe who dwell upon the German and Baltic seas, as well as those of the islands in the Mediterranean Sea, every *fourth year;* those who are within the confines of Europe in provinces farther off than these, as well as those of Africa just opposite to our shores, and those of the ocean North and West of Europe and Africa on this side of the new world, every *fifth year;* those of Asia, and those beyond Asia and in other newly discovered countries to the east, the south, the west and north, whether islands or continents, and finally those who are in any part of the world whatsoever, every *tenth year.*"

4. But the question has frequently been raised as to when the triennium, quadriennium, &c., should begin. Some have held that Bishops should reckon the time from the day of their preconisation to the Episcopal See in Consistory; others from the day of their consecration; others from the day on which they took possession of the See. Some also have considered that the time for the Visit to the Sacred Threshold should commence from the day on which the diocese was constituted. Hence it has come to the knowledge of the Sacred Congregation that in various countries various practices have begun to get into vogue in this matter.

5. It is enough to look carefully into what Sixtus V. decreed in order to do away with all conjectures of this kind; for it is clearly specified in Section 8 of the aforesaid Constitution, that Bishops are bound to visit the tombs of the Apostles from the date of the publication of the same Constitution. Therefore, as Fagnanus writes:[1] The aforesaid number of years begins for all from the day on which the Bull of Sixtus V. was published, that is, from December 20th, 1585. Nor does what we read in Section 7 create any difficulty; for, as the same author observes, "the words of the Bull—*this number of years*—are not to be understood in such a way that the beginning of the reckoning should be taken from the day of the consecration, taking possession, or translation, but have this meaning, that from the very fact of one's being consecrated the obligation begins to lie upon him of visiting the Threshold, but not that the aforesaid space of time must be

---

1. In ii. Lib. Decret. in Cap. Ego N. Episcopus, iv. de jurejur, n. 36.

reckoned from that moment. And these words have always received this interpretation in the Sacred Congregation of the Council. And this reckoning must be made from the very day of the publication of the Bull exclusively, and thus at the end of each triennium, &c., or decennium, the whole of the 20th of December is at the Bishop's disposal, inasmuch as the time for the said visit lasts to the very end of that day. For it is laid down as a rule, that the day on which the term ends should not be counted as part of the term." And indeed, the said Sacred Congregation of the Council, to remove all doubt, by an encyclical letter to the Prelates of the whole Catholic world, November 16th, 1673, informed them that for ever and by all one and the same term for the Sacred Visit must be observed, and that the very day of the publication of the Sixtine Constitution.[1]

6. This Sacred Congregation of Propaganda made the same announcement in 1802 to the Bishops of Ireland; and in 1865 to one of the Archbishops of the United States of America it wrote, "the trienniums and decenniums must be computed in such a way that beginning with the day on which the aforesaid Constitution was published, namely December 20th, 1585, they should go on continuously and uninterruptedly for all succeeding Bishops."

7. But recently the question has been raised, as to "*whether in the case of newly erected Sees the time for the sacred visit must be reckoned from the day of the publication of the Sixtine Constitution.*" And some modern canonists decided that the trienniums, quadrieniums, &c., in the case of Dioceses established since the time of Sixtus V., must be reckoned from the day on which the first Bishop of a newly established Diocese undertook the administration of it.

8. But there is no reason why Bishops of new Dioceses should follow any other rule for computing the time for the Visit to the Sacred Threshold than that of the others; for they also must adhere to the Sixtine Constitution, as in the rest of its contents, so likewise in this. Hence in regard to the question subsequently raised the Most Eminent Fathers of this Sacred Council, at a general meeting of May 3rd, 1875, after mature deliberation, decreed that the reply should be *affirmatively*; that is, that the said rule should be observed even by those Bishops who are governing Sees recently erected.[2]

9. This being the case, when anyone is raised to an Episcopal See, whether it be one of the old ones or the new, let him keep before his eyes the day on which the law of Sixtus V. was issued; and if, beginning the reckoning of bygone time from it, he finds that his predecessor, when the triennium, quadriennium, &c., came round, did not properly fulfil his obligation of Visiting the Sacred Threshold, let him understand that he is bound to make up for it. It will be useful to hear again Fagnanus, who writes thus: "According to the prescription of Sixtus V., §. *Ad hoc autem*, paragraph *Quae ne longius differantur, &c.*, whatsoever length of time lies to the account of any Bishop, who through being forestalled by death or some other cause has not visited the Threshold by reason of the prescribed time not having elapsed, this must be understood to have descended to and devolved upon his successor in such way, that as soon as the period implied in his predecessor's oath is

---

1. V. caus. Carpectoraten, dici 19 Febr. 1718, in princ.   2. Loco cit., n. 46

completed, he is bound to make the visit due; not that these words imply that the succeeding bishop is bound to make up all the triennial, quadriennial, &c., visits that his predecessor failed to make, but they must be understood to mean that a newly consecrated Bishop is bound to pay the visit if during the current triennium, &c., his predecessor has failed to do so." If, accordingly, at the beginning of the triennium, &c., the Bishop goes to the sacred Threshold and gives an account of his diocese, and subsequently dies, his successor is not bound to either duty; for the fulfilment of it by his predecessor stands good for the successor.[1]

10. On the other hand, if any one has taken charge of a diocese a short time before the triennium, &c., begun by his predecessor has come to an end, since by reason of the shortness of the time he cannot as yet have ready what is required to give an account of the state of his church, the remedy of asking for a delay comes in, and this, particularly under such circumstances, is easily obtained from the Holy See.

11. It is known that the Sixtine regulation takes into account the case of those Bishops who are kept away by some lawful impediment, and cannot in person betake themselves to the tombs of the Apostles; for they are allowed to do this through a Procurator. Indeed, as regards deputing a Procurator, the custom has become more easy and free, as Benedict XIV. of blessed memory remarked in regard to his own time,[2] and the strictness of olden times has been exceedingly relaxed as years passed by. "Wherefore, if a Bishop is kept away through any just impediment, and asks of the Sacred Congregation permission to visit the Threshold by a Procurator or to depute for this purpose some canon or priest of his diocese already in the city and attending to his own business, or even his own ordinary business man and agent well posted in the affairs of the church and diocese, provided he is an ecclesiastic, and after a report of the case has been made by the secretary of the same Congregation to the Roman Pontiff, a refusal is not so usual as it was formerly, but the leave and faculty asked for are generally granted." In the same way, a regular priest was not formerly allowed the office of Procurator, unless upon proof of the lack of a chapter and secular clergy, except perhaps in the case of churches in very remote countries;[3] but in this respect also, of late years, the Holy See has shown itself more lenient.

12. What are the more usual and valid impediments which are cause of exemption for Bishops from making the journey to Rome, may be seen in writers upon canonical matters, on *Chap. IV. Ego. N. de jurejur.* Catalani thus enumerates them.[4] "Duty and office in the State combined with the bishopric . . . . . likewise great age, hostilities or fear of the enemy, robbers, pestilence, and other causes of this kind, some of which, however, excuse Bishops merely from the personal visit, but not from that by means of a special messenger, such as ill-health, old age, some duty combined with the episcopacy, which are personal to the Bishop himself. But there are others which excuse Bishops from even sending a special messenger to Rome, for instance, pestilence, the roads in possession of an enemy, war—provided they are of such a nature as to prevent members of the diocese from going to the

---

1. Fagn. loc. cit. n. 47. 2. De Syno. Diœc. L. XIII. cap. VI., n. 3.
3. Ibid. 4. Comment. Pont. Rom. Tom. I., § IV.

City." Obstacles of this description may be as numerous as the peculiar circumstances of each individual, by reason of which it may not be possible to journey to Rome without great difficulty and serious inconvenience.

13. But everyone will readily understand that the ordinary obstacles that may stand in the way of a personal visit do not now-a-days usually exist; for the ingenuity of man has invented such means of travelling long distances, that with almost incredible speed and ease the longest journeys, whether by land or sea, can be accomplished. And, if Sixtus V. prescribed the aforesaid times with a view to the duty of Visitation being fulfilled *without inconvenience*, as he himself says, with the utmost prudence *taking into account*, to use Benedict XIV.'s words,[1] *the various distances of places and dioceses from the City*; what can be more easy at present, than to visit the City within these times? The Sacred Congregation, therefore, is persuaded that Bishops will never be wanting in this duty to which by oath they have bound themselves, not merely at the times fixed by Sixtus V.; but as it hopes, much oftener, out of veneration for the tombs of the teachers of truth, Peter and Paul, which enlighten the hearts of the faithful. And this certainly they will willingly do, if they but reflect upon what the Council of Sardica has said:[2] "It is very important and exceedingly befitting that chief Priests should give an account of each and all of their districts to their head, that is to the See of Peter the Apostle." For thus does it come to pass that the Roman Pontiff, to whom is entrusted the care of all the churches, is enabled by the labour and aid of Prelates coming to Rome to become cognizant of the necessities of the Christian flock in every part, to understand the infirmities of his spiritual sheep, and to apply suitable remedies for them; and thus nothing escapes his knowledge in respect to matters which he ought of necessity to be aware of for the increase of God's glory, the propagation of religion, and the promotion of the good of souls. True, that many matters can be managed by letter; but you will find no one deny that there are many others which cannot be better treated than by word of mouth. It likewise happens that sometimes there are matters which require such secrecy that it would be dangerous to commit them to writing: and hence Benedict XIII., of happy memory, in his Roman Synod of 1725,[3] warns Bishops, "not easily to dispense themselves from this personal Visit, since by the intercession of the same Holy Princes of the Church and the word of the living voice of the Supreme Pontiff, they will here receive many and profitable suggestions, which cannot at times be committed to writing."

14. Let not, therefore, prelates be backward in hastening even from far distant lands to the City which the Princes of the Apostles have consecrated by their blood, to the end that bound by faster bonds even to the Supreme Head of the Church, and in union with their Chief, they may so much the more boldly proceed to fight the battles of the Lord, the more the enemies of the Christian Commonwealth strive daily by their attacks and onslaughts to overwhelm it.

15. This Instruction of the Sacred Congregation having been

---

1. Loc. cit. n. 5.   3. Tit. XIII. Cap. I.
2. Epist. Syn. ad Jul. I. Rom. Pont. apud Labbaeum, Tom. II., col. 690. edit. Venet.

laid before our Most Holy Lord Pius IX., Supreme Pontiff, by me the undersigned Secretary, at an audience of the 13th of last month, His Holiness graciously approved thereof upon all points, and gave to it the weight of his Apostolic authority.

Given at Rome, at the Office of the said Sacred Congregation, June 1st, 1877.

Letter of the Most Eminent Cardinal Fransoni to the Most Eminent Cardinal Archbishop of Westminster.

My Most Em., Most Rev., and Most Hon. Lord,

Although I am persuaded that your Eminence, in arranging the matters to be discussed in the Provincial Synod, has not overlooked the very important subject of Clerical Education, still you will allow me to recommend to you this matter in an especial manner, since on it the progress of Religion eminently depends. On the occasion when all the Bishops shall have assembled together, it would be very opportune to consider the method followed in colleges and in Seminaries for the thorough training of young ecclesiastics in piety and in learning, and to lay down at least the fundamental principles of the improvements to be introduced in order to obtain happier results. It is quite unnecessary to remind Your Eminence of the most wise Tridentine prescriptions on this matter, and of the regulations introduced by Holy Prelates and recommended by a happy experience; it will belong to the discernment and enlightened zeal of Your Eminence and Colleagues to make whatever useful regulations they may believe feasible and opportune, taking into account the state of Ecclesiastical Establishments in England and other circumstances.

Meanwhile with profound respect I humbly kiss your hand.

Your Eminence's

Most humble and devoted Servant,

G. F. CARD. FRANSONI, Prefect.

AL. BARNABÒ, Secretary.

Rome, Propaganda, June 27th, 1855.

Instruction of the Sacred Congregation of Propaganda upon Duplication.

1. Permission to binate Mass, which the Holy See usually gives to Ordinaries of Missions with the power to extend the same to the Missioners, has raised many doubts which has been submitted by them to this Sacred Congregation. The grounds of the doubts owe their origin to the severity of the clauses which by command of Alexander VII. were subjoined to the Article of the Formulæ having reference thereto. Hence it appears opportune to gather together in the present instruction the more usual laws and regulations that should be kept in view in the use of the said permission.

2. Everybody is aware that by the the general law, in the present discipline of the church, Priests are allowed to offer up the Holy Sacrifice but once daily. This is settled by Innocent III.:[1] "We reply that with the exception of our Lord's Nativity it is sufficient if a Priest celebrates only one Mass once daily, unless necessity demands otherwise."

3. In a case of necessity, therefore Priests are allowed to repeat the Mass on the same day. This must however be understood, as follows plainly from the very terms of the Formulæ, as permission to say two Masses only, notwithstanding the greatness of the need for celebrating a larger number. The Prefect of the Missions of the Capuchins of Tunis put the question, as to whether, when all his missioners were in prison, he should have the power, *in case of necessity*, to celebrate oftener than twice on the same day. And the General Congregation replied, August 7th, 1614, "that the faculties gave no permission to celebrate more than two Masses." And this had already been the reply of the General Congregation held in presence of His Holiness, February 17th, 1648; when the abuse that had been introduced amongst Priests enslaved in Algeria of celebrating three Masses being discussed, "His Holiness ordered that a command should be sent through the said Prefect (of Algeria) in the name of His Holiness to the Priests . . . . that in cases where the Apostolic See had given power or permission in the Missionary faculties for celebrating twice in the day, where there was necessity, they should not for the future celebrate more than two Masses." The same was repeated in the years 1818 and 1820 to the Prefect Apostolic of Tunis.

4. Necessity is therefore the only title which authorizes Priests to say two Masses. It is useful here to notice also with Verricelli,[2] that "this necessity must not be determined by taking into account the scarcity of priests, but the spiritual needs of the people and the want of priests." This principle being laid down, it is easy to lay down negative rules as to the use of the faculty in question.

5. 1. In the first place, it is clear that he would be mistaken who should affirm that anyone could binate on the suppressed feasts, when there is no obligation of hearing Mass, as was stated by the Sacred Congregation in 1837: "After due deliberation, it was clear from the words of the formula itself that the faculties could not be extended to suppressed feasts. For since in the said formula it is laid down that the faculty holds good in a case of present necessity, it follows that, Mass cannot be celebrated twice by the same Priest on these days merely because they were formerly of obligation."

6. 2. It is likewise forbidden to binate for the convenience of persons who might wish to fulfil the precept of Mass in their private chapels. In 1842 the Vicar Apostolic of Limburg had represented that the custom had become established of permitting bination in the private oratories of the castles of noblemen, and as he did not consider that on such occasions the necessity required by the formula existed, he asked as well by reason of the custom as of the moral utility arising from it, to be allowed to give permission for the same. But the Holy Office judged

---

1. Cap. *Consuluisti* de celebratione Missarum.
1. De Apost. Missionibus Tit. iv. Q. 98. Dub. 18, n. 201.

that "*so far as the case went it was not expedient.*" And the Vicar Apostolic having replied that some priests on the strength of the faculty formerly given by his predecessor, continued to binate, the Supreme (Congregation) decreed, "that the faculty should be recalled, in so far as the Vicar Apostolic of Limburg should consider this might be done with prudence."

7. 3. From these resolutions it follows that custom is not a sufficient reason for one and the same priest offering up twice on one day the Holy Sacrifice. And this is in accordance with the teaching of Benedict XIV. in the Constitution "Declarasti nobis," addressed to the Bishop of Huesca in Arragon, March 16th, 1746. "We have only gone into the question," says the Pontiff, "whether this custom has acquired anything in the shape of prescription or presumption, and we decide that both of these have no foundation and are foreign to it." And as regards prescription he says: "For if according to civil law there can be no prescription in the case of things sacred, it is in every sense absurd to say that anything has been obtained or acquired by prescription, which is opposed to the general laws of the church, the observance of which in reference to the celebration of Masses the Holy Council of Trent has commanded to all Priests." He then subjoins as to presumption: "But to pass by other considerations, we submit that these must be understood to refer to those privileges, which might have been granted by the Apostolic See if anyone had asked for them, but not to those which are usually altogether refused when asked for; otherwise presumption would have more force and weight than fact." Hence it was that when the Sacred Congregation had discovered that in any place the custom of binating Mass without necessity had grown up, it did not fail to stigmatize such a custom as an abuse, and arouse the zeal of Bishops to eliminate it.

8. 4. Neither does the poverty of priests justify binating of Mass, as has been already seen in Verricelli.[1] An Archbishop of Ireland asked, in 1688, whether by reason "of their poverty alone Regulars could celebrate two Masses on feast days, doing this in private houses, notwithstanding that all the parishes and convents had their churches and chapels." The reply of the Sacred Congregation was in the negative; and when it was laid before two private Congregations of Propaganda, March 7th, 1743, and July 28th, 1750, that the said abuse still existed in Ireland, inasmuch as many Priests made use of "the faculty to binate with no other end than to get more abundant alms, and hence to be able to support themselves more easily," the most Eminent Fathers ordered: *Let Priests be seriously warned against abusing the faculty of celebrating twice in the day, in order to receive a more abundant and ample stipend.* And in Benedict XIV.[2] the practice of giving a priest the faculty to binate *to the end that by double alms he may live more becomingly* is styled *an intolerable abuse.* It was solely out of consideration for poor religions of that country, who had complained of a similar prohibition made in 1817 by the Provincial Synod of Tuam, by reason of the loss they sustained by having taken from them the alms that at Mass-times they were in the habit of receiving at the entrance of the church, living as they did by the contributions of the faithful, that

---

1. Cost. *Apostolicum ministerium*, May 30th, 1653, § 11.   2. Loc. cit.

the Sacred Congregation wished Bishops to be reminded that, "in granting by authority from the Apostolic See permission to Priests to celebrate two Masses on feast days of precept in cases of necessity approved of by the Apostolic Constitutions, they should take into account the case of regular Priests and especially of those who were living in poor convents." Finally, the Sacred Congregation of the Council having declared that "by general custom Priests are not allowed to take an alms for the second Mass, even when there is a question of those who having the charge of a parish cannot take any stipend for their first Mass, seeing that they are bound to apply this *for the people*," as was made known in the subjoined circular from Propaganda, October 15th, 1863, to the Ordinaries of missions; every excuse for the abuse of binating Mass with a view to the stipend is nowadays taken away. In consideration, however, of the peculiar circumstances of some missions, the Holy Father has deigned to authorize, as is plain from the circular itself, the aforesaid Ordinaries to allow "the priests under them to take a stipend even for the second Mass celebrated on the same day for a just and good reason."

9. 5. It is not out of place, finally, to observe, that a priest is forbidden to say Mass twice, whenever another Priest can be had, by means of whom the necessity so far as the people are concerned can be obviated, as Benedict XIV. expressly teaches in the Constitution already referred to—"*Declarasti nobis.*" And hence, before having resource to bination, it is necessary to examine as to whether there is at hand any one of the alternatives laid down by law for providing for the spiritual need of the people; and, to begin with, the parish priest himself is bound to give a stipend to some other priest; should he be unable to do this, the people are so bound; and lastly, if the people by reason of their poverty could not be so bound, the Ordinary would have to supply it.[1]

10. So much for cases in which it is forbidden to repeat the Mass. Coming now to cases in which the necessity requisite for so doing exists, these are set forth in the Constitution—"*Declarasti nobis.*" First of all it is therein noted, that, according to the unanimous consent of Theologians, a Priest is allowed to binate Mass, "who has two parishes, or two sets of people, so far apart that one or other cannot by any means, by reason of the very great distance, hear their parish priest's Mass on feast days." And this is the first and most common case; the other specified therein is, "when there is but one church in which Mass is celebrated, and all the people cannot get into it together."

11. In the cases enumerated above, Mass can be repeated even though one is not furnished with the faculty in the Formula which are usually granted by Propaganda, the common law itself allowing it, always however dependently upon the Ordinary, to whom it belongs to judge whether there is real necessity, as well as in reference to the possibility of making use of the canonical alternatives. (§ 9). After having laid down such alternatives Benedict XIV. subjoins: "what has been said so far rests upon canonical and general law." And it is moreover the common opinion of Theologians, as Benedict XIV. observes, that in the case of only one parish priest with two parishes "the parish priest is

---

1. Benedict XIV., loc. cit. Voto del Card. Zelada Thesaur. resolutionum, Tom. 37, in causa Derthusen, 25 Agosto, 1768.

not only able, but evidently bound to celebrate Mass twice on the same day."[1] And from this it readily follows that the analogous article in the Formulæ, being of an empowering character, extends likewise to other cases of necessity not contemplated in the common law, otherwise it would be rendered useless, at least in places where parishes are canonically instituted, as the common law itself would provide for them. This is conformable to what the same Pontiff says in his work *De Sacrosancto Missæ Sacrificio*,[2] where after stating that "the case which really occurs, is when a parish priest has two parishes, &c.," he goes on as follows: "nor do we wish to prejudge any other cases that occur on Missions, for which provision has been made by granting missioners the faculty of celebrating several Masses on the same day; nor likewise those other cases, in which by reason of distance, the scarcity of Priests, or persecution at the hands of heretics and unbelievers, Priests must celebrate two Masses lest the faithful should be without Mass." And it was precisely of these cases, which occur on Missions and for which the faculty is given to the superiors of the same, that mention was made at Propaganda in 1832, when a letter was sent to a missionary of Philippopoli, who did not celebrate more than one Mass although his people were of more than one rite. For having commanded him to binate by an order of the General Congregation, it subjoined: "If he asked why those rigorous clauses were added to the faculty of binating Mass in the Formula of the indult, he would find the reply in the Formula itself, observing, that the indult is not restricted to the needs of the people on feast days, but that being in general terms it contemplates also the other cases in question, such as the necessity for administering the Viaticum to the sick in two parishes, and it is in these other cases that the prescribed cautions must be attended to."

12. It is by such less obvious cases that Bishops and Missioners not unfrequently become embarrassed in the use of the faculty, doubting chiefly as to the sufficiency of the reasons that are required by the clauses that are attached to it. On the other hand, so numerous and so various are the cases that may arise in this matter upon Missions, that one cannot easily foresee them, much less bring them under a general rule, opinion being liable to change, according to the various circumstances as to places, times, and persons that may arise. This is the reason why the solution of the particular doubts submitted is for the most part left to the wise discretion of the Superiors of the Missions.

13. To begin with, a rule is frequently asked for as to the number of the faithful for whose benefit Mass may be repeated. In the Constitution *Apostolicum Ministerium* for England it is laid down, that use can be made of the faculty "when the number of those who are bound to assist at Mass on feast days shows such a necessity, that unless power be given to some Priest to celebrate two Masses on the same day, *several* would not fulfil the precept of the Church." This general rule, does not remove all doubt as to the number necessary for bination. The same might be said of a reply in the negative of the Holy Office in 1688 to some Capuchin Missioners in Greece. These having asked: "Whether

---

1. De Syn. Diœc., L. vi., cap. viii. n. 2.   2. Lib. III., cap. v. n. 4.

a Missionary Priest living alone in a place can say two Masses on Sundays and feast days for fifteen or twenty persons, who through some lawful impediment have not been able to be present at the first Mass." And the Supreme Congregation, on January 28th of the same year, decreed that *it was not lawful*. If, on the other hand, twenty in number is insufficient for it, it may finally be asked what is the least number that will suffice.

14. But as regards this doubt, as well as those that have reference to distance, the Sacred Congregation has adhered to the practice of allowing it to be settled by the judgment of the Ordinaries of the Missions, upon whom depends the faculty, they alone being able by being on the spot to give due weight to all the circumstances that surround each case. And indeed, towards the end of 1688 the Prefect of Missions of Tunis in Barbary asked generally that it should be declared what number of the faithful otherwise deprived of Mass there must be, in consideration of whom one could binate; and the General Congregation of Propaganda replied, November 16th: *Let it be left to the charity and conscience of the Father Prefect*. In the same way, the Bishop of St. Louis in the United States of America having, in 1828, submitted as well his own fears as those of the Bishops in respect of burthening their consciences by reason of the clauses of the Formula, asked: "whether they might celebrate Mass twice, as often as thirty or fifty of the faithful were exposed to the danger of not hearing a Mass of obligation." In a letter of March 13th, it was intimated to him by Leo XII's orders: "You must lay aside all anxiety and, without being disturbed at the strictness of the terms, trust to your conscience and prudence to judge what cases, account being taken of the circumstances of your diocese, are to be considered to possess sufficient reasons for imparting the faculty in question to priests. And where in conscience you deem such reasons weighty, His Holiness has graciously declared that you can make use of the faculty without any hesitation."

15. A similar reply was also given in 1851 to the Vicar Apostolic of Limburg, who had submitted a doubt as to distance. "In this country (he said), leave to binate is sometimes given in accordance with an old custom by reason of a moral necessity, although the nearest parish is only a half a league off: is this right?" Propaganda, in a letter July 31st, replied: "It being premised that it is the duty of Bishops to endeavour as best they can that there shall be no necessity for making use of this faculty for supplying the needs of the faithful, a general rule cannot be laid down for observance in each instance. Hence in special cases such as the above, when there is a scarcity of priests, and after taking into careful consideration all the circumstances of the case, it must be left to the prudent judgment of the Superior to decide, whether such weighty reasons exist as constitute what Doctors term a case of necessity (such as the one submitted seems to be), in which there are grounds for a dispensation from the general law of the same Priest not saying two Masses on one and the same day, and for giving the faculty of bination, which it is clearly seen from the words of the Apostolic indult he must make use of with the utmost reserve." And this instruction was repeated in the same terms to the Bishop of Treves in 1853, upon whose part several doubts in reference to binating Mass had

been submitted; for he was informed September 28th, that after studying his questions, "the Sacred Congregation considered that the instruction should be given him which . . . the Vicar-Apostolic of Limburg received July 31st, 1851."

16. Among the various replies which guide the judgment of Superiors in reference to the weight of the reasons adduced, there are some that demand special attention, inasmuch as, without departing from the ordinary rule of requiring the Superior himself to judge of the reasons, they, when taken together, indicate in some sense the kind or degree of necessity required for bination, and at the same time soften somewhat the impression and allay the consequent anxiety of Bishops and Missioners caused by the clauses by which this Faculty is restricted in the Formulæ. One of these replies was given in 1848 to a Bishop of the United States of America: "I come to an inquiry of yours (thus ran a letter of May 9th) in reference to the manner of interpreting the necessity requisite for the lawful use of the faculty of celebrating Mass twice on the same day . . . . Your Lordship should therefore be aware that a necessity of this kind must be understood to be a real but still a moral and not an absolute necessity, to come to a determination in reference to which in each case pertains to your prudent judgment after examination of the circumstances. You must, therefore, beware of too much anxiety in coming to a determination, lest the said faculty may seem to have been granted to no purpose, or hardly any, when it comes to be reduced to practice." More remarkable is the declaration which was issued in 1824 to a Prefect Apostolic in the Antilles of America. This Prefect mistrusting his ability to make use of the faculty in question without scruples owing to the severe conditions which accompany it, had begged for "a more extended faculty from the Apostolic See of giving power to priests to celebrate Mass twice on Sundays and festivals of obligation, whensoever necessity or the spiritual benefit of the faithful might require it." The matter was laid before the Pope at an audience of April 13th, and an answer was sent to the following effect: "Such is the opinion of your virtue and prudence, that our Most Holy Lord has ordered you should lay aside all anxiety, and if you consider it necessary or extremely serviceable to the faithful that the priests should say Mass twice on the same day, you must not be disturbed by the stringency of the words in which the rescript appears to be couched. His Holiness therefore refers it to the conscience of your Reverence to judge of the necessity and the gravity of the several cases, and has graciously declared that under such circumstances you have the faculty by virtue of the said rescript to empower priests to say two Masses."

17. The same rule of referring to the judgment or charity of the Superiors of Missions the application of general principles to practical cases was likewise observed when in these, as they were reported, there was not that grave urgency, considered at least in itself and in the abstract, which the clauses of this faculty require; and this abundantly confirms the fact that much consideration in determining the reasons that justify its use must be given to all the circumstances and to the condition of the faithful. A proof of this is the reply given by this Sacred Congregation in 1688 to the Vice-Prefect of the Mission of Tripoli. In his uncertainty arising from the oft quoted clauses he had asked: "For what precise number of slaves or free people the second

Mass could be celebrated, instancing at the same time the case, that in the prison outside Tripoli there are not ten or fifteen enslaved persons present at the Sacrifice; and whether, in a deficiency of priests, a second Mass could on days of obligation be celebrated for these alone." Now, notwithstanding the adverse decision sent forth in the very same year from the Holy Office in a similar case, as has been stated § 12, the Sacred Congregation of Propaganda gave the order on October 5th, that "It should be left to the charity and conscience of the Father Prefect." Nor is it to be wondered at, if Propaganda considered that it could find room for a more lenient interpretation, as it was a question of slaves, who by their condition were worthy of particular indulgence, it being perchance their only comfort to assist at the Sacred Sacrifice. Another proof of the leaning to a more mild interpretation or connivance in view of the circumstances of the case, the Supreme Congregation gave in 1610; for although, June 20th, it had replied to the Vicar Apostolic of a country on the borders of China, "the wish of Neophytes to receive the Most Holy Eucharist twice or three times in the year was not in itself a most urgent reason, in the case in question," that is for saying Mass twice in accordance with the faculty, nevertheless it subjoined: "but considering all the circumstances of place and people, it must be left to the judgment of the Reverend Father the Lord Vicar Apostolic." Whence it follows that those reasons which of themselves and in many places are not weighty, may become so in others owing to the circumstances connected with them.

18. These are the principles which have been kept in view as regards the faculty of binating, and which certainly tend to ease the minds of the Ordinaries of Missions, in the exercise of the same. If it is true that it is usual to defer therein to the wise discretion of the Ordinaries of Missions, it is nevertheless plain from what has been said, how much caution must be used, as their conscience remains always burthened with the legitimate exercise of the said extraordinary faculty. Nevertheless, the clauses in the Formulæ "must not be interpreted in the *most rigorous* manner" (to conclude with the advice tendered by the Sacred Congregation in 1832 to the Bishop of Nicopoli in Bulgaria), "having always in view that the Apostolic See grants the said faculty for the spiritual advantage of the faithful, in its desire that all should have the convenience of fulfilling the ecclesiastical precept."

19. It remains now to speak of the rite, or mode to be followed in binating Mass. And upon this point it is not necessary to observe that it is always prescribed for Missioners by the Sacred Congregation and by Benedict XIV. himself, that he who binates must not take the accustomed ablutions of the chalice, by reason of the fast, so that "if he has taken the ablution at the first Mass after receiving the Body and Blood, he must not say second a Mass in the above mentioned cases,"[1] even though they are such that the people would otherwise be deprived of Mass on a feast day. Although, however, it was prescribed in a decree of the Sacred Congregation of Rites *in Ebusitana* September 16th, 1815, that only one chalice should be used by the person saying two Masses, since the observance of such a decree involved no small difficulty when one had to celebrate in two churches at a distance from each other; the venerable Sacred Congregation at a general meeting, September 12th,

---

1. Council of Nismes, 1284. See Bened. XIV. De Sanct. Missæ Sacrif. L. III. v. n. 4.

1857, relaxed the aforesaid decree, and decided that "the use of two chalices could, in the case before them, be permitted." And the instruction given herewith, which was drawn up by order of the same Sacred Congregation, treats of the manner of purifying the chalice at the first Mass.

Propaganda, May 24th, 1870.

For the instruction referred to in the last sentence of th above see *Synodi Diœc. Suth.*, p. 113.

CHAPTER THE FIFTH.

CHAPTERS, CANONS, AND VICAR-CAPITULAR.

I.

PRELIMINARY DOCUMENTS REFERRED TO IN VARIOUS DECREES OF THE FIRST SYNOD OF WESTMINSTER.

1. Westminster, Appendix, I., p. 125.

THE APOSTOLIC LETTER INSTITUTING CATHEDRAL CHAPTERS.

PIUS IX. POPE.

For all time to come. In our Apostolic letter, dated September 29th last, under the seal of the Fisherman, We restored in the most prosperous kingdom of England the ordinary episcopal hierarchy, appointing therein Westminster the metropolitan church with its suffragan episcopal churches of Southwark, Hexham, Beverley, Liverpool, Salford, Clifton, Plymouth, Nottingham, Birmingham, Northampton, Shrewsbury, and Newport with Menevia. We, moreover, declared that the administration of all these was to be carried on according to the common rules of ecclesiastical law. These We decreed should be kept in that kingdom in all matters connected with the Catholic religion and the Church, as was clearly expressed in the aforesaid letter. Subsequently, by another Apostolic letter, given likewise under the seal of the Fisherman, We appointed pastors to the archiepiscopal church of Westminster as well as to seven other churches, to wit, Hexham, Beverley, Liverpool, Clifton, Birmingham, Northampton, and to the united churches of Menevia and Newport. And pending the time when We shall be able to appoint Bishops to the remainder, We have committed the administration of the church of Southwark to the Archbishop of Westminster, the administration of the church of Salford to the Bishop of Liverpool, the administration of the church of Plymouth to the Bishop of Clifton, the administration of the church of Nottingham to the Bishop of Birmingham, and, finally, We gave the administration of the church of Shrewsbury to the Bishop of the united churches of Menevia and Newport. These matters having, therefore, been settled by the above mentioned Apostolic letter, We now turn our attention to the institution of canonical colleges, and consider that the task of bringing this about without delay should be handed over to the prelates already appointed. Therefore, of our own accord, and from the fulness of our Apostolical authority, We empower and command our beloved son the Cardinal Archbishop of Westminster, and his venerable brethren the Bishops of Hexham, Beverley, Liverpool, Clifton, Birmingham, Northampton, and the Bishop of the united churches of Menevia and Newport, that each one of them in our name and by the power delegated to them by Us, shall establish a chapter in his diocese, consisting of at least one dignitary and ten canons. As to the united churches already mentioned of Menevia and Newport, we deem it sufficient for the present that but one capitular college should be formed for both. We command likewise and give power to the same metropolitan Archbishop and the Bishops of Liverpool, Clifton, Birmingham, as well as to the Bishop of the united churches of Menevia and Newport, to establish, each of them, in the church entrusted to their administration by Us, a cathedral chapter, precisely in the same way and by the power delegated to them by Us. And these chapters, from the moment of their institution, shall enjoy all rights and be bound by all the obligations, which by the common law of the sacred canons are attached to metropolitan or cathedral chapters.

Therefore, so often as it shall happen that the metropolitan or any one of the episcopal churches of England is deprived of its pastor, and there is no one to whom the administration has been consigned by this Holy See, it shall pertain to the chapter established therein to look after the business of the diocese by its deputy the vicar-capitular, and this in the way prescribed by the common law of the canons and the decree of the Council of Trent. But if a vacancy occurs in any one of these churches before the chapter has been established in it, or if the chapter has been established but has not duly and in the prescribed time performed its duty, the regulations of the common law of the Church and of the Council of Trent are likewise to be observed. According to these, this care and the appointment of a Vicar will fall to the metropolitan Archbishop, or to the oldest of the other Bishops according to circumstances. These things we decree, order, appoint, and declare, notwithstanding all that We have decreed to be notwithstanding in our abovementioned Apostolic letter of September the 29th of this year, and everything else whatsoever to the contrary.

Given at Rome, at St. Peter's, under the seal of the Fisherman, November 19th, 1850, in the fifth year of our Pontificate.

A. CARD. LAMBRUSCHINI.

L. ✠ S.

EXTENSION OF THE ABOVE-MENTIONED FACULTIES.

Ib. App. ii., p. 127.

At an audience of his Holiness, granted August 10th, 1851, Our Most Holy Lord Pius, by divine Providence Pope Pius IX., at the instance of me the undersigned secretary of the Sacred Congregation of Propaganda, on the petition of the Right Rev. Thomas Grant, Bishop of Southwark, graciously consented that, inasmuch as in all or at least some of the churches in the kingdom of England chapters of canons have not been established by the Bishops, to whom the matter was entrusted by the Apostolic letter of November 19th, 1850, the duty should be committed for fulfilment to the Bishops who are placed over the aforesaid churches, to whom accordingly all the faculties granted in the aforesaid Apostolical letter are given, all things whatsoever to the contrary notwithstanding.

Given at Rome, at the office of the said Sacred Congregation, the day and year as above.

AL. BARNABÒ, Secretary.

L. ✠ S.

DECREE OF THE SACRED CONGREGATION OF PROPAGANDA WITH REGARD TO THE CATHEDRAL CHAPTERS FOR THE CHURCHES NEWLY CONSTITUTED IN THE KINGDOM OF ENGLAND.

Ib. App. iii., p. 128.

April 21st, 1852.

The questions referred to by the most Eminent and Reverend Lord Nicholas Wiseman, Archbishop of Westminster, with respect to the establishment of Cathedral Chapters, after a meeting of the English Bishops held in the previous year, were laid before the Sacred Congregation on April 5th, 1852. And since it is clear that, owing to the circumstances of the newly appointed churches, several things concerning the chapter of a cathedral church which are in canon law laid down, cannot at once be carried out in regard to the churches in question; their Eminences have concluded that, subject to the good pleasure of his Holiness, an instruction should be sent giving the course to be pursued in the matter until some further decree shall be made.

Inasmuch as there are no canonical prebends, and the canons have to devote themselves to the cure of souls, to teaching, and to other duties for the good of religion in the diocese, and considering also the small number of priests; their Eminences have thought that consent might be given to their exemption from the duty of residence at the cathedral and of attending to the sacred office, provided that the Bishops at the next Provincial Synod name some days upon which the canons shall be bound to be present at choir and go through the office, and that they meet the Bishop especially when business is on hand of such a kind that, according to the sacred Canons, the opinion of the chapter must be taken with regard to it.

Likewise, the method proposed for the election of canons seems a proper one—viz., that in the first instance all, dignitaries included, should be chosen by the Bishop, in accordance with the Apostolic brief, but for the future (with due regard to the months in which the appointment has to be made by rescript from the Holy See),[1] the nomination should be made for the remaining months alternately either by the Bishop or by the Chapter. So far at least by the Chapter, that three ecclesiastics shall be presented once, again and even a third time to the Bishop, in order that a fit and in every way commendable person may be appointed by him a canon; otherwise the election falls to the freewill of the Bishop.

Their Eminences have also approved of the proposition of the Bishops that the dignitary designated in the Apostolic letter for each Cathedral Chapter should be known by the title of Provost.

Canons theologian and penitentiary will likewise have to be appointed, and may this first time be chosen without concursus by the Bishops; but in future according to the prescriptions of the Sacred Canons. The penitentiary should live as far as possible at the cathedral church; and at the next Synod arrangement should be made for the canon theologian's lectures according to the plan laid down by the Sacred Canons, due regard being paid, however, to the circumstances of time and place.

---

1. See note to p. 105.

And since, in fine, it is very proper that those who form the church's senate, and are the Bishops advisers and chief assistants in the administration of the diocese, should be in some way known by their garb, the petition of the Bishops was granted that canons, without any distinction by reason of diocese or grade, might wear a black mozzetta over their surplice, but not of silk, like the pattern to be decided upon by the most Eminent and Reverend the Archbishop of Westminster. This decision of the Sacred Congregation, laid before our most Holy Lord Pope Pius IX. by me the undersigned secretary at an audience on April 6th, His Holiness graciously confirmed, and granting the faculties required, commanded the same to be observed, all things whatsoever to the contrary notwithstanding.

Given, &c.

AL. BARNABÒ, Secretary.

Decree of the Sacred Congregation of Propaganda concerning the Chapter of Plymouth.

April 21st., 1852.

Ib., App. iv., 130.

Seeing that in the establishment of the cathedral chapter of Plymouth, in accordance with the Apostolic letter of our most Holy Lord, dated November 19th, 1850, difficulties may occur as to the immediate appointment of canons to the number prescribed in the letter referred to; the Sacred Congregation of Propaganda, at a general meeting on April 5th., 1852, at the instance of the most Eminent and Reverend the Archbishop of Westminster, and their Right Reverend Lordships, the Bishops of England, have judged that his Holiness might be petitioned to allow the Chapter of Plymouth to be established even without the prescribed number of canons being at once made up, the arrangements as to other matters in the brief remaining unaltered.

This decision of the Sacred Congregation, was laid before our most Holy Lord, Pope Pius, IX., by me the undersigned secretary at an audience granted the sixth day of the same month and year, and his Holiness graciously approved thereof upon every point, all things whatsoever to the contrary notwithstanding.

Given, &c.

AL. BARNABÒ, Secretary.

Decree of the Sacred Congregation of Propaganda upon Cathedral Churches.

April 21st., 1852.

Ib., App. vi., p. 132.

Now that the episcopal hierarchy has been re-established in the realm of England and that an Apostolic letter has been issued for the establishment of cathedral chapters, cathedral churches for the arch-diocese of Westminster and for each of the other dioceses must be appointed in the way laid down by the sacred canons. Accordingly, his most Eminent and Right Reverend Lordship, Cardinal of the Holy Roman Church, Nicholas Wiseman, Archbishop of Westminster, having taken counsel with their Right Reverend Lordships the Bishops of England, has stated that several cities chosen as episcopal Sees do not as yet possess churches of sufficient size, appearance and convenience of every kind, to be used for good and all as cathedrals.

A petition is, therefore, presented that for Birmingham the church dedicated to the honour of St. Chad, Bishop and Confessor, be appointed the cathedral; for Southwark, that of St. George; for Nottingham, that of St. Barnabas, Apostle; for Salford, that of St. John, Apostle: but that the faculty be granted to the Archbishop of Westminster and the rest of the Bishops of England to appoint provisionally, in lieu of a cathedral, some church which may do for the present, and that in the meanwhile everything may be carried on therein as in the cathedral, which as time goes on must be provided and appointed for good and all.

Seeing that this petition seemed a just one to their Eminences of the Sacred Congregation when considered by them at a general meeting on April 5th., 1852, our most Holy Lord, Pope Pius, IX., having in an audience of the sixth day of the same month and year, had the matter in question laid before him by the undersigned secretary of the same Sacred Congregation, approved of the decision, and upon both points yielded to the prayer of the petition, all things whatsoever to the contrary notwithstanding.

Given, &c. Al. BARNABÒ, Secretary.

II. On Cathedral Chapters

I West., D, xi., p. 50.

Although by an Apostolic brief of November 19th, 1850, permission was graciously given for each Bishop to establish a Chapter, and already in almost every diocese, by virtue of this grant, a lawfully appointed Chapter exists; it has been deemed advisable that for the fuller understanding of such an institution, there should be brought here together and ever remain for reference, the regulations and other arrangements fully sanctioned by the decrees of the Sacred Congregation of Propaganda, April 21st of the present year; the matter of which should be added to the decrees of this Synod. (*See Appendix, i., iii., iv., v., vi.*)[1]

1.—The Chapter shall consist of ten canons and one Dignitary.

2.—Considering, however, the want of priests, it may consist of less than that number in the diocese of Plymouth.

3.—In the Diocese of Newport and Menevia the cathedral chapter shall be the monastic chapter that is to be established therein by the Anglo-Benedictines.[2]

4.—Since, with the exception of the dioceses of Southwark, Birmingham, Salford and Nottingham, no other dioceses of England possess churches worthy of the name of Cathedrals, in every one of these the Bishop shall name some church to hold the place of a provisional Cathedral, until by God's help a fitting temple is provided, and a Cathedral church named and appointed for good and all.

---

1. All of these are given above with the exception of No. 5, for which see p. 122.
2. Ibid.

5.—The Dignitary in each chapter shall be honoured with the title of Provost.

6.—In each chapter also a canon theologian and canon penitentiary must be appointed. These, after the first appointment which has been granted to the Bishop, must be elected in the way set down in the sacred Canons. The canon penitentiary should dwell, as far as possible, at the Cathedral church. But the canon theologian shall discharge his duty, in the manner prescribed in the sacred Canons, at the times and place appointed by the Bishop. The Bishop shall likewise decide upon the subject of his lectures.

7.—The rule for the appointment of canons shall be as follows: After the first appointments have been made at the Bishop's sole will, by virtue of the Apostolic Brief referred to, the nomination shall for the future alternate between the Bishop and the Chapter, that is, in the months left after the exceptions in which this has to be done by rescript from the Holy See.[1] With this proviso, however, that whensoever the nomination falls to the Chapter, three ecclesiastics shall be named to the Bishop once, twice, and a third time, in order that a fitting and in every way commendable canon may be appointed. Otherwise the election will devolve upon the freewill of the Bishop.

8.—As we have no canonical prebends and the canons have to devote themselves generally to the cure of souls or to teaching in the seminaries, they are exempted by pontifical authority from the duty of residence and from keeping choir in the Cathedral; provided that once a month they are bound to attend choir and go through the divine office on the days selected by the Bishop at the commencement of each year, who should take note for this end of any particular festival that happens to occur within each month. On such occasions the Chapter meetings may be held. But the Bishop will settle as to the time of holding a Chapter in his own residence, especially for the discussion of those matters concerning

---

1. Bishop Grant, in Appendix XV., of the Synods of the Diocese of Southwark, thus explains the Rule as to Papal months, &c. "Certain benefices are said to be affected to the Pope, whilst others are reserved to him in the Corpus Juris, in the Extravagantes, and in later Constitutions. In addition to such reservations, the Pope is accustomed on the day after his elevation, to confirm the Regulæ Cancellariæ which contain other reservations, of his right to appoint to benefices falling vacant under certain conditions. The IXth Rule, first published by Martin V. in the Council of Constance, reserves to the reigning Pope the right of nominating to all benefices falling vacant otherwise than by resignation during the months of January, February, April, May, July, August, October, and November. But, as a reward for his fidelity in observing the law of residence, a Bishop may obtain an Indult which secures to him the right of nominating to all benefices, not otherwise affected or reserved, in the months of February, April, June, August, October, December, (Benedict XIV. *Ad Universæ*, Sept. 3, 1746.) The position, therefore, of our Chapters may be thus briefly described. The Pope names to the dignity of the Præpositum by the fourth of the Rules of the Chancery, and he names to all Canonries which are reserved to his nomination by the IX., and by other rules, or by the Canons, Extravagantes, or later Bulls. The Rule IX. leaves to the Bishop the nominations which occur in March, June, September and December, and in these months the Bishop may name to unreserved and unaffected Canonries, with this exception, that the Theologian and Penitentiary must be named after a Concursus, and with the further exception that during these four months every alternate nomination to other Canonries supposes the presentation of three names by the Chapter. An Indult of Residence adds to the number of episcopal months, and in the six months thus belonging to the Bishop, if resident, every alternate nomination will rest with him absolutely, whilst in the others the Chapters must forward one, two, or three lists, of three names, from which the nomination is to be made if the names are otherwise suitable." (*I. West.* p. 129).

which, according to the sacred Canons, the opinion of the Chapter has to be taken. The Bishop's permission must be obtained for an extraordinary meeting of the Chapter.

9.—There is to be no distinction of orders amongst the canons, that is, no division into priests and deacons.

10.—Since it is very proper that those who are promoted to the Senatorship of the church and to be the Bishop's advisers and chief assistants in the administration of the diocese, should also be in some way known by their dress; the canons may, by pontifical leave, wear a black mozzetta, but not of silk, over the surplice, of the pattern approved of by his Eminence the Archbishop, without any distinction as to the diocese or rank.

11.—Merely titular or, as they are called, honorary canons we forbid to be made.

12.—Finally we order the capitular statutes which have been read and approved of in this Synod to be strictly observed.

III. THE MANNER IN WHICH RECOMMENDATIONS TO THE EPISCOPACY ARE TO BE MADE.—THE VICAR-CAPITULAR.

Ib. xii. p. 53.

If by reason of the position they occupy and the duty they discharge in the diocese, canons should be examples to the rest of the clergy in goodness of life, in piety, in learning and in zeal, how much more is it becoming that they should be adorned with every virtue, to whom is committed the government itself of the church when it is deprived of its pastor, and the honourable office most graciously granted by the Holy See, of recommending those whom they deem worthy of promotion to the burthen of the episcopacy. And for this great boon granted to the clergy at our request, we in this Synod assembled desire that our most humble and devoted thanks be given to our most Holy Lord, Pius IX., in a letter which will accompany the acts of this Provincial Synod.

1.—On the death, therefore, of a Bishop, the canons shall meet together after the funeral ceremony has been duly performed, and under the presidency of the Provost they shall go through everything prescribed by law for the election of a Vicar-Capitular. And this should be done within eight days.

2.—Within a month (or, when they are summoned, in case it is for the election of a Bishop to succeed another who is not dead) the Provost and canons of the church in question must assemble as for Chapter, under the presidency of the Archbishop, or, if he cannot be present, or it is a case of the vacancy of the Archbishopric, of the Senior Bishop. He, however, is to take no part in the business. But they, then and there, are to proceed to the recommendation in the way set down in the late Instruction upon this matter by the Sacred Congregation of Propaganda, April 21st of the present year, to be added to the acts of this Synod. (*See below*).

3. After that, as is therein to be found, the act of the Chapter must be handed over to the Archbishop or to the Senior Suffragan, that the Bishops at their meeting may confer together as to the three names sent in in alphabetical order, and forward them to the Sacred Congregation, giving their opinion as to each of those thus recommended.

4. If any canon is lawfully hindered from being present at the Chapter at which this recommendation has to be made, he shall be allowed to hand in, through a proxy, chosen from the Chapter, three notes containing the names and surnames of those to be recommended by him.

5. This faculty of recommendation we refer in such manner to the gracious liberality of the Holy See, that no right of election or nomination can be advanced; but that it shall ever pertain to the free will of the Holy Father, to exercise his own right of election of any other than those recommended, as often as he shall deem it necessary.

Instruction of the Sacred Congregation of Propaganda as to Recommendations to the Episcopate in England.

April 21st., 1852.

Ib., Appendix vii., p. 133.

That the churches recently established in the realm of England by our most Holy Lord may day by day increase, and that Bishops may be always appointed to them who are well known for their goodness of life, their learning, zeal and prudence; it has seemed in every way befitting that by ecclesiastics who have been prominent in the discharge of sacred duties, and especially by the Bishops for the time being, certain names should be brought to the notice of the Apostolic See, in order that from amongst them it may select the fittest for elevation to the episcopal rank.

Such a recommendation is a matter so weighty, that after considering the observations made by his most Eminent and Reverend Lordship, Nicholas, of the Holy Roman Church, Cardinal Wiseman, and their Right Reverend Lordships the Bishops of England, and a thorough examination into the matter, the Sacred Congregation of Propaganda has thought it well, at a general meeting held April 5th, 1852, to lay down the method to be pursued in a special Instruction.

When a Bishop has to be appointed, the Provost and canons of the church in question shall meet together capitularly, and after the customary prayers and the oath of secrecy, votes shall be given three times for persons to be recommended as worthy of the office to the Holy See. If at any of the three times there is not a clear majority in favour of some one, the voting shall not count, but take place again.

The act of the Chapter duly recorded and signed must be handed to the Archbishop, or to the Suffragan Senior Bishop should the Archiepiscopal See be vacant or in case it is for the appointment to the Archiepiscopal See itself; in order that the Bishops at their meeting may confer together and refer the three names written in alphabetical order, which have obtained at each voting a majority, to the Sacred Congregation, giving their own opinion, and the authentic deed of the capitular resolution being also sent. Finally, seeing that it may happen sometimes that canons may be lawfully hindered from being present at the Chapter at which this recommendation is to be made, the Sacred Congregation has thought fit that their proxies should be admitted, but only empowered to hand in a paper with the name and surname of the person to be elected.[1]

But the Sacred Congregation has deemed it proper to notice and declare that in all this there is to be merely a recommendation; so that the Apostolic See may exercise its right of choosing others than those nominated, so often as it seems necessary or opportune to do so.

And when all these points were laid before our most Holy Lord Pope Pius IX. by the under-signed Secretary of the Sacred Congregation at an audience on the sixth day of the same month and year, His Holiness graciously approved thereof and ordered that they should be observed, all things whatsoever to the contrary notwithstanding.

Given, &c.

AL. BARNABÒ, Secretary.

IV. ADDITIONAL DECREES AND RESCRIPTS IN REFERENCE TO CHAPTERS.

IV. Westminster. viii., p. 35.

At the first Synod of Westminster sufficient consideration was given and statutes were made in regard to the establishment, obligations and privileges of Cathedral Chapters. Experience, however, has taught us that additional regulations or remarks must be made.

1. The remarkable earnestness with which members of Chapters have abundantly fulfilled their duties is worthy of special praise; all the more so, as every one is aware of the many and great difficulties that stand in the way of the discharge of these duties. Chief amongst them the absence of prebends is to be noted, and hence, that as the canons cannot live at the Cathedral church, they are dispersed up and down the diocese, attending to duties on missions, at colleges, or in other ecclesiastical ways, and for these and other reasons of a similar nature they are to a great extent exempted by Pontifical authority from the obligation of residence and keeping choir.

Nevertheless, those who take unto themselves honours and offices

---

[1] Or, as was subsequently explained by the Sacred Congregation, three papers, with the names of those to be proposed. And speaking generally, whenever any discrepancy appears between the Decrees of this Synod and the Documents referred to, it arises from the fact that these have been modified by subsequent directions from the Sacred Congregation itself. In practice, therefore, the text of the Synod must be followed. N. C. W.

should remember that they also take the burthens; and that canons, according to the statutes of Chapter, are bound to be present at choir and to attend the Chapter meeting every month on the day fixed by the Bishop, unless they have obtained leave of absence from the Bishop, this power having been granted to him by the Holy See. (*See—Rescript of the Sacred Congregation of Propaganda, January 21st, 1855, p. 118*).

Hence if for grave reasons they cannot attend the Chapter on the appointed day, they are bound to acquaint the Secretary of the Chapter by letter with the cause of absence. This letter the Secretary shall himself read out to the Provost and canons, and shall keep for the Bishop to examine at his visitation. The Provost should be aware that it is part of his duty to see that the statutes for Chapters are kept, and to admit only a legitimate excuse. And in the discharge of this duty he should be supported by the other members of the Chapter. And if any canon stays away from Chapter without excuse, he must know that he is to blame.

2. Amongst the Statutes for Chapters in the First Synod of Westminster, in chap. IX. on the duties and functions of canons, it was decreed that: "Copies of resolutions of Chapter cannot be withheld from the Bishop by the canons, should he require them; inasmuch as it is his duty to watch and see that nothing is decreed by the members of the chapter contrary to law or prejudicial to the Church." Now, to meet questions which might arise from this passage, we judge that it should be added that the canons must lay before the Bishop in residence even the books of the Chapter, as often as he reasonably requires them to do so.—*See Appendix, v., (p. 108)*.

3. By the gracious permission of the Holy See it devolves upon the Chapter at the death of the Bishop to elect three ecclesiastics by secret voting, and, in the way prescribed by the same above-mentioned Synod, in its twelfth Decree, to recommend them to the Supreme Pontiff for the vacant See. The members of the Chapter should, therefore, bear in mind the greatness of this privilege and its responsibility as regards the happiness and prosperity of the diocese; seeing that on their judgment and honesty depend the unity of the clergy, the good estate of the diocese, the peace of the flock. For as the Bishop is, so is the church. Hence in selecting names, the members of the Chapter should not confine themselves to the Chapter or to the diocese, but should take note of men especially fit even out of the diocese, who shall be not merely endowed with the necessary gifts, but eminent also for their ability in human affairs as well as divine.

That this may be the more easily done by the canons, we deem it wise to subjoin to the acts of this Synod, a list of the qualities that should be found in a Bishop.—*See Appendix, vi., (p. 108)*.

In sending on the names of those nominated by the Chapter, the canons should not neglect to send also to the Metropolitan, or to the Bishop who has taken his place, any facts concerning the persons recommended, so far as they can do so.

The two Instructions referred to are as follows:—*IV. Westminster, Appendix v., p. 137.*

RESCRIPTS OF THE SACRED CONGREGATION OF THE COUNCIL ON LAYING THE BOOKS OF THE CHAPTER BEFORE THE BISHOP.—*Decree viii, 2.*

August 2nd, 1869, the Sacred Congregation of their Eminences of the Cardinals of the Holy Roman Church, Interpreters of the Council of Trent, ordered a rescript to the effect that[1] it was settled by the Synod of Westminster of 1852, the decrees of which were printed in 1853, and were examined and approved of by the Sacred Congregation of Propaganda May 14th, 1853, in the second Part, upon Chapter Statutes iv., n 50, p. 100—that "Copies of resolutions of Chapter cannot be withheld from the Bishop by the canons should he require them; inasmuch as it is his duty to watch and see that nothing is decreed by the members of the Chapter contrary to law or prejudicial to the Church; and he can exact them from the canons by recourse to penalties and censures." It, moreover, ordered the answer to be given of the Sacred Congregation of Rites, at a Special Meeting, on September 19th, 1710, *in Alben.*, to questions 34 and 35: 34 being, "Is the Chapter bound to keep a book in which all the resolutions of the Chapter are entered; as well as one in which are likewise entered the income and expenditure of the Chapter Revenue?" And 35, "Is the Chapter bound to shew the Bishop the said book as often as he shall think fit?" The Sacred Congregation replied, to 34.—Affirmatively; to 35, Affirmatively, when there is a reasonable cause.

L. ✠ S.   P. CARD. CATERINI, Prefect.
P. ARCHBISHOP OF SARDIS, Secretary.

IV. Westminster, App. vi., p. 138.

ON THOSE WHO SHOULD BE RAISED TO THE EPISCOPACY.—*Decree viii, 3.*

Information and queries in reference to the qualities necessary for the episcopal office and dignity.

1. Name, surname, age, and country of the candidate.
2. His ecclesiastical diocese and province.
3. Place where he made his theological course, and proficiency therein.
4. His degrees, if he has taken any.
5. Has he acted as Professor, and of what subject?
6. Has he had any sacred business matters to transact, and what kind of experience has he gained therein?
7. In how many and what languages is he skilled.
8. What offices has he held, and how has he succeeded in them?
9. Has he shewn prudence in discussion and in action.
10. Is he in good health? thrifty, not hasty, and accustomed to the management of temporalities?
11. Is he determined, or changeable?

---

1. The question raised was, whether a Chapter is bound to lay the whole Chapter book before the Bishop in residence demanding it, and not merely copies of the deliberations of Chapter; and also, whether at the time of his visitation, the Chapter is bound to lay open its archives to the Bishop, without any reservation.

12. Is he of good fame, and has there ever been anything immoral about him?

13. Is he devoted to the discharge of his priestly duties, of an edifying comportment, and a careful observer of the rubrics.

14. Does he shew signs of seriousness and religion in his dress, his carriage, his appearance, speech and every other way?

V. Capitular Statutes Approved of at the First Provincial Synod of Westminster.
I. West., p. 90.

1.—On Canons in General.

1. Canons should bear in mind that they have been called to the Senate of the Bishop of the diocese, and therefore that they should assist him, and be an example to the clergy throughout the diocese by the practice of those virtues that especially become the ecclesiastical state.

2. They should often read over the statutes of chapter, the better and more surely to keep the decrees thereof.

3. They should carefully gather from the sacred canons and authentic interpretations of the same, what are the obligations and what the rights of Canons, that whilst they give due consideration to the latter they may rigorously fulfil the former.

4. We especially recommend the Canons to direct their attention and means to the formation by degrees of prebends attached to the Cathedral church, to the end that, by God's help, Canons may dwell at the church itself and perform the divine office therein, as well as with greater readiness assist the Bishop in governing the diocese.

5. The Canons should for this end often call upon the help and intercession of the Saint to whom the Cathedral church is dedicated.

2.—The Admission of Canons.

6. A Canon on receipt of the letter of his promotion, shall personally or by letter transmit a copy of the same to the Very Rev. the Provost, and shall request that he should be admitted to possession of his canonry. The Provost shall then make known to him the day for the next chapter meeting, for him to present thereat the aforesaid letter. The Canon cannot use any of his privileges or exercise any of his rights until he has taken possession of his canonry.

7. On the day named by the chapter, the new Canon, supported by two Canons asked by him, one on each side, shall present his letter of nomination to the chapter (*Council of Trent, Session xxiv, c. 12. On Reformation.*) Moreover, what the Council of Trent[1]

---

[1]. "Those also who are promoted to any benefices whatsoever having care of souls, shall within two months at the latest from the day of their taking possession be bound to make a public profession of their orthodox faith before the Bishop, or if he be hindered, his Vicar-General or Official; and shall promise and swear that they will continue in obedience to the Roman Church. But those who are promoted to canonries and dignities in Cathedral churches shall be bound to do this, not only before the Bishop or his Official, but also in the Chapter.

commands under the penalties specified, must be fulfilled, to wit, "he is bound to make public profession of his orthodox faith in the presence of the Bishop himself, or if he cannot be present, of his Vicar-general or substitute, within two months at the most from the day of his taking possession; and to promise and swear that he will remain in obedience to the Roman Church." And after that he shall make the following declaration: "I. N., elected Canon of this Cathedral church, declare that I receive with due reverence the statutes of this chapter, and I promise obedience as to secrecy, even under pain of mortal sin, as often as the Bishop or the chapter shall order it."

8. Thereupon the Provost shall assign a stall to the Canon-elect, and in the name of the whole chapter shall address him in seasonable language.

9. The chapter cannot exact or receive anything from the new Canon on account of his nomination or installation. It is to be desired that all expense may as far as possible be avoided at all chapter meetings, and particularly when the admission of a new Canon is kept. (*On this subject Monacelli's excellent remarks should be borne in mind. Legal Formulary, Part iii, title, 3, formula ix.*).[1]

3.—THE PRECEDENCE OF CANONS.

10. To the Provost belongs the first stall or first seat after the Bishop.

11. Next to him shall sit the Canon who is senior, counting from the date of taking possession; and then the other Canons must take their places successively.

12. Episcopal ceremonial functions do not fall to the Vicar-Capitular but to the chief Dignitary of the chapter. (*S.R.C., August 7th, 1627*).

13. Precedence is due to the Vicar-Capitular before all the members of the chapter with the exception of the Dignitary or representative of the chapter. (*S.R.C., June 12th, 1638; April 2nd, 1667*).

14. The proper place of the Vicar-Capitular both in choir and at processions is at the left of the Dignitary: or, should the Dignitary be bearing the most Holy Sacrament, at the left of the chief

---

[1]. The Formula referred to is as follows: Having considered the case laid before Us on the part of N. appointed by the Apostolic See to a Canonry in the Cathedral church of N., as is clear from the Apostolic letter in evidence, who complains that possession of the Canonry is held back by the Chapter and canons, because he will not promise to remit the payment of interest (or some other payment); and having seen the notice to the Chapter to show cause why it should not be declared to have incurred the censure of Interdict contained in the Constitution of Pius V., and in the absence of any defence, we declare that the aforesaid Chapter has fallen under the Interdict contained in the Bull quoted by reason of the said unlawful demand for payment and the retarding of the possession of the Canonry, and we denounce it as lying under Ecclesiastical Interdict, and will and order that it shall be publicly so denounced.
    N. Vic. Gen.   N. Actuary.

Formula N. consists of the Denunciation by the ordinary authority of the Chapter of the Cathedral (or Collegiate) church of N. as subject to and lying under Ecclesiastical Interdict, for refusing and delaying to yield permission of the Canonry to one who has obtained it, upon the plea of the non-performance of an illicit promise (or payment) on the part of N. appointed by the Apostolic See, in direct opposition to the Decree of the Council of Trent, session 23, c. 14, and the Bull of Pius V.
    N. Vic. Gen   N. Actuary.

and most dignified Canon, representing the Chapter. *(S.R.C., March 16th, 1658).*

15. The Bishop's Vicar-general takes precedence of all the Canons and the Provost in choir, in the church, and everywhere. *(S.C.R., in Nicien, October 2nd, 1677).* But functions which belong to the Bishop are in his absence to be performed by the Dignitary and Canons successively, not by the Vicar-general. *(S.R.C., February 25th, 1606).*

16. Particular attention should be paid to the decree, *in Casalensi*, of July 5th., 1614: "As to the question of precedence between the Vicar-general and the Canons of the church of Casala, the Sacred Congregation of Rites has considered that there should be no deviation from the decrees made in other similar cases; and that precedence should be yielded to the Vicar-general before all Dignitaries and Canons, provided the Vicar is not of the number of these same Dignitaries and Canons; because in this latter case he must take his seat in his own stall and walk in his own place, in order to take his share in the daily distribution, provided that the Canons are not clad in their sacred vestments, inasmuch as in this case, by reason of the vestments, the Vicar must give place to the vested Canons. *On the Dress of the Canons, see Rescript in Appendix xxiv. (p.* 118).

4.—ON THE DIVINE OFFICE AND KEEPING CHOIR.

17. Following the decree of the Sacred Congregation of Propaganda, we enjoin that every Canon not legitimately hindered shall repair to the Cathedral church every month on the days named by the Bishop at the beginning of each year, for the purpose of singing Tierce of the day and assisting at High Mass (saving, of course, the right of the chapter to assemble more frequently, with the Bishop's consent, however, and also the right of the Bishop to convoke one whensoever he wishes). The duties of celebrating and ministering are to be so divided as to be filled in turns by all the Canons. But whenever the Bishop celebrates, he has the right to choose his assistants without any regard to the order of precedence.

18. Tierce shall begin about ten o'clock, and all should be present at it. The Senior Canon present at choir shall take the place of Hebdomadary, should the Provost have to leave in order to put on his vestments. Two of the Canons, selected annually for this duty, shall be named Cantors, and must take the lead in the singing.

19. They shall recite the canonical hours in a high and clear tone, worthily, attentively and devoutly, all together, nor shall one side of the choir begin its verse until the other has finished, a fitting slight pause being always made at the asterisk. Everyone reciting the office with others is bound to share in the whole recitation, supplying by listening for the part not recited by him. *(Synod of Foligno).*

20. Following the rubrics and with due regard to the particular time and office, all should be together and alike, in rising, standing, sitting, genuflecting, removing or putting on the biretta, and in bowing; and all together should sing or assist in the same position, with one accord of voice and upraising of the mind.

21. The Canons should remember that at the Mass they are bound not only to be present but to use their voices, and must two and two recite in a low tone those portions prescribed by the rubrics.

22. Since the Cathedral should excel all the other churches in matters concerning the divine worship, all should assist at the celebration of Mass with devotion and respect, and adhere strictly to the rubrics of the missal and ceremonial, and to the authentic answers and decrees of the Sacred Congregation of Rites.

23. Following the decree of the Sacred Congregation of Cardinals Interpreters of the Holy Council of Trent, two Canons, one appointed by the Bishop the other by the chapter, shall be charged to watch over the exact observance of everything pertaining to the proper conduct of Mass and of the divine office. *(June 18th, 1589. See Crespin., On Visitation, p. 387).*

5.—THE CATHEDRAL CHURCH.

24. The right of the temporal and spiritual administration of the Cathedral church shall belong exclusively to the Bishop, unless some other arrangement has been made by the authority of the Holy See. The chapter, however, have the power to carry on the divine office therein.

25. Following the Council of Trent, the chapter shall depute one of its number as administrator, when the See is vacant, to attend to the Cathedral church.

6.—THE DIGNITARY, OFFICES AND OFFICIALS.

26. There shall be one Dignitary only—the Provostship, and the appointment to this is reserved to the Holy See.

27. In the chapter there shall be a Canon Theologian who must give lectures upon the subjects appointed by the Bishop, at the place, day and hour also prescribed by him.

28. There shall be likewise a Canon Penitentiary, who shall be obliged to hear confessions in the church appointed by the Bishop, in Advent, Lent, and at any other time prescribed by the Bishop.

29. When a vacancy occurs in the post of Canon Theologian or Canon Penitentiary, there shall be a concursus among those who have obtained their own Bishop's permission and been accepted by the Bishop of the diocese, in order that the Holy See or the Bishop may select the most fitting from those who have passed the concursus with approval. Others besides Canons can stand if they have been duly admitted to do so.

30. The alternating proposition of three candidates for a vacant

canonry, granted by the Holy See, does not hold for the nomination of a Canon Theologian or Penitentiary, if the nomination happens on the occasion to fall to the chapter. The alternating appointment of candidates must go on just as though the nomination of the theologian, penitentiary or dignitary had not intervened.

31. At the first meeting in each year, the Canons shall choose a secretary of the chapter, treasurer, sacristan and master of ceremonies, to attend to the duties that concern the chapter.

32. The Secretary must write out accurately the acts of the chapter, and read before the whole chapter at the next meeting all the documents to be issued in its name, or that have been addressed to it. For these documents to be deemed authentic, they must have the seal of the chapter and the signature of the Provost and of the secretary, or of those who by the authority of the chapter happen to be taking their places. The custody of the seal belongs to the Provost and to the secretary, and should be under two different kinds of lock and key.

33. At the January meeting, the treasurer shall give an account of all the moneys in any way belonging to the chapter, and he cannot part with any of them without a decree of the chapter.

34. The master of ceremonies and the sacristan must take care that the church is got ready for the capitular functions that have to be carried on therein. They shall likewise fulfil the duty of "pricking" the attendances; that is, they must note those Canons who are absent, and keep a record in the chapter book of those who are present. It shall be open to the Bishop to ask for and examine the book containing the attendances of the Canons.

7.—Meetings of the Chapter.

35. Ordinary meetings should be held on the days indicated above immediately after Mass; extraordinary meetings as often as the Bishop wishes them, or the Provost of the chapter convenes them. When requested by a majority of the Canons to convoke a chapter, the Provost is bound to do so, provided the petition for it be couched in the following terms: "We, the undersigned, pray that chapter may be convened on the ...... day of ......, in the year ......, at ...... o'clock, we ourselves testifying that we require this for weighty reasons, and that the time named will be convenient for all the chapter." But the Bishop's assent to an extraordinary chapter of this nature must of necessity be obtained; and he will also direct when it is to be held in his own house.

36. The Canons must be summoned to both ordinary and extraordinary meetings by a letter of the following kind: "Rev. Sir,—A chapter meeting will be held in the chapter room or at the house of his Right Rev. Lordship the Bishop, on ...., at ...... o'clock. By command of the Bishop, or Provost. N., Secretary."

37. A quarter of an hour after the appointed time, the Provost or senior Canon shall warn the Canons by ringing a bell that the

meeting has begun; and all shall kneel down and say the prayer: *Adsumus, Domine.*

38. The Antiphon of the B. Virgin Mary, for the time of the year, shall be said at the end of the chapter.

39. Then all shall take their seats in the order of canonries, that is to say, of the date of taking possession. Beginning with the youngest member of the chapter, all who wish to speak shall give their opinions as to the business laid before them by the Provost or by any other Canon called upon by him, if possible by the one who has suggested the question to be discussed. When anyone has once stated his opinion, he shall remain silent, and cannot speak again without leave of the chapter. Finally, by the 36th constitution of Alexander VII., each one shall give his vote secretly, under pain of nullity.

40. Whenever it is a question which touches upon the interest of any member of the chapter or of his relatives to the second degree inclusively, such Canon cannot be present at the chapter, so far as that business is concerned, in order that the votes of the others may be the more free; otherwise, the act itself must be deemed void. *(Synod of Foligno).*

41. If three Canons are present at the appointed time, the business of the chapter may be gone on with, even though the Dignitary is absent, provided that the summoning of the chapter was made canonically.

42. On the death of the Bishop, all the Canons shall meet together to assist with due respect at the funeral. And within eight days from the Bishop's death the chapter shall by a free election appoint its Vicar, with power to govern the diocese in accordance with the canon law. And he, when once appointed, cannot be set aside by the chapter or have anyone associated with him in his office.

43. Then, at the place and time arranged by the Archbishop or, when he is hindered or deceased, by the senior Bishop, but not more than a month from the day of the Bishop's death, the chapter shall be convened; and after Mass of the Holy Ghost has been sung by the principal Canon and the oath of secrecy made by all, the Canons shall place in a receptacle expressly prepared their secret votes. At the first voting each shall give the name of the ecclesiastic whom he considers before the Lord to be the most fit to fill the vacant see. These votes shall be given in writing without any previous discussion at the chapter meeting, and shall be taken charge of by three scrutators chosen at the commencement of the meeting. And they are to be so folded that the name of the person proposed only can be seen. The name of the proposer should be written inside and the voting paper well secured by some unknown seal. The writing should also be different from the usual hand of the voter. Then, by adding up the votes it will be seen if anyone has a complete majority of the votes of those present and of those absent but represented by proxies, but not of those who

are absent and not so represented. As soon as the names have been made known, after each scrutiny, the votes should be burnt.

44. Absentees cannot vote by letter, but only by proxies chosen from the chapter and duly authorised. And this authorization cannot be made without a really necessary cause for the absence fully set forth and to be submitted to the chapter. If it is a case of ill health, it should be stated that in the opinion of at least one doctor and one Canon, whose signatures must be attached to the document, the member of the chapter in question cannot be present. The proxy must only be allowed to present three papers containing the names and surnames of those voted for.

45. But if on the first scrutiny no one has a majority, the votes should again be taken until some one has.

46. The appointment of second and third candidate must be managed in the same way. And a document shall be drawn up in the following terms:

"The See of N. being vacant by reason of the death or.........of his Right Reverend Lordship, N.N., the chapter has held a meeting under secrecy, on this the.........day of......, in presence of his Right Reverend Lordship the Archbishop or........., at which after Mass of the Holy Ghost had been offered up, the *Rev.* ...., the *Rev.*.............., and the *Rev.*.............. were chosen scrutators.

It appears that upon the three scrutinies those ecclesiastics whose names are here written in alphabetical order have by a majority of the votes to be submitted to the judgment of the Holy Father.—The *Rev. A. B.*, the *Rev. C. D.*, the *Rev. E. F.* Everything was carried out in accordance with the decrees of the Sacred Congregation of Propaganda.

In testimony of which the chapter has ordered this present document to be issued after being duly read out in the chapter, sealed with the chapter seal, and signed by the Provost, the secretary and the scrutators, on the ......day......of......, in the year..........

The Seal	*A.—Provost* *D.—Secretary*	*G.* *M.* } *Scrutators.*" *N.*

Three authentic copies should be made, one of which should be kept by the chapter, another by the Archbishop, and the third sent by the Archbishop to the Sacred Congregation of Propaganda.

47. The same order in voting and in handing over the votes to the scrutators should be kept in the nomination of three ecclesiastics to vacant canonries, when the nomination falls to the chapter. But the above-mentioned document should be omitted and in place of it another drawn up in this wise.

48. "A canonry being vacant by reason of the death, resignation, etc., the chapter held a meeting on the......day of......in the year......, at which after a Mass of the Holy Ghost, *A. B.* and *D.* were chosen scrutators. After three scrutinies it is found that the three ecclesiastics whose names follow are by a majority of the votes to be proposed to the most Illustrious and Reverend Bishop.

Scrutiny I.—*Titus.*
„ II.—*Francis.*
„ III.—*Joseph.*

In testimony of which, &c.

A.—*Provost* E.
D.—*Secretary* G. } *Scrutators.*"
  L.

8.—ON THE DECEASE OF CANONS.

49. Whenever the chapter cannot assemble at the funeral of a departed Canon, we exhort every Canon to offer up the sacrifice of the Mass as soon as possible for his brother Canon.

9.—ON THE STATUTES IN GENERAL.

50. 1. Copies of resolutions of chapter cannot be witheld from the Bishop by the Canons should he require them; inasmuch as it is his duty to watch and see that nothing is decreed by the chapter contrary to law or prejudicial to the the Church; and he can exact them from the Canons by recourse to penalties and censures. And this notwithstanding any contentions there may be between the Bishop and the chapter; not only because in them the motives, merits and secret reasons connected with any case are not put down, but especially for this reason that, although the Bishop cannot interfere in the chapter lest freedom of voting should be taken from the Canons, yet when they have passed a resolution, such a reason for withholding such resolutions no longer exists.

51. 2. The interpretation of statutes must be based upon the principles of common law.

52. 3. It must be remarked that by common law the consent of all the Canons is sometimes requisite for the validity of capitular acts; but it is always necessary that there should be at least a majority of all those present, and, if it is a case of making new statutes, of at least two thirds of the votes.

VI. MISCELLANEOUS DECREES HAVING REFERENCE TO CANONS.

ON THE APPOINTMENT OF CANONS.

I. West. XI. 7, p. 51. (See p. 79.)
II. Westminster, Appendix, iv., p. 73.

In appointment to canonries not otherwise reserved and affected an Indult is granted to the Bishop who resides for the months of February, April, June, August, October, December. *(Benedict XIV., September 3rd, 1746).*

MOST HOLY FATHER,

The Bishop of Southwark in England hearing that the approaching Provincial Synod will be of considerable duration, owing to the multiplicity of matters to be discussed therein, would venture to implore your Holiness, in order that there may be a certain uniformity in the capitular statutes of which they will certainly treat, for the Apostolic grant of the enjoyment of the six months in favour of resident Bishops, inasmuch as it might happen that some Bishop would be unaware of the obligation of asking for himself the two months given in favour of residents over and above the usual four months, and cause of dissension might arise, when a Bishop was seen conferring in a month, in which another Bishop not enjoying the above privilege could not of course make use of it.

At an audience of his Holiness granted June 27th, 1852, Our most Holy Lord Pope by divine Providence Pius IX., at the instance of me the undersigned secretary to the Sacred Congregation of Propaganda, graciously yielded to the prayer of the petition, on the understanding that the Bishops in question really keep residence. All things whatsoever to the contrary notwithstanding.

Given at Rome, at the office at the said Sacred Congregation, on the day and in the year as above.

AL. BARNABÒ, Secretary.

L. ✠ S.

III. Westminster, App. ii, p. 81.
ON ALTERNATE APPOINTMENTS OF CANONS.

MOST HOLY FATHER,

The Cardinal Archbishop of Westminster and the Suffragan Bishops of England most humbly beg :—

1. That Your Holiness would grant to the petitioners a five years' Indult, in virtue of which they may bestow canonries that fall vacant during two of the months reserved to the Sovereign Pontiff, provided they are not reserved or affected to the Sovereign Pontiff by any other than the monthly title, and on the understanding that the said Bishops really keep residence.

At an audience of His Holiness granted April 22nd, 1860, our most Holy Lord Pius by divine Providence Pope Pius IX., at the instance of me the undersigned secretary of the Sacred Congregation of Propaganda, and having heard the resolutions agreed to by their Eminences the Cardinals of the same Sacred Congregation, on the 15th of April, 1860, graciously consented to all things embodied in the petition.

Given at Rome, at the office of the said Sacred Congregation, the aforesaid day and year.

CAJET. ARCHBISHOP OF THEBES, Secretary.

L. ✠ S.

II. Westminster, App. v. p. 74.

Chapter Meetings.

(See Chapter Statutes, iv., n, 1. p. 83).

The Bishop is empowered to dispense with attendance, for good reasons.

At an audience of His Holiness granted January 21st, 1855, our most Holy Lord by Divine Providence Pope Pius IX., when the case was laid before him by the undersigned Secretary of the Sacred Congregation of Propaganda, graciously yielding to the prayer of some of the Bishops of England, and seeing the difficulties which sometimes stand in the way of all the Canons of the Metropolitan church of Westminster and of the Cathedral churches of England being present at the meetings that have to be held each month, has granted to the Archbishop of Westminster and to the rest of the Bishops of England permission to dispense with one or two of the Canons under them, for good reasons, from taking part in the monthly meeting, yet so, however, that the aforesaid meetings are not omitted.

Given at Rome, at the office of the said Sacred Congregation, January 23rd, 1855.

AL. BARNABÒ, Secretary.

L. ✠ S.

Brief Concerning the Choir Dress of Chapters.

III. Westminster, Appendix, Part ii, 1., p. 95.

POPE PIUS IX.

For all time to come.

It has been found that priestly robes add much majesty to sacred rites. And, therefore, our Predecessors the Roman Pontiffs have been wont to allow special marks of honour to those ecclesiastics who perform the sacred functions in Cathedral churches, that with the aid of these they may carry out the sacred rites with all the more solemnity and grandeur, seeing that thus the faithful are wonderfully turned to piety and religion. Therefore, when our venerable Brother the present Archbishop of Westminster besought us to allow special kinds of robes during sacred functions both to the chapter of the Metropolital Church and to the Suffragan chapters, We were easily led to favour this petition, and all the more so, as We had heard great things of the religious spirit of these chapters and their zealous observance of ecclesiastical discipline. Wherefore, wishful to bestow upon each and all of those whom this letter concerns a special mark of favour, and absolving them by virtue thereof and holding them henceforth absolved, from all sentences, censures and penalties of excommunication and of interdict, or any others of an ecclesiastical nature, in what way soever or for whatsoever causes inflicted, should they happen to have incurred them, by our Apostolic authority, in the terms of this present Letter, We grant and allow that the Canons of the Metropolitan chapter of Westminster may wear during sacred functions purple cassocks of other material than silk, and the Canons of the Suffragan chapters black cassocks, likewise not of silk, with a red hem and buttons; and that both the Metropolitan and Suffragan chapters may wear the garment with sleeves, commonly called the Rochet, with border of lace, not more than twelve English inches in depth, as well as a purple cape, or Mozzetta, not of silk, with its borders of the white fur of the Alpine weasel, commonly called ermine, and likewise a purple lining of wool, with red buttons. But We wish that the decree of May the 14th, 1853, be carefully attended to as regards the use of canonical robes in the several churches, and likewise that the ecclesiastical regulations as to the time and place at which canonical robes can be used and worn, be adhered to. This We grant and allow, notwithstanding the decisions of our Predecessor of happy memory, Benedict XIV., and other Popes, and all general or special constitutions and ordinances made at Universal, Provincial, or Synodal Councils, "On the arrangement of Material," and all things else whatever to the contrary.

Given at Castle Gandolfi, under the seal of the Fisherman, May 14th, 1858, in the twelfth year of our Pontificate.

L. ✠ S.   V. CARD. MACCHI.

ON CANONS WEARING THE CANONICAL DRESS IN THEIR OWN CHURCHES.

1. Westminster, Appendix xxciv., p. 150.

MOST HOLY FATHER,

Since the Canons in England are rarely able to meet together, and yet it seems fit that they should use more frequently the distinguished kind of dress granted to them, the Archbishop of Westminster and the Bishops assembled in Provincial Council most humbly beg that any Canon may wear his canonical dress in the church to which he is attached, even though it is not the Cathedral.

At an audience of his Holiness granted March 13th, 1853, Our most Holy Lord, Pius IX., by divine Providence Chief Pontiff, at the instance of me the undersigned secretary of the Sacred Congregation of Propaganda, in accordance with the decree of the Sacred Congregation, graciously yielded to the petition, all things whatsoever to the contrary notwithstanding.

Given at Rome, at the office of the Sacred Congregation, May 14th, 1853.

L. ✠ S.   AL. BARNABÒ, Secretary.

VII. THE REGULAR CHAPTER AND CANONS OF THE DIOCESE OF NEWPORT AND MENEVIA.

Their Statutes differ as follows from those laid down at the First Synod of Westminster. And wherever the word Provost occurs in the latter it is changed into Prior in the former.

4. Since the Canons of the Diocese of Newport, are equally with the other Religious of the Anglo-Benedictine Congregation bound by the vow of poverty, they are accordingly, by their Constitutions C. IX., n. 1. which have ever in this matter been maintained, ordered under Holy Obedience, and under the penalty due to a most grevious fault, not to keep any money either themselves or in the hands of anyone whatsoever, nor to spend any without the express permission of their Superior, but to give up to the Superior within twenty-four hours whatsoever money anyone of them has, either in his own possession or in the hands of another; and thus, they cannot enjoy prebends. This, however, should not be held to be any obstacle to their being bound to devote all their powers that with the blessing of God the Catholic Religion may be extended in the Missions, and Churches and Schools erected.

9. A chapter can neither exact nor receive anything from a new Canon on occasion of his nomination or installation. And although according to the Statutes of our Congregation, a Monk may incur certain expenses with the permission of his Superior; nevertheless, we do not allow any such, even with the Superior's permission, in the case of a new Canon for celebrating his installation; but we command the Constitution of St. Pius V., of May 31st, 1570, which begins "*Durum nimis*" to be observed.

11. After him (the Prior), the Canons must take their places according to antiquity in the habit, in accordance with the Rule of the Holy Father St. Benedict and the Constitutions of the Congregation, except under the special circumstances laid down in the same rule and Constitutions.

17. Nothing shall be preferred to the Work of God. As often, therefore, as this greatest of works, which comprises the recitation of the whole of the Divine Office in Choir, is to be performed, the Canons should hasten with ready piety to the appointed place, and at the given sign enter the church, two and two, each in his proper place. Always should the cowl be worn in choir; and the whole of the external appearance should bespeak humility and modesty, testifying thereby that there is mindfulness of the presence of God. The duties of celebrant and ministers shall be distributed in such a way that they may be regularly fulfilled by all the Canons in turn. But when the Bishop celebrates, he has the right to select his attendants, without any consideration of the order of precedence.

18. As to the times for Matins and the other portions of the Divine Office, and of private Masses, considering the peculiar circumstances of the present time, the existing custom and practice shall be continued; but when by the blessing of God these circumstances have changed, the Bishop and Superiors of the Monastery should take counsel with the Sacred Congregation and decide upon what they may deem befitting in the Lord for the glory of the church and the convenience of the people.

24. So long as things remain in their present state, the right as to the administration of the Cathedral church shall be under the Bishop and chapter conjointly; as to the power of arranging about the manner and time for singing the Divine Office, of saying private Masses and other matters of this kind, which Regulars are accustomed to settle as they will in their own churches, the arrangements made in above Art. 18 shall be adhered to for the present; but all other rights and duties, such as fall to

the other Bishops in their churches, should be reserved to the Bishop of this Diocese.

26. There shall be one Dignity, to wit, the Priorship. By the special indulgence of the Holy See, the election of the Prior of the Chapter of Newport shall be conducted in the way that the Priors are chosen in the Anglo-Benedictine Congregation. In the election of Prior all the Canons shall enjoy the right of voting.

Whilst the General Chapter is sitting, the Canons shall send secret votes to the Chapter; and the Definitor-Electors appointed to this duty shall elect and declare elected one of those whom the Canons have named, and who has obtained a clear majority of the votes of the Definitor-Electors.

If it is necessary that an election should be made previous to the General Chapter, the Canons themselves shall elect the Prior, and their votes must be examined by Scrutators bound by oath, and these shall declare him to be elected, who in the same way has obtained a clear majority of the votes. If the votes are equal, he shall be declared elected, who has precedence by reason of the offices he has held that are enumerated in the Constitutions or by the earlier reception of the habit.

In both cases, the President General shall be bound to make known the election, without delay, to the Bishop; and, should he have grave reasons against it, he should lay them before the Holy See.

29. When the office of either Canon Theologian or Penitentiary is vacant, the Very Reverend President and the Fathers of the Regimen shall present to the Right Reverend the Bishop three priests suitable and able to teach Theology.

30. From the three thus presented, the Bishop shall select the one whom, upon examination, he shall judge to be most fit.

47. The same course as to giving the votes and putting them into the hands of the scrutators shall be followed by the General Chapter, or when it is not sitting by the Very Reverend President and the Fathers of the Regimen, when choice has to be made of three ecclesiastics to be presented to the Right Reverend the Bishop for vacant canonries, since, by the favour of the Holy See it has been settled that there shall be no reservation of months as regards this chapter.

48. A document must be sent to the Bishop within eight days after the election in this style:—"A canonry being vacant by reason of the death, resignation, &c., the General Chapter of the Anglo-Benedictine Congregation," (or when it is not sitting, "the President General of the Anglo-Benedictine Congregation and the Definitors of the same,") "after a Mass of the Holy Ghost, have chosen as Scrutators *A.*, *B.*, and *D.* On a third scrutiny it appears that by a majority of the votes the three ecclesiastics have to be proposed to the most Illustrious and Right Reverend Bishop whose names follow.

Scrutiny I.—*Titus*.
„ II.—*Francis*.
„ III.—*Joseph*.

In testimony of which &c. *E.*
A. *President General.* *G.* } *Scrutators.*
D. *Secretary.* *L.*

(Seal.)

49. When a Canon dies, everything should be done at the Cathedral Monastery that is prescribed by the Constitutions for the other Religious.

VIII. Rescripts that have reference to the Regular Chapter of Newport and Menevia.

Decree of the Sacred Congregation of Propaganda concerning the Chapter of Newport and Menevia.

April 22nd, 1852.

1. Westminster. Appendix c., p. 130.

Seeing that the singular merit of the Monastic Order of St. Benedict in reference to the extension of the Christian religion throughout England is manifest, and to such an extent that this Institute has deserved to be enriched with special privileges for the good of that church; and that now also the English Benedictine Congregation is willing to devote itself with the greatest earnestness to the good of the church of Newport and Menevia; the most Eminent and Right Reverend Nicholas Wiseman, Cardinal of the Holy Roman Church, Archbishop of Westminster, and their Right Reverend Lordships, the Bishops of England, have made known their desire to the Sacred Congregation, that the Cathedral chapter, which according to the Apostolic Letter of November 19th, 1850, should be only one for the above-mentioned church, should be drawn from the chapter of the Anglo-Benedictine Congregation to be established at Newport, the faculty being added of electing less than ten should that number, which was named in the Apostolic letter, not be obtainable at once.

When the matter had been placed before the Sacred Congregation at a general meeting of April 5th, 1852, the most Eminent Fathers having given due consideration to all points connected therewith concluded that consent should be given, but with the understanding that the Holy Apostolic See's right to select the Bishop even from amongst those who were not monks so often as necessity or utility might demand it, should remain intact; and that the Archbishop and Bishops should take care, after learning the opinions of the Superiors of the aforesaid Congregation, to draw up an instruction to be submitted to the examination of the Sacred Congregation, in order that whatever arrangements were made generally for the government of the churches of England, might be adapted to the church of Newport and Menevia subject to the terms of this indult.

This decision of the Sacred Congregation was laid before our Most Holy Lord, Pope Pius IX., by me the undersigned secretary at an audience on the sixth day of the same month and year, and His Holiness approved of it in every way, and ratified it according to the terms above described, all things whatsoever to the contrary notwithstanding, &c.

Given, &c.

AL. BARNABÒ, Secretary.

The Chapter is Allowed to Consist of a Prior and Six Canons for the Space of Two Years.

May 13th, 1855.

Most Holy Father,

On April 5th, 1852, your Holiness graciously consented that the Monastic Cathedral chapter of Newport might be formed with a less number of Canons than the eleven there ought to be. The Anglo-Benedictine Congregation is now engaged in forming the chapter, and seeing that its members are serving upon Missions, it most humbly begs that your Holiness will allow the chapter to consist of a Prior and four or at the most six Canons, and that this indulgence may be extended to not more than two or three years.

At an audience of His Holiness, granted May 13th, 1855; Our Most Holy Lord by divine Providence, Pope Pius IX., at the instance of me the undersigned secretary of the Sacred Congregation of Propaganda, by desire of the same Sacred Congregation, graciously consented that for the term of two years the chapter might consist of a Prior and six Canons, whatsoever things to the contrary notwithstanding.

Given, &c.   AL. BARNABÒ, Secretary.

L. ✠ S.

The Church of St. Michael at Belmont is provisionally appointed as the Cathedral.

May 13th, 1855.

Most Holy Father,

Since Mr. Francis Wegg-Prosser has offered to the Anglo-Benedictine Congregation a new church of sufficient size, which is being built at his expense in the County of Hereford, and which he has arranged to endow with an annual income, and also offers five acres of land for a Monastery there, Thomas Joseph Brown, Bishop of Newport and Menevia, and Paulinus Heptonstall, in the name of the Anglo-Benedictine Congregation, humbly beg that, as long as a Cathedral church with its Monastery cannot be erected in the city of Newport itself, the aforesaid church at Belmont may be provisionally regarded as the Cathedral of the Diocese of Newport.

At an audience of His Holiness, granted May 13th, 1855, our most Holy Lord by divine Providence Pope Pius IX., at the instance of me the undersigned Secretary of the Sacred Congregation of Propaganda, by desire of the same Sacred Congregation, graciously consented to what was asked for; with the understanding, however, that care should be taken to erect a Cathedral and capitular Monastery as soon as possible in the city of Newport itself; whatsoever things to the contrary notwithstanding.

Given, &c.   AL. BARNABÒ, Secretary.

L. ✠ S.

The Method of Electing the Cathedral Prior.

May 13th, 1855.

Most Holy Father,

Although the election of Prior for the chapter of Newport must be made, according to the rescript of the Holy See, as was arranged for the Provosts of the chapters of England; yet, considering the peculiar circumstances of that monastic chapter, the Anglo-Benedictine Congregation earnestly begs your Holiness to allow the election of the said Prior to be made in the same way as the elections of the other Priors in the same Anglo-Benedictine Congregation, yet so, however, that the name of the person elected be made known without delay to the Bishop of Newport and Menevia for his approbation, and should he have grave reasons for refusing it he shall submit them to the Holy See.

At an audience with His Holiness, granted May 13th, 1855. Our Most Holy Lord by divine Providence Pope Pius IX., at the instance of me the undersigned Secretary of the Sacred Congregation of Propaganda, by desire of the same Sacred Congregation, graciously granted the favour asked for; and allowed that the election of Prior should be conducted in the way to be prescribed in an instruction of the Sacred Congregation, whatsoever things to the contrary notwithstanding.

Given &c.,   AL. BARNABÒ, Secretary.
L. ✠ S.

Relaxation of the Preservation of Months.
May 13th, 1855.

Most Holy Father,

Considering the difference that exists between the other chapters of the Cathedral churches of England and the Monastic chapter of the Diocese of Newport, the Anglo Benedictine Congregation humbly begs that your Holiness will graciously vouchsafe to relax the rule of reservation to the Holy Apostolic See as regards the election of the Canons of the aforesaid Monastic chapter of Newport.

At an audience of His Holiness, granted May 13th, 1855, our most Holy Lord by divine Providence Pope Pius IX., at the instance of me the undersigned Secretary of the Sacred Congregation of Propaganda, by desire of the same Sacred Congregation, graciously yielded to the petition, provided that the election of the Monastic Canons should be always conducted in a special manner in conformity with the instructions to be issued by the Sacred Congregation, whatever things to the contrary notwithstanding.

Given &c.   AL. BARNABÒ, Secretary.
L. ✠ S.

Approbation of the Statutes with Emendations.
August 13th, 1855.

Most Illustrious and Reverend Lord,

Seeing that a Monastic Cathedral chapter of the Anglo-Benedictine Congregation was decreed for the Diocese of Newport, the Sacred Congregation has graciously accepted the statutes which your Lordship and D. Paulinus Heptonstall, by command of the Very Reverend Placid Burchall, President of the Anglo-Benedictine Congregation, had proposed for the said chapter. After due consideration of all matters at a general meeting on May 7th, 1855, the aforesaid Statutes with the emendations and in the form shewn in the printed copy sent herewith, were approved of; and it was decreed that in the establishment of the chapter of Newport the same should be observed.

Wherefore similar copies of the Statutes are sent to your Lordship, to the most Eminent and Reverend the Archbishop of Westminster, and to the President of the Anglo-Benedictine Congregation.

I pray God long to preserve you in health and strength.

Rome, at the Sacred Congregation of Propaganda, August 13th, 1855.

  Your Highness's
    Most faithful Brother,
      J. PH. CARDINAL FRANSONI, Prefect.
      AL. BARNABÒ, Secretary.

To the Right Reverend T. Brown, Bishop of Newport and Menevia.

Additions to the Statutes in Reference to the Resignations of the Prior and of the Canons.

February 20th, 1856.

Most Illustrious and Reverend Lord,

The letters of your Highness of August 20th and September 30th, 1855, were laid before a general meeting of the Sacred Congregation, together with those of the Reverend Father Burchall, President of the Anglo-Benedictine Congregation, and it was thought proper to yield assent to an article being added to one of the Capitular Statutes for Newport, to the following effect :—"The Prior thus elected shall be bound to resign his office to each General Chapter, just as do the Very Reverend President and all the other Superiors of the Anglo-Benedictine Congregation; he shall enjoy, however, a passive voice. And, to prevent the dependence of a Religious Canon upon his lawful Superiors from becoming nugatory and unreal, each shall be bound to resign his Canonry, should the General Chapter deem it expedient and require it; and this he shall also be bound to do before the assembling of Chapter at the instance and by command of the Very Reverend President, unless the Bishop should object, provided that the majority of the chapter is not changed at one and the same time."

I pray God to preserve you long in health.

Rome, at the S. Congregation of Propaganda,
  Your Lordship's
    Most dutiful Brother,
      J. P. CARDINAL FRANSONI, Prefect.
      AL. BARNABÒ, Secretary.

To the Right Reverend Thomas Joseph Brown,
  Bishop of Newport and Menevia.

The Cathedral Monastery is Placed under the Protection of St. Michael the Archangel.

December 18th, 1859.

Most Holy Father,

Monsignor Brown, Bishop of Newport, begs to place the new Monastery adjoining his Cathedral under the title and protection of St. Michael.

At an audience of his Holiness granted Dec. 18th, 1859, our most Holy Lord by Divine Providence Pope Pius IX., at the instance of me the undersigned Secretary of the Sacred Congregation of Propaganda, graciously yielded the favour as asked for.

Given, &c.

   CAJETAN, ARCHBISHOP OF THEBES, Secretary.

L. ✠ S.

The Reverend Father Norbert Sweeney is named to be the First Prior.

December 18th, 1859.

Most Holy Father,

 Thomas Brown, Bishop of Newport, humbly begs your Holiness to name the Reverend Father Norbert Sweeney Prior of the Monastery of St. Michael, the same, who has already been proposed by the President and Chapter of the Anglo-Benedictine Congregation; but inasmuch as the Prior is the first Dignitary of the Regular Chapter of St. Michael, it is deemed necessary that your Holiness should nominate and confirm him.

 At an audience of his Holiness, granted Dec. 18th, 1859, our most Holy Lord by divine Providence Pope Pius IX., at the instance of me the undersigned Secretary of the Congregation of Propaganda, graciously yielded the favour as asked.

Given, &c.

   CAJETAN, ARCHBISHOP OF THEBES, Secretary.

L. ✠ S.

Apostolic Letter in Reference to the Monastery and Chapter of St. Michael.

March 1st, 1860.

POPE PIUS IX.

Venerable Brother, Health and Apostolical Benediction.

 Your most dutiful letter of the 13th of last February has reached Us, in which, Venerable Brother, you desired to return Us best thanks, that We had most willingly yielded, especially to your own wishes, in regard to that Cathedral monastery and chapter. We unite with you in the hope that, by God's grace, no small profit may redound therefrom to our holy religion and to monastic discipline. And it was with no small pleasure that We gathered from that letter how great is your faith, your affection and your submission towards Ourselves and this Chair of St. Peter. We see, again, how acute is your grief of soul at the too manifest trials which beset Us through the most iniquitous designs and machinations of men, who in their bitter animosity and opposition to the Catholic Church and this Holy See seek and strive for the overthrow of the princedom of the same See and the patrimony of Blessed Peter, and for the complete destruction of rights both divine and human. And this excellent feeling on your part, well worthy of a Catholic Prelate and to be honoured with every kind of praise, has brought Us no small degree of comfort, amid Our overwhelming straits and anxieties. Continue, Venerable Brother, with your clergy and faithful people to pray and beseech the good and great God to rescue His holy Church from calamities so great and so manifold, to honour it with splendid conquests on all sides, to aid and console Us in Our trouble, and to vouchsafe in

His omnipotent power to bring back to the ways of truth, of justice, and of salvation all the enemies of the Church and of this Apostolic See. But seeing that you are not unaware of the direful attacks to which our religion is exposed, We therefore doubt not, Venerable Brother, that in reliance upon the help from above you will with your well-known devotion and your especial zeal strenuously defend the cause of the same religion with even increased readiness and care, and with forethought and wisdom provide for the safety of your flock and expose the wiles of its enemies, refute their errors and meet their attacks. Finally, in token of Our great paternal love for you and as a pledge of all heavenly gifts, We most lovingly and with all the affection of Our heart bestow upon you, Venerable Brother, and all the faithful clergy and laity committed to your care, Our Apostolical Benediction.

Given at Rome, at St. Peter's, March 1st. 1860, in the fourteenth year of Our Pontificate.

POPE PIUS IX.

To Our Venerable Brother, Thomas, Bishop of Newport and Menevia, Newport, England.

Permission is Given for Temporally having only Five Resident and Four Non Resident Canons.

April 22nd, 1860.

Most Holy Father,

The President of the Anglo-Benedictine Congregation humbly begs the faculty of leaving the Monastic Chapter of St. Michael in the diocese of Newport for a time with a Prior and five resident Canons instead of six, and four non-resident Canons serving the missions which support them. Monsignor Brown, the Bishop, approves of this application.

At an audience of his Holiness, granted April 22nd, 1860, our most Holy Lord by Divine Providence, Pope Pius IX., at the instance of me the undersigned, Secretary of the Sacred Congregation of Propaganda, graciously yielded to the petition as asked for.

Given &c.

CAJETAN, ARCHBISHOP OF THEBES, Secretary.

L. ✠ S.

SANATORIUM.
June 6th, 1861.

Most Holy Father,

Mgr. Thomas Joseph Brown, Bishop of Newport and St. David's, in the District of Wales in England, in his letter of November 16th, last year, 1860, writes as follows:—

"If Propaganda had the intention of giving instructions relative to the formation of our first chapter differing from those concerning secular chapters it would certainly have taken care to send them to us. I have not however received any.

The Prior was proposed to the Holy See by the President and Regimen, and thereupon elected. Our special statutes lay down the forms to be used in the election of the Canons Theologian and Penitentiary, when such canonries are vacant *(Chap. VI., 29)*, and for filling vacancies in the chapter, *(Chap. VII., 47)*, but they do not give any special instructions for the formation of the first chapter. Perhaps there was no intention of giving any instructions. But the words of the Rescript which made me fearful of taking a false step from the beginning, and hence of compromising the validity of all the future acts of the chapter, were the following:—

'At an audience of his Holiness, March 13th, 1855, Our most Holy Lord Pius, at the instance of me the undersigned, Secretary of the Sacred Congregation, graciously yielded to the petition, in suchwise that the election of the Monastic Canons should be always conducted in the special manner laid down in the instruction to be issued by the Sacred Congregation, all things to the contrary notwithstanding. Given &c.

AL. BARNABÒ, Secretary.'

Not having any instructions for the formation of the first chapter, we believed ourselves able to proceed as in the case of secular chapters, which were first set up by the Bishop alone in accordance with the Brief of November 19th, 1850, page 125 of our general Statutes.

Nevertheless, in order to insure as perfectly as possible the validity of the first chapter, I engaged the President and Regimen of the Anglo-Benedictine Congregation (in case there were any instructions similar to those issued for filling vacancies) to elect Scrutators and to propose to me by secret votes those whom they might deem fit to become members of the first chapter. But there was no Mass of the Holy Ghost, because on that morning I had to consecrate the church, nor was the oath of secrecy taken. Accordingly, the first formation of the chapter was exclusively in my hands. I nominated the several members of it, availing myself, however, of the individuals elected by the President and Regimen. If in all this there has been any notable defect, I beg of you to grant me a SANATORIUM."

At an audience of his Holiness, June 6th, 1861, Our most Holy Lord by Divine Providence Pope Pius IX., at the instance of me the undersigned, Cardinal Prefect of the Sacred Congregation of Propaganda, graciously granted the Sanatorium in so far as it is necessary.

AL. BARNABÒ, Prefect.

THE CHOIR DRESS.
April 20th, 1865.

MOST HOLY FATHER.

Seeing that the Monastic Canons of the church of Newport and Menevia in England, whether in the Cathedral church or in attendance upon the Bishop in the Diocese, can in no way be distinguished from the other brethren of the same Congregation; and that it is clear both from the pattern of the Hood of the Anglo-Benedictine choir monks, as well as from ancient statutes, that the monks of the Anglo-Benedictine Congregation formerly wore the monastic Almuce granted by Pope Clement V., at the council of Vienna to all black monks *(Clement. "Ne in agro," On the Monastic State)*, and, likewise, that the fur of this Almuce must not be used again without express permission from the Apostolic See: Thomas Joseph, Bishop of Newport and Menevia, with the approval and concurrence of all the Bishops of England at their late meeting in Birmingham, humbly prostrate at the feet of your Holiness, begs your Holiness to vouchsafe to grant to the Canons of the chapter of Newport and Menevia, in the pro-Cathedral church, in place of the ordinary Hood, the use of a Monastic Hood (formerly styled the Almuce), of black cloth, closed at the bottom over the breast, and with its border fringed with black sheep's wool.

The aforesaid petitioner also most humbly begs that, as the use of the choir cowl is by reason of its large sleeves extremely inconvenient for Canons assisting the Bishop in his mitre, permission be graciously granted by your Holiness to wear the Almuce over a surplice, without the choir cowl, to those Canons who are attending the Bishop at the throne.

At an audience granted by his Holiness, April 20th, 1865, our most Holy Lord by Divine Providence, Pope Pius IX., at the instance of me the undersigned, Cardinal Prefect of the Sacred Congregation of Propaganda, graciously yielded to the petition as asked for, whatsoever to the contrary notwithstanding.

Given &c.

AL. BARNABÒ, Prefect.

THE CONCESSION AS TO NON-RESIDENT CANONS IS RENEWED.
December 5th, 1865.

MOST HOLY FATHER,

The President of the Anglo-Benedictine Congregation in England, humbly begs from your Holiness a renewal of the dispensation for having non-resident Canons in the regular Chapter of St. Michael's, and this by reason of the necessity there exists for sending Priests upon the missions which, &c.

At an audience with his Holiness, granted Dec. 5th, 1865, our most Holy Lord by Divine Providence, Pope Pius IX., at the instance of me the undersigned Cardinal Prefect of the Sacred Congregation of Propaganda, graciously yielded to the request in the form and precise terms of the preceding concession, provided, however, that the Ordinary of Newport and St. David's assents.

Given &c.

AL. BARNABÒ, Prefect.

L. ✠ S.

We willingly accept the dispensation.
February 16th, 1866.
THOMAS JOSEPH, O.S.B., Bishop of Newport and Menevia.

CHAPTER THE SIXTH.

PRIESTS.

I.—ON ORTHODOX FAITH.

I. Westminster. Decree vii., p. 45.

1. Since, as the Apostle teaches, without faith it is impossible to please God *(Heb. xi., 6)*, and since faith, as the Holy Council of Trent declares, "is the beginning of man's salvation, the foundation and root of all justification" *(Sess. vi., c. 8)*, therefore, before all things, we must hold and preserve inviolate the sound and orthodox faith, which the Holy Catholic Church holds, and has ever held. Whatever, therefore, has been defined in Œcumenical Councils, but especially all and everything that has been sanctioned, defined, or promulgated by the Sacred Council of Trent, we embrace with heartfelt reverence and love, we profess, and, with the grace of God, we intend to hold to our last breath. All depraved teachings, and all heresies and errors condemned in the said Councils, we likewise reject and condemn.

2. But since the Lord exhorts us by the mouth of the prophet, saying, "Look unto the rock, whence you are hewn . . . . Look unto Abraham your father" *(Isaiah li., 1)*, it is right, that we, who have received our faith, our priesthood, and the true religion immediately from the Apostolic See, should beyond others be bound to it by the bonds of love and veneration. Wherefore, the foundation of true and orthodox faith we rest on the same basis on which our Lord and Saviour Jesus Christ was pleased to place it, namely, on the immovable chair of Peter, the Holy Roman Church, the mistress and mother of the whole world. Whatever has been defined by her, we, on that account hold to be certain and sure: her traditions, rites, pious uses, and all apostolic constitutions regarding discipline, with our whole heart we embrace and venerate. Finally, with all sincerity we profess obedience and reverence to the Supreme Pontiff, as the Vicar of Christ, and cling to him in the closest bonds of Catholic communion.

3. As then in these times and in this country, error has put on a new mask, and there are numbers of persons, who profess to hold the doctrines of the Church, and who copy her rites and practices, and who, though cut off from the society of the spouse of Christ, nevertheless pass themselves off as Catholics, and delude simple souls with the fallacious hope that they can obtain salvation out of

the Church: against this kind of error we must put forward, as the firmest shield of faith, the doctrine of the unity of the Church, and of the necessity of being in indissoluble communion with the centre of unity. Consequently, whoever may have to deal with such kind of persons, either in writing or in conversation, let them be careful not to strengthen them in their error. On the contrary, let us continually cry out with St. Jerome: "Whoever eats of the lamb out of this house is unclean; whoever is not in Noe's ark, will perish in the raging flood."—*(Ad Damas)*.

II.—On the Means of Defending the Faith.
Ib. viii., p. 47.

Those who build up the city of God must gird themselves for the safeguard of their work, in the same manner as we read of the Jewish people, on their return from captivity. "Each one with one hand did the work, and with the other he held a sword; for every one of the builders was girded with a sword about his loins." *(II. Esdras iv., 17).* Thus in the conflict in which we are engaged, not indeed against flesh and blood, but against the spirits of wickedness *(Eph. vi., 12)*, there is, as it were, a twofold work imposed upon us, namely, by piety and virtue **calmly to fashion our people**, as living and chosen stones for the building up of the body of Christ, and, at the same time, bravely to ward off every danger from them. This duty is the more urgent upon us in these times, because the malignant adversary is now prowling around the fold of Jesus Christ, seeking whom he may devour, sometimes snatching the sheep by main force, at other times seeking to ensnare them by artful cunning.

1. Wherefore, our first care should be to attend to the education of children. And first of all we exhort the priests of the Lord to establish schools, large enough for the boys and girls in their congregations; and if there be schools already built, but too small, to enlarge them, or add to their number. We likewise beseech and implore the faithful, through the bowels of the mercy of Jesus Christ, to assist the clergy in their work; since in no other way can they better provide for their own welfare before God, than in promoting the training up of little ones in faith and piety. In these schools the Christian doctrine, that is, the Catechism duly approved of, shall be taught to all Catholic children; nor should the pastor so far make over this duty to others, however good or religious they may be, as not to visit the schools frequently and instil into the tender minds of youth the principles of true faith and piety.

2. Priests should in every lawful way oppose the efforts of enemies, who strive to seduce Catholics to send their children to non-Catholic schools. They should often speak in their sermons of the necessity of faith, of the duties of parents to their children, and of the account they will have to give to God at His strict judgment,

if the children are lost through their fault. But especially in the sacred tribunal, they should deter parents from impiously trading in the souls confided to them, warning them of the severe threats which God has uttered by His prophet against Israel, "because he sold the just man for silver and the poor man for a pair of shoes"—*(Amos ii., 6)*. How much more, they will rightly argue, will God be angry with parents, who for money or promises of clothes to themselves or to their children, have no scruple in sending their offspring to schools that are not Catholic, with the danger of at least weakening their faith! They should also arouse the zeal of Catholics who, by giving more abundant alms, are often able to prevent poor parents being guilty of such wickedness.

3. Besides having Catechism taught every day in school, there shall also, on every Sunday, be a public catechetical instruction in the church, in which the mysteries of the faith, and the commandments of God and the Church, and the doctrine of the sacraments, shall be explained in a plain and clear manner. Moreover, whilst the priest accommodates his language to the understanding of little ones, he should speak in a way not too tedious to the well instructed; on the contrary, by his weighty words, and by aptly illustrating his discourse with numerous appropriate texts of Holy Scripture and by the examples of the Saints, he should attract even adults to listen and to learn.

4. Since the vilest tracts attacking the Catholic religion or assailing it with calumnies, lies and abuse, are in a marvellous way scattered abroad everywhere and even brought into the houses of Catholics or put into their hands, the faithful should be admonished to refrain from reading them; nay more, to cast them away altogether, remembering the penalties declared by the Church against those who read such kind of books. But the more effectually to check this pestilence, the priest should furnish himself with a supply of pious and edifying books, or provide a library suited to the capacity of his people, whence even the poor and ignorant may imbibe useful knowledge by having books lent out to them for a time to read. He should also do his best to spread amongst his flock the pious works of Catholics, which are daily issuing from the press.

5. What we have decreed concerning poor schools, we wish also to apply to schools for the education of the higher classes. Therefore should priests admonish parents not to send their children to schools, in which mere secular knowledge is taught, to the loss or danger of religion.

III.—On the Sacraments in General.
Ib., xv., p. 57.

Since our Lord Jesus Christ has been pleased to treasure up in the sacraments an abundance of grace overflowing unto eternal life, the priests of the Church should have nothing more at heart, than that the faithful may draw waters in joy from the fountains of Our Saviour. But as there is nothing more holy, nothing more sacred than these institutions, we must anxiously and earnestly take care that there be no negligence or irreverence in the administration of them. Purity is requisite in administering what is pure, holiness in administering what is holy, and as far as human frailty will permit, perfection in the disposition of mind and of the whole soul in him who administers what is divine. Nothing regarding the administration of the sacraments, neither ceremonies, nor words, nor circumstances of place and time, are to be made light of: on the contrary, even the most minute directions of the Church must be considered of great importance and be observed with the greatest care. And on this account, if owing to local circumstances it is difficult, or almost impossible, to administer the sacraments with becoming splendour and outward honour, we should the more zealously endeavour to supply the deficiency by inward devotion, and inflame the minds of the recipients and assistants with more fervent piety. We, therefore, decree as follows:—

1. Since the church is the proper place for the administration of the sacraments, let the priest take care that all who wish to receive them come to the church; and to avoid confusion, he should make known to all the time and place appointed for the administration of each. However, he should not refuse to administer the sacraments, whenever they are asked for: especially in cases of necessity, or when there is danger that the applicants, if rejected, will not come again.

2. In order to make the sacraments revered, it is of the highest importance that the priest administer them in the proper vestments, viz., surplice and stole; unless necessity compel him to dispense with these, or circumstances of time and place forbid the use of them.

3. Let him also seize the occasion of the administration of a sacrament to explain in plain and simple words to those present the doctrine of the Church on the sacraments generally or particularly.

4. He should be careful to keep everything used in the administration of the sacraments clean and neat, and thus increase the reverence of the faithful.

5. Lastly, he should follow the rubrics exactly and observe them carefully.

IV.—On Baptism.

Ib., xvi., p. 59.

As among Protestants there is no dogma which has been more corrupted in these times, than that regarding the baptismal regeneration of infants, on this account it is the more necessary that the sound and clear doctrine of the Church on this matter be lucidly and frequently explained. Moreover, so great a sacrament ought to be administered with the greatest decorum. Wherefore, we command that the following directions be observed:—

1. In every church to which is annexed the cure of souls, there shall be a baptismal font, unless the Bishop dispense with it for a time. This font should be placed in a conspicuous and convenient situation, and the baptismal water always kept in it. It should be becomingly ornamented, kept locked, and, if the situation will permit, be surrounded with rails. We, therefore, recommend that the rules for the safe keeping of the font, published by St. Charles Borromeo, be observed.[1] We also admonish all that, except in case of necessity, baptism is not to be administered with unblessed water, nor with water blessed for other sacred purposes, in accordance with the constitution of Benedict XIV. *Inter omnigenas*, §10. It should be noticed also, that where there are parish priests or missionary rectors appointed, the administration of solemn baptism belongs to them; and it is only by their permission that other priests can baptize solemnly.

2. The oil of catechumens and the holy chrism, and, if it be thought proper, the salt also and all the other requisites for the administration of baptism, must be kept by themselves in the baptistry, or in the sacristy with all reverence and with the greatest cleanliness. When new churches are built, a place should be prepared for their reception in the baptistry.

3. The priest also should keep in the sacristy, carefully and safely, the baptismal register, in which are to be entered the names of the persons baptized, and the names of the godfather and godmother, according to the prescribed form; so that uniformity in the keeping of baptismal registers may prevail throughout the whole province.

4. Unless in the exceptional cases mentioned in the ritual, baptism ought always to be administered in the church, and never out of the church without leave of the Bishop, except in case of danger of death or of great inconvenience. Baptisms conferred at stations, at a distance from the principal church or chapel, on occasion of the priest visiting them, or when he is called thither, are excepted.

5. Persons who are not Catholics must not be allowed to stand godfathers or godmothers, nor those excluded by ecclesiastical law: namely, persons under the age of puberty, persons excommunicated by the greater excommunication, persons who have not been confirmed, persons who do not fulfil the precept of paschal communion, and ecclesiastics. On account of danger to the faith of infants, which may easily occur on the death of their parents, the priest should take care that, if possible, there are two sponsors.

6. The priest may baptize infants born of parents who are not Catholics, provided that it is agreed that they be brought up in the true religion, and that they have a Catholic godfather or godmother.

---

[1] See page 136.

7. Since the reasons which induced the vicars-apostolic, at the beginning of this century, to decree that all persons born after the year 1773 and baptized by Protestants, should on their conversion to the faith, be baptized conditionally, are now even stronger, we renew this rule absolutely, and command, that all converts from Protestantism be baptized conditionally, unless it be most surely ascertained, from evidence beyond all doubt, that all that regards the matter and form of the sacrament was duly performed.[1]

8. Conditional baptism must not be administered publicly, but altogether privately, with holy water and without the ceremonies.[2] Sacramental confession is likewise always in such cases to be required. See p. 142.

9. Since Catholic mothers are frequently attended by surgeons or midwives who are not Catholics, and who care nothing about the baptism of infants in danger of death, the faithful of both sexes must be carefully instructed as to the manner of baptizing in cases of necessity as they are called; so that no child may depart this life without the saving laver of regeneration. Should the child recover, it must be brought to the church, that the ceremonies may be supplied. The priest, however, should make diligent inquiry into the way in which the baptism was administered, and in coming to a decision, he should rather incline to the safer side; and should he think proper, he need not hesitate to confer conditional baptism.

10. Parents should be frequently admonished not to put off the baptism of their children, but to be careful that as soon as they are born into the world, they may be born again to eternal life.

Appendix xi., p. 139.

On the Custody of the Baptismal Font.

(Taken from the Acts of the Fourth Council of Milan.)

The baptismal font should be of marble or of good stone; and if it is of such a kind that the water gradually escapes, either through leaks or in any other way, one of another kind of stone—hard, solid and sound—should be prepared as soon as possible.

---

1 See Rescript p. 58, and also p. 142. Full particulars as to the mode in which converts are to be received may be gathered from these and from Synodi Diœc. Suthwarcensis," p. 76.—Ed.

2 It would seem that this applies to adults only, as the following replies were sent to the Bishop of Nottingham. Ed.

Wednesday, April 2nd, 1879.

At a general Congregation of the Holy Roman and Universal Inquisition assembled under their Most Eminent and Reverend Lordships the Cardinals of the Holy Roman Church, acting as General Inquisitors in matters of Faith, the following doubts, sent by the Reverend Father the Lord Bishop of Nottingham, were raised.

1. Is it lawful to baptize conditionally in public and with the sacred ceremonies, children not arrived at the age of reason, who having been baptized doubtfully as Protestants and without the ceremonies, have to be baptized conditionally?

2. Supposing that this may be done, is it obligatory under precept to use the sacred ceremonies in the case of such children in conditional baptism?

3. And if the replies are affirmative, what should be done with the number of this class who were years ago in their childhood baptized conditionally without the ceremonies.

And they decide that the reply should be: *To the first*, Conditional baptism to such children is to be given privately and with the ceremonies prescribed in the Roman Ritual. *To the second* provided for in *the first*. *To the Third*, it must be passed over; but if mooted, submitted to the private decision of the Right Rev. Ordinary. F. Pelami, Notary of the Holy Roman and Universal Inquisition.

Meanwhile, that the baptismal water may be safely retained until the other font is ready, a receptacle not of glass or any other such material, but of bronze lined inside with tin, and of exactly the same size as the bowl of the font, should be inserted therein, so that fitting exactly into it, it may form as it were one with it.

It should have a cover or top fitted for keeping the holy oils with safety and decorum, unless in accordance with instructions given by us it has to be differently constructed. It should also have a covering at least of some kind of stuff.

It should likewise have a lid divided into two parts, one only of which should open. This should shut up closely, and so keep the water completely free from dust or any other impurities.

This lid should be in all fonts at which baptism is administered by infusion; but in those where it is by immersion, only in case the stonework is of sufficient size to admit of it without any obstacle to the immersion.

Every baptistry should be railed off completely, by wooden rails at least, if in the judgment of the bishop it cannot be by iron or stone ones.

Moreover, should it not be altogether or partially under a vaulted roof or in a semicircular recess within the wall, there must in this case be a covering either of marble or tile-work, or at any rate of some texture appropriately embroidered.

It will also be proper to have a representation of St. John baptizing Christ our Lord either in the chapel or on the adjoining wall.

The baptismal font should be placed near the entrance of the church and on the left hand side, unless the bishop considers that it should stand on the other side. But those baptistries should not be interfered with, which already exist in churches or inside chapels adjoining cathedral or parochial churches, and expressly constructed for that purpose. But these churches or chapels, where there are such, should be repaired and refitted. Where, however, there are none, especially in the principal churches, the bishop should take care that such churches or chapels be erected and baptistries constructed within them.

As regards baptismal fonts where baptism is administered by infusion, care must evidently be taken lest the water that has been poured over the head of the child should flow back into the font instead of into the sacrarium; and hence the sacrarium should be built of marble or good stone close to the font, according to the tenor of our instructions.

Two towels should be kept in the cupboard of the font, both white and perfectly clean, to be used for wiping the head of the child. A good number, therefore, of these towels should be kept in a fixed place in the sacristy.

But if towels or kerchiefs are sometimes brought for this purpose, only new ones should be used; and when the new ones have been used, they should be given up, not to profane purposes, but to such use of the church, as they may serve; otherwise they should be burned.

V.—On Confirmation.
Ib. xvii., p. 61.

Since, in this country, Catholics, and especially the poor and ignorant, are exposed to daily attempts made to undermine their faith; in order to resist these temptations, there is need of the greatest diligence to have them fortified by the sacrament of Confirmation, that they may persevere firm and steadfast in faith and good works.

1. In order that they may receive more abundantly the grace of the Holy Ghost communicated in this sacrament, both children and adults must be well instructed before they are confirmed, as to its nature and effects; and no one should be admitted, who has not a sufficient knowledge of Christian Doctrine. We exhort the clergy, that according to a commendable custom, they take occasion at the time of preparing for confirmation to perfect those who are to be confirmed in the knowledge of the catechism.

2. As it often happens that children are taken away from school and sent to work when very young, and since it is difficult to recall them to instructions; it is desirable to have them confirmed early, provided they are old enough to make the requisite preparation.

3. Converts also must be urged not to neglect this grace, and not to defer it unnecessarily for a length of time.

4. In every church should be kept a register of those who are confirmed, and it should also record the name of the godfather and godmother. A list of the persons confirmed must also be given to the Bishop.

5. To each person to be confirmed a godfather or godmother, according to sex, should be assigned. In the choice of sponsors for confirmation, the same conditions hold good as those above named in Decree XVI., No. 15, on Baptism. *(See p. 134).*

VI.—On the Most Holy Sacrament of the Eucharist.
Ib. xviii., p. 62.

Among so many pledges of love bequeathed to us by the Divine Saviour of mankind, as there is none more sacred none more magnificent, than that by which He has given us His own most sacred body for our food, and His own most precious blood for our drink, so there is none against which the bitter enemy of mankind has raged with more unbridled fury. Hence it is scarcely possible to express in words, how wickedly and how impiously both in acts and in writings, this most Divine Sacrament of the Eucharist has been attacked in this country. Not to mention sacrilegious outrages, there is no limit to the invective, railing and blasphemy, by which it has been, and to this day continues to be, assailed.

But the more insane is the rage of unbelievers, the more grievous the injury done to the divine bounty, the more ardent on that account ought to be the faith and gratitude of the faithful, and the more fervent their worship and devotion. Wherefore this Synod has nothing more at heart than to cherish and promote everywhere, and by every means, piety and devotion to our Lord in the Holy Eucharist; that the hearts of priests being filled with the richness of the Spirit may advance from virtue to virtue, and the children of the Church, like young olive branches surrounding daily the table of the Lord, may be refreshed with the sweetness of this heavenly bread, and in the strength of this food walk forward even to the mountain of God.

1. Whatever therefore, is dedicated to the service of this divine sacrament and of the unbloody sacrifice, altars, sacred vessels, sacred furniture—all, if not splendid and costly, should be at least neat, clean and becoming. The priest, when saying Mass, should allow nothing to be seen about him that is torn, soiled or less precious than it ought to be. The cup at least of the chalice and of the pyx should, if possible, be of silver, gilt in the inside; the paten also the same. The sacred robes must be made of silk, the other vestments and altar cloths of linen only. That uniformity may prevail in these things, we must strive to shape our sacred vestments according to the pattern of the Roman Church.

2. It were desirable that Mass should be said by all priests every day; however, they should at least frequently receive Christ at the altar, that He may renew their youth in grace; and they should give notice to the faithful of the days and hours when Mass will be said in the church during the week.

3. On Sundays and Festivals Mass should be celebrated with as much solemnity as possible. But the rubrics should be exactly observed, especially when Mass is sung without the assistance of sacred ministers. For it is not lawful in such masses to make changes at pleasure; but all should be done according to order and in a uniform manner.

4. Benediction of the most Holy Sacrament cannot be given without leave of the Bishop. Much less processions, those excepted which are prescribed by the rubrics. Nor can solemn exposition of the most Holy Sacrament be allowed without permission from the Bishop.[1] In exposition and benediction, the rite should be followed, which has been already printed with the approbation of the Bishops; since this is conformable to the Roman rite, and has been prescribed for Ireland by the Synod of Thurles, which has been approved by the Holy See.

5. A lamp should burn day and night before the Holy Eucharist when reposing in the tabernacle. The pyx should be covered with a veil of white or gold-coloured silk.

---

[1]. That is, when the Monstrance is used. For the less solemn Benediction with the Pyx alone does not need the Bishop's permission, as is clear from Benedict XIV's letter to the Bishop of Worms April 17th, 1746, as well as from another to the Cardinal Vicar of the city, July 27th, 1755.

6. If, on account of danger of sacrilege, the Holy Sacrament cannot be kept safely on the altar or even in the church, there should be fitted up a suitable retired place, approved of by the Bishop, where it may be preserved with a lamp always burning, according to the last decree.

7. The most Holy Sacrament ought not to be kept in oratories,[1] unless they belong to the mission, and are therefore considered to be public. But even in this case, the key of the tabernacle ought not to be entrusted to the sacristan or to any other person; but the priest should keep it in his own possession, and burthen his conscience with the duty of frequently renewing the sacred hosts.

8. The faithful must be exhorted and urged to frequent communion, and must be seasonably reminded of the necessity of communion to gain the holy indulgences, not only on certain appointed times during the year, but as frequently as possible; provided they lead lives worthy of such a grace, and dispose themselves by a devout preparation.

9. In order to promote devotion to the Blessed Sacrament more and more, it is very desirable that the doors of the church be kept open during the whole day, or in country places for some hours, and that all the faithful be taught to make visits to their most loving Saviour in the most Holy Eucharist, to make fervent supplications to Him, and at the same time to refresh their souls by a spiritual communion.

10. To increase the piety of the faithful, it seems also highly expedient to establish all over England the Forty Hours' prayer, so that at every instant of time reparation may be made to Our Lord for the grievous offences committed against Him in this Sacrament, and prayers offered for the peace of the Church and the salvation of souls.

11. It is expedient also, in order to promote devotion to the Divine Sacrament, that, where it is practicable, the Sodality of the most Holy Sacrament be established; the members of which shall provide for the service of the altar, for processions and other functions. This Sodality and the Confraternity of Christian Doctrine should, according to the first Provincial Council of Milan, be established in every congregation prior to all others.

12. Although, on account of the state of things around us, the most Holy Viaticum cannot, without danger of sacrilege and scandal, be taken to the sick publicly and solemnly, and consequently the Holy See has allowed us to carry It without a light and secretly; nevertheless no priest should forget that he has His hidden God clinging to his breast, and that he is bearing Him along with him for the solace of his people. Reverently therefore, nay devoutly and as if fixed in contemplation, he should convey to the house of the sick the most Holy Sacrament, having it suspended from his neck in a bag becomingly or richly adorned. And as the dwellings

---

[1] See p. 65.

of the poor are often most wretched, so much so, that the Sacred Viaticum can scarcely be administered in them with decency, we declare it to be a commendable practice, and recommend it for general adoption, that the priest carry with him or send on beforehand a small case furnished with the requisites for the decent administration of the Blessed Sacrament. As soon as possible after the communion of the sick, the pyx must be brought back to the church, and replaced in the tabernacle till it is purified.

13. The consecrated hosts must be frequently renewed,[1] both those for the communion of the faithful and for Benediction of the Blessed Sacrament. The pyx should also be purified to prevent the accumulation of particles and the danger of irreverence in giving communion.

14. Also, "Let all corporals, palls, and other altar linen be kept whole and very clean, and let them be often washed by the persons appointed by the canons" (viz. corporals and palls by the priest himself, where there is no sub-deacon) "through reverence and on account of the presence of Our Saviour and of the whole court of heaven, who, there is no doubt, are present both at the time when this Sacrament is consecrated and also where it is reserved after consecration."[2]

15. The tabernacle must be kept empty of every thing else; "wherefore let neither the holy oil vessels, nor relic case, nor purificatory be kept there. The Holy Eucharist alone with the vessel containing it must abide there; nothing else."—*IV. Council of Milan, p. ii.*).

16. That there may be no doubt regarding the matter of the Sacrament, it is not to be allowed to every one to prepare the sacred hosts, but this duty should be entrusted to confidential persons only, and, if it be thought proper, to nuns. The wine also for the sacrifice should not be procured from innkeepers, nor from any wine merchant indiscriminately, as it is well known that such persons frequently do not sell pure wine; but every care must be taken, and the Bishops must see that their priests are everywhere supplied with the genuine fruit of the vine.[3]

17. Since, on account of the scarcity of priests, it is impossible to hear the confessions of all the faithful within the limits of the Paschal term, it seems advisable to petition the Sovereign Pontiff to extend the time for all England from Ash Wednesday to Low Sunday inclusively.[4]

18. Let no priest, at the risk of incurring the penalties named in Canon Law, presume to celebrate mass twice on the same day (except on the Festival of the Nativity), unless he obtains a written permission from the Bishop or his Vicar, empowered to grant it by apostolic delegation.

---

1. The Provincial Council of Oxford, held in the year 1222, directs that, "*The consecrated hosts should not be kept beyond seven days, but that they be renewed every week.*"
2. *Ibid.*   3. See p. 6.
4. A petition to this effect was presented by the Archbishop and Bishops on the 12th of March 1853, and granted on the 14th of May, 1853.

19. Likewise let the rubrics of the Roman Missal and of the little Ritual of Benedict XIII.,[1] of blessed memory, be strictly observed, as far as may be, during the three last days of Holy Week, so that only one Mass be celebrated in each church on Maundy Thursday and Holy Saturday. On the latter day, if Mass is celebrated, the whole of the office must be gone through (with the sole exception of the blessing of the font, in a church where there is no font), nor can the priest omit at pleasure any portion of it.

20. Finally, priests should remember that the infinite value of this sacrament and sacrifice consists in the presence of Our Lord Jesus Christ, not in the display of external worship; consequently, it is better to give the faithful a simple low Mass, than to attempt, beyond one's capabilities, a more solemn rite with ceremonies often sadly mutilated, and with wretched music more likely to drive away than to excite devotion. The singing, especially at Mass and Benediction, should be grave and devotional, so that the faithful listening to it may at one time with St. Augustine be moved to tears, at another time join the angels with great joy in a canticle of praise to God and the Lamb. The children also should be taught music at school, in order to exclude from church choirs women singers, especially those who sing for hire. Thus, by degrees, will be brought about, what we so much desire to be accomplished, that the whole congregation will join with one voice and heart in the psalmody.

The singing should not be protracted, so as to stop the Mass in places where the rubrics do not allow it.

VII.—ON THE SACRAMENT OF PENANCE.

Ib., xix., p. 68.

As this sacrament is rightly designated the plank after shipwreck, and as we have all sinned and need the glory of God (Rom. iii., 23), the efficacy of this saving medicine must be inculcated on all from their tender years, and all must be sedulously trained to the use of it. The faithful must also be exhorted to have recourse to this laver of the soul, not merely once a year, and at long intervals, but frequently; even as often as they have contracted the stain of sin, so often let them seek to be cleansed; as often as they feel sickness, let them hasten to apply the remedy. On the administration of this sacrament we therefore decree as follows:—

1. In every church, where confessionals have not already been erected, we direct that they be erected in proportion to the number of priests. If the place will not admit of them, the matter must be referred to the judgment of the Bishop. The confessions of women must be heard in no place but in the confessional, unless sickness or deafness require otherwise. But even in this case, women must be heard in an open place, where they can be easily seen by others.

---

1. See p. 184.

2. The priest should sit in the confessional, vested in surplice and purple stole.

3. Children capable of commiting sin must not only be admitted, but must be brought to confession, and absolution given them if they are in proper dispositions. Wherefore, the practice of deferring absolution till they make their first communion is not to be approved of. On the contrary, even backward and dull children must be prepared for this sacrament with the greatest care.

4. The medicinal nature of this sacrament makes it urgent that it should be received as soon as possible after the infliction of the mortal wound of sin. On this account, those who contritely confess their sins must not be remanded for absolution to another time. The general confessions of converts especially must not be put off from day to day; but if they are sufficiently instructed, and if moved with sincere sorrow of heart they ask forgiveness, the minister of a merciful God should mercifully impart it to them. As to the less intelligent kind of converts, the priest should take care that they are well instructed before he admits them to the sacraments.

5. He must question even Catholics on the mysteries of faith, when he finds or suspects that they are ignorant; and he must not let them proceed further, till they are sufficiently instructed. Moreover, the priest should strive by appropriate questioning to assist the ignorant and particularly young persons to make a clear and complete confession.

6. The faithful are at liberty, even at Easter, to make their confessions to any priest duly approved of, nor must they ever be sent away by the priest of their choice on the pretext that they do not belong to his congregation. Nor should the priest, to whose charge they do belong, put any obstacle in their way, or presume to hinder any one from having recourse to another priest, but rather let him rejoice that his sheep is saved, though snatched from destruction by another hand.

7. Priests should beware of receiving any retribution from penitents on account of confession.

8. There should be fixed days and hours for confession in each church, and the times appointed should be faithfully observed.

The following Letter and Reply find their proper place under the head of the Sacrament of Penance.

ON THE COMPLETE CONFESSION TO BE REQUIRED FROM CONVERTS.

IV. Westminster. Appendix xviii., p. 170.

In the decrees of the first Provincial Synod of Westminster, c. xvi., n. 8, where the abjuration of adult Protestants and the conditional baptism to be given them are treated of, it is added, "Sacramental Confession is likewise always in such cases to be required." In the notes which Father Ballerini has subjoined to the Roman Edition of Father Gury's Moral Theology, it is stated that such confession is more in conformity with the instruction upon the way of reconciling heretics issued by the Supreme Congregation of the Holy Office, and from this Instruction it is concluded that a complete confession of sins is befitting. In the text of Father Gury it is held that it is advisable in practice.

But inasmuch as this author both in his Theology and Cases of Conscience has quoted the opinion of other authors to the effect that, by reason of the doubtful previous baptism in their infancy of converts (so that if it were invalid the real baptism would be that given at the time of their abjuration), the obligation of integral confession of sins previous to this conditional baptism is doubtful; some confessors in England have considered that, according to these authors, the doubtful obligation of integral confession is no obligation; and that owing to the repugnance on the part of converts to making it, and the danger of imperfection in it, or even of sacrilege, it is quite enough for converts to mention only some sins to the confessor in order to get the benefit of sacramental absolution at his hands, if there be necessity for it.

On the other hand, there is the constant practice of the majority of the confessors of the kingdom, as well previously as subsequently to the approbation of this course by the Provincial Council, who not only advise but exact it; there is the difficulty on the part of converts of captivating their understandings to the obedience of faith, except through the humility and submission of mind which Christ our Lord has deigned to connect with the sacrament of Penance; there is also the impossibility of knowing, except by the integral manifestation of sins, whether the convert is duly disposed for baptism itself, and is willing, for instance, to make restitution of character or of goods (if he happen to be bound to do so), to shun the proximate occasions of sin, to withdraw from a marriage invalidly contracted, and which perhaps cannot be remedied by dispensation from the Holy See (as in cases, daily of more frequent occurrence, of marriage contracted with a party separated by civil divorce); there is, moreover, the necessity of providing for one's salvation by justification in the sacrament of Penance, from the integrity of which no one once baptized in infancy can be exempt; especially, when one considers the care taken by the rising generation of the Anglican clergy as regards faithfully adhering to the rite of baptism, and therefore the greater number of those concerning whose baptism in infancy there can be no doubt.

But since it is certain that after some years the obligation of a complete confession will entirely lose its force, if theologians may in practice follow as safe the opinion of the said authors, the Archbishop of Westminster and the Bishops of England earnestly beg that your Holiness, in Your goodwill towards the missions of England, will deign to declare the mind of the Church upon this important question:

Must Sacramental Confession be required from converts in England, according to the Decree of the Provincial Synod, which was approved of by the Holy See? And should it be complete?

Thursday, December 17th, 1868.

At a general congregation of the Holy Roman and Urban Inquisition held in the Convent of *Santa Maria sopra Minerva*, in the presence of their most Eminent and Right Reverend Lordships the Cardinals Inquisitor-General, against heretical depravity, the subjoined doubt was proposed and after taking the opinions of the consultors, the same most Eminent and right Reverend Fathers considered that the following reply should be given to each particular of the doubt: *Affirmatively; and that the Decree of Thursday, June 17th, 1715, should be issued.*

On the same day of the month and week, our most holy Lord Pius IX. by divine Providence Pope, at his accustomed audience, granted to the Reverend Father the Assessor of the Holy Office, deigned to approve and confirm the Resolution of their Eminences; and commanded the same together with the Decree mentioned to be sent to the Reverend Father, the Lord Archbishop of Westminster.

L. ✠ S.
ANGELO ARGENTI, Notary of the Holy Roman and Universal Inquisition.

Thursday, June 17th, 1715.

DOUBT.

Is full credence to be given to Charles Ferdinand Wipperman, a preacher of Rostoch in the Duchy of Mechlenburgh, and Chief Lector upon Lutheran quietest theology, and leading doctor of the sect of Lutheran Quietists, reconciled with the Holy Catholic Faith before the Holy Office at Parma, and is he to be believed as to what he states in reference to certain mistakes discovered in his baptism; and should the reply be in the affirmative, both for the sake of his safety and for that of others of that sect or country, especially who are in ignorance:

The question is asked, as to whether Wipperman must be re-baptized, and if so, absolutely or conditionally; again, if so, must he confess all the sins of his past life; and if so, must the confession be previous or subsequent to the conditional Baptism.

His Holiness, having heard the opinions of their Eminences, said:— "Charles Ferdinand must be rebaptized conditionally; and after baptism let him confess the sins of his past life and receive conditional absolution for them."

This decree agrees with the original,

So it is.
L. ✠ S.
ANGELO ARGENTI, Notary of the Holy Roman and Urban Inquisition.

VIII.—ON THE SACRAMENT OF EXTREME UNCTION.

Ib. xx., p. 70.

Greatly to be prized is the institution of this sacrament, by which, in our last contact with the enemy of our salvation, we are anointed and strengthened for victory.

1. Wherefore, the priest should be careful that none of the faithful under his charge depart this life without this medicine of soul and body, through any negligence of his or lack of pastoral vigilance.

2. He should, therefore, exhort the faithful not to put off receiving this most wholesome sacrament to the last extremity, when their senses have begun to fail them; but rather as soon as the malady grows serious and they are in danger of death, let them call in the priests of the church to anoint them with oil, and afford them strength and protection in their last agony.

3. On this account, the priest should admonish the friends of the sick man, and oftentimes also remind the faithful, when in health, that, if they are attended by a doctor who is not a Catholic, they should insist and frequently urge him to let them know, as soon as ever there is danger, lest by some sudden attack their soul be deprived of the benefit of this sacrament.

4. A suitable place, secured with a lock, should be fitted up, if possible, in the church or in the sacristy, for keeping the *oleum infirmorum;* or even " in the house, in a decent and safe place," as directed in the Fourth Provincial Council of Milan. In building new churches an ambry should be made near the high altar, bearing the inscription *oleum infirmorum*, with a door that will lock.

5. When the priest is called to a dying person, " who, owing to the violence of his disease, or to some accident, has entirely lost the use of his senses, so that he can understand nothing," nevertheless he ought to administer the sacrament of extreme unction, " provided the person is alive, and that when in his senses he showed sufficient signs of piety to lead to suppose that he would now ask for this sacrament, if he were capable of doing so."— *III. Provincial Council of Milan.*

IX.—On the Sacrament of Order.
Ib. xxi., p. 71.

It is a pre-eminent object of pastoral solicitude to train up and establish in the church, as the ministers of Christ and the dispensers of the mysteries of God, upright and faithful men, distinguished for every kind of virtue.

Wherefore, as regards the promotion and ordination of clerics, we enjoin that what follows be carefully observed.

1. Bishops should hold ordinations as far as possible at the times prescribed by the Canons, either in their Cathedral churches, or in the churches or chapels of their seminaries. These ordinations should be held with the greatest solemnity, and with all the rites of the Roman Pontifical.

2. As among those to be ordained there are frequently some, who on account of being converts from heresy, or being born of convert parents, or from other causes, have contracted irregularity, the Bishop should inquire diligently on this point; so that, if any one of those about to be promoted to orders be found with this taint, he may be freed from it before he is ordained. It seems desirable also to petition the Holy See that the prelate who confers orders in seminaries belonging in common to several Bishops, may have faculties to absolve from irregularity even those who are not his own subjects, provided he obtain the consent of their ordinaries. And since a doubt arose whether the faculty of ordaining out of the usual times could be exercised in favour of the alumni of such

seminaries, the Sacred Congregation of the Propagation of the Faith published a decree on the 21st of April, last year (1851), by which faculties are granted to Bishops, in whose Dioceses such colleges are situated, to ordain out of the usual times alumni, not their own subjects, having first however obtained the consent of their respective ordinaries.[1]

3. Those about to be ordained must be strictly examined by examiners on the order they are about to receive. Those to be promoted to the tonsure and minor orders must be examined in literature, those about to receive the sub-diaconate, in one treatise of sacred theology; those about to be advanced to the diaconate, in two treatises of theology; and those to be raised to the priesthood, in three treatises at least, or, if it seem proper, in the whole course of dogmatic theology. If practicable, there should also be proclamations made beforehand of those to be ordained.

4. As far as possible, the interstices should be duly observed, so that each one, before he is raised to a higher order, may have frequent opportunity of exercising the order he has already received, and thus maturely learn the rubrics.

5. As to the sum required for the decent maintenance of persons promoted to the sub-diaconate under the title of *patrimony*, the Bishops are of opinion, that no one ought to be ordained on this title, who has not a legally sure income of at least £40 sterling. On this matter the *Institution xxvi. of Benedict XIV.* and the rules there laid down should be attended to.[2]

6. But those who are ordained under the title of *patrimony* should understand that they are not at liberty to leave their own diocese without the consent of the Bishop, to whom at their ordination they promised reverence and obedience. For as Benedict XIV. (Constit. xxv., *Ex quo dilectus*) declares, " this solemn promise of obedience and reverence we do not consider a mere empty form .... may we freely acknowledge that a priest by virtue of this engagement is bound, among other obligations, not to quit the service of the church to which he belongs by his ordination, without leave of his Bishop."

X.—On the Sacrament of Matrimony.
Ib. xxii., p. 73.

There is scarcely any sacrament of the church the administration of which is attended with more serious difficulties, especially in a country where the civil laws do not recognize marriages contracted before the Church, and where the faithful live in the midst of non-catholics. Priests having the care of souls must therefore act with the greatest prudence in matters that regard the administration of this sacrament.

1. They should frequently impress upon their people the

---

1. See p. 54.   2. p. 74.

sanctity of holy Matrimony, inasmuch as it was instituted by our Lord Jesus Christ and honoured by His first miracle; teach them to hold in abhorrence all marriages not contracted according to the Catholic rite; and severely rebuke those who get married in the Protestant church.

2. The law of publishing in the church the banns of marriage must be observed. But it seems best to leave the manner and time of introducing this practice to the discretion of each Bishop, who will act according to circumstances.

3. Priests must exhort and try every means to induce those who are about to contract marriage, to go to confession previously and make a worthy communion.

4. Marriages are not to be celebrated in churches to which no district is attached with cure of souls.

5. A marriage register should be carefully kept in every church where marriages are celebrated.

6. No priest should celebrate a mixed marriage, without obtaining a promise both from the Catholic and non-Catholic party, that their children of both sexes shall be brought up in the Catholic religion; a promise from the non-Catholic party of allowing the Catholic party the free exercise of religion; and a promise from the Catholic party to strive to bring about the conversion of the non-Catholic party.

7. As it often happens that foreigners come into England for the purpose of contracting marriage, priests should be very careful not to take part in a marriage *in fraudem legis*. Wherefore, in every such case, they should have recourse to the Bishop; and the instruction of the Holy Office, dated 21st August, 1670, which treats of cases of this kind, and also of the practice to be followed in regard to persons who have no fixed abode, should be attended to.[1]

8. When there is a case of impediment to marriage, the priest must send a petition to the Bishop, stating the case and explaining accurately the degrees of relationship or other matter in which dispensation is asked for; and he must at the same time set forth the reasons for which he considers it may be granted. If the Bishop thinks proper to grant the dispensation, either by virtue of his own faculties, or after petitioning and obtaining leave from the Holy See (if the case in question exceeds his power), he must then either himself, or through his Vicar, deliver in writing the dispensation with all the clauses of canon law to the priest who has petitioned for it, and with it also a schedule to attest the execution of the dispensation. To this schedule the priest must subscribe his name and return it to the Bishop to be kept in the archives, as evidence that the marriage was lawful.[2]

9. Matrimonial dispensations are therefore never to be granted by word of mouth nor in an ordinary letter, but in a formal document accurately drawn up.

---

1. & 2. See pp. 58, &c.

XI.—On the Precepts of the Church.

Ib. xxiii., p. 75.

It were much to be desired that the exact observance of Holidays should prevail amongst us; but since it is difficult, especially to those who are dependent on Protestant masters, to abstain from servile work, we must labour most earnestly that the faithful hear Mass at least on Holidays which fall on week days. And therefore missionaries ought, if possible, to have at least one Mass celebrated early, to satisfy the devotion of their people. But they should admonish their flocks, that it is not on their own authority, but by leave of the priest, that they may engage in business and work on those days.

2. To increase the devotion of the people to the holy Patrons of their dioceses and of their churches, we shall have to petition the Sovereign Pontiff that he would graciously grant permission to transfer these festivals to the following Sundays, unless the rubrics forbid it.

3. Priests should explain carefully the rules of fasting, particularly at the beginning of Lent; should forbid the use of fish and fleshmeat at the same meal on fasting days; and display a holy severity, tempered with charity, in the exercise of the dispensing power confided to them.

4. As the obligation of paying tithes is no longer in force amongst us, the faithful should be reminded that they are not on this account exempt from the duty of providing for divine worship, and for the proper support of sacred ministers.

5. The faithful, who through devotion or for any other reason, do not frequent the quasi-parochial or missionary church of the district in which they reside, must not think themselves dispensed from the obligation of aiding it and supporting its pastors. Moreover, with regard to relieving the wants of the poor and providing for the education of children, they ought to be as solicitous as those who go to their own church. Therefore, let them, according to their means, help, in the fulfilment of these duties, their lawful pastors, who have to bear the burden of the day and the heat, in cultivating the vineyard of the Lord.

The following is the Rescript referred to above (2). *I. Westminster, p. 146.*

Most Holy Father,

Desirous of promoting devotion towards Patron Saints throughout England, the Archbishop and Bishops in Provincial Council assembled ask for each Bishop the faculty of permitting, in cases where he thinks it expedient, that the Mass of the Patron Saints of the place, or of the Saint under whose invocation the church is, may be said on the Sunday immediately following the Feast without any interference with the office of the day in other respects, and this even though the Patron Saint has not been chosen in the way laid down by the Constitution of Urban VIII. for choosing Patron Saints, or the church been consecrated.

At an audience of His Holiness granted March 13th, 1853, Our Most Holy Lord Pius IX. by Divine Providence Chief Pontiff, at the instance of me the undersigned Secretary of the Sacred Congregation of Propaganda, and in accordance with the opinion of the Most Eminent Fathers of the Sacred Congregation, graciously permitted this, provided the Sunday or Festival be not of the more solemn class; and he granted this, all things whatever to the contrary notwithstanding.

Given at Rome, at the office of the said Sacred Congregation. May 14th, 1853.

L. ✠ S. AL. BARNABÒ, Secretary.

Two other Rescripts follow granting indulgences for the Festivals of SS. George and Patrick, and allowing the latter to be kept in England as a double.

XII.—On the Life and Good Conduct of Clerics.[1]
Ib. xxiv. p. 76.

Justly are those styled by Our Lord the salt of the earth, by whose ministry men are to be preserved from the corruption of vice; and whom, if they lose their savour, it is scarcely possible to restore to a better state, for then, with the people entrusted to their care, they will hasten to ruin, and *it shall be as with the people, so with the priest (Isai. xxiv., 2; Osee iv., 9)*. But if the light of the pastor so shine before men that they shall glorify his Father Who is in heaven, and if the priest shew himself *an example of good works, in doctrine, in integrity, in gravity (Tit. ii., 7)*, so that those who are opposed to us may fear, having no evil to say of us; then, assuredly, will he build up the house of God with living and elect stones, and as the offspring of the Church and the multitude of the faithful increase, he will enlarge the place of his tent and stretch out the skins of his tabernacle (*Isai. liv., 2*). We, therefore, with the greatest solicitude, exhort all our fellow labourers in the cultivation of the Lord's vineyard, that with the new birth of the Ecclesiastical Hierarchy, they be renewed in the spirit of their mind, and stir up the grace that is in them by the imposition of our hands (*Eph. iv., 23*). Wherefore we decree that what follows be carefully observed.

1. Priests should keep away from all spectacles unworthy of an ecclesiastic; from clamorous hunting with horse and hounds, from public dances, from unlawful games, and from feastings protracted to a late hour of the night. *(Council of Trent, Session xxiv., On Reformation, and I. Provincial Council of Milan).*

The passage probably referred to is from c. xii, although it refers to Canons. Ordinary Clerics are dealt with in session xxii. c. i.

The passages from the first Provincial Council of Milan, are the following:—

"Clerics should not leave the house by night after the first hour, unless for some just cause, and then should have a light," *c. xxiv.*

"The Apostle instructs us not to live in feastings and drunkenness

---
[1] See p. 174, &c.

but soberly; hence Clerics should not be present at disreputable banquets, and should not invite anyone to drink. But if at times, on occasion of the more solemn festivals, or when meeting together for a function or for a funeral, invitations have to be given; they should not ask more than six at a time, and those clerics. In order to remove from clerics the occasion of wrongdoing which is seldom absent from inns and taverns, we altogether forbid them to enter or make use of them, unless when on a journey by reason of necessity."

Nos. 1 and 2 of this Decree are coupled together in the Acts of the Synod of Maynooth, 1875, under the penalty of suspension *ipso facto*.

2. We strictly forbid all in holy orders to be present at stage plays in public theatres; and impose on all who transgress this command the penalty of suspension, to be incurred *ipso facto*, and reserved to each one's Ordinary, according to a regulation which has been in force in England up to this time.[1]

3. The beauty of cleanliness with simplicity should shine forth in the houses of priests; and nothing in their furniture or ornaments should savour of luxury or of worldliness. No ludicrous and foolish pictures, or such as are unbecoming to a priest, should be seen there; but in each of his rooms there should be an image of Our Lord Crucified, or of the Most Holy Mother of God, or figures of Saints, or pictures illustrating the life of Our Saviour or sacred history.

4. In compliance with the injunctions of the canons, the female domestics of priests should be advanced in years, and known for their modesty, prudence, and blameless lives.

5. The dress of ecclesiastics ought to distinguish them from laymen, but not confound them with heterodox ministers. It should be black or of a dark shade; and they should not, under pretext of travelling, return to the ignominy of the secular habit, from which they have been freed. As to the shape or cut, we recommend that which has recently begun to be used by secular priests. At home their most becoming dress is the cassock (or if they prefer it, what is called the *zimarra*), with the biretta.

6. But as the distinguishing badge of the Catholic clergy, in nearly all parts of the world, is what is known as the *Roman collar*, and as it this now recognized as such even by Protestants without provoking injury or insult, we desire it to be worn by all priests when exercising the sacred ministry, unless, considering the state of things, the Bishops at their discretion may for a time determine otherwise. And for greater decency in divine worship, and also for greater uniformity in the church services, we command that all secular priests, and also Regulars when not wearing the distinctive habit of their order, shall, as often as they celebrate Mass in public or preach the word of God, or clad in sacred vestments officiate, or assist at any office in church, appear in the Roman collar, so worn that no shirt-collar appears.[2]

---

[1]. See p. 176, where the addition is made (IV. West., xl. 9.) "or n places temporarily made use of as public Theatres." Ed.

[2]. See p. 177.

7. As the fervour of devotion easily cools down, and, as St. Leo observes, even pious souls become sullied with the dust of the world, each priest should, at least every two years, attend the spiritual exercises, which the Bishop will provide.

8. It is our express will, that conferences on theological and liturgical subjects be held at certain fixed times in all our dioceses. The Bishop will determine, according to circumstances, whether there be only one conference of the clergy of the whole diocese under his own superintendence, or a number of conferences under the presidency of the rural deans in their respective deaneries. All priests, both secular and regular, who have the cure of souls (saving the rights of the latter), must attend these conferences and come prepared with their answers (*Benedict XIV., Instit.*). The conferences must send their solutions of the cases or conclusions to the Bishop for examination and correction. As to the method of holding these conferences, and as to the subjects to be discussed, each Bishop will arrange for his own diocese.

9. Since "*no man being a soldier to God entangleth himself in secular business*" (*II. Tim. ii., 4*), it is our will, that no priest exercise a trade, or engage in anything savouring of trade, or in occupations pursued for mere gain (*Provincial Council of Milan, I. Constit. Prov. Conc. of Oxford, c. Ne clerici*). Likewise let no priest undertake the office of guardian or executor, without the leave of the Bishop.

The passages referred to are :—

"We also strictly forbid a business of any description, (But we allow of any honourable artistic kind of work for the purpose of procuring the means of living by employment of one's hands.) No cleric should rent land of anyone for the sake of gain, nor undertake the guardianship or responsibility of anyone, nor become surety for anyone." c. xxvi.

10. Priests who have entered on the duties of the sacred ministry, must not on that account bid farewell to study, and especially they must not give up the pursuit of sacred knowledge; but inasmuch as *from the lips of the priest the people have to seek knowledge* (*Malach ii., 7*), they should be assiduous in reading the Holy Scriptures and studying dogmatic and moral, as well as ascetic, theology. Thus, in instructing their flocks, they will not merely fill their ears with empty words, they will not fight with adversaries as men beating the air, but they will nourish the former effectually with the true bread of life, and put to flight the latter with solid reasoning. Priests should also refrain from reading books that treat of frivolous and worldly subjects; for such reading wastes their time and energy to no purpose, and easily opens the door to temptations.

11. It is expedient that all, except Missionary Rectors, should have their faculties limited as to time; so that at first they may receive them for a year, and then gradually for longer periods. But all priests should bear in mind, that the Bishops have a right,

and it is one exercised in many places and most highly commended by Benedict XIV., to subject priests again to examination, especially junior ones, before they renew their faculties. If priests will in this way persevere in sacred studies and in reading the word of God, they will find the wisdom that sitteth by the throne of God meeting them in their sacred ministry as an honourable mother.—(*Eccli. xv., 2*).

12. But since both *we and our words, and all wisdom and the knowledge and skill of works* (*Wisdom vii., 16*) are in the hands of God, let us therefore invoke Him, that the spirit of wisdom may come upon us. On this account, a priest ought frequently to devote himself to prayer to obtain this gift which descends from the Father of light. He should practise daily meditation, strive to say the divine office devoutly, make a visit at least once a day to the Sacrament of the most Holy Eucharist, and honour with signal devotion the Blessed Virgin Mary.

XIII.—INCUMBENTS OF CHURCHES.
Ib. xxv., p. 80.

Whoever presides over a church, whether he be a simple missionary, or one who is honoured with the title of Missionary Rector, must be considered as God's steward, to whom a certain portion of the Lord's vineyard is entrusted for cultivation. He should therefore be a profitable and faithful servant, labouring incessantly; mindful that the captain of the ship runs the same chance of loss or safety as his freight.

1. Whoever, therefore, is set over a congregation, should make a profession of faith before the Bishop or his Vicar, and this faith he will engage to preach in all its integrity to the faithful committed to his charge.

2. In case this has not been already done, he should go through the whole extent of the district under his pastoral care, and write an exact report of it, and make out a *Liber status animarum,* in the manner prescribed in the Roman Ritual, as far as circumstances will permit.[1]

3. Registers of baptisms, of confirmations, of deaths and of marriages must be accurately kept by him.

4. All sacred edifices, schools, presbytery and all appurtenances of the church, he must be careful to keep in good repair. There should be no change either by way of addition or alienation, or any material alteration of church property undertaken by him, without consulting the Bishop.

5. He should examine carefully into his obligations[2] as to Masses, and have a list of them hung up in the sacristy; but he should not accept new obligations without the approbation of the

---

[1] See p. 172.   [2] See p. 173.

Bishop. If the obligations of Masses already attached to his church appear too burthensome, and the endowment for them inadequate, he should apply to the Bishop, or lay the matter before him at the time of his visitation.

6. If any of the faithful wish to make a foundation for an anniversary or daily Mass, the matter must be referred to the determination of the Bishop; and the sum contributed for this object must be profitably invested, so as to produce annual interest for a perpetual endowment, in accordance with the regulations of canon law, as far as circumstances of time and place will allow.

7. He should be attentive in visiting and assisting the sick and dying; and by no means abandon them altogether, after they have received the sacraments; but continue to visit them often, even daily if he have time, and assist them in their agony. In a long illness where the sick person is never out of danger, he should administer the Holy Viaticum frequently. It is a truly laudable practice, where there is no cemetery, to perform the funeral rites at the house of the deceased, if the corpse cannot, as is desirable, be brought to the church. But we exhort Catholics, that they everywhere provide cemeteries of their own, blessed according to the Catholic rite, or where public cemeteries are made at the common cost, that they see that a portion be set aside exclusively for themselves.

8. A priest should be careful not to incur any suspicion of avarice by meddling with the making of wills, especially, if the testator leaves a portion of his possessions for the benefit of the church or the poor. He should, however, not be deterred by the foolish clamour of some persons from doing his duty, by admonishing those who have been guilty of unjust rapine, that now at length they make restitution; and also by exhorting those who have never shown mercy to the poor, that now at least they redeem their sins with alms.

9. He should establish among his flock whatever is calculated to foster piety; he should open both day and Sunday schools, and also evening, or what are called night schools; he should found a Confraternity of Christian Doctrine, the members of which may help in the schools, and he should frequently visit his schools *(Conc. Prov. Mediol. II. Dec. II)*. He should promote devotion to the Passion of Our Lord, and to the Blessed Virgin; for instance, by erecting the Stations of the Cross, by reciting the Rosary, and also by directing the piety of the faithful to the most Sacred Heart of Jesus and to the Immaculate Heart of His most Holy Mother; and by having frequently Benediction of the most Holy Sacrament.

The decree referred to prescribes the foundation of a Sodality of Christian Doctrine or something similar.

" To enable parish priests to apply themselves with greater zeal to this work (the Christian education of the young), which in the constitution concerning the rudiments of the faith being taught by the parish priest was ordered at a foregoing Council; the Bishop should also see that in every town and village of his Diocese a Sodality of Christian Doctrine should be formed for the purpose of assisting the parish priest in this labour."

10. But he should take care to introduce nothing that has not been approved of by the Church. And, as in lesser churches, especially in the country, it is the custom to recite certain prayers both before and after Mass in the vernacular tongue, it is our wish that no prayers, and particularly that no Litanies, be said, which have not been sanctioned by the Church or approved of by the Bishop. It would also seem desirable, that this Synod should depute certain pious persons to compile prayers from approved sources, to be recited everywhere according to a uniform rite.

11. But we especially desire that the priest provide for his flock a mission or spiritual exercises, to be given by religious or by some of the clergy, as often as the Bishop shall deem it expedient. The result will be, that those who have fallen asleep in sin will be awakened and arise, that the tepid and weak will be animated and strengthened, and the just and devout be inflamed with more fervent piety.

12. The appointment of the Incumbent of a church, either ordinary or Missionary Rector, belongs to the Bishop: so that no right of preferment is acquired by serving as second priest on a mission, or even temporarily administering it.

13. He should avoid taking upon himself burthens, either temporal or spiritual, that will devolve upon his successors; for example, receiving money for which he engages to pay interest, or promising Masses in perpetuity to benefactors, in order to induce them to found some work of piety or even to build churches.

14. Those who have the cure of souls should remember that they are bound to residence; and consequently, no priest should be absent without just cause, nor frequently from the place of his ministry. If he wish to leave home for more than a few days, he should obtain a written permission from the Bishop or the Vicar. (Council of Trent. *Session xxiii., c. 1. On Reformation; and also Session v., c. 2., Ib.*)

For an explanation of this injunction see *II. Westminster. Decree, x. p. 80, (p. 164.)*

The passages alluded to above (14) refer to the duty of residence and of preaching on the part of those "who hold any ecclesiastical benefice having care of souls."

I. Westminster, D. xix. c. 7, p. 89.

A priest who wishes to leave the diocese to which he is attached must be furnished with a letter of excorporation[1] from his Ordinary, and no Bishop can aggregate to his diocese any strange priest who is not possessed of such a letter.

Necessity of having with them commendatory letters for all priests who have left their diocese. *IV. Westminster, p. 136. (See page 42.)*

---

(1) Commonly termed an "Exeat."

XIV.—The Management of Congregations or Missions.

1. Westminster, D. xiii. p. 54.

Now that the ecclesiastical hierarchy has been re-established by our most Holy Lord, it is in every way desirable that a plan of management in consonance with it should, as far as circumstances permit, be restored. This cannot be done altogether. For neither can we define the limits of parishes or make canonical institution of them, both by reason of the distance of churches from each other, and of the fact that in many instances the chapels attached to the houses of laics are used for the missions instead of churches, as well as for many other reasons which it were superfluous to enumerate here. Hence, the Archbishops and Bishops have determined to beg, that our most Holy Lord would deign to allow and to ratify a plan of management proposed by them, by means of which the inconveniences enumerated would be avoided, and the system of parochial management introduced by degrees. And to this our petition his Holiness yielded, as may be seen by the decree of the Sacred Congregation of Propaganda, April 21st of the present year, the substance of which will be added to the acts of this Synod. *(See App. viii. p. 135).*

1. By virtue, therefore, of this, and until some further provision be made by the Holy See, let certain churches be selected in each diocese, by the authority of the Bishop after advising with his chapter, which seem suitable for being regarded as quasi-parishes.

2. And over these, as a rule, let there be placed a priest with the title of *Missionary Rector*, to attend to the care of the church and of souls, just as do other heads of churches in England; but let him be considered to be fixed permanently.

3. Let the Bishop select five of his most trustworthy priests at his diocesan Synod, to form a *Commission of Inquiry*, and let one of the commission be appointed by the Bishop president thereof. *(See p. 157).*

4. A Missionary Rector permanently appointed shall not be definitively removed until three members at least of the said commission have examined into the case and their advice listened to. *(See also pp. 156).*

The method of procedure in an inquiry of this kind will be laid down in a special statute, which will be prepared by those Bishops set aside in this Synod for this purpose, and submitted to the Sacred Congregation for its approval. *(App. ix and x., p. 136).*

5. To forestall any questions that may arise, we declare that the Bishop with the advice of his chapter and in spite of the opposition of the Missionary Rector, may build new churches within the limits of his district, and give them a portion thereof, should necessity or utility in regard to the faithful demand it. But these limits let the Bishops take care to have defined as soon as possible.

In the other churches or missions mere missioners, removable at the Bishop's pleasure, shall have charge of souls, within the bounds fixed for each mission for the time being by the Bishop. But in places where the Bishop happens not to have fixed upon any boundaries, we wish that the line midway between the two nearest churches should be regarded as far as possible as the boundary.

6. If there are two or more priests at the same mission, we decree that one is to be appointed the head, to attend to the cure of souls and the management of the church or congregation.

The following Instructions having direct reference to this Decree are inserted here.

DECREE OF THE SACRED CONGREGATION OF PROPAGANDA CONCERNING THE APPOINTMENT OF MISSIONARY RECTORS.

Ib. App. viii., p. 135.

April 21st, 1852.

Although when the episcopal hierarchy was re-established throughout the realm of England the observance of the common ecclesiastical law was prescribed generally, yet it appears that this can hardly be done at once, seeing that the pre-requisites thereof are on many points wanting; so that the missionary state has to some extent to be reconciled with the establishment of dioceses, just as in several other cases it happens, until by God's goodness the common ecclesiastical laws can be completely followed. Of this description is that part of the canon law which refers to the establishment of parishes. Hence it has occurred that the most Eminent and Reverend Lord Nicholas Wiseman, Archbishop of Westminster, and their Right Reverend Lordships the Bishops of England have submitted the following rules for the approval of the Holy See.

In each diocese let churches be selected by the Bishop's authority and with the advice of the Chapter, which seem suitable to be considered as quasi-parishes.

Over these let there usually be placed a *Missionary Rector*, to attend to the church and souls just as the other head priests do at their churches; but let him be considered as permanently fixed.

At the diocesan Synod let the Bishop choose five of his most trustworthy priests to form a *Commission of Inquiry*, and let one of the number be appointed by the Bishop president of the commission.

Let no Missionary Rector permanently appointed be definitively deprived without his case being examined into by at least three members of the said commission, and their advice received.

These matters having been brought before the Sacred Congregation at a general meeting on April 5th, 1852, their Eminences considered that permission might be given. And our most Holy Lord at an audience on April 6th, having received the report from me the undersigned Secretary of the Sacred Congregation of Propaganda, approved of the decision of the Sacred Congregation and of the above-mentioned plan, and willed that for the time being it should be followed, all things whatever to the contrary notwithstanding.

Given, &c.

A. BARNABÒ, Secretary.

Decree of the Sacred Congregation of Propaganda in which Approval is given to the Mode of Proceeding in the case of a Missionary Rector.[1]

Ib. ix., p. 136.

At a general meeting of the Sacred Congregation, held March 8th, 1853, at the instance of the most Eminent and Reverend Lord Cardinal Raphael Fornari, on the occasion of the recognition of the acts and decrees of the provincial Synod held by the Bishops of England, a plan was also presented for examination, which was drawn up at the instance of this Synod and forwarded by his Eminence the Archbishop of Westminster, and was entitled: *Method of proceeding in taking the opinion of the Council of Inquiry before the final deprivation of a Missionary Rector*, and was comprised in fourteen articles. The question having been put as to whether the plan mentioned should be approved of, the most Eminent and Reverend Fathers replied in the affirmative.

Given at Rome, at the Office of the Sacred Congregation of Propaganda, August 4th, 1853.

L. ✠ S.   J. PH. CARD. FRANSONI, Prefect.

The Mode of proceeding in taking the opinion of the Commission of Inquiry before the final deprivation of a Missionary Rector.[2]

Ib., x., p. 137.

1. Recourse should not be had to the Council of Inquiry, unless the Missionary Rector prefers this course to giving up his position and office of his own accord, on the Bishop explaining to him in clear and precise terms the reasons impelling him to remove him altogether.

2. When the Bishop has determined to take the opinion of the Council of Inquiry in reference to depriving a Missionary Rector, he should entrust his Vicar-general or some other priest appointed by him for the work, with the task of committing to writing an account of his reasons for proceeding to the deprivation, together with the results of any preceding inquiry, and a record of any circumstances which may have especial reference to the case or to the conduct of it.

3. He should make known by letter to each of the members of the Council the place, day and hour of meeting.

4. He should summon by letter the Missionary Rector in question to the place fixed for holding the Council on the day appointed; and set forth in full his reasons for proceeding to deprive him, unless motives of prudence suggest otherwise. And he should warn the said Rector to prepare a reply supported by proofs in writing to all that has been brought forward in the account of the case, either previously by word of mouth or at present in writing.

---

1. See note,. p 184.
2. This is copied in full in the Appendix to the Decrees of the Synod of Maynooth, 1875, p. 248. It is also prescribed (*IV. West. xii. 5*) before sentence of deprivation is passed upon any Missioner. See p. 182.

5. As soon as the members of the Council have assembled together at the appointed time and place, the Bishop shall order secrecy to be kept as to all matters that transpire at the Council. He should likewise remind them that the inquiry is not a judicial procedure, but set on foot for the purpose, and to be conducted with a view, of arriving by any means whatsoever at the knowledge of the truth; so that each member, weighing all matters in the sight of God, may form as accurate a judgment as is possible as to the truth of the facts upon which the case rests. He should also warn them against doing anything in the course of the inquiry which might render themselves or others liable to loss or difficulties, and especially which might expose them to the danger of an action for libel or of any trial before a civil tribunal.

6. The account of the case should be read to the Council by the Bishop's official, and his reply to the questions put to him by the president or by any of the other members through the president for their farther enlightenment.

7. The Missionary Rector should thereupon be admitted and should read his reply, as well as answer the questions similarly put to him.

8. Then, after consulting together, if, in the judgment of two-thirds at least of the members[1] the facts appear to be proven, each should give his opinion in writing and the reasons upon which it is founded; the opinions should be compared; the proceedings of the Council drawn up by the Bishop's official and signed by the president in the name of the Council, and forwarded to the Bishop with the opinion of each in full.

9. If any farther inquiry seems to be necessary or advisable, on the same day or on any other fixed by the Council for a meeting, the witnesses whom the Council judge to be requisite should be summoned, and the Missionary Rector heard as to those whom he wishes also to be summoned.

10. The witnesses for the case should be examined separately by the president and by the other members through the president, and first of all in the absence of the Missionary Rector; and this as minutely as possible, but not upon oath. But if the witnesses are willing they may depose that they are ready to repeat their testimony upon oath if the opportunity is given them.

11. With the consent of the witnesses and at the discretion of the Council, the evidence must be repeated in the presence of the Missionary Rector, and he may examine the witnesses through the president.

12. In the same way the witnesses against the case should be examined.

13. Having thereupon consulted together, the course mentioned above (n. 8) should be followed.

---

[1]. In America, a bare majority suffices. See the whole Instruction, given in Smith's Ecclesiastical Law, vol. II. p. 415. [Ed.]

14. But if the witnesses are unwilling or unable to attend the Council, or in case their evidence is not as complete as it might be two at least of the members should be deputed by the Council to go to them, and after visiting this or that place or in any other way whatsoever in their power seeking out means for settling any doubts, they should give an account of their inquiries to the Council, so that no means should be left untried for arriving at the truth with moral certainty.

On the Commission of Inquiry.
III. Westminster xviii., p. 55.

At our first Provincial Synod we made some decrees in reference to a Commission of Inquiry, in accordance with an Instruction from the Sacred Congregation of Propaganda. But, inasmuch as some doubts have since arisen as to the mode of carrying out what was authorized, we have weighed the whole matter carefully again, and proposed that the following should be adopted :—

Those who have been named as members of the above mentioned Commission at a Diocesan Synod, should retain office until the next Diocesan Synod, when they may be re-appointed or others put in their places. But if, meanwhile, by the death or resignation of any one of those appointed the Commission should be decreased, the Bishop shall nominate another member, with due regard to the proportion between the Chapter and the body of the Clergy, which was suggested at the first Provincial Synod.

XV.—Church Property.
II. Westminster viii., p. 24.

1. Offerings of the faithful for the propagation and ornament of religion, for the support of the clergy, the relief of the poor and other pious uses, are considered as made to God and the Church; and the administrators or guardians of them, whether ecclesiastics or laymen, are to be deemed merely dispensers of them, under obligation of rendering an account to God of their stewardship. As *here now it is required among the dispensers, that a man be found faithful* in those things, which concern the rightful administration of Church property, it seems proper, that in this Synod, we should treat this matter more fully, inasmuch as having been occupied with matters more important in the first Provincial Council, we deferred the consideration of this subject to a more convenient opportunity.

2. Every effort must be made to determine, if there be any doubt, the intention and purpose of the donor or testator of each fund, and that the proceeds of it may be rigidly applied to the use prescribed by him.

3. If this intention cannot be ascertained from any trustworthy document, rules or canons by which a safe judgment may be formed in such cases, should be observed.

4. Whenever a church, or school, or any other building intended for religious uses, is erected or provided, either wholly or in part from money contributed by the faithful, or granted by any society administering the alms of pious Catholics, every edifice of this kind is to be considered as belonging for ever to the place where it stands.

5. The same judgment must be passed on buildings erected by any benefactor, unless it is clearly proved that he made a declaration, that, in erecting such an edifice, he did not intend it for the advantage of the faithful of that place, but that he wished to confer a benefit on some particular Order. The rules laid down in this and the preceding number as to rights in foundations, are in the case of Regulars to be applied to new foundations only.

6. But the Bishop shall not be allowed, on this account, to take away a mission lawfully entrusted to any religious order. These rules regard merely a case, in which a religious body either cannot or will not retain the care of a mission ; for example, if a superior remove it to some other place, or for any other reason it there cease to exist altogether, and not for a time only.

7. If, however, any mission be founded altogether or for the most part by funds belonging to any religious body, which for good reasons may wish to leave entirely and go elsewhere, we recommend that a distinct agreement be made between the Bishop and the superiors of the order as to what has to be done ; so that, on the one hand, just rights may not suffer, and on the other no scandal may arise nor grievous loss of souls ensue.

8. Much less is it lawful for any cleric, or even for the Bishop himself, to alienate Church property ; as is evident from almost numberless decrees of canon law. If, however, on account of reasons approved of by the canons, such an alienation become necessary, the priest can never act in this matter without the authority of the Bishop, nor the Bishop without the precautions required by canon law.

9. In every mission, where money is contributed by the faithful in the ways hereafter described, it is to be accounted Church property, and not a donation to the priest. For from this money he must provide not only for his own decent support, but for the expense of religious worship, for the maintenance of the fabric, for payment of debts, where there are any, and for other wants. Wherefore, if any priest leave a mission during the course of the year, he has not a right to his proportion of the yearly income, until the amount justly due for expenses be deducted. In like manner, what he has provided for the use of the church from the income of the church, for example—wax candles, wine for the most holy sacrifice, sacred furniture—these he should leave behind him,

without any compensation, unless he can clearly show that the supply is excessive.

10. All are aware that there are now in operation different methods of raising money for the support of missions. The following in particular we do not disapprove of, till the charity of the faithful shall provide in a better way.

They are:

1. Letting of seats or places in the church to certain persons or families at a fixed rent, to be paid to the church.

2. Church collections made at the Offertory.

3. According to a custom prevailing generally in England, payment of a fixed sum according to the part of the church which they occupy, by those who do not rent seats, yet are not content to occupy what is called the free space.

4. Sermons by some distinguished preacher of the word of God, after which the alms of the congregation, whose number is often swelled by a concourse of strangers, are collected for the general or particular use of the church, or for some special purpose.

5. Collections which are either made from house to house, by persons appointed for the purpose, or by societies and confraternities lawfully appointed, or which are gathered from *tens* or *hundreds* as is done in the excellent society called the Society for the Propagation of the Faith, or contributions made by the more wealthy portion of the congregation at fixed times, or yearly.

11. Although it is certainly much to be desired that many of these methods of maintaining the church were done away with, yet experience has taught that it is as yet impossible altogether to dispense with them. Wherefore, in those places where one or more of these methods prevail, they ought to be so kept on, that no innovations be introduced without the authority of the Bishop. Especially, should not the free space be diminished nor narrowed without consulting him. But whatever money comes to the mission by these means, it should be considered as belonging not to the priest personally, but to the general wants of the mission. Therefore, whatever furniture, either sacred or domestic, he acquires from these sources, or whatever he expends in keeping in repair the church, or other buildings in any way belonging to it, in this expenditure, he is not making provision for himself, but is providing for the mission from mission property.

12. As soon therefore as any priest enters on a mission, an inventory of all property belonging to the mission should be placed in his hands by the dean, or by some one deputed by the Bishop. The missionary is bound to keep the furniture and buildings in good repair, yea rather to improve them, that he may deliver to his successor as much at least as he received himself. Should he provide for the renewing of what is grown old and mean, or procure something new and more elegant to ornament the

place, a distinction must be made as regards the sources from which the expense is defrayed.

1. If the priest has procured these things from his own property, or from the gifts of friends well disposed towards him, or, in fine, from that portion of the income of the church which he might have expended on his own decent maintenance, they are to be considered as his own property, provided he has kept all that he received in good order.

2. But if these things were procured out of the general revenues of the church, or by gifts and collections from the congregation, or by money granted by the Bishop or the administrators of the temporalities of the diocese, they are to be deemed entirely the property of the mission, nor is it lawful for the priest on any account to claim them.

13. It is also to be generally understood, according to a rule of canon law, that things adapted for ecclesiastical purposes given to a missionary, are, unless there is proof to the contrary, given to the mission; but things adapted for personal use are presumed to be given to the priest personally, as are also such church things as are given by a flock to a priest as tokens of gratitude or affection.

14. Retributions for Masses are the property of the priest. In like manner, where it is the custom, which is a very ancient one in England, of making presents to each priest at Easter and Christmas, these gifts of right belong to them. But the priest should be on his guard, lest he incur the suspicion of avarice, by receiving anything on account of his administering the sacrament of penance.

15. As to the application of money derived from stole fees, there is no uniform practice throughout the whole Church. For though the Church detests all filthy lucre in extorting or exacting money for the administration of the sacraments, yet the Council of Lateran, held under Innocent III. in the year 1215, prescribed that the laudable customs, in accordance with which offerings were made by the faithful to the ministers of the altar on occasion of the administration of the sacraments, should be observed. The proceeds derived from this source should be ordinarily considered as belonging to the priests; though they are distributed in different ways, in different places. That distribution seems to be the best, which is most conducive to alleviate the burthens of the mission.

16. Whilst therefore we forbid anything to be asked for and much more anything to be exacted before the celebration of baptism and matrimony, and even after the celebration as a right, we leave it to the prudence of Bishops to determine in their Diocesan Synods, what seems best adapted to the customs and state of places.[1]

---

[1] "The Sacraments should never be withheld on the plea that the usual offerings are not forthcoming." Synod, Maynooth, (1875) p. 74. "Lest through individual avarice any abuse may creep in, and this Sacrament (of Baptism) so absolutely essential to salvation should be withheld from anyone, no Parish Priest or his Curate should enter into the matter of offerings before administering Baptism. We likewise forbid them, and under pain of suspension *ipso facto*, to refuse baptism to any infant on the plea that no offering, or less than the usual sum, is forthcoming." Ib. p. 77.   Ed.

Especially should they most vigilantly correct all abuses, if any exist, as to the amount, or to the exaction of these offerings, by enforcing everywhere an equitable arrangement.

17. Whoever presides over the administration of any mission, whatever title he may bear, should by all means keep a day book of all the receipts and expenses of the mission, both of which should be entered most exactly every day, in their proper order. He should also keep another book, commonly called a Ledger, to which he will transfer every month or three months, all the entries in the other book arranged in order, according to the heads under which each sum received or expended ought to be placed.

18. Every administrator should keep what is called an open account at some Bank, in the names of two respectable persons and his own. These persons should be made aware that they are named merely to secure the money from any danger of being lost, and they must not interfere in the administration of it. If any one of these fail, through any cause, the two that remain will take care that another be chosen by the Bishop to fill his place. Wherefore, no administrator should keep on hand more than twenty pounds of money belonging to the mission; that is, of money which is not his own property; but should carefully place it in the Bank.

19. No administrator of a mission should draw up any legal documents concerning church property, without the express authority of the Bishop, who will not fail to consult lawyers most skilled in these matters, and subject everything to the most careful revision.

20. All buildings belonging to a mission should be insured against fire by an annual payment to some insurance company.

21. Every one seeking alms of the faithful ought to be furnished with the autograph of his Ordinary or of his own superior, stating the object of his pious quest; and this must be verified by the Ordinary of the place, in which he is begging; and also must contain an express proviso, that he is bound to give an exact account to the Bishop, or to his own superior, of all the sums collected by him, specifying also the places in which he has been, the persons who have contributed, and the length of time he has remained in each place.

XVI.—On a Translation of the Canonical Scriptures.
Ib. p. 30.

That an accurate version of the Holy Scriptures from the Latin Vulgate may be had as soon as possible, the Bishops are of opinion, that this undertaking should be entrusted to learned men, be be selected by his Eminence, the Archbishop, care being taken, however, to observe the rules of the Index, as to the revision of the work, and as to adding notes from the Holy Fathers and pious authors, and as to the permission and approbation for its perusal.

XVII.—ON THE ABSENCE OF PRIESTS.

For the clearer understanding of Decree XIV. c. xxv. of the I. Council of Westminster, we determine that assistant priests ought to inform the head priest of each church, as often as they leave home even for a day, and that no Missionaries, either principal or assistants, ought to be absent on a Sunday or a Holiday of obligation without leave of the Bishop or Vicar-general, except in case of urgency, in which case, the priest on leaving home ought as soon as possible to inform the Bishop of the said urgency, and should leave a suitable priest to supply his place.

XVIII.—THE BOUNDARIES OF MISSIONS.
III. *Westminster xvi., p. 51.*

From new limits being assigned to dioceses, or from other causes, it may easily happen, that some Catholics are found to be nearer a church or mission in a neighbouring diocese, than they are to any yet established in their own. In this case, questions may arise, both as to the obligations of neighbouring priests, and as to the rights of the aforesaid Catholics to their ministry; and as a case of this kind has already been before the Holy See, and His Holiness has been pleased to refer it to this Provincial Synod that provision may be also made for similar cases, the Fathers have made the following decrees, to suit as far as possible a variety of circumstances.

1. When neighbouring Catholics are so near a church of another diocese, that they repair to it for divine service and to receive the sacraments, and also give their alms to it; with the consent of their own Ordinary, they are to be considered attached to it; and the Ordinary will grant the necessary faculties to the priest of that mission. The said priest will be deemed their missionary, and will be bound to visit and instruct them, and to attend to the sick; and his conscience will be burthened with the salvation of their souls.

Therefore

a.—Neighbouring Bishops should by common consent determine the boundaries of this extra-diocesan cure of souls, and the limits within which the said priest ought to exercise his ministry.

b.—The names of the Catholics living within these bounds shall be entered in the *Liber status animarum* of the church to which they are aggregated. Their baptisms, marriages and deaths shall be recorded in the respective books of the same mission, with a notice of the diocese whose subjects they are, so that at any time the Ordinary may be furnished with faithful extracts from them.

c.—But as to Lenten Indults and instructions on all matters which directly depend on or proceed from the Ordinary, these they shall receive from him and observe them; and the priest, who has the care of them, shall be bound to make them known to them. And, in the same manner, they ought to be admonished to contribute, according to their abilities, to the collections made in their own diocese.

2. If they be too far distant from both churches to be reasonably considered as attached to either, or to be able to attend either conveniently, then the Bishops should by common consent give them in charge to that priest who can most easily and efficiently take care of them, regard being had to the following considerations:—

a.—The relative distances of the outlying place from the two neighbouring missionaries, when in other respects they are similarly situated; according to the rule laid down in I. Synod of Westminster.—(*Chap. xiii., 5*).

b.—The conveniences for the journey; as for example, when there is a railway or public conveyance to the place in question or to somewhere near it; as in this case, although the distance may be greater, the journey may very possibly be shorter.

c.—The state of health, age and strength of each priest: the junior, especially if the journey has to be made on foot, will be better able to bear the burthen.

But whatever the Bishops may agree upon in this or in any better way, regarding such cases, their decision must be the rule; for the first thing to be looked to is the salvation of souls; the manner of accomplishing this, if a lawful one, need not be too anxiously dwelt upon.

XIX.—On Payment of the Cathedraticum.
(Ib. xvii., p. 53).

His Eminence the Prefect of the Sacred Congregation of Propaganda, in the name of their Eminences of that Sacred Council in a letter of the 12th of February of the present year, directed to the most Illustrious and Right Reverend the Lord Bishop of Liverpool, was pleased to lay before this Synod certain doubts as to the yearly payment of the Cathedraticum to the Bishop, which had found expression in his diocese. These doubts had been brought before the Holy See by one of the priests of his diocese, in order that a decision might be made as to what course should be adopted in that diocese. Whereupon, the said Sacred Congregation, most wisely as is its wont, cleared up and solved most of these doubts.

But at the fifth question, the Sacred Congregation hesitated and made the declaration: "Deferred, and let the wish of the Provincial Council be asked for." This fifth question is expressed as follows:

"Is it for the Holy See to decide upon the sum to be paid under this head in England, and especially in the Diocese of Liverpool?"

Two points therefore have to be considered by us in reference to the amount of Cathedraticum, and submitted to the judgment of the Holy See.

1. What should the Holy See declare as to the proper Cathedraticum for the clergy of Liverpool?
2. What should be settled for England in general?

To the first question, after careful consideration, our answer is that, having regard to the condition and good will of that most edifying clerical body, the sum of one pound sterling is not too much, as will appear more clearly from what follows.

To the second question we accordingly reply before coming to any decree, that four years ago the Bishops at their extra-Synodal meeting took this whole matter into consideration, and almost unanimously agreed that throughout the whole of England the sum of one pound should be fixed for the Cathedraticum. In accordance with this decision several Bishops have at their Diocesan Synods exacted the pound from their clergy, namely his Eminence the Metropolitan, the Bishops of Liverpool, Beverley, Birmingham, Salford and Nottingham. Now, however, that at the bidding of the Sacred Congregation we have gone again into the whole matter, some of the Bishops have laid before the meeting that owing to the poverty of many of their priests it would be impossible to get this sum except from a few. Hence, desirous as we are of ever acting kindly and considerately towards the clergy, we decree as follows:

a.—Since it is highly expedient that uniformity should be established throughout all the Dioceses of England, as to the amount to be paid annually by way of Cathedraticum; but whereas in some Dioceses, which God has blessed with greater abundance, one pound would not be too much, yet in others labouring under poverty, it would be too great a burthen upon the clergy; and since, in fine, it is by no means according to equity that the rich should be the rule for the poor, but the contrary ought to hold good; we decree that in future the amount to be paid for Cathedraticum shall be the same in all the Dioceses, and shall be fixed at one-half the pound sterling.

2. But as, in addition to the amount of the Cathedraticum; the Sacred Congregation has directed us to determine also from whom payment of the Cathedraticum is due, taking into consideration the condition of our clergy and their means of subsistence, we decree that the undernamed ecclesiastics are bound to pay it:—

a.—All chapters from their common stock.

b.—Priests ordained under the title of *the mission*, who are in the receipt of stipends from any church or oratory.

c.—Those who have the cure of souls.

d.—Those who preside over churches or public oratories, unless they are able to prove a special exemption.

XX. MISCELLANEOUS RESCRIPTS.

III. Westminster, Appendix iii, p. 82.

MASSES FOR DEPARTED PRIESTS.

Most Holy Father,

The Cardinal Archbishop of Westminster, and the other Fathers of the Synod beg your Holiness to deign to allow and sanction the following arrangements, seeing that—subject to the approbation of the Holy See—they are considered just by the Priests among the worthy Secular Clergy, who have gone into the question.

There being no certainty as to the existence of any law for the pious practice of saying Mass for each and every Priest in the kingdom, and no possibility of producing any authoritative approbation in its favour, Your Holiness is asked, for the peace of consciences, to abolish any such custom if it is in force, and absolve anyone who has either in good or doubtful faith not acted in accordance therewith; and also to substitute in its place the following practice, which shall be considered to hold good until it is altered at a subsequent Provincial Synod.

England shall be divided into two parts, of which the Southern shall comprise the counties which form the Dioceses of Westminster, Southwark, Newport, Clifton, Plymouth, Birmingham, Northampton, and Nottingham containing about 363 Secular Priests, while the Northern, shall comprise the Counties which form the other Dioceses, &c., containing about 367 Secular Priests. The practice of applying the Mass should in future be limited to the Bishops (even though Regulars) and the Secular Priests of that division to which the deceased belonged, on condition that an exact list be kept of the Priests in each Diocese, and that no one has the right to any Mass, who has not personally or by proxy been entered upon the list as undertaking to say one Mass during his lifetime for every Bishop or Priest entered upon the respective lists for the South and North.

Priests who for any cause are permanently transferred from one division to the other, shall have their names transferred from one list to the other, and shall reap the benefit of the Masses of that division in which they are at the time of their death. Those however who cease to belong to the jurisdiction of the Bishops of England, or die whilst under supension, lose all right to the Masses. Priests of the English Colleges abroad, as well as those attached to the Pontifical Court, may enjoy these suffrages by having themselves entered upon the lists of their several Dioceses. Everyone who inscribes himself on the new list, thereby cedes every right real or doubtful to any advantage arising from the old custom, which, by virtue of the Apostolical sanction hereby humbly sought for, will be abrogated.

The Bishops likewise beg that the Mass to be applied in accordance with this arrangement may by the favour of your Holiness be privileged.

At an audience with his Holiness granted April 22nd, 1860, our most Holy Lord Pius IX. by divine Providence Pope, on the representation of the case by me the undersigned Secretary of the Sacred

Congregation of Propaganda, having heard the opinions of their Eminences the Cardinals of the same Sacred Congregation given April 15th, 1860, graciously yielded to the prayer of the petition.

Given at Rome, at the office of the said Sacred Congregation, the day and year as above.

    CAJET. ARCHBISHOP OF THEBES, Secretary.

L. ✠ S.

ADDITIONAL RESCRIPT IN REFERENCE TO THE ABOVE.

MOST HOLY FATHER,

John Virtue, Chamberlain to your Holiness, begs that, as several English and Irish Army Chaplains have in conformity with the Rescripts of the Sacred Congregation of April, 1860, said Masses for deceased Confrères, and as they or other English priests who may some day be selected as army chaplains may well be considered to be in England, although at the risk of their lives they must betake themselves with the troops to distant regions, your Holiness will declare that Chaplains belonging to one of the Districts of England, and those of the English clergy who may be hereafter appointed, are to enjoy participation in the Masses offered up by their Confrères of the District, provided that in other matters they have kept the conditions laid down in the Rescript, and that at the time of their death they are occupied in attending to the care of the troops, saving the wish of any future Provincial Synod as to other Chaplains asking in the future to be enrolled.

At an audience with His Holiness on August 23rd, 1866, Our most Holy Lord Pius IX. by Divine Providence Pope, at the instance of me the undersigned Cardinal Prefect of the Sacred Congregation of Propaganda, having maturely considered all points and noted also the wish of the Bishops of England, has declared that English Army Chaplains, as well as those who may become so, can enjoy the Masses specified in the Rescript of April 22nd, 1860, as well as Chaplains who have come from other countries and been engaged for some time in England, and having been entered on the list of priests have pledged themselves to say Masses for their English Confrères, and indeed have all along done so, thinking that after their death the Masses of their surviving Confrères would have to be said for them; provided they have fulfilled the conditions laid down in the aforesaid Rescript; even though their death should occur when living out of the district in which they were enrolled; but as to others belonging to other countries and who have not already made such compact with these Priests, He ordered that they must have recourse to some future Provincial Synod if they wish to share in the benefit of the Masses.

Given at Rome, at the office of the Sacred Congregation of Propaganda, on the day and in the year as above.

    AL. CARD. BARNABÒ, Prefect.

L. ✠ S.

Indulgence for the Mission Vow. *(See p. 183).*
Ib., iv., p. 98,

At an audience granted me, the undersigned Secretary of the Sacred Congregation of Propaganda, May 7th, 1775.

Our most Holy Lord by divine Providence Pope Pius VI., in his ardent zeal for the spread of the Catholic Religion, seeing that it might tend greatly to the welfare and increase of the Apostolic Missions, if those who have been brought up as future preachers of the Gospel, whether seculars or regulars, in Colleges or Seminaries, or who under the title of the Mission have been raised to ecclesiastical Orders, should call to mind the vow by which they have bound themselves to co-operate with God, in the salvation of souls; he earnestly exhorts them to renew that vow every year on the anniversary of their taking it, carefully reflecting upon the divine goodness towards them in making them the Ministers of His Word to announce the wonders of His goodness and power; upon the crown of imperishable glory prepared for them in heaven if they holily and duly fulfil their duty; and upon the severe judgment awaiting them if anyone should perish,—but may this never happen!—through their carelessness or sloth.

To encourage them to do this readily and cheerfully, His Holiness most affectionately grants each of them for all time to come a Plenary Indulgence applicable to the souls in Purgatory, only not when they take the aforesaid vow first of all, but also when they renew it on the day fixed; provided that in each case they do not neglect to cleanse their conscience by means of the Sacrament of Penance, and receive the Holy Eucharist or offer up the sacrifice of the Mass.

Given at Rome, at the office of the same Sacred Congregation, May 7th, 1775.

STEFANO BORGIA, Secretary.

XXI.—On the Duties of those Entrusted with the Cure of Souls.
IV. Westminster, Decree x., p. 46.

1. The Holy and Œcumenical Council of the Vatican in its definition of the primacy of the Roman Pontiff, gives us a clear insight also into the pastoral duty of Bishops, in these words:— "To Peter alone did Jesus after His resurrection entrust the jurisdiction over the whole flock, saying 'Feed my lambs, feed my sheep.'"[1] "Bishops," the Synods goes on, "who, chosen by the Holy Ghost, have succeeded the Apostles, feed and govern, each his own distinct flock,"[2] and will have to render a strict account to the divine Shepherd of the sheep entrusted to him.

2. We most affectionately, in the Lord, therefore, admonish all rectors of churches or missions and all who are appointed to assist them, to understand well and constantly to reflect that they are bound to attend to the salvation of souls by many ties both of

---

[1] The Vatican Council, First Dogmatic Constitution on the Church of Christ, c. 1. [2] Ib. c. 3.

conscience and of affection. And seeing that, in the 1st Council of Westminster, *Decree xiii.*, 6, it was settled that "where there are two or more priests at the same mission, one is to be appointed the head and be entrusted with the cure of souls and the management of the church or congregation," we now for the better maintenance of order decree moreover that all the others are to carry on their share of the care of souls in complete dependence upon the head priest.

3. It is altogether just that those who preach the Gospel should live by the Gospel; and indeed a missionary priest receives the offerings of the faithful solely by reason of his being a missionary; and therefore are they who live by the Gospel bound in season and out of season to teach, and imbue the minds of the faithful with the Gospel. If in the fulfilment of a duty of such moment they prove slothful, from the mouth of the Judge will they hear those reproaches which the Prophet of old uttered to the pastors of the people:—"Woe to the pastors of Israel who fed themselves. Ye drank the milk and were clothed with the wool, and that which was fat ye killed; but my flock ye fed not." [1]

4. Moreover, if God has given every one charge of his neighbour and all Christians are therefore bound in charity to have a regard for the salvation of their neighbours, how much more is a priest bound, who by virtue of his ordination takes the place of Christ, dispenses the mysteries of God, administers the Sacraments of eternal salvation, and holds jurisdiction over the mystical body of Jesus Christ. Priests should remember, therefore, that they have to render an account to their own Pastor upon earth, and to the Chief Pastor of all at His dread tribunal, if by their negligence even one of the sheep should perish. Woe to the worthless servant, who digging it into the earth hides the talent confided to him by Christ. Most humbly do we pray God that our missionaries, in imitation of St. Paul, may be prepared to spend themselves and be spent for the salvation of souls. [2]

5. Missionary priests are likewise bound by obedience to labour unwearily for the salvation of the souls committed to their care. Let them call to mind that solemn moment when, just raised to the unspeakable dignity of the priesthood, they on bended knees promised obedience and reverence towards their Ordinary. Since, therefore, they have been chosen and sent forth by the Bishop, to whose commands they have willingly subjected themselves, to fulfil their pastoral duty towards the sheep entrusted to them, it is clear that they are bound by the bond of obedience to the due discharge of so great an office.

6. Moreover, by the favour of the Apostolic See it was arranged some three centuries ago that missionary priests in England, deprived as they were by sacrilegious hands of every kind of support, might be raised to sacred orders under the title of the *mission*, taking that truly Apostolical and additional vow, with a

---

1. Ezech. xxxiv., 2, 3. 2. Cor. xii., 15.

view to the good of the Universal Church (the which Alexander VII. in his Brief "*Cum circa juramenti vinculum,*" July 20th, 1660, has in befitting terms explained), of applying themselves for the future, as far as in their power, to seek out and save the lost sheep of the nation of England. From the power of this most stringent bond, through years of cruellest persecution, came forth and waxed strong even unto martyrdom that wondrous constancy and patience, which is the crown and glory of our clergy. Hence the Holy See, whilst it still gives its usual permission to the Bishops of England to ordain their subjects under the above-mentioned title, exhorts our missioners, with the inducement even of a Plenary Indulgence, not to forget to renew the vow they have taken each year on the anniversary itself thereof : "Seriously reflecting upon the divine goodness towards them, in having appointed them ministers of the Word, to announce the wonders of his greatness and power ; upon the imperishable crown of glory prepared for them in heaven if they holily fulfil their duty ; and upon the severe judgment awaiting them if by reason of their negligence or sloth (and may this never happen!) anyone should perish."[1]

7. To sum up :—It is from all these sources taken together, that is, from justice, from priestly charity, from the promise of obedience, from the sanctity of the oath, that the mutual bond arises between a priest and his own Bishop, by means of which they are happily united in the faithful discharge of their several duties, linked together as they are by a common work and mutual assistance in it.

8. All therefore to whom the cure of souls has been entrusted should know, that their mission is to all persons, non-Catholics as well as Catholics, throughout the whole of the district over which they have been placed. We are debtors to all, nor do we know to whom the Lord may reveal by means of us his salutary grace. "Other sheep I have, that are not of this fold ; and them also I must bring, and they shall hear my voice, and there shall be one fold and one shepherd." [2] It is, therefore, not enough to hold forth the word of life and the aids to piety towards those only who come for them of their own accord ; but we are bound to seek out and to bring back to God those sheep especially that are lost and those that being fallen away from virtue and plunged and sunk in the abyss of many vices will not listen to the pastor's voice. And there is another Apostolic mission that we have. For there are many in England, who being born of Catholic parents are Catholics in faith at least and name, yet brought up in non-Catholic orphanages or at law-established schools, having had no Catholic education, have completely given up the worship of God. Truly these are the sheep of whom the Saviour speaks when He says : "The Son of Man cometh to seek and to save that which was lost." [3] Finally, before the eyes of our missioners lies our own

---

1. Instruction of the Sacred Congregation of Propaganda, upon the Title to Ordination, n. xv. April 27th, 1871. (p. 77.)   2. John x 16.   3. Luke xix., 10.

England—holy of old, beloved of God, fertile in Saints as the Paradise of the Lord; but now woefully changed indeed, yet beauteous still and exceedingly dear for the memories of its Saints. The harvest is therefore great indeed: the crops are ripening: let us apply the sickle; let us with unwearied patience, with a firm trust and an inexhaustible charity bind up the sheaves.

9. Every four years,[1] by the constitution of Sixtus V., *Romanus Pontifex*, § 4, the Bishops of England are bound to visit the threshold of the Apostles, and to lay before the Supreme Pontiff as accurately a prepared account as possible of the flock entrusted to them. That this may be completed, it is altogether essential that the rectors of churches and missioners should do their part, and should send to the Bishop an accurately prepared account of the state of the souls confided to their care. Therefore, wherever it is possible, an accurate census of the people should be taken by every rector of a church assisted by the missioners associated with him. In this should be noted the number of families and the members thereof, with the names of both children and adults, as well as all matters that have reference to their faith, character and virtue, and above all the education of the children. And since, in the lapse not of years only but sometimes of months, changes are apt to take place, a census of this kind with its accompanying state of souls should be kept carefully looked over and corrected.

10. At every mission there should be a chest or place for the archives, of sufficient size and security, and in it should be kept all the books and other documents relating to the mission. In accordance with the I. Council of Westminster, books of those baptized should be as carefully kept as possible and preserved, note being taken when the baptism is conditional; likewise, of those confirmed and of the dead, as well as those married, and if possible there should be a book too of the burials. The rector of the church has the duty by virtue of his office of keeping the archives, although he may assign it to another; he, however, will have to bear the responsibility both of filling up the books and of the custody of all things consigned to the repository of the archives. In this repository there should be placed and carefully kept all the Decrees of Provincial and Diocesan Synods, a complete series of the Bishop's Pastorals, and copies issued by the Ordinary of all instructions of that nature.

11. The Rectors of churches of the secular clergy should bear in mind that the Bishop alone has the right to fix the obligation of Masses, whether temporarily or for ever, upon churches; and the obligations already imposed cannot be changed or lessened without recourse to the Holy See.[2]

12. At the first Council of Westminster priests were cautioned against undertaking the management of worldly business.[3] And,

---

1. See p. 84.   2. See below, and p. 153.   3. p. 161.

taught by experience, we judge that this most wise prohibition should be renewed. Moreover, we command all to persist in refusing the custody of money; and that they should not keep other people's savings in their hands, especially those of the poor, or allow them to be invested in their names; lest, deceived by the snares of wicked people or misled by their own want of care and attention, they should allow these deposits to be lost in such a way as to render themselves liable to be brought before a secular court of law; or, still worse, tarnish the priestly name with the suspicion of broken faith, or avarice, or even injustice.

THE OBLIGATION OF MASSES *(referred to above—n 11.)*

Ib. App. vii. p. 139.

From the Decrees of the Sacred Congregation of the Council, confirmed by Urban VIII. and Innocent XII. (*See Ferraris, Prompta Bibliotheca, on the Sacrifice of the Mass, Art. 2*).

"§ 3 . . . The Sacred Congregation commands and orders, under threat of the Divine judgments, that just as many Masses be offered up as have been prescribed for the sum given in alms; so that those whose business it is, and who do not fulfil their duty, sin greviously and are bound to restitution.

"§ 5. And moreover, wishing to keep from the Church everything of a filthy lucre nature, it forbids a priest who undertakes to say Mass for a specified offering, to pass this Mass on to another to say, keeping for himself some portion of this offering.

"§ 6. Moreover, lest in churches burthened for ever with Mass obligations the priests become tepid and slothful in saying them as in justice bound, by reason of their bringing little or nothing with them, it has determined and decreed that money and movable goods to be hereafter acquired with the obligation of Masses by churches, chapters, colleges, hospitals, societies, congregations, monasteries, convents, and all places as well secular as regular and their inhabitants shall, under pain of being interdicted from entry into the church *ipso facto* incurred from the day of the actual acquisition, be immediately set apart in some sacred repository, or under some trustworthy person with the proper authority, to the end that they, or their value, may as soon as possible be invested in interest-bearing real property, with the express and particular mention of the obligations attached thereto.

"§ 7. And if this real property has subsequently to be alienated with the leave of the Apostolic See, the value of the same must under the same penalty be set aside and devoted to some other equal interest-bearing safe investment, with a full account of the obligations attached thereto.

"§ 8. In addition, the Sacred Congregation strictly forbids all chapters, colleges, societies, and congregations, as well as all and each of the superiors of religious places, both secular and regular, or others whom it concerns, to undertake for the future perpetual obligations for Masses, *i.e.*, seculars without the leave and consent given gratis in writing by the Bishop and his Vicar-General, regulars that of the General or Provincial

Let any secular who transgresses this rule be interdicted from entry into the Church *ipso facto;* and any regular incur, without any sentence, the penalty of privation of all the offices he is then filling and perpetual inability to fill any others, with the loss of both active and passive voice.

"§ 26. . . . Let the same be bound *(i.e.*, rectors, superiors, and ministers of all churches whatsoever, whether secular or regular,) to draw up and always keep in an open and obvious place a list of all the perpetual and temporary obligations, written in plain and legible characters.

"§ 27. Let the same also *(i.e.*, rectors, &c., as above,) be bound moreover to keep two books in the sacristy, and carefully and accurately enter in one of them, and see to the other points being entered, each of the perpetual and temporary obligations, and in the other the manual Masses, together with the fulfilment and alms given in both cases, and also to send in to his superior an exact account every year of the aforesaid fulfilments, alms, and obligations."

XXII.—Arrangements to be observed in Priests' Houses.
Ib. xi. p. 50.

1. Presbyteries should be everywhere the true abodes of peace and charity, of sobriety and modesty; in all things a worthy pattern to the faithful, "that he who is opposed may fear, having no evil to speak against us."[1] "Simple cleanliness should appear throughout; and neither in the furniture nor the adornments should there be anything ministering to luxury or to worldly tastes. Ludicrous and foolish pictures or such as are unsuitable in other respects for priests should not be before their eyes; but there should be in every room the figure of our Lord crucified, or of the most Holy Mother of God or of some Saint, or pictures illustrative of the life of our Saviour or of sacred history."[2]

2. There should be regularity in everything. The priest should say Mass at an appointed time; and although he should be always ready to hear confessions, he should especially be at hand in the confessional or at least in the church on the days and at the hours given out, lest through lack of order and method, scandal and loss to souls may arise. Preserve order and order will preserve you.

3. Women should not live in a priest's house without leave of the Ordinary. Schoolmistresses also and pupil teachers should be strictly forbidden ever to live in any presbytery with the priest, unless for some reason known to the Bishop and approved of by him in writing; for these being by their intelligence and education more refined are more exposed to the tongues of calumniators. "But the women who act as servants in the presbyteries should be of advanced years, well known for their modesty, prudence, and irreproachable lives, so that the prescriptions of the canons may be

---

1. Titus ii., 8.   2. I. Westminster xxiv. 9. See p. 150.

kept."[1] And therefore, Priests should beware of certain women who by their domineering ways, their contempt for Christ's poor, and their mischief-making spirit, become real plagues in a mission.

4. "No priests should reside in a rented or in a **private** house without the previous permission of the Bishop."[2]

5. "Whosoever is head of a church, whether he be simply a missioner or possessed of the title of missionary rector, must be regarded as the steward of God to whom a portion of the Lord's vineyard has been entrusted for cultivation. He should, therefore, be useful and faithful, unsparing of pains in all things, remembering that the captain of a ship runs the same risk as to either safety or danger as his freight."[3] Where there are two or more priests at a mission, one of them alone independently of anyone save the Ordinary shall fill the office entrusted to him; but the others in dependence upon him. The assistants receive indeed their faculties from the Bishop; but for the preservation of order we command them to make use of these only with submission to the rector of the church; and hence in the paper of faculties there should be the following or similar words: "dependently upon the rector of the church to which you are appointed."

6. For the Rector has charge of the church and the people, the schools and the presbytery, and all the goods of the mission, and in fine of all the clergy who serve it; and hence he alone and exclusively is accountable for everything to the Bishop. It is true that by law or by custom, all rectors and their assistants usually dwell in the same presbytery; but the presbytery is the rector's house, so long as he discharges the duty of rector and has faculties in the diocese, and to him alone belongs the right of managing and ruling over it. And not the right only, but the obligation as well: "if any one knoweth not how to rule his own household, how shall he have care over the Church of God?"[4] Let him understand, however, of what spirit he is, and how mutual charity and true respect between all the priests should constantly be maintained: he himself, therefore, should be as an elder amongst his assistants, not domineering over them but rather acting as their father or even as an elder brother. But they should be trained and instructed as true ministers of the Good Shepherd, worthy and capable of presiding over a mission in their turn. From the fact, however, that the cure of souls depends chiefly upon the rectors of missions, their assistants should not imagine that they are free from this weighty burthen. For it is their duty, under the rector, to help him by preaching, by hearing confessions, by teaching children the catechism, by visiting the sick and administering to them the sacraments, and by fulfilling the other duties of a missioner.

7. The common table in presbyteries is the mark and sign of fraternal charity, and absence from it lessens this, yea, if frequent, completely banishes it. Rarely, therefore, should they

---

1. Ib. 4. 2. Synod of Thurles. On the life and good estate of the clergy, n. 16, p. 33.
3. 1 Westminster, xxv., See p. 128. 4. 1 Tim. iii., 5.

take meals elsewhere, much less habitually: "having food and raiment, let us with these be content."[1]

Would that regularly at home rather than elsewhere recreation in common were enjoyed by priests. "How good and how pleasant it is for brethren to dwell together."[2] For being present at recreation in common establishes and strengthens charity, and daily brings out opportunities of exercising it by words and deeds.

9. "Priests should keep away from scenes unbecoming the ecclesiastic, from hunting of the noisy kind with horses and dogs, from public dances, from unlawful sports, and from parties that are kept up to a late hour of the night."[3] Moreover, "we strictly prohibit ecclesiastics who have received sacred orders from being present at stage representations in public theatres," or in places temporarily made use of as public theatres, "under the penalty to transgressors of suspension to be incurred *ipso facto*, such as has hitherto been the rule in all parts of England, with reservation to the respective Ordinaries."[4]

10. Priests should have before their eyes that golden axiom of sacerdotal life of the Apostle's, "all things are lawful for me, but all are not expedient,"[5] and also, "all things are lawful for me, but all things do not edify,"[6] and direct all their aims to the good of their neighbours and the increase of grace. They should not readily betake themselves too much or over frequently to places of public resort and amusement, even though of an innocent nature, lest uselessly wasting their time, they become suspected of a want of the sacerdotal spirit. They should at night time be back early at the presbytery unless the call of duty or of charity demand otherwise. For it is of small account to keep themselves from things unlawful, unless, emulous of the better things, they learn how to use things lawful sparingly and to edification. Most affectionately, therefore, do we exhort our well-beloved clergy in the Lord, not to interpret the afore-mentioned prohibitions according to the letter, but with all piety according to the spirit, and to keep them religiously.

11. A harsh and severe temperament is unbecoming in a priest who is labouring amongst the people. A modest cheerfulness, provided it is not out of season, is not to be reprehended but rather encouraged. Hence we give praise to those missioners who following in the footsteps of the saints strive by means of innocent amusements to withdraw the young people committed to their care from dangerous scenes. And in this they should aim at giving recreation to their minds and not at relaxing them; nor whilst endeavouring to give pleasure to others, should they do harm to themselves. And this is especially worthy of note in the case of confraternities of women, amongst whom the amusements should, as far as possible, be managed by other women rather than by the

---

1. Tim. vi., 8.
2. Psalm cxxxii., 1.
3. 1 Westminster xxiv., 1.
4. 1 Westminster xxiv., 2.
5. 1 Cor., vi, 12.
6. 3 Cor., x, 23.

priest in person, lest an opportunity be given to the tongues of calumniators. But priests should check the abuse which is springing up in some places of getting up dances for the purpose of making money for schools or for other good works.

As to those public kinds of amusements called *excursions*, we have heard with grief that a multitude of evils spring therefrom. Hence we consider that they should be rather checked than promoted. However, not to appear to act too harshly in matters of themselves innocent, we advise the pastors of souls to refrain from getting up excursions without the permission of the Vicar-General.

12. "The dress of ecclesiastics should be such as to completely distinguish them from the laity, and yet not render them liable to be mistaken for non-Catholic ministers. It should therefore be black or nearly black; and clerics should not lower themselves by reverting to the dress of seculars they have cast off, even on the plea of travelling. We approve of the style which the secular clergy a few years ago began to make use of. In the house it is particularly becoming for them to wear the cassock, or if they prefer it the zimarra (as it is called,) with the biretta."

"But seeing that the distinguishing mark of the Catholic clergy in almost all parts of the world is the collar, commonly called the Roman collar, and that with Protestants amongst us it is already so regarded without provoking insult or injury, we wish that it be worn by all priests exercising the sacred ministry, unless perhaps temporarily and owing to circumstances it be otherwise enacted by the will of the Bishop. And for the increase of the beauty of the divine worship, as well as for greater uniformity in the sacred offices, we ordain that secular priests, and regulars also who do not wear the peculiar habit of their order, so often as they say Mass, preach the word of God, or in any other way, clad in their sacred vestments, carry on any function of the church or assist therein, shall so conspicuously wear this collar that no part of the shirt shall appear about the neck."[1]

13. To these Decrees this Fourth Synod considers that some additions are needed. We order, therefore, that every priest shall wear the Roman collar, not merely whilst he is fulfilling his sacred duty, but at all times, in order that he may be recognised by all as a priest. We decree likewise that the custom in vogue amongst ecclesiastics in Rome of not wearing whiskers or beard should be strictly followed.[2]

14. And if any priest so completely lays aside the clerical garb, unless in some very rare case approved of by the Ordinary, that he can no longer be recognised by everybody as belonging to the clerical body of this province, and is an object of suspicion to the faithful or of notable scandal, he should not be allowed to say Mass nor to assist in the sanctuary at the divine offices.

---

1. Westminster xxiv., 5 and 6. (See p. 150.)
2. See page 178 and Appendix to IV. Westminster ix., p. 142.

15. It was judged by our forefathers assembled at the Council of London in the year 1248, that to lay aside the clerical dress was an exceedingly great and evil abuse, by which mockery was shewn to God, the glory of the Church beclouded, the high standing of the clerical order lowered, Christ deserted by his soldiers resuming the uniform of another, the honour of the Church tarnished; whilst the beholder distinguishes not the cleric from the laymen, and he becomes to all the truly faithful an object of scandal and contempt. [1]

16. The Bishop of Chalcedon, the second Ordinary after the subversion of the Hierarchy in these realms of England and Scotland, thus addressed our predecessors, who were the fellows of martyrs and themselves true confessors for the faith:—" Let missioners be content with the food that is set before them, and not ask for anything special unless their health requires it. Let them wear nothing in the way of clothing that betokens vanity or expense. And let them refrain from rude laughter and from every kind of action which may savour of dissipation, knowing for certain, as saith Ecclesiasticus, that the attire of the body, and the laughter of the teeth, and the gait of the man show what he is.

Let them shun laziness as the surest source of evil temptations; and therefore have with them the Sacred Scriptures, at least, and constantly meditate thereon.

Let there be no altercations with other priests, especially those who are older; for to these they should pay all reverence and due honour, that by their example they may teach the laity how to treat all priests.

Let them guard against the habit of raising objections to or of contradicting the words of others, which for practice sake they have made use of in the schools; because in private life this is extremely objectionable.

Let them not be ready to believe anything bad of their fellow priests or brethren, nor let them refer to such things before others, nor listen to those who do so." [2]

This is the Letter referred to above:—

On Clerics Wearing the Beard.

Ib. App. ix., p. 142.

LETTER OF THE APOSTOLIC NUNCIO TO THE ARCHBISHOP OF MUNICH.
(Decree xi., 13.)

Most Excellent and Right Rev. Lord.

It has reached the ear of the Holy Father that there are ecclesiastics in some dioceses of Bavaria, who led away by the spirit of novelty, or rather of levity, are striving to introduce again the long obsolete practice of wearing beards, and to entice others by their example to

---

1. Labbe's Councils, Tome xiv., p. 408.
2. Some useful hints for Priests, Seminarists and Missioners of England. By Richard Smith, Bishop of Chalcedon, and Ordinary of England and Scotland. London, 1695.

follow it. Whatever is to be said of bygone days, there is no question that the modern and existing discipline of the Latin Church is altogether at variance with this practice, and that the legitimate introduction of a new custom necessarily requires at least the tacit consent of the supreme Pastor of the Church. But he declares that he completely repudiates any such novelty; and all the more so, because in these sad latter days the spirit of innovation is leading astray not a few, and from one form of novelty it is easy to pass on to others. This being the case, it has pleased His Holiness to command me to notify to all the Bishops of Baravia in his name, that they are to take special care not only to forbid the aforesaid practice but also to keep, or if needs be restore, in all matters and consequently in the dress and tonsure of clerics, uniformity of discipline, as well as complete conformity with the Roman Church, the mistress of all; and to forbid any new custom whatsoever that has not been made clearly known to the Supreme Head of the Church and approved of by Him.

And whilst writing to your most Illustrious and Right Reverend Excellency by command and in the name of the Most Holy Father, I beg of you to let me know when you have received this letter, and to state what your Excellency thinks had better be done that the aforesaid practice, should it have begun to make any appearance in your Diocese, may at once be given up, and that nobody may ever dream of introducing it.

Meanwhile, with sincere feelings of deference and respect,

I remain,

Your Most Illustrious and Right Reverend Excellency's Most humble and devoted Servant,

MATTHEW EUSTACE, Archbishop of Neo-Cæsarea, Apostolic Nuncio.

Munich, June, 1863.

XXIII.—ON PRIESTLY LIFE.

IV. Westminster sii., p. 56.

1. "Those who are not holy, should not deal with holy things."[1] All Christ's faithful, are, according to the Apostle, called Saints;[2] but priests should scale the heights of sanctity. "For a priest by the exigencies of his position has to speak of the highest matters, and must by force of these same exigencies show the highest example."[3] And terrible indeed is the warning:—"He should not rashly make himself the leader in divine light to others, who has not completely and habitually made himself like unto God."[4] "But they who are engaged in the divine mysteries acquire a Regal dignity, and should be of perfect virtue."[5] And this are we taught by the Catholic Church during the solemn rite and in the act itself when the priesthood is conferred. For as

---

1. Council of Carthage.   2. 1 Cor., i, 2.
3. St. Gregory, on the Pastoral Care, p. 2, c. 3.   4. On the Hierarchy of the Church, c. 5.
5. St. Thomas, Fourth Book of the Sentences, Supplement to P. B. Question xl., § 1.

God commanded Moses "to choose as helpers seventy men from the whole of Israel, amongst whom the Holy Spirit should distribute His gifts," so has the Lord Jesus chosen priests of the second grade as helpers to the Apostles, that is the Catholic Bishops, "that by word and by deed he might teach" His Church, "that the ministers of His Church should be perfect in belief and works, in other words, grounded in the virtue of a twofold love, of God that is, and their neighbour."[1] For they have been chosen by God in order that being distinguished for that wisdom which comes from on high, for soundness of character and for a lengthened course of godliness, "keeping the commandments of the law by the help of the sevenfold Spirit, they may be seasoned and ripe in knowledge and in deed," and that they may keep "unimpaired chastity and sanctity of life," and the pattern of perfect justice may be manifested in them.[2]

2. Priests should, therefore, bear in mind that holiness is presupposed in them. "But that simple sanctifying grace by no means suffices for the reception of holy orders, and that interior perfection is requisite in addition, is clear from the common consent of the Holy Fathers and Doctors, who with one accord maintain this."[3] But no kind of sanctity whatever will be deemed by the Church of God and by God the Author of the priesthood as in keeping with priestly perfection, which does not shew marks of likeness to that of the Supreme Priest, our Lord Jesus Christ. For the priest is set before the world as the living image of the life of Jesus, as He endured the straits of seclusion and poverty, and bore with the contradictions of men.

3. Hence the dignity of the priesthood is mainly traceable to two chief sources. For Priests are the beloved companions of Jesus, and share with Him the mission given unto Him by His Father. "As the Father has sent me, I also send you."[4] They are likewise associates in the priesthood of Christ, as well as participators in the twofold power over His natural and mystic Body. For by their sacred order they are appointed "to the highest of all ministries, by which service is paid to Christ Himself in the Sacrament of the Altar; and for this there is requisite a greater interior holiness than even the religious state demands."[5] They are accordingly His friends, and to them in familiar love He spoke: —"I will not now call you servants but my friends; because you have known all that I have done in your midst."[6] And inasmuch as in the dispensation of the Redeemer's grace it has been ordained that God's servants receive the help of the Holy Spirit according to the height of their dignity or the arduous nature of their duty, to none assuredly are given graces more abundant than to the friends and associates in the priesthood and mission of Jesus the Saviour.

---

1. Roman Pontifical. The Ordination of Priests.   2. Ib.
3. St. Alphonsus, Book vi,, n. 3.   4. St. John xx. 21.
5. St. Thomas's Theological Summary, 2nd of the 2nd., q. 184, a. 8.   6. St. John xv. 15

4. How great a love of God and of souls should therefore be enkindled in us, how ardent a fire should inflame our hearts! "The Pastor's flame is the flock's light." [1] For in a priest should live and reign the most holy Heart of Jesus, the principle and source of love and of fervour. Inflamed, therefore, with the fire of zeal for souls, our missioners will strive by accurate teaching to set before the people committed to them God's commandment in its exceeding breadth of fulness of every kind and holiness. They should beware of shewing darkness for light, and of deeming it sufficient to keep Christ's faithful from deadly sin.

5. Since the dividings of the Holy Spirit are manifold and inscrutable, and the faithful are called to various degrees of perfection, some to one, others to another, it is not sufficient for a priest to distinguish clearly "between leprosy and leprosy," without understanding how to distinguish between spirit and spirit; otherwise he may give ear to the spirit of man or even of the evil one instead of the Spirit of God, and thus, led astray himself, may drag others with him. For not only those of the faithful of cultivated intellect, but also uneducated and simple people, are at times called to the highest state of perfection. The director of souls, therefore, should have such a knowledge and skill, if not experience of his own, in the approaches of the heart to God and progress in prayer, as to be able to uphold beginners in the purgative way, direct those who have made progress in the illuminative way, and lead on the more perfect in the unitive way to higher paths. For in every flock there are some who are called by God to the life of the counsels, and who look for a knowledge of the spiritual life to the lips of the priest. Hence, let us strive, lest in the hidden life in God the sheep be found to be out-running the shepherds.

That is a wondrous saying of the Apostle's:—"Christ did not send me to baptize, but to preach the gospel." [2] Accordingly, we have it in the Council of Trent, that the chief duty of Bishops is to announce God's word to men:[3] and that which is chief in a Bishop's duty, must assuredly be regarded as of the utmost moment in all. But as the simple and vigorous announcement of the Gospel is the salvation of hearers, so vain and empty declamation is a scandal to the faithful and ruin to the preacher. The mysteries of the kingdom of heaven must not be treated as subjects for rhetorical exercises or studies in literature. The testimony of the Holy Spirit needeth not the persuasive words of human wisdom, yea, the simplicity of divine truth loathes and rejects the loftiness of our speech, in order that our faith "may not be in the wisdom of men, but in the power of God." [4] Let all directors of souls, therefore, diligently strive to introduce nothing but what is full of simplicity and importance in their treatment of the mysteries of faith, and in their exhortations to piety.

---

1. St. Bernard.
2. 1. Cor., I. 17.
3. Council of Trent, Session xixx. On Reformation, c. 4.
4. Cor. II., 5.

6. Surely difficult is the life of a priest; but yet is he girt about and supported by innumerable means and aids to the acquirement of perfection. For our thoughtful mother the Church, by placing upon the clergy the duty of divine praise, secures and protects for her ministers a term of repose amid their labours of charity. Seven times each day she orders us to raise ourselves heart and soul to the king of the Saints and to the Heavenly Court; and, if by receiving once only the Body and Blood of Jesus men may be turned into saints, nothing can be wanting to make saints of the companions, priests and friends of Jesus, who are fed daily at the Holy Sacrifice of the Mass with the most holy Body and Blood of Jesus. Indeed everything in a priest's life contributes to this end: his daily meditation; his intimate intercourse with the Most Holy Sacrament; his sacred pursuits, almost without interruption; his offices of charity, which while they exhaust the body refresh the soul; his robes also of religion and dignity has he received with the tonsure, the emblems of royalty and perfection.

7. Moreover, special assistance towards acquiring priestly perfection is given us by the Lord, the compassionator of our weaknesses, in our combat in England for the kingdom of truth. For the priesthood of our missioners is entrusted with the care of souls, and consequently all the spiritual graces attached to the pastoral office are theirs. Now they are specially the pastors of Jesus's friends, the poor, "who have no means of paying us;"[1] and they themselves are likewise poor, and kept by and contented with the offerings of the poor. There is also the daily and almost continuous self-denial necessary day and night for lightening the burthens of others, for comforting the sick, and assisting the dying. Finally, there remains both the grace and the privilege of that missionary vow,[2] which they took on the threshold of the apostolate, and by which, in imitation of the oblation made by Jesus on the Cross, they day by day freely offer themselves a living and acceptable sacrifice to God the Father.

8. Wherefore, should it ever happen that anyone should fall off from the manifold graces of his state,—and this may God avert,—he should understand that matters which are of little moment in others must be held of serious importance in the case of priests; oftentimes that which in lay persons is no fault is a sin in those raised to Holy Orders.

Priests, to whom the exercise of their ministry has been forbidden by the sentence of the Ordinary, have no claim upon him for support, since by their own fault they have rendered themselves incapable of working upon missions.[3] However, before sentence of this kind of deprivation is pronounced, the accused should be admonished; and should he not improve, the same process should be followed in his case, as the Sacred Congregation of Propaganda, by its decree of August 4th, 1853, forwarded to

---

1. 1 Council of Trent. 2. See below. 3. Plenary Council of Baltimore ii., p. 57.

the Bishops of England, prescribed previous to the final rejection of a missionary rector.[1]

Form of the Oath taken by those who are Ordained under the title of the Mission.

I. N. son of N. of the Diocese (or Vicariate) of N. promise and swear that when promoted to Holy Orders I will not without special permission from the Apostolic See or the Sacred Congregation of Propaganda, enter any Religious Order, Society, or Congregation, or make any Profession in any one of them.

I likewise vow and swear, that in this Diocese (or Vicariate, or the Mission[2] to which the Holy See or the Sacred Congregation of Propaganda may please to send me), I will ever labour and work for the salvation of souls under the complete direction and jurisdiction of the Right Rev. Ordinary for the time being; and that this I will also do, if by leave of the aforesaid Apostolic See I enter any Religious Order, Society or Congregation, and make my profession therein.

I likewise vow and swear that I understand and will keep the aforesaid oath and its obligation. So help me God and these Holy Gospels of God.

---

1. I. Westminster App. x., p. 137. (See p. 157).
2. Those who are not yet placed at any Mission must use this form.

Notes to the Foregoing Chapter.

Note to page 141.

Most Holy Father,

The Vicars-Apostolic of England prostrate at your Holiness's feet most humbly beg you graciously to allow – by reason of the scarcity of priests and other circumstances – that on those days when, by the Rubrics, high Mass alone should be celebrated, low Mass may be said if it is the parochial or principal Mass, and, as far as possible, the prescriptions of the lesser Ritual of Benedict XIII., of blessed memory, are followed. Wherefore, &c.,

At an audience with his Holiness, March 7th, 1847, our most holy Lord Pius IX., by Divine Providence Chief Pontiff, at the instance of me the undersigned Secretary of the Sacred Congregation of Propaganda, after due deliberation, graciously assented to the request upon all the points asked for, whatsoever to the contrary notwithstanding.

Given at Rome, at the office of the said Sacred Congregation, the day and year as above.

Gratis, without any payment whatsoever, under any pretext.

Place ✠ of Seal.   JOHN, Archbishop of Thessalonica, Secretary.

Decree of the Holy Office with regard to the Administration of the Sacrament of Penance at Sea.

Wednesday, March 17th, 1860.

Seeing that from time to time the faculty which priests going to sea usually obtain from Ordinaries, namely of hearing the confessions of their fellow voyagers, has been discussed by Theologians, and that neither the opinions of Doctors nor even the judgments of the Sacred Congregation had always been one and the same in the matter; and that lately the very question had been submitted, under the form of a doubt, to the judgment of the Supreme Congregation of the Holy Office, on behalf of the Right Rev. the Bishop of Nantes: "*Can priests about to undertake a sea voyage get faculties for hearing confessions of the faithful during the passage from the Ordinary of the place whence they set sail?*" the most Eminent Fathers, the Cardinals Inquisitor-Generals of the whole Christian State, that for the future all occasion for doubt or anxiety with regard to so important a matter affecting the good of souls might be removed, formally discussed the question, and on Wednesday, March 17th, 1860, decreed: "*Priests starting upon a voyage can be approved of by the Ordinaries of the place whence they set sail, so that during the passage they can validly and lawfully hear the confessions of their fellow voyagers, until they arrive at some place where some other ecclesiastical superior holds jurisdiction. But the Ordinaries must beware of giving faculties of this kind to priests who are not recognised as fit according to the prescriptions of the Council of Trent. (Session 23 on Reformation, c. 15.)*" And this resolution, at the instance of the Reverend Father, the Assessor of the Holy Office, at his ordinary audience on the same day, our most Holy Lord Pius by Divine Providence Pope Pius IX., vouchsafed fully to approve and confirm. And the same most Eminent Fathers commanded that this should be the reply given to the Right Reverend the Bishop of Nantes and the other petitioning Ordinaries.

Given at the Chancery of the Holy Office, March 29th, 1860.

Note to page 157.

Dr. Smith in his Elements of Ecclesiastical Law, vol. ii., p. 417, writes in reference to a similar Instruction sent to the Bishops of the United States, as follows:

"The mode of procedure is substantially the same as that existing in England, and also recommended by the late Synod of Maynooth for Ireland, though its application is much wider with us than in England. In England this method was established in 1853, in the following manner: A Committee of Bishops was appointed in the First Provincial Council of Westminster, held July 6th, 1852, for the purpose of preparing a mode of procedure to be followed in deposing a missionary rector from his parish. The method agreed upon by this committee was submitted by Cardinal Wiseman to the Sacred Congregation of Propaganda, and approved by this Congregation by decree of August 4th, 1853; . . . . A comparison of the two documents shows that the Sacred Congregation of Propaganda of Faith took the English document as the model for ours. For the latter is almost word for word the same with the former. The following are the only points of difference: According to the English document, it is necessary that two-thirds of the Councillors should agree on a verdict or opinion; according to ours, it is sufficient that a bare majority should agree. Then again, §§ 8, 10, and 17 of our Instruction are omitted in the English mode of procedure."

"But apart from the form of trial, there are substantial points of difference as to its application with us and in England. In the latter country, at least by the virtue of the First Provincial Council of Westminster, the benefit of the prescribed trial need be accorded only in the case of the final removal of a missionary rector from his parish. In the United States this trial must be given a defendant, not only where a rector (and with us all duly appointed pastors are rectors, whereas in England only a few pastors—namely those of the principal parishes—are rectors), is to be dismissed, but also where a censure or an ecclesiastical punishment or a grave disciplinary chastisement is to be inflicted upon an ecclesiastic, whether he be a rector, or merely an assistant, whether he be a priest, or only deacon or sub-deacon."

He also gives (p. 422) the reply of the Sacred Congregation of Propaganda to certain questions raised by the American Bishops in reference to this Instruction.

CHAPTER THE SEVENTH.

SINGERS AND ECCLESIASTICAL MUSIC.

IV. Westminster, xiii, p. 60.

As of the other things which are wont to be dedicated to the honour of God and by means of which men's affections are upraised to Him, so does the Church take up music, both for more worthily magnifying God, and that by pleasure to the ear weaker souls may be drawn to devotion. For in proportion as man upraises his affections by means of divine praise to God, is he by this means withdrawn from all that is opposed to God.[1] Hence from the very beginning vocal music has found place in the Church, and during the time of the Apostles and for many following ages the whole body of the faithful was accustomed to sing together with the clergy, and to assist by singing and with the responses when the priest celebrated solemnly.[2] But owing to the absence of skill on the people's part as they sang with the clergy, there was discord in the church singing, and the Fathers of the Council of Laodicea[3] decreed, c. xviii., "that no one must sing in the church but the canonical singers, who mount the lectern and sing from the book." Again the Council of Antun decreed,[4] "that it was unlawful for choirs of seculars and young girls to take the singing in the church." In the following century Pope Zachary, in his letter to Pepin, declares, "that it was wrong for women to serve at the holy altars or to take upon themselves any of those duties which pertained to men." The same Pontiff praises the decree of St. Gelasius, and goes on to reject and put down an abuse that was springing up in France. "Nevertheless," he says, "we have heard with annoyance that there is so little respect for the sacred rites, that women are reported to be ministering at the sacred altars, and are attending to those things which have been assigned to the task of men, and for which the other sex is not competent."[5] Accordingly, the ecclesiastical music began to be rendered by clerics alone who were at least of the rank of Lectors, especially after the change or revision of the same made by St. Gregory, Pope. Hence

---

1. St. Thomas, 2nd, of the 2nd, q. 91.
2. Cardinal, Bona or Liturgical Matters, c. xxv., n. 19.
3. A.D., 320.
4. A.D., 578.
5. Labbe's Councils, viii., col. 244; P. Rodotá's Commentary upon Benedict xiv.'s Letter, February 19th., 1749.

the Bishops everywhere took care that the clergy were taught psalmody from their earliest years, and, as history relates, several of the Roman Pontiffs themselves spent their youth in the work of cantorship. Thomassin holds up to admiration the humility of the most holy Pontiff, Gregory, the Great, in these words: "Gregory himself, than whom none even of the Roman Pontiffs penetrated so deeply into the recesses of theological dogmas or the contemplation of things eternal, came to the determination within himself that it would not be degrading to the majesty of the highest and holiest dignity upon the earth and to the kingship of the priesthood, if he should set himself to teach boys ecclesiastical music."[1]

This Gregorian music, which, according to John the Deacon, St. Augustine, the Apostle of England and first Archbishop of Canterbury, brought to our island, greatly flourished there. Nor can there be a doubt but that the disciples of Gregory the Great, the announcers of the divine Word in England, took care to teach the Roman singing to those whom they had converted to the Roman faith. In the seventh century the blessed Benedict, surnamed Biscop, as he was returning to Britain obtained from Pope Agatho at Rome as his companion the chief musician of the Basilica of St. Peter, named John, for the purpose of teaching in his monastery the course of singing for the whole year, just as was practised at St. Peter's in Rome.[2]

And frequently, we find in reading, that of old other nations sent messengers to Rome, and begged books of chants from the Roman Pontiffs, and that some Englishmen held the Roman pratice of singing in such respect that they went to Rome for the purpose of learning it. According to Bede: "Wilfrid an English monk, in the flower of his age, hastened to Rome that he might be trained in the more enlightened rules of piety, of faith, of ritual, and of the chant."[3]

It is therefore abundantly clear that this Roman Chant, handed down to us from St. Gregory, is truly and specially ecclesiastical. Justly, therefore, did Guy of Arezzo write: "He goes directly against the authority of the Church, who sets aside altogether the Chant of Blessed Gregory for other kinds."[4] "For this is the chant," says Benedict, in the passage quoted,[5] "which stirs up the souls of the faithful to devotion and piety."

Clerics used to fulfil this ecclesiastical duty of singing not far from the altar. And therefore it was decreed that at all functions the singers should be clad in a clerical habit or robe. For they who co-operate in the duty of singing are doing the work of clerics, and so should conduct themselves as clerics. And from this it is clear, how opposed to the tradition and practice of the Church is the custom of placing the choir over the principal entrance of the Church.

---

1. On Ecclesiastical Discipline. P. i., l. 2., c. 31., n. 9.
2. Ven. Bede's History of England, B. iv., c. 18.
3. Ven. Bede, B. v., cc. 20 and 21.
4. D. Avena, Reg. Mus., c. 74.
5. Encyclical of Febraury 19th., 1749.

And in this constitution, "*Apostolicum Ministerium*," Benedict XIV. gives us an admonition that in the Seminaries and colleges from which missioners of the secular clergy are sent to England, no exertion or care should be wanting that the students intended for the sacred mission may be as far as possible trained in the Gregorian Chant.

1. In accordance therefore with the traditions of the Church and the authority of the Council of Trent, as well as the decree of the First Council of Westminster, (xxvi., 5, p. 84),[1] we peremptorily order that both the theory and practice of the Gregorian Chant be accurately taught in our ecclesiastical Seminaries and Colleges; so that all clerics, whether at the altar, or in the sanctuary, or in the choir, may know how to sing properly everything that is to be sung either singly, or by the choir, or by everybody, according to the notes in the Ceremonial of the Bishops, the Gradual, the Antiphonary, the Choir Directory, and other ritual books.

2. The Bishops should make it their care, and in union with them the rectors of churches should strive, to restore as far as possible the practice of this most admirable Chant. And hence the Cathedral churches in particular, and the greater churches throughout the Province, should take the lead in rendering the Gregorian Chant in this way. "Let boys also," according to the Decree of the first Council of Westminster, (xviii., 20, p. 68),[2] be taught music in the schools, so that the singing of women in the choir, especially of those hired for the purpose, may be banished from our churches. And thus by degrees it will be brought about (as it is our especial desire) that the whole body of the faithful may be heard singing with voices and hearts in unison."

3. As to the precise nature of this ecclesiastical chant, we renew the Decree of the First Council of Westminster *(xxvi., 5, and xxvii. 1,)*: "That uniformity may be introduced, we wish that in all places, but especially in Colleges, whenever at Mass and the Offices Plain or Gregorian Chant is used, the Roman Chant alone be adhered to"; yet, so, however, as not to forbid any rite and chant there may be, legitimately authorized for a religious order serving any Church, or the use of their own calendar.

But as hitherto a perfect copy of the Roman Chant could hardly or indeed scarcely ever be got, now by the goodness of his Holiness, our Lord Pope Pius IX, there is one ready to hand for anybody. Wherefore, in furtherance of the wish of his Holiness, we adopt by name, as the style for all, that edition of the Roman Chant which is now edited at Ratisbon, that by degrees the desired uniformity may be obtained the Chant in all our dioceses. Thus at length will be brought about what the Chief Pontiff declares he most earnestly desires, "that as in other matters pertaining to the sacred

---

1. See Chapter ix.   2. See p. 141

Liturgy, so also in the Chant, one and the same kind for all places and dioceses may be adhered to, and that the one which the Roman Church makes use of."[1]

4. It is not for us to condemn the use of harmony or figured music, seeing that it has long been introduced into the Church and not condemned by her. Let it not be, however, that music should bring down the vigour of the Christian soul to effeminate softness, for this kind of music even the pagans avoided. "Let the tune or melody," as saith St. Nicetius, "be subservient to holy religion; not that which bursts out into theatrical display, but which shows forth in us true Christianity; not that which savours of the stage but produces compunction in sinners."[2] "Surely there is no one," says Benedict XIV., "who does not wish to see a certain distance kept between the sacred chant and the singing on the stage."[3] Hence as the chant and the singers in the Church, so also is the organ regulated by the practice and laws of the Church as well as by the arrangements of the rector of the Church, but certainly not by the impulses of anyone.

We wish, therefore, and command:—

1. That, as far as is practicable, the laws as to the use and non-use of the organ in the "Ceremonial of Bishops," which is binding everywhere, should be kept.

2. That harmonised singing be severe and simple; that the words be intelligible; that there be no frequent repetition that there be no addition, omission or change in the sacred Liturgy; and "that the singing should be of such a length as not to necessitate an interruption in the course of the Mass, save where the Rubrics so permit."[4] Likewise, the music should as much as possible be in accord with the season of the year and the nature of the Feast.

3. Priests should remember that the custom, still prevailing in some places of alluring Catholics and non-Catholics to the divine office by advertisements and by placards giving the names of the singers and musicians as well as the kind of music and the pieces that are to be sung, is exceedingly opposed to the glory and reverence of the most holy Sacrament of the Eucharist and seriously unbecoming the worship of the omnipotent God. But if invitations and advertisements of this kind are made use of, the name of the celebrant and preacher, the subject of the sermon the purpose of the collection if there is to be one, and those matters that refer to the divine worship should alone be published.

We wish, likewise, that rectors of churches should not themselves publish in the papers, nor allow anyone else to do so, accounts savouring of the theatre and criticisms as to the ability and style of the singers, just as is the practice in connection with the stage.

---

1. See in the Appendix, x., the Apostolic Briefs concerning the Association of St. Cecily and the Ratisbon edition of the Gregorian Chant. 2. Quoted in the Encyclical of Benedict XIV.
3. The Encyclical quoted above. 4. I Westminster xviii., viii, 20.

The following are the Briefs alluded to above.

Ib App. x., p. 144.

ON ECCLESIASTICAL SINGING.

1.—APOSTOLIC BRIEF IN REFERENCE TO THE ASSOCIATION OF ST. CECILY.

PIUS IX., POPE.

For the future remembrance of the matter.

Sacred Music when accompanying the solemn supplications of the church is of much avail towards arousing souls and exciting them to piety, provided it is so composed and performed as to befit the sanctity of the Divine House and the majesty of its rites. In this noblest of arts many have gained the highest praise, whose harmonies adapted as they are to the august splendour of the temple and to the serious character of the ceremonies, in proportion as they are far apart from the profane and enervating style of the theatre, recal the mind from the attractions of human affairs and upraise them to the thought and contemplation of heavenly good. But it is a matter of great regret that these excellent masters in Sacred Music have been set aside, and that in many churches, both in the City and out of it, a kind of music has been introduced truly worthy only of the stage; and therefore, justly blamed and proscribed by canonical law, by our Predecessors, and by Ourselves. Bishops of several Dioceses, whose inhabitants use the German language, revolving this matter, have taken the good and promising resolve of establishing in these Dioceses pious sodalities, taking their name from St. Cecily, with the especial aim of bringing back Sacred Music to an ecclesiastical and pure style. As the model for these sodalities they have wished to take the Congregation called after St. Cecily in this city, and the following rules for their guidance:—

GENERAL STATUTES OF THE ASSOCIATION OF ST. CECILY, ESTABLISHED FOR THE PROMOTION OF SACRED MUSIC IN ALL COUNTRIES WHERE THE GERMAN LANGUAGE IS SPOKEN.

"I. The Association is favoured with the protection of a most eminent Cardinal to be graciously nominated by the Holy Father and the surveillance of the Ordinaries of the Diocese in which the members live. A President-General shall manage the affairs of the Association, with the assistance of Presidents of each Diocese. The President-General shall be appointed in accordance with the statutes especially referring to his election, and with the previous assent of the most Eminent Protector. In addition, the members elect eight gentlemen skilled in music, to search out musical compositions worthy of being produced in God's churches. And this number may be increased to twenty. II. That the end of the Association may be gained, to wit, the promotion of sacred and liturgical music after the spirit of the Church and of the strictest observance of ecclesiastical regulations, it must have a care: 1. That the Gregorian or plain Chant be everywhere studied, and that figured music, in so far as it is in conformity with ecclesiastical law, whether its compositions belong to past or modern times, be encouraged. 2. Sacred hymns, used by the people at their devotions, are permitted so far as the canon law allows. 3. The laws of the Church as to the use of the organ and the permission for other instruments shall be accurately attended to. 4. Inasmuch as in some churches, notably those that are small and in the country, what has been laid down cannot all at once be brought into practice, yet every effort must be made that the liturgical music be brought by degrees to a better state. III. The President-General shall every year send an account to the most Eminent Cardinal Protector of the doings and progress of the Association, and in the same way the Presidents of the Dioceses to the right Reverend Ordinary."

Now seeing that the above-named Bishops on their coming to this City for the Œcumenical Vatican Synod earnestly begged of us to confirm the aforesaid rules by our Apostolic Authority, we most willingly assenting to their petition, took counsel with our Venerable Brothers, the Cardinals of the Holy Roman Church belonging to the Congregation established for ascertaining the lawful Rites of the Church, and in accordance with their opinion, consigned these aforesaid laws for examination and consideration to the distinguished members of what is known by the name of the Council of this City for the Gregorian Chant. This being the case, we received the decision of these gentlemen, and in accordance with the opinion of our aforesaid Venerable Brothers, by virtue of this present letter we, of our Apostolic Authority, approve and ratify the Laws or Statutes of which mention has been made, and which are contained and expressed word for word in this Letter; and to them we give the full weight of our approbation and sanction; decreeing, moreover, that this our Letter remains, and shall remain firm, valid, and efficacious, and that it gains and obtains its full and complete effect, and now and for all times to come imparts its fullest benefits to all concerned, and that thus in all matters as aforesaid, shall judgment and decision be given by all Judges whether ordinary or delegated, even though Auditors of cases connected with the Apostolic Palace, and that it would be invalid and to no purpose if it should happen that any attempt in controvention was made by any one whatsoever, by any authority whatever, whether knowingly or in ignorance. Notwithstanding Apostolic Constitutions and Ordinances, and anything else whatsoever to the contrary. And we wish that to copies of this letter, even to printed ones, when countersigned by some Public Notary and sealed with the seal of some ecclesiastical dignitary, the same credence be given, as would be to the letter itself, were it presented or shewn.

Given at Rome, at St. Peter's under the Fisherman's ring, December 16th, 1870, in the twenty-fifth of our Pontificate.

For the LORD CARDINAL, PARACCIANI CLARELLI,

FELIX PROFILI, Substitute.

2. APOSTOLIC BRIEF UPON THE RATISBON EDITION OF THE GREGORIAN CHANT.

PIUS IX., POPE.

BELOVED SON, Health and the Apostolical Blessing.

Those who have devoted themselves to printing the choir books of the Church and have brought to their work the skill they excelled in, in the art of typography, we deem to have deserved well of the Catholic

Religion, and to have proved themselves worthy of the praise of their Bishops and even of the Roman Pontiffs. Amongst these, you, beloved son, hold a place of honour. For, under the honourable title of Typographer to the Pontifical Court and to the congregation of Sacred Rites, by your splendid editions of ecclesiastical works, and especially by your carefully edited books of the Gregorian Chant, you have never ceased to aid, so far as lay in your art, the Catholic cause, in these grievous times in which we live. And it was most pleasing to us to hear lately that you had brought to completion a beautiful and magnificent edition of the Roman Gradual, as it is called, and that you had produced it after the fashion of the Medici edition and on the lines laid down for you by the Congregation of Sacred Rites. Hence we could not do otherwise than earnestly applaud the labour and industry devoted by you to it; seeing that great profit will thereby accrue to the sacred rites of the Church both in the way of ornament and of utility. And so we earnestly recommend this edition of the said Roman Gradual, which has been completed at your expense and by your labour, to the Right Reverend Ordinaries of all places, and to all interested in the science of music. And this all the more because it is our special wish that, as in other matters that pertain to the Sacred Liturgy so also in the singing, one and the same style as the Roman Church makes use of, should be everywhere followed. Meanwhile, beloved son, while we again and again exhort you in the Lord to keep the path you have commenced to tread and to follow in the footsteps of your past praiseworthy efforts, we look for one more proof of your industry, namely, that you should publish the volumes still to be edited upon the Gregorian Chant, which will complete the edition formerly commenced by our predecessor of happy memory Pope Paul V. And that you may the more readily do this, we by this Letter confirm and, if there be any necessity, again grant all the rights and privileges which have been bestowed upon you by this Holy See through the Congregation of Sacred Rites for your past publications; and at the same time we from our heart impart to you and yours the Apostolic Blessing, as the surest pledge of our goodwill.

Given at Rome, at St. Peter's, under the Fisherman's ring, May 30th, 1873. In the twenty-seventh year of our Pontificate.

P. ✠ S.   FABIUS CARD. ASQUINI.

To our beloved Son, Frederic Pustet, Knight, of the Diocese of Ratisbon, &c.

The following are the Regulations in the *Ceremoniale Episcoporum* (c. xxviii.) referred to :—

1. On all Sundays, and on all festivals of the year on which the people are accustomed to rest from servile works, it is right that the organ and singing should be heard in the churches.

2. The Sundays of Advent (with the exception of the third), and of Lent (with the exception of the fourth) are not included in the above rule. And the third of Advent and fourth of Lent are excepted only as regards Mass. Other exceptions in Advent and Lent, such as great festivals, &c.

3. As the Bishop is entering the Church, when about to sing High Mass or to assist at High Mass celebrated by another; as also, during his

departure at the end of Mass, it is right that the organ should be played.

4. So also at the entrance of Legates, Cardinals, &c.

5, 6, and 7. Rules as to organ and singing at certain canonical hours.

8. At High Vespers it is usual to play the organ at the end of each Psalm; and between alternate verses of the Hymn and of the Magnificat, &c.

9. At High Mass the organ is played (1) whilst the *Kyrie Eleison* and *Gloria in Excelsis* are gone through at the beginning of the Mass; also when the Epistle is over; likewise at the Offertory; also at the Sanctus, &c.; (2) again during the Elevation of the Most Blessed Sacrament—solemnly and softly; also at the Agnus Dei, alternately; and at the Versicle before the Post Communion, and at the end of the Mass.

10. But during the Creed at Mass it must not be played; but the Symbol should be sung out plainly by the choir.

11. But care must be taken lest the organ-playing be of a lascivious or improper character, and lest the singing be foreign to the function that is going on, and much more lest it savour of profanity or folly; nor should there be any other instruments besides the organ.

12. The singers and musicians should likewise be careful lest their singing, which is provided for the increase of devotion, should savour of levity or effeminacy, and so be calculated rather to drawing off the minds of their hearers from the thought of things divine; but it should be devout, distinct, and easy to follow.

13. At Masses and functions for the Dead, we make use neither of the organ nor of figured music, but of plain chant; and this it is proper to observe also on all non-festival days in Advent and in Lent

CHAPTER THE EIGHTH.

REGULARS.

§ 1.

I. Westminster, c. xviii., p. 84.

Since in England those who are bound to regular life live for the most part out of their Monasteries, and that without blame, engaged as they are in the Sacred Ministry, it is expedient likewise that their case should be treated of; yet in such a way as to show that we readily admit and in no way propose to interfere with the privileges and exemptions they lawfully enjoy, either in their houses or out of them.

1. Missionary and public churches served by regulars are subject to the Bishop's visitation. For by him, according to the Holy Synod of Trent, "it is proper that all that pertains to the divine worship in the Diocese should be carefully attended to and provision for wants made."[1] The Bishop, therefore, must keep an eye to these, just as he does to churches served by secular Priests, as regards all matters that concern the divine worship, the administration of the Sacraments, preaching the word of God, and the care of souls generally: yet so as not to prohibit any peculiarities of rite, should there be any, in the celebration of the Mass, lawfully approved of for the order attached to any church, or their keeping to their own calendar.

2. Seeing that serious inconvenience may easily arise from the sudden removal or recall of regular missioners, particularly if this happens against the wish or without any consultation with the Bishop, this Synod earnestly begs the provincials and superiors of orders, for the sake of peace and the salvation of souls, to act cordially with the Bishops with reference to the appointment or removal of their subjects. For as the shepherd knoweth best the face of his sheep and considereth his own flock (Proverbs xxvii.), and since to him the care of the sheep has been committed by the Lord, it seems befitting that what must necessarily be greatly to the harm or to the benefit thereof, should not be arranged without his knowledge, but rather, if possible, with his approval.[2]

---

[1] Council of Trent, Session xxv. c. 8, on Regulars; lib. iii. Decret., tit. xxxvii., De capellis monach, Sec. iii. 18.   [2] See the Letter upon this subject given in the Appendix, n. xxii. (p. 194).

3 A regular priest appointed by a regular superior to any mission or to hear the confessions of seculars, must be presented to the Bishop; and it will be for him to judge of his knowledge of theology, even if he thinks fit by his examiners, before giving him the asked for approbation.

4. Religious men, who are in discharge of the duty of missioners, should excel others in greater strictness of life, contempt of the world, and attention to higher contemplation. Wherefore, as long as they apply themselves to the service of missions, they must be bound by those decrees which we have given above for the protection and confirmation of the clergy in goodness of life. It is therefore to be desired that they should dress as do secular priests, unless they wear the habit of their order; refrain from the same things; and conduct themselves in the same or even a better way.

5. No new religious house shall be founded without the express permission of the Ordinary.[1]

The following is the Letter referred to above.

I. Westminster, Appendix xcii., p. 149.

On the Removal of Regular Missioners.

Most Eminent and Right Rev. Lord,

That the missions in England entrusted to regulars may be properly managed, seeing also that there are not many such missionaries there, the Sacred Congregation, when passing under examination the Provincial Synod, not only approved of the wish of the Bishops in reference to the course to be followed in cases of removal which is contained in Decree xxvii., n. 2., but declared that this course should be specially recommended, and that, moreover, the instruction lately issued for regular missioners in China should be forwarded.[2] The judgment of the Sacred Congregation, with the approval of our Most Holy Lord, is communicated to your Eminence in a special letter which may form portion of the appendix to the decrees of the aforesaid Synod, and together therewith are sent some copies of the said instruction, that the same may be shown by your Eminence to the bishops and the superiors of regular orders.

Meanwhile, reverently kissing your hand,
    I remain your Eminence's most humble and devout servant,

        J. PH. CARDINAL FRANSONI, Prefect.
        AL. BARNABÒ, Secretary.

To the Most Eminent and Rev. Lord Cardinal N. Wiseman, Archbishop of Westminster, London.

---

1. Trid. sess. xxv., cap. 3. *De Regul.*   2. See p. 212.

IV. West., D. xiv., p. 66.

* * * In a reply of the Sacred Congregation of Propaganda approved of by the Supreme Pontiff, and forwarded to the bishops of England and to the superiors of religious orders having missions in England, it was laid down that :—

1. Missionary regulars are not bound to give a return to the bishops of those goods they possess as regulars.

2. The bishops have the right to demand of missionary regulars an account of the goods given to regular missions or to missioners for the benefit of the missions to which they belong, just in the same way as they can exact the same from parochial secular clergy. As to doubtful cases, the Sacred Congregation has decided that the bishops and regular superiors are to arrange them by mutual agreement; or if adverse opinions cannot be reconciled, the case must be referred to the Holy See.

3. In all churches which are served by missioners, whether secular or regular, the sum which is paid for seat rents or for sittings must be approved of by the bishop; and in all other public churches it must be in conformity with the rules laid down in the diocese. Likewise, it pertains to the bishop to determine the amount of space that shall be kept free in the church for the poor.

4. The mission schools are subject, saving the legitimate privileges of regulars, to episcopal visitation, both as regards the buildings and accounts, the discipline and management, and their relation with the civil government. But the buildings, if they do not belong to the mission, are to be exempt from visitation.

The following are the documents referred to above.

IV. Westminster, Appendix, xi., D. xiv., p. 148.

THE TEMPORALITIES OF REGULAR MISSIONERS.

MOST ILLUSTRIOUS AND RIGHT REV. LORD,

The fresh observations made to Propaganda by your Lordship during your stay in Rome last winter, concerning the relations between the bishops of England and the religious attached to English missions were submitted to their most Eminent and Rev. Lordships the Cardinals of this Congregation at a general meeting which took place on April 19th last. Their Eminences, after full consideration of all that had been freshly brought forward by your Lordship, agreed to the following decisions :—

1. Regular missioners are not bound to give an account to the bishops of the temporalities belonging to them as religious.

2. The bishops have the right to demand from regular missioners, just as they can exact from parish priests of the secular clergy, an account of the temporalities given to the missions or to the missionary regulars for the support of the missions to which they belong.

As to doubtful cases the Sacred Congregation decides that the bishops and regular superiors shall arrange matters by mutual agreement, and that whenever the difference between them cannot be thus settled, the question must be referred to the Holy See.

His Holiness, to whom at an audience on May 2nd last the above decisions were referred, graciously vouchsafed to approve of them. Your Lordship will, therefore, please to make them known to your suffragans, whilst Propaganda will do so to the superiors of those religious orders that have missions in England. And I pray that our Lord may long preserve your Lordship.

Rome, Propaganda, July 16th, 1869.

Your Lordship's most affectionate servant,

AL. CARDINAL BARNABÒ, Prefect.
JOHN SIMEONI, Secretary.

The Lord Archbishop of Westminster.

Ib. p. 149.

NOTES TO THE FIRST AND LAST PARAGRAPHS OF DECREE XIV.

1. "No derogation has been made (i.e. by the quotation from the Bull *Firmandis*) from the latest decisions upon regulars in general, nor is the obligation incumbent upon them of giving an account of the revenues of the missions entrusted to them by the bishops as mere incumbents in any way lessened." (From a letter of his Eminence the Prefect of the Sacred Congregation of Propaganda, Aug. 29th, 1874).

2. "When a religious is appointed individually by the bishop to manage a school of the diocese, not in dependence upon the order to which he belongs, but upon the ordinary, he must be regarded as being in the same condition as a simple priest, without any power of falling back upon the privileges of his order." (From the same letter).

Appendix xii. D. xiv. l. pp. 149, &c.

THE TEMPORALITIES AND RESIDENCE OF REGULARS.

MOST ILLUSTRIOUS AND RIGHT REV. LORD,

Their most Eminent and Rev. Lordships the Cardinals of the Sacred Congregation of Propaganda, on the 4th of May last, at a general meeting undertook to examine the important questions which your Lordship and the bishops of your ecclesiastical province have submitted to the Sacred Council, in reference to their relations with the religious of the several orders in England; and they gave special attention to that well-known one which refers to the temporalities administered by religious. * * * Partly in order to preserve with greater security the possessions of the Catholic Church in England, the most Eminent Fathers have ordered the Regulars on their part to furnish an exact account of the temporalities of the different missions administered by them, making a distinction between those goods which are the exclusive property of the same missions, and those which belong to their respective institutes, and that a similar statement shall be furnished by the bishops as to the missions served by the secular clergy. Moreover, his Holiness, to whom the whole of this matter was referred at an audience of May 6th last, has willed that missionary regulars should be reminded through their superiors, that it is their bounden duty to expend upon the missions under their charge whatsoever is over and above, after their own proper support, from the goods under their administration and from the offerings made them by the faithful towards these same missions . . .

Moreover, having discussed at the said general meeting the other doubt—*Are the regular missioners equally with the seculars bound to the observance of the 1st and 2nd Synods of Westminster as to residence?*—the Sacred Council did not hesitate to declare that regular missioners in charge of the care of souls are bound to observe these decrees, and hence to the question referred the reply should be—*Affirmatively.*

Finally, at the same Congregation the notable inconveniences were discussed which arise in England from the number of secularized religious who go about through the several dioceses. And upon this matter the most Eminent Fathers decided that on the one hand the superiors of regulars possessing houses in England should be exhorted to redouble the necessary precautions towards ascertaining every particular concerning the subjects they admit to the noviciate and afterwards to profession. And on the other hand, that the bishops should be urged to avail themselves at proper seasons of their rights in reference to the admission of religious to Sacred Orders, and to the admission into their dioceses of those religious who have obtained an indult of secularization.

All this your Lordship will please to communicate to each of your suffragans for their guidance and instruction, and in conclusion I pray our Lord to preserve and bless your Lordship.

Rome, Propaganda, July 9th, 1868.

Your Lordship's most affectionate servant,

AL. CARDINAL BARNABÒ, Prefect.
JOHN SIMEONI, Secretary.

To Monsignor, the Archbishop of Westminster.

The following Constitution,[1] commonly called the "Romanos Pontifices," has been issued since the last Synod of Westminster, and determines several doubts which had previously existed.

CONSTITUTION OF OUR MOST HOLY LORD LEO XIII. BY DIVINE PROVIDENCE POPE, IN WHICH SUNDRY POINTS OF CONTROVERSY BETWEEN THE BISHOPS AND REGULAR MISSIONARIES OF ENGLAND AND SCOTLAND ARE DEFINED.

LEO, BISHOP,

SERVANT OF THE SERVANTS OF GOD, FOR A PERPETUAL REMEMBRANCE OF THE MATTER.

The warm and paternal love which the Roman Pontiffs Our Predecessors have ever cherished towards the noble English people is evidenced by the monuments of history, and has received a clear and striking proof in the Letters *Universalis Ecclesiae* published by Pius IX., of happy memory, on the 29th day of September of the year of

---

1. As translated in the Tablet with a few alterations.

Our Lord 1850. When by means of those Letters the said Pontiff restored amongst the English the episcopal hierarchy, as far as the circumstances of the times would permit, he placed, so to say, the crowning grace on those favours of which the Apostolic See had been so profuse to that nation. For by the restoration of dioceses that portion of the Lord's flock which had already been called to the espousals of the Lamb and joined to His mystic body, acquired still greater stability of truth and order through the government and rule of Bishops. *For Bishops,* says St. Irenæus, *are the successors of the Apostles, and with the Episcopal succession have received, according to the decree of the Father, the sure gift of truth.*[1] Hence it is, as St. Cyprian remarks,[2] *that the Church is established on the Bishops, and every action of the Church is regulated by these rulers.*

The event has answered in a wonderful manner to this wise resolve; several provincial Councils have been held, at which most salutary laws have been passed regulating the religious affairs of the dioceses: day by day the Catholic faith has been more widely spread, and many persons distinguished by the nobility of their birth and by their learning have been led back into the Church; the clergy has greatly increased in number; so also have the religious houses, not only those belonging to regular orders, but those appertaining to institutions of more recent date, which, by devoting themselves to the training of youth, or to the exercise of works of charity, have deserved well of the christian body and of civil society; pious confraternities of laymen have been established; new missions have been opened and many new churches have been built, enriched with noble ornament and splendid with the beauty of worship; a great many establishments have also been founded for the maintenance of orphans, as also seminaries, colleges, and schools, in which a considerable number of children and youths are trained in piety and learning.

For all these things no small degree of praise is due to the character of the British people, who steadfast and unconquered when opposed by force, readily yield to the voice of truth and reason, so that Tertullian truly said of them "Strongholds of the Britons inaccessible to the Romans are subject to Christ."[3] But the chief meed of praise is due to the constant watchfulness of the bishops, on the one hand, and to the docile obedience and ready activity of all the clergy, on the other.

Nevertheless, from the very nature of things, it has happened that certain difficulties and disagreements which have arisen between the bishops and the members of religious orders have impeded the gathering of more abundant fruits. For whereas in the aforesaid letters of Our predecessor the observance of the common law of the church was enjoined, the former were of opinion they were free to decree whatever appertained to the carrying out of the said law, and which according to the general discipline of the church had been intrusted to the authority of the bishops. On the other hand, many and grave reasons forbade that the special discipline belonging to missionary countries, which had been long in use, should be at once totally abolished. In order, therefore, to remove these difficulties, and put an end to these controversies, the bishops of England, with that deference which they ever show for this

---

1. *Adv. hær.* lib. IV. cap. 26. h. 2.   2. Epist. 29 *ad lapsos.*
3. Lib *Adv. Judæos.* cap. 5.

Apostolic See, addressed themselves to Us, entreating Us to settle these questions by Our supreme authority.

We, on Our part, have not unwillingly acceded to their request, both on account of the good will which We, no less than Our predecessors, cherish towards that noble nation, and also because there is nothing We desire more than to see the occasions of discord removed, and durable peace and mutual charity everywhere flourishing. But in order that We might act with greater weight and caution in giving Our award, not only did We apply Ourselves to a diligent consideration of the laws and authorities brought forward on either side, but moreover We earnestly sought the opinion of a Congregation of some of the cardinals of the Holy Roman Church specially appointed for this purpose and chosen from two sacred congregations, one of which presides over the transaction affairs relating to bishops and regulars, the other over the Propagation of the Christian faith. These, having accurately investigated all the subjects under deliberation, and having weighed the arguments alleged on either side, faithfully laid before Us what it seemed to them in the Lord most equitable and best to determine regarding each of the questions proposed. Wherefore, having taken the opinion of the aforesaid cardinals, and with full knowledge of the cause, We deliver Our supreme judgment on the controversies and doubts proposed, by means of this Constitution.

Manifold and intricate as is the list of matters which come under discussion, they may, nevertheless, in our opinion, all be conveniently ranged under three principal heads, the first of which relates to the exemption of religious bodies from the jurisdiction of the bishops; the next regards the ministrations performed by missionary regulars; and the third embraces questions on temporal goods and the use to which these are to be devoted.

As regards the exemption of regulars, the rules laid down by canon law are positive and well-known. To wit, although in the ecclesiastical hierarchy, as by *divine ordinance* established, priests and ministers are inferior to bishops and subject to their authority,[1] nevertheless the better to connect and fit together all things appertaining to the religious orders, and to secure for each of their members a quiet and orderly method of life, in order, lastly, to provide for the increase and perfecting of *religious conversation*,[2] the Roman Pontiffs, whose right it is to fix the limits of dioceses and to assign to the head of each diocese the subjects to be ruled by his sacred authority, has not without reason ordained that the regular clergy shall be exempted from the jurisdiction of the bishops. The reason for which ordinance is grounded, not on any wish that the religious bodies should enjoy a higher position than the secular clergy, but on the circumstance that their houses are regarded by a legal fiction as if they were territories cut off from their diocese in which they are placed. Hence it happens that religious communities which by common law ought to be immediately subject both to the Bishops on account of their hierarchical pre-eminence, and to the Supreme Pontiff by reason of the Papal Primacy,[3] have remained under the power of the latter, and have by privilege passed out of that of the Bishops. But since, as a matter of fact, the Religious lead their lives within the limits of the

---

1. Council Trid Sess 23, *de Sacram ord.* con. 7.
2. Gregor. M. Epist. III. lib. ix.—Bened. xiv. Epist. Decret. *Apostolicæ servitatis*, prid. Idus Mart. 1742.
3 Concil. Vatic, Constit. *Pastor æternus*, Cap. 3.

diocese, the action of this privilege has been so far modified as to preserve intact diocesan discipline, so that in many things the Regular clergy must be subject to the authority, whether ordinary or delegated, of the Bishops.

Now, as regards this privilege of exemption, a doubt has been raised whether it be enjoyed by the members of Religious bodies dwelling as missionaries in England and Scotland, inasmuch as these reside for the most part two or three together, and sometimes alone, in private houses. And although Benedict XIV., in his Apostolic Constitution, begining with the words *Apostolicum Ministerium* and dated the 30th of May, A.D. 1753, has declared that the aforesaid missionaries were in the enjoyment of that privilege, the Bishops nevertheless considered that there was some doubt whether they did so at present, inasmuch as, since the restoration of the episcopal hierarchy, Catholic affairs were to be governed in those parts in conformity with common law. Now, common law provides [1] that houses occupied by Religious men in number less than six shall be altogether under the power of the Bishops. Moreover, the author of that very Constitution seems to have declared that the reason for which the privilege was granted was on account of the " civil laws of the kingdom . . . according to which all communities were forbidden"; but this reason is well-known to have ceased to exist, since, for many years past, it has been lawful according to the laws of that kingdom for Religious men to live in communities.

Nevertheless these reasons are not such as to lead Us to judge that the privilege has really ceased to exist. For although the re-establishment of the Hierarchy has the effect of *rendering possible* the adoption of the ordinary discipline of the Church in the management of Catholic affairs amongst the English, nevertheless things continue to be managed there as yet very much in the same manner in which they are managed in missions. Now the Sacred Congregation of Propaganda has repeatedly declared that the Constitutions of Clement VIII., *Quoniam* dated 23rd of June, 1603 ; of Gregory XV., *Cum alias*, dated 17th August, 1622 ; of Urban VIII., *Romanus Pontifex*, dated 28th of August, 1624 ; as also the Constitutions of Innocent X., are not to be understood as applying to houses and residences in missions. [2] And rightly so ; for when long ago the doubt was proposed to Clement VIII., whether Religious men sent to India for the good of souls were to be considered as leading extraclaustral lives, and therefore, as ordered by the Council of Trent to be subject to the Bishops, that Pontiff decreed by the Constitution *Religiosorum quorumcumque*, dated the 8th of November, 1601, "that they were to be reputed as Religious living in convents ;" wherefore " that in all things concerning the cure of souls they were under the local Ordinary ; but in others matters they remained subject not to the local Ordinary but to their own superiors." Such was also the opinion held by Benedict XIV., and the award given by him in his Constitutions *Quamvis*, dated the 25th of February, 1746 ; *Cum nuper*, dated the 8th of November, 1751 ; and *Cum alias*, dated the 9th of July, 1753. From all which things it is clear that even residences and houses tenanted by ever so small a number of inmates are comprised under the terms of the privilege here

---

1. Innocent. X. Constit. *Instaurandae*, die 15 Octob, 1651. Constit. *Ut in parvis*, die 10 Februar. 1654.
2 Cong. de Prop. fide 30 Jan. 1627 ; 27 Mart. 1631 ; 5 Oct. 1655 ; 23 Sept. 1805 ; 29 Mart. 1834.

referred to, and that not only in places where there are Vicars-Apostolic but in those also presided over by Bishops; for it is Bishops that are spoken of in the Constitutions alluded to. Moreover, it appears that the chief ground for exemption of missionary Regulars in England is to be sought, not in the opposition raised by the laws of the country to the erection of convents, but rather in that salutary and most noble ministry exercised by apostolic men. This is not obscurely pointed out by Benedict XIV. when he says that "the Regulars sent on the mission in England go there for the advantage of our holy religion." The same reason was adduced by Clement VII., when, speaking of the Religious men who had started for India, he explained that they had gone there by order of their own superiors, and lived there under the rule of the prefect of the province "in order to preach the holy Gospel of God, and to show forth the way of truth and salvation." Wherefore, after the repeal of the laws hostile to the Religious Orders, and after the full restoration of the Catholic Hierarchy, the British Bishops themselves bore witness in the first Synod of Westminster that they held as valid the privileges "lawfully enjoyed by Religious men both in their own houses and outside the same," although "in most cases they dwell outside monasteries."

Wherefore, also in the present condition of the Catholic Church in Great Britain, We hesitate not to declare: That Regulars dwelling in residences on the mission are exempt from the jurisdiction of the Ordinary, no less than Regulars living within cloisters, except in cases expressly mentioned by the law, and, speaking generally, in those matters that have reference to the cure of souls and the administration of the Sacraments.

Akin to this main controversy which We have decided, is another regarding the obligation of Rectors of missions to whom is confided the cure of souls, their vicars, and their other Religious brethren furnished with faculties such as are usually granted to missionaries, to attend those meetings of the clergy known as *Conferences* as also at the diocesan Synods. The better to understand the force and bearing of this question, it will be well to recall what the Fourth Council of Westminster ordains in the following words: "If two or more than two priests reside in the same mission only one of them shall be denominated head priest, and shall be charged with the cure of souls and the administration of the church . . . all the others shall exercise the cure of souls confided to them dependently on the first."[1] The nature of the fact about which We are treating being thus made clear, and setting aside for the present that portion of the question which relates to Synods, it cannot be called in question that the Rectors of missions are bound to attend the meetings of the clergy called *Conferences*. For their case is almost the same as that of a parish priest; and Benedict XIV. in his Constitution *Firmandis*, § 6, dated 8th Nov., 1744, and the Sacred Congregration presiding over the interpretation of the decrees of the Council of Trent have repeatedly declared that parish priests, even when Regulars, are so bound to attend.[2] Wherefore it was rightly decreed in the aforesaid Synod of Westminster that "all secular priests, and regulars also (saving their rights) who have the care of souls, are bound to attend their respective Conferences." It may seem to be otherwise as regards vicars

---

1. Dec. n. 10.   2. *Forasmproniem.* 5 Sept. 1650, Lib. 19 Decret.

and other Religious men exercising the apostolic ministry. For, according to the *established law*, these are free to absent themselves from the said Conferences, according as the Sacred Congregation of the Council has on other occasions declared.[1] But it does not escape Our memory that the Roman Council, held in the year 1725 by authority of Benedict XIII., ordered all Confessors, even belonging to Regular Orders, residing within the province, to take part in those meetings, "unless moral lectures were held in their own convents." But inasmuch as that which is ineffectually done may be considered as not done at all, the Sacred Congregation of Propaganda, rightly judging that in certain missionary localities the domestic conferences of Regulars could bear but little fruit owing to the very small number of members who could attend, gave orders that all and each of those who exercise that office should attend the conferences of the clergy. Moved therefore by these reasons, We declare that all Rectors of missions are bound by their office to attend the Conferences of the clergy, and moreover We ordain and command that vicars also and other Religious men holding ordinary missionary faculties and who live in residences and in small mission-houses shall do the same.

As regards the duty of attending Synods, the Tridentine law is well known :[2] "Diocesan Synods also shall be held each year, at which all, even exempt, persons, who otherwise would be bound to attend if the exemption ceased, and who are not subject to General Chapters, are bound to be present. Those who have charge either of parochial or other churches of seculars, even if annexed, whoever they may be, are bound on account of the said churches to be present at the Synod."[3] And this law has been admirably explained by Benedict XIV. Nor do We imagine that any difficulty can arise on account of a decree of Alexander VIII. dated 30th March, 1691, wherein all abbots, rectors, prefects, and all superiors of Religious houses who had been subjected by Innocent X. to the power of the Bishop are forbidden to go to the Synod. For inasmuch as the Innocentian Constitution has no reference to apostolic men who are employed in sacred missions, it is easy to see that neither does the decree of Alexander VIII. affect those persons of whom we are at present treating, Wherefore to this latter part of the question We briefly reply ; let the decrees of the Council of Trent be observed.

Next in order comes a question regarding appeals made from the interpretation published by the Bishop of Synodical decrees. For Religious men, no less than others, are required to render obedience to such decrees in matters regarding the cure of souls and the administration of the Sacraments, as well as in other things[4] "in which the Canon Law bids them to submit to the jurisdiction of the Bishops."[5] There cannot, indeed, be any doubt that it is lawful to appeal from such interpretations to the Apostolic See, "for Gelasius I.[6] and Nicholas I."[7] assert that the Canons "authorise an appeal to this See from whatever part of the world it may come, whilst, on the other hand, nobody is allowed to appeal from its decisions." A doubt, therefore, can only be

---

1. *Firmismprovica*, 12 Maii 1681 Lib. 53 Decr. fol. 258. *Aquipendien* VV. SS. LL. 12 Mart. 1718.
2. 24 cap. 2 *de reform*.   3. De Synod. dioec. lib. 3. cap. 1 § 11.
4. Concil Trid. sess. 25. cap. 11 *de regular*.   5. Innoc. IV. Cap. 1. *de privileg*. in 6.
6. Epist. 7. *ad Epise. Dardan*. anno 495. Tom. 2 collect. Harduini.
7. Epist. 8. *ad Michael Imperat*. Tom. 5 collect, Harduini.

raised as to the force and the effect of such an appeal. But such a doubt may easily be removed, provided a proper distinction be made between different causes. Thus it is lawful for Regulars to appeal, but only *in devolutivo* [*i.e.*, without arrest of judgment] in the case of an interpretation of such decrees as by common law either ordinary or delegated affect also Regulars; and in the case of the interpretation of other decrees also *in suspensivo* [*i.e.*, with arrest of judgment pending the appeal]. For the authenticity of an interpretation issued by the Bishops, with whom the Synods originate, is on a par with that of the decrees themselves. It follows, therefore, as a necessary consequence, that members of a Religious body may appeal from the first class of decrees referred to by the same right, and in the same manner that it is lawful for any member of a diocese to appeal from the common law; that is to say, *in devolutivo*.[1] But as regards other decrees, they certainly, when issued against Regulars, lose the force and essence of law: and so it is certain that the Regulars retain their exemption from Episcopal jurisdiction the same as before, until such time as the authority of the Supreme Pontiff shall decide whether they have been dealt with according to law or otherwise.

Thus far regarding the privilege of exemption: We shall now proceed to treat those questions to which certain ministrations exercised by Regulars have given rise. Foremost amongst these is the office of the cure of souls, which, as already noticed, is often deputed to Religious men within certain limits prescribed by the Bishops. The district comprised within those limits is designated *a mission*. Now a controversy has arisen with regard to these missions, whether, and in what manner, they may be by the Bishop divided, or, as the phrase is, dismembered. For they who maintained the rights of the Regulars denied that such division could be made except for legitimate reasons, and subject to the legal formalities prescribed by Alexander III.,[2] and by the Council of Trent.[3] The Bishops, on the other hand, held a different opinion.

Of course, where the case is one of dividing a parish properly so-called, whether of ancient origin or legally constituted within a recent period, it is undoubtedly unlawful for the Bishop to disregard what is prescribed by the Canon Law. But the British missions, generally speaking, have not been erected into parishes in the way marked out by law: and for this reason the Sacred Congregation of Propaganda Fide, in the year 1866, decided that the duty of applying the Mass for the people rested with the Bishop, inasmuch as the British dioceses were not constituted in such a way as to be distributed into real parishes. So that the customary legal formalities which have been drawn up for the dismemberment of parishes must not be applied to the division of a simple mission: the more so because, owing to the nature of the missions and their special circumstances, more numerous and less weighty reasons may present themselves in favour of their being divided, than those which have been laid down by law as necessary for the division of parishes. Nor should the similarity existing between the two be urged; for the obligation of observing the customary formalities of law being a check

---

1. Bened. XIV. de Synod. Diœc. Lib. 13. Cap. 5, § 2.
2. Cap. *ad audientiam* de eccles. ædific. 3. Sess 21. Cap. 4 *de reform*.

upon freedom of action, it must not be drawn into a precedent for cases that are similar. Therefore as the general laws of the Church are silent on this subject, the authority of the Provincial Council of Westminster must be enforced, which decrees as follows: "Notwithstanding the appointment of a missionary rector, the Bishop shall be at liberty, with the advice of the Chapter, to establish within the limits of the mission which has been intrusted to the charge of the said rector new churches, and to assign to them a part of the district if necessity or the good of the faithful require it." Under these circumstances, to the question proposed We reply: The Bishops are at liberty to divide Missions, provided they keep to the form laid down by the Sacred Council of Trent,[1] in respect to missions which are really and properly so-called parishes; but in respect to all the others, provided they act in conformity with the First Provincial Synod of Westminster.[2] Moreover, in order that the interests of the mission and those who serve it may be the better provided for, We will and ordain that the opinion of the rector shall likewise be asked for, which laudable practice, as We are informed, is already customary: and if the mission is served by members of a Religious body, then shall the Superior of the Order be consulted: leaving intact the right of appealing, if the matter requires it, from the decree of the Bishop to the Holy See, but only *in devolutivo*.

Another question arises where the dismemberment of a mission in charge of Regulars has been effected—whether namely, the Bishop, in the appointment of a Rector to the newly created mission, is bound to give the preference to the members of such Religious body. Although the latter claim this as their right, it is easy to foresee that such a claim would give rise to difficulties and disagreeable incidents. Besides in the case of the new erection of which we are now speaking one of two things must happen; that is to say, either a parish properly so called, or else a simple mission, is being established. If the former, then to select a parish priest from a Religious community and give him the preference would be most contrary to the discipline of the Church; for by the law now in force so strictly are Regulars inhibited from accepting the office of parish priest that before accepting it they require the leave of the Holy See. On this point Benedict XIV., in the Constitution *Cum nuper*, dated November 8th, 1751, says, "Just as it cannot be denied that, according to ancient canon law, monks and Regulars were eligible for the charge of parochial churches, so it is now certain that in virtue of more recent canonical discipline Regulars are forbidden to take charge of parishes without a dispensation from the Apostolic See." Hence the Sacred Congregation appointed for the interpretation of the Tridentine Decrees,[3] in reply to the question "whether the petition of the Augustinian Fathers to have a new parish assigned to them should be complied with," issued a rescript in the negative, directing that the matter should not be again brought forward. But if (as named in the second place) a simple mission has to be formed, it is true that the law is not so far adverse to the Religions as to forbid the Rector being chosen from amongst them, but neither does it favour their claim to be chosen in preference to others. The Bishop, therefore, on approaching the question

---

1. Cap. 4, sess. 21 de reform.   2. *De regimine congregationum seu missionum*, n. 5.
3. In Iannen. *Dismembrationis*, XXV. Januarii. MDCCCLXXIX.

finds it and his power untouched, and is free to follow his own choice; for when the law is silent the authority of the Bishop stands in the place of law; the more so as, according to the adage of the jurists, *that which is in the mind of the Bishop has the support of the law* in all matters that regard the administration of his diocese. Hence the claim put forward by the Regulars to the presidency of the new mission is either destitute of all support in law or else runs counter to what the law clearly enacts.

The duty of the cure of souls, as confided to the care of the Regulars, gives rise to further doubts. These have reference to places comprised within the limits of missions under their charge. For it began to be questioned whether the Bishop had a right to visit the cemeteries and pious establishments existing within those limits. But as regards cemeteries, an easy distinction readily presents itself which settles the controversy. For if there be question of cemeteries exclusively reserved for the interment of Religious communities, they are clearly exempt from the jurisdiction of the Bishop and, consequently, from his visitation; but other cemeteries which are open to the multitude of the faithful, inasmuch as they are of the nature of parochial cemeteries, are beyond all doubt subject to the jurisdiction of the Ordinary, and therefore are of full right visited by the Bishop, as Benedict XIV. decreed in his Constitution *Firmandis*, dated Nov. 6, 1744. So the question regarding pious establishments is settled by making a similar distinction, and separating such as are exempt from such as are subject to the Bishop, either by ordinary or by delegated right. Therefore, both as regards cemeteries and pious establishments, We briefly pronounce Our decision, which is, that the regulations of the Sacred Canons and of the Apostolic Constitutions be observed.

Closely connected with the preceding doubts is that other in which the question is proposed, whether poor schools, called *elementary*, *primary*, or *children's* schools, should be subject to the Bishops; for the ministry of teaching is most sacred, and the schools in question occupy a rank very closely allied to pious establishments. The scope of these schools is discernible from their very name. They are directed, that is, to the due instruction of young children in the first elements of letters, and the primary truths of faith and precepts of morality: an instruction which is necessary for all times, places, and kinds of life, and is of the greatest importance to the well-being, no less of human society in general, than of individuals; for on the education which a man receives in childhood depends, for the most part, how he will behave during the rest of his life. Pius IX. therefore wisely set forth the chief duties of teachers in such schools when he wrote: " In these schools especially all children of every class of the people, even from their tender years, are to be carefully instructed in the mysteries and precepts of our most Holy Religion, and carefully formed both to piety and moral virtue, and to the duties of religion and civil life: and in these schools religious doctrine in particular ought to hold so primary and dominant a place in instruction and education, that all other kinds of knowledge which are there imparted to the young should plainly appear to be merely accessory to this."[1] Hence it is obvious to every one that this education of children must be ranked

---

1. Epist. ad Archiep. Friburg. *Cum non sine maxima*, 14 Julii, 1864. Acta vol. 3.

among the duties of Bishops, and that the schools in question, whether in populous cities, or in small villages, are comprised among those works which belong in the strictest sense to the management of the diocese.

Moreover the dictates of reason are confirmed by the light of history. For there never was a time in which the care of Councils in establishing and fostering such schools has not been singularly conspicuous, and they have made many wise ordinances concerning them. Thus by the decrees of Councils it has been provided that Bishops shall cause these schools to be restored or increased, both in towns and villages,[1] and that children shall be admitted as scholars, if possible, without any payment whatsoever.[2] By the same authority regulations have been made for the training of the pupils in religion and piety;[3] the qualifications and dispositions which the masters ought to possess have been defined;[4] and these have been commanded to make sworn profession of the Catholic Faith;[5] lastly, inspectors of schools have been appointed to visit them, and observe carefully that nothing faulty or unsuitable be introduced, nor anything omitted which the laws of the diocese have enacted concerning the discipline to be maintained.[6] In addition to this, as the Fathers of the Councils were well aware that parish priests also are participators in the pastoral ministry, they assigned to these no small part of the management of the children's schools, the care of which is so intimately connected with the care of souls.

It was ordained therefore that in every parish schools for children should be established,[7] which were styled *parochial schools*;[8] parish priests were commanded to undertake the duty of teaching, and to associate to themselves masters and mistresses as assistants;[9] they were required to exercise the utmost diligence in the direction and care of their schools;[10] should these functions not be performed with fidelity and completeness they are charged with having neglected their duty,[11] and held to be deserving of Episcopal censure.[12] Arguments therefore derived from reason and from facts converge to prove that the so-called poor schools are by special legal right to be numbered among diocesan and parochial institutions; and for this reason, the British Bishops down to the present time, both in Regular and Secular Missions, have been accustomed, as far as was in their power, to visit them. And this We also approve, and declare that Bishops have the right to visit in regard to all things such poor schools in the missions and parishes of Regulars just the same as in those of Seculars.

Quite different is the case of other schools and colleges in which Religious men, according to the rules of their Order, devote themselves

---

1. Synod. I. Provincial. Camerac. tit. *de scholis* cap. 1. Synod. provinc. Mechlin. tit. *de scholis*. cap. 2.
2. Synod. Namurcen. an. 1604. tit. 2. cap. 1.
3. Synod. Antuerpien. sub. Mirco tit. 9. cap. 3.
4. Synod. Cameracen. an. 1550.
5. Synod. II. Provinc. Mechlinien. tit. 1. cap. 3.
6. Synod. II. Provinc. Mechlinien. tit. 20. cap. 4. Synod. provinc. Pragen. an. 1860. tit. 2. cap. 7.
7. Synod. Valens. an. 529. can. 1. Synod. Nannet. relat. in cap. 3. de vit. et hon. clericor.—Synod. Burdigal. an. 1583. tit. 27.
8. Synod I. Provin. Mechlin. tit. *de scholis* cap. 2. Synod. Provin. Colocen. an. 1863. tit. 6.—Synod. Provin. apud Maynooth, anno 1875.
9. Synod. Namnet. sup. cit. Synod. Antuerp. sup. cit. Synod. Prov. Burdig. an. 1850. tit. 6, cap. 3.
10. Synod. Prov. Vienn. ann. 1858. tit. 6, cap. 8. Synod. Prov. Ultraject. an. 1865. tit. 3, cap. 2.
11. Synod. Prov. Colocen. an. 1863. tit. 6, cap. 5. Synod. Prov. Colonien. an. 1860. tit. 2. cap. 23. Synod. Prov. Ultraject. an. 1863. tit. 9, cap. 5.
12. Synod. I. Prov. Cameracen. tit. de scholis, cap. 2.

to the education of Catholic youth. For in these both reason requires, and Our will is, that the privileges bestowed upon them by the Apostolic See should remain firm and entire, as was plainly declared in the year 1874, by the Sacred Congregation of Propaganda, when revising the acts of the Fourth Provincial Council of Westminster.[1]

This much being settled with respect to the schools and colleges of the Regulars already established, a doubt still remains when it is a question of opening new ones. In the case of these is the permission of a superior to be obtained? and of what superior? Moreover since this doubt has a wider extension, and affects also the establishment of churches and monasteries, we comprise all these within the limits of one question and decision. And here in the first place we are met by the ancient Decretals,[2] in which it is provided that no such institution be established by any one without special permission of the Apostolic See. Subsequently the Council of Trent forbade any establishments of this kind to be undertaken without first obtaining the license of the Bishop in whose diocese they are to be erected. But by this decree of the Council no derogation was intended to be made from the more ancient laws, which require that permission be obtained from the Apostolic See.[3] Wherefore, as too great freedom in this matter was everywhere prevalent, Urban VIII.,[4] with the view of amending this irregular practice, disapproved of all works of this kind undertaken either without the permission of the Bishop, or by his sole authority; and decreed that the laws as well of the ancient canons as of the Council of Trent should be absolutely observed for the future. In the same sense Innocent X., in the Constitution *Instaurandæ*, Oct. 15th, 1652, forbade any member of a Religious Order "to presume to receive or found new houses or establishments of whatever kind without special permission of the Apostolic See." Wherefore it is now the common opinion, supported also universally by the authority of judicial decisions, that it is not lawful for Regulars, whether within or without the limits of Italy, to found new monasteries, convents, or colleges, with the sole permission of the Bishop, but that there is further required a faculty from the Apostolic See.[5] Following the same track, the Sacred Congregation of Propaganda has several times decreed, that for the erection of churches and colleges, even in missions where Religious Orders possess houses and residences, the permission of the Apostolic See and of the Bishop or Vicar Apostolic is absolutely necessary.[6] For these reasons, therefore, We reply to the doubt proposed, that it is unlawful for Religious Orders to create for themselves new establishments, by erecting new churches, or opening monasteries, colleges, or schools, without having first obtained the express license of the local Ordinary, and Apostolic See.

It is usual, indeed, to raise a more subtle point, and to ask whether this twofold consent is necessary when a religious body is not undertaking a work that is entirely new, but wishes to apply to other purposes an existing foundation. But the answer to be given is neither obscure

---

1. Decret. 26.
2. Cap. Religiosorum, § *confirmatus de relig. domib.* et cap. *Ex eo de excess. prælat.* lib 6.
3. Concil. Trident. sess. 25., cap. 3 *de Regular.*
4. Constit. Romanus Pontifex xiii. Kalen. Septembris, 1624.
5. Bened. xiv., *de synod. diœces.* lib. 9, cap. 1, num. 9. Monacelli *formul. legal.* part 1, tit. 6, form. 19, num. 31.
6. Sac. Congreg. de Prop. Fide in cœtibus habitis diebus 22 Martii 1669; 3 Nov., 1668, 1704, 1768; 23 Aug. 1858; 30 Maii 1864; 17 Julii 1865.

nor doubtful, if we discriminate between the various cases that may present themselves. For, in the first place, who can entertain a serious doubt as to whether it is lawful to apply charitable and religious foundations to uses alien to charity and religion? Therefore we have to confine our inquiry to the following three points, namely, whether it is allowable to remove foundations from one place to another, or to divert them to some kindred use, such as would be the change of a school into a church, of a Religious house into a college, an orphanage, or a hospital, or *vice versâ*; or, lastly, whether, while keeping such establishments to their original use, it would be permissible to unite therewith some new scope or use? Now, as to the first two cases, members of Religious bodies are inhibited from acting on their own private authority by a decree of Boniface VIII., who forbade them "to receive in future dwelling-houses or places of any kind whatever, or to make a change in those already in their possession."[1] How, again, is it possible to do either the one or the other without such act being tantamount to a fresh foundation "of Monasteries, Colleges, houses, convents, and other erections of this kind?" But this was prohibited by Urban VIII. in his Constitution *Romanus Pontifex*, unless "in perfect conformity with the Sacred Canons of the Council of Trent." Therefore, one point alone remains for discussion; whether, while keeping to the existing use, it is permissible to add thereto another scope or use. In this case, it is necessary to press the question still further, and to examine carefully whether such additional use regards internal administration and domestic discipline, as when an elementary school or house of studies is set up in a Monastery for the benefit of the younger members of the community; or whether it goes beyond the limits of internal administration, as when, for instance, a school or college is there set up for the admission of externs likewise. It is clear that if those limits are transgressed the proceeding is identical in character with one or other of those which, as we have said, Boniface VIII. and Urban VIII. prohibit being done at will. But if the change be confined within the limits of domestic discipline, Regulars will, of course, avail themselves of their right: unless it should happen that the conditions of the foundation are contrary thereto. Taking all these several considerations into account, it clearly results that members of a religious body are not allowed to convert existing institutions to other uses without the express permission of the Apostolic See and of the Ordinary of the place, except in the case where the conversion regards merely internal government and Regular discipline, the conditions of the foundation being left intact.

We now come to that part of the controversy which relates to the discussion about the temporal goods of the missions. These goods have their origin in the generosity of the faithful, who, in the spontaneous and voluntary bestowal of their gifts, have in view either the mission or else the person who has charge of the mission. Where the donation has been made with a view to the mission, it is debated whether the Religious to whom the donation has been made are bound to give an account of receipts and expenses. Now that this is obligatory results from the following words of the Rescript published by the Sacred Congregation of Propaganda, April 19th, 1869, in answer to a question proposed in

---

1. Cap. *Cum ex eo de excess. prælat.* in 6.

reference to Missions in Great Britain intrusted to Religious Orders or Institutes: 1st. Missionary Regulars are not bound to give an account to the Bishops of temporal goods belonging to them as *Regulars*. 2nd. The Bishops, however, have the right to exact from the said Missionary Regulars, just the same as from the parish priests of the secular clergy, an account of those goods which have been given to the mission, or the Regulars *with a view to the mission.*" And in order that an accurate account might be kept of receipts and expenses, the said Sacred Congregation, on May 10th, 1868, had given orders for a careful description of the property of the missions, setting forth such as belonged to the missions separately from those which belonged to the Religious bodies or the individual members.

There was nothing in these decrees and injunctions in the least at variance with the commonest teaching of general law. For any offering whatever made to a parish priest or other Rector of a church with a view to some pious purpose accrues to the purpose itself. And hence it follows that he who receives the thing or sum of money offered holds the place of administrator, and is bound to dispose of it according to the mind and intention of the donor.[1] But as the office of administrator involves the obligations of drawing up an account of what he has done, and presenting it to the person in whose behalf it has been done,[2] therefore the parish priest or Rector of the church cannot but give an account to the Ordinary of the place, to whom belongs the jurisdiction and the guardianship of the pious purpose.[3] But the missions, about which we have been appealed to, belong to the Bishop *pleno jure* (of full legal right); to him, therefore, must an account be rendered of any offering whatever that has been received for their benefit. Nor is the force of what we have just said weakened by the fact that Urban II. in the Council of Clermont, and other Roman Pontiffs after him, have decreed[4] in reference to parochial churches, united to monasteries as to the temporalities, that the vicars are bound to account to the Bishops for the care of the people, but not so with regard to the temporalities, since they are subject to their own monastery; for even apart from the historical consideration as to the origin of that legal provision,[5] it is well known that in those Pontifical decrees the revenues of the benefice and the profits accruing to the person of him who holds it, are signified by the designation of temporalities.

Wherefore, in confirmation of the Rescripts and injunctions of the Sacred Congregation of Propaganda Fide, We decree that members of Religious bodies, are bound to render account to the Bishop, and to inform him of the money given to them with a view to the missions, and how much of it and for what purposes it has been spent, just as missionaries of the secular clergy are bound, in accordance with the above-mentioned decisions of the said Congregation dated April 19th, 1869, and the Instruction of May 10th, 1868.

---

1. Fagnan. in cap. *Pastoralis, de his quæ fiunt a Prælatis*, n. 20—Card. de Luca *in Con. Trid* discur. 18, n. 5.—Reiffenst. Lib. 3. *Decret.* tit. 30, n. 193.
2. L. 1 § *officio* ff. *de tutela et rat. distr.*—L. 2 § *et sane* ff. de negot. gest. L. *Curator.* Cod. de negot. gest.
3. Sac. Cong. Concilii *Nullius*, seu *Nonantulan. jurium parochialium*, 27 Junii, 1744, ad dub. xii.
4. Lucius II. *ad Priorem S. Pancratii in Anglia.* Alexander III. *ad Monaster. S. Arnulph* Lucius III. *ad Superior. Præmonstrat. et ad Abbatissam S. Hilarii in diœcesi Fesulana.*
5. Gonzal. Comment. in cap. I. *de Cappel. Monach.*

O

Lastly, to obviate the risk of error or disagreement in the execution of what We have just decreed, We think it necessary to define what monies and what things are understood to be offered to members of Religious bodies with a view to the missions. For on this point it is a received maxim that the wish of the donor should be looked to in the first place; and, failing evidence of that, it is held that the donation should be presumed to have been in favour of the parish priest or the rector of the church.[1] But this rule has been widely departed from owing to a custom asserted by some skilled in ecclesiastical law to have become almost general, in force of which " at the present day almost the only offerings which belong to the parish priest are those which are made in the church during Mass at the altar, and those which are specially made for the administration of the Sacraments, for the blessing of marriages, or of women after childbirth, for funeral services and burials, or other similar functions; nearly all the rest being applied by custom to the churches or chapels themselves, or to other definite objects."[2] Moreover, if a gift may not unreasonably be presumed to have been made in favour of the parish priest or the rector, from whom the faithful receive spiritual aid,[3] where a church possesses endowments sufficient to provide for religious decorum and the maintenance of the ministers, a very different judgment must be formed where a church is not so abundantly endowed, and is maintained solely or chiefly by the contributions of the faithful. For then the donors would have to be regarded as having intended to provide for the splendour of divine worship, and the dignity of religion, in such manner and measure as ecclesiastical authority should determine. And so among the Christians of the early Church it was made a law that all money received as a gift should be divided between the Church, the Bishop, the clergy, and the poor. Moreover, when the authority of law intervenes and prescribes times and reasons for the making of offerings, it produces this effect also, namely, that the faithful are not allowed in all cases to fix at will the manner and object in and to which the offering shall be applied; for the will of private individuals cannot deprive of due effect that which is ordered by legitimate authority for the common good. Bearing all this in mind it has seemed to us that the Fathers of the Second Provincial Council of Westminster acted prudently and opportunely, when, partly interpreting the pious and just wish of the donors, partly availing themselves of that power which Bishops possess of ordering collections to be made and of deciding the time and scope of such collections, they decreed, in the chapter *concerning ecclesiastical property*, what was to be regarded as having been given *intuitu missionis* (for the good of the mission). Therefore reason prescribes, and We also ordain, that in this matter members of Religious bodies shall entirely conform to the regulations of the Synod of Westminster.

And now that we have disposed of the points in dispute which have been brought to Our cognisance, We trust that the care which We have bestowed on the settlement of them will so far avail as to contribute in no slight degree to peace and the progress of Catholicity in England.

---

1. Argum. ex cap. *Pastoral.* 9 *de his quæ fiunt a Prælat.* cap. *Transmissa, de Verb. sign.* ac præsertim cap. 1. *de Statu Monach.*
2. Reiffent. L. 3. *Decretal.* tit. 30 n. 193, Van Espen. *jus eccles. univ.* part. 2, sect. 4, tit. 2, cap. 10, no. 20 et 21.
3. Argum, ex cap. *Quia Sacerdotes* 13 caus. 10 Quæst. 1.

For We have studiously and religiously tested Our decisions by the rule of law and equity, and We do not doubt that those between whom We have delivered judgment will display a like diligence and conscientiousness in the execution of them. For thus it will come to pass that under the guidance and by the prudence of the Bishops Religious bodies, which have deserved especially well of the English missions, will continue with vigour and alacrity to bring forth from their labours most joyful fruits of salvation, and both of them (to use the words of Gregory the Great to the Bishops of England) "with common . . . . accord and united action prepare together all that they have to undertake for the zeal of Christ, be righteous in the resolutions they come to, and carry out without difference amongst themselves their common resolves."[1] This spirit of union is required by the fatherly charity which Bishops ought to show towards their co-operators and the respect which on their part the clergy should render to Bishops; it is demanded by the end which they have in common, and which consists in seeking the salvation of souls by unity of will and effort; it is rendered necessary by the obligation of resisting the enemies of the Catholic Faith. This concord is the source of strength; this it is which makes even the feeble equal to the greatest undertakings; this is the mark by which the true disciples of Christ are distinguished from those who falsely claim that title. To this, therefore, do We earnestly exhort one and all, beseeching them with St. Paul to fulfil Our joy, that they be of one mind, having the same charity, being of one accord, agreeing in sentiment.[2]

Finally, in order to give strength and durability to all that We have ordained, We will and decree that these present Letters and all that is contained therein shall not at any future time, either on the plea of surreptitiousness or of obreptitiousness, or of nullity or want of intention on Our part, or of absence of the consent of the parties interested in the case, or any other defect, be it ever so great and substantial, and requiring special mention, ever be impugned, infringed, revoked, called in question, or reduced to the terms of law. Neither shall anybody seek or obtain against them restitution *in integrum* or any other legal remedy whatsoever, even on the ground that the aforesaid members of Religious bodies and others whosoever having interest in the premises of whatever state, grade, order and dignity they may be, or who are otherwise entitled to special mention, refuse to assent to them, or plead that they have not been cited or heard, or that the causes leading to the publication of these presents have not been sufficiently set forth, verified and proved, or on any other, be it ever so juridical or privileged cause, colour, or reason even if included in the Corpus Juris. But that these present letters shall ever remain and be firm, valid and efficacious, and they shall have full and plenary effect notwithstanding any defect in law or in fact that may be pleaded against them under any form by whosoever he may be for the purpose of causing let or hindrance in the execution of the same. And therefore, every let and hindrance being utterly cast aside, they shall be, by all those whom it may concern, inviolably kept. And thus and not otherwise all judges whether ordinary or delegated in these matters shall adjudicate and define, and all attempts to rule otherwise on the part of any man whatsoever, or by whatever authority, whether knowingly or in ignorance, shall be null and void.

---

1. Apud Bedam *Histor. Angl.* II. 29. 2. Philip. ii., 2.

Notwithstanding the above, and, in so far as is necessary, the rule published by Us and the Apostolic Chancery, "*de jure quæsito non tollendo*" (that acquired rights may not be taken away), and other Apostolic Constitutions, and those published in General, Provincial, and Synodical Councils; notwithstanding also the statutes and customs of all Orders, Congregations, Institutes, and Societies whatsoever, including the Society of Jesus, and of all churches, and all other statutes, usages, prescriptions, even from time immemorial; also all privileges, indults, and Apostolic letters, granted, published, and executed in any form whatsoever contrary to the premises, even if several times renewed. From all, and each of these, even if requiring a special form of derogation, and the tenor of which We hold to be fully and sufficiently described herein, in so far only as they effect these presents, We specially and expressly derogate, all other things whatsoever notwithstanding.

Moreover, in whatever manner copies of these same letters shall be published in England, We will that, forthwith after such publication has been made, they shall take effect in regard to all and each of the persons whom they concern, or hereafter may concern, as if they had been intimated and notified to each of them individually.

Let no man, therefore, infringe or rashly contravene these Our decisions, declarations, decrees, precepts, and will, in these pages set forth. And if any man shall presume to essay to do so, let him know that he will incur the anger of God, and of His blessed Apostles, Peter and Paul.

Given at Rome, at St. Peter's, in the year of our Lord, 1881, eight days before the Ides of May, in the fourth year of Our Pontificate.

C. CARD. SACCONI, Pro-Datarius.
T. CARD. MERTEL.

Seen
De Curia I. De Aquila De' Visconti.

L. ✠ S.

Registered in the Secretary of Briefs.

I. CUGNIONI.

Instruction as to the Dependence of Regular Missioners upon the Vicars-Apostolic and other Superiors of Missions.

Appendix ad I. Syn., Ed. Salf., *p. 92.*

The Sacred Congregation is very sorry that the authority of the Vicars-Apostolic and other Superiors of Missions is not unfrequently disputed by some Missioners, notably Regulars, and that from time to time are brought forward questions about dependence, inexhaustible sources of consequences most fatal to the well-being and progress of the said Missions; although such questions have oftentimes been examined into and settled by the same Sacred Congregation, there are also the most wise prescriptions of the Holy See itself upon the subject.

It was in order to eliminate such unpleasant differences that Clement IX., A.D. 1669, in his Bull *Speculatores, &c.*, laid down the rules regarding the dependence of the said Missioners, ordaining:

1. That such Missioners must present their letters patent to the Vicars-Apostolic, even though they may have been sent on the Mission

directly by the Holy See or by the Sacred Congregation of Propaganda, and that if they should refuse to present them, the said Vicars may, as Delegates of the Holy See, forbid them to exercise the sacred ministry.

2. That the same Missioners are bound to ask permission from the Vicars-Apostolic to exercise their faculties; although the latter cannot without a serious reason deny such exercise to them.

3. That they undertake the cure of souls when there is an insufficiency of secular priests; and this, not only *ex charitate* but even *ex justitia*, so that they may be constrained thereto by the Vicars-Apostolic.

4. That in the exercise of the cure of souls and in regard to parochial duties, they are to be subject to the visitation and correction of the Vicars.

5. That when requested to do so they must render an account to the Vicars-Apostolic of the fulfilment of such pious bequests as they may have been deputed to execute.

6. That if amongst themselves any dispute arise, the Vicars-Apostolic may, as Delegates of the Holy See, decide and put an end to them, &c.

These rules were in the course of time placed in a still clearer light and inculcated anew, according as difficulties were met with in the observance of them or doubts were proposed in reference to them. Thus, in 1677, the Holy See declared the aforesaid Missioners, not excepting the Fathers of the Society of Jesus, bound to submit to and obey the Vicars-Apostolic "*in regard to all the business and direction of the Missions.*" In 1680, to remove all misunderstanding concerning the relations between Religious and Regular Superiors, the Holy See wished it to be understood, that although they were subject to the Superiors of the Institute as regards regular discipline, yet these could not remove them from the Mission without the consent of their respective Vicars-Apostolic. In 1701, it was confirmed that the aforesaid Missioners, in regard to the administration of the Sacraments and the other duties of the Mission, were *immediately* subject to the Sacred Congregation of Propaganda, or to whomsoever it may place over them, i.e., to the Vicars-Apostolic. Likewise, in 1702, the decree was re-enacted that the Regular Missioners in China, of whatever Institute, must be entirely subject to the Vicars-Apostolic as regards the administration of the Sacraments and the cure of souls, &c., and so on, successively.

From all this it is easy to deduce in what respects Religious of whatever Institute or Society are bound to be in dependence upon and submission to the Vicar-Apostolic or the Prelate Superior of the Mission, under whatever title he may govern. Finally, to exclude every cause of doubt, the Congregation specially appointed for the affairs of China has in conformity with the above regulations, and with the sanction of the Holy Father, ordered it to be declared to your Lordship as a rule to go by, that, *with the sole exception of internal regular discipline*, Regular Missioners, including as expressly mentioned the Fathers of the Society of Jesus, *are under the jurisdiction of the Vicars-Apostolic as regards the entire business and direction of the Missions.* Moreover, the same Congregation expressly declares and wishes it to be understood, that if the Missionary is to be considered bound by a two-fold obedience, one towards the Head of the mission the other towards the Regular Superior, the former must always outweigh the latter; and hence, in case of conflict between the two, the first must always prevail and not be paralysed by scruples about the latter. A very strange idea indeed would it be if anyone thought that a Religious should set the obedience which he has professed towards the Superior of his Order before that which is above every other kind of obedience, viz., the obedience due to the supreme authority of the Holy See and the Vicar of Jesus Christ, or that he should allow any point whatever of regular internal discipline to outweigh the chief and most serious duties of the Missionary, or that he should prefer a private good to a public one and to the eternal salvation of the vast number of souls committed to his care. The Sacred Congregation is intimately persuaded that the aforesaid conflict will never occur if the Regular Superior is animated by the true spirit of the Gospel and by a lively sense of the obedience and respect which are due to the Holy See and to the Representative or Vicars of the same; and if the latter on their part, act solely for the good of Religion, which certainly depends a great deal upon the sanctity of its Ministers. It will be your Lordship's duty both to follow the above rules and regulations Yourself, and to require the most exact observance of the same from your Missioners.

Propaganda, September 30th, 1848.

JAMES PHILIP CARD. FRANSONI, Prefect.
AL. BARNABÒ, Secretary.

Glory to God and to the Immaculate Virgin Mary.

Testimonial Letters for Religious.

Decree of the Sacred Congregation upon the state of Regulars published by Authority of our Most Holy Lord Pius IX., Chief Pontiff, in reference to the Testimonial letters that have to be obtained from the Ordinaries at the reception of persons asking to be admitted to the religious habit.

The Roman Pontiffs in that pastoral care with which they have never failed to provide for the well-being and good repute of Regular bodies, have done their best to recommend Superiors to make diligent inquiry into the life, character, and other endowments and particulars of the Postulants before admitting them to the religious habit, lest they might open the door to religious bodies in favour of unworthy persons, to the greatest possible detriment of the former. But take whatever care the Superiors of Orders may, they are for the most part in great danger of being deceived unless they obtain the testimony of the local Prelates in reference to the qualities of those who beg to be admitted to the religious habit : for Ordinaries by virtue of their pastoral office are able to know better than others their sheep, and oftentimes to make known impediments which others are unaware of. Perceiving this, our Most Holy Lord Pius IX., Supreme Pontiff, having listened to the opinion of the Most Eminent Cardinals of this Sacred Congregation on the state of Regulars, and noted the requests of several Bishops, by his Apostolic authority determines and decrees what follows, by the present decree which is to be observed everywhere for the future.

1. In every Order, Congregation, Society, Institute, Monastery, or House, whether solemn or simple vows are made therein, and even in

Orders, Congregations, Societies, Institutes, Monasteries, and Houses, which by reason of some privilege are not included in ordinary law, or for some reason or another are not included in general decrees, unless special individual and express mention is made of them, let no one be admitted to the habit without testimonial letters both from the Ordinary of the place of his birth, and from the Ordinary of any place where the Postulant has spent more than one year after completing his fifteenth year.

2. The Ordinaries having first of all made diligent inquiries, even by secret means, as to the character of the Postulant, shall, in such letters, state his birth, age, character, life, repute, condition, education, learning; whether he has been prosecuted, or is under censure, irregularity, or any other canonical impediment, in debt, or liable to have to give an account for any trust. And let Ordinaries understand that their conscience remains burthened as to the trustworthiness of their report; and that they are never free to refuse testimonial letters of this kind; that, however, they need only testify therein to those points in the aforesaid details on which they conscientiously deem in the Lord that they can affirm.

3. The observance of this decree is strictly enjoined, even by virtue of holy obedience, upon all and every Regular Superior, and upon all other Religious concerned whatever their position, and though their institute is exempt and privileged, and necessarily to be mentioned; and whoever in opposition to the tenor of this decree admits anyone to the religious habit, by so doing incurs the penalty of privation of all offices and of active voice, and perpetual inability as to obtaining in future any offices; and can only be dispensed from this by the Apostolic See.

4. In virtue of any whatsoever privilege, faculty, indult, dispensation, or approbation of rules and constitutions, even if obtained in a specific form by any Order, Institute, or Religious Superior from the Apostolic See, never must it be considered that any derogation is made from this decree, unless the derogation be made expressly and by name, even though in the concession general derogations, however unlimited, are included. But if to any Institute a dispensation in regard to this decree be at any time granted expressly and by name, by no means can it be extended to others by virtue of any privilege whatsoever or communication of privileges.

5. Every year on the 1st of January, let this decree be read at the public meal, under pain or privation of office and of active and passive voice to be incurred *ipso facto* by Superiors.

And lest the observance of this decree should for any reason, or upon any title or pretext be hindered, His Holiness completely annuls and declares null all whatsoever constitutions, rules and statutes tending to the contrary of any Order, Congregation, Institute, Monastery, or House, even if approved of in specific form by the Apostolic See, as well as every privilege, even if embodied in the law and confirmed by Apostolic Constitutions and decrees, and needing express, individual, special, and most special mention, and whatsoever else to the contrary.

Given at Rome, at the Sacred Congregation upon the State of Regulars, January 25th, 1848.

ANDREW CANON. BIZZARRI, Secretary.

§ II.—Nuns.

I. *Westminster, xxviii. p. 86.*

1. No monastery, that is, no new house for religious women, shall be founded without leave of the Bishop, who must be well informed as to the kind of institute to which it belongs, and the rules thereof.[1]

2. With the exception of exempt monasteries, which are already lawfully under some regular Superior, all the rest are subject to the Bishop's visitation, even though they are in dependence upon some other houses, and that perhaps across the sea.

3. Inasmuch as by reason of alteration in the circumstances of place and time many things in the approved Constitutions of nuns are oftentimes difficult of observance, and indeed sometimes impossible, such as abstinence and fasting, it seems better in such cases, for the removal of scruples, to make a change in the rule itself, after obtaining the Apostolical authority, than to grant a perpetual dispensation, as now seems to be done, with danger of detriment to conscience.

4. For hearing the confessions of nuns, ecclesiastics conspicuous for their gravity, prudence and virtue should be selected; and an extraordinary confessor should be appointed at stated times for every monastery.

5. The Bishop should pay careful attention to the business concerns of non-exempt monasteries, and make provision either personally or through some other for the proper management of their worldly goods. The state of the temporalities must be made known to the Bishop, even in the case of nuns subject to a regular Order. The dowries of the nuns should be placed in good investments so as to produce a certain annual return,—nor should any extraordinary expenditure be incurred without the Bishop's approval.

§ III.—Mendicants.

IV. *Westminster, xvi., p. 68.*

1. As no one can be unaware of how serious an unseemliness and scandal it is that nuns and sisters consecrated to God should wander about out of their monasteries, without control and contrary to the rules of their institute; sitting at table with seculars; and, without any great necessity, sleeping in their houses; we strictly order the Superiors of these not to allow their subjects, under any pretence whatever, to go out collecting alms without the previous permission in writing of the Bishop.

By this Decree we by no means wish to lessen or fetter the

---

1. Council of Trent, Session xxv. c. 8, on **Regulars**.

privileges of any institute granted by the Holy See; but let them make use of the same in moderation and with the holy fear of God.

2. Moreover, in reference to the Brethren of the Mendicant Orders, who are in the habit of going out to collect alms for the support of their convents, in accordance with the privilege granted by the Holy See, we think that their Superiors should be reminded that the privilege they enjoy within the diocese in which their convent is, by no means extends beyond those limits, unless leave in writing has been previously obtained from the Ordinary of such places.

The superiors should likewise be careful to select for this duty those only who are advanced in virtue and modesty of character, for it is one exposed to manifold dangers; and they should strictly enjoin them not to make themselves annoying to the faithful by over-importunity. The Brothers are strictly forbidden to wear the Roman collars or the dress of a priest.

4. In the Lord we beseech the clergy of the Province of Westminster to take care to send us speedily as possible to the Ordinaries any information concerning those who transgress this Decree, should there be any.

CHAPTER THE NINTH.

COLLEGES AND SEMINARIES.

COLLEGES OR SEMINARIES.

I. Westminster, Decree xxvi., p. 83.

We hold that it would exceedingly avail to the increase of religion if Seminaries could be established in which the clergy could be educated apart from others. But seeing that they are now brought up mingled with secular youths, we must use every endeavour to keep up in them the Ecclesiastical spirit, that their hearts be not turned aside to worldly desires.

1. Young men or boys should therefore be selected who have shewn clear signs of a vocation; in whom already there has begun to appear innocency of life, docility and piety, joined with fair talent. Examiners should be appointed to subject to examination all those who are to be admitted into College amongst the clerical students, and to inquire into their past life not less than their mental qualities.

2. It will be a gain also if students be admitted to the College by competitive examination; yet so, however, as that this should not stand in the way of any existing or future rights.

3. Each year the Rector of the College shall send in an account to the Bishop or Bishops of the progress and character of each student.

4. They should be carefully instructed in asceticism at monthly conferences, apart, if it is thought fit, from the others; they should be taught the method of meditation, and learn thoroughly the Rubrics and Ceremonies of the Church.

5. They should be practised in Ecclesiastical Music after having studied the theory of it. And for the introduction of uniformity, we wish that in all places, but particularly in Colleges, wheresoever at Mass or the Office, the plain or Gregorian Chant is used, the Roman Chant alone should be made use of. The Prayers, therefore, Responsories, the Epistle, Gospel, and other things of the kind, should be sung in the way laid down in the Ceremonial of Bishops or in other authentic books. The same is to be said of the Rubrics and Ecclesiastical Ceremonies; for, in regard to them, the customs of other countries must not be taken up at pleasure; but the definitions and rules, and where these are wanting, the usage and practice, of the Holy Roman Church, must be strictly followed.

On the Establishment of Seminaries.

Title I.

III. Westminster, xiii., p. 28

The Holy Bride of Our Lord Jesus Christ, the Church Catholic, is united to her Divine Spouse by such a bond of love that she not only eagerly and lovingly receives from Him the precepts and maxims of eternal life, but finds in His every word and action the model and exemplar of her own operations. Hence, whatsoever she originates after deliberation, or, as it were, gives life to spontaneously, takes its pattern from Him, to Whom her eyes are ever raised, upon Whom her heart is ever fixed.

What wonder, therefore, that those Colleges which have sprung up in the Church, as it were by instinct, and grown by degrees into perfection, for the education of priests, took their origin from the very source of the priesthood itself. For our Redeemer withdrew from the world and from their homes to Himself those whom He willed and destined to be His successors in His sublime ministry; He attached them to Himself, and honoured them with His own companionship.

Thus, He instructed and prepared those whom He had called to the Apostolate, not only apart from the multitude, but even from His disciples. Those things that He preached obscurely to the people, He to them explained clearly, treating with them more minutely of Himself, and of His mission, and of His Kingdom that was to be established upon earth. To the rest He spoke in parables, delivering His doctrine still as it were enshrouded in the smoke and clouds of Sinai; them He now taught in the brightness of the Divine countenance, even as God speaking face to face had done with Moses on the mountain top. Nor, in forming His ministers did He merely do this, but He treated them with such familiarity as to have everything in common with them; to settle their almost childish disputes, to shield them from Pharisaic cavillings, and to solve even the smallest of their doubts; He comforted them; He supported them; He reproved and He rebuked them—and why say more? He called Himself the Master and them His disciples. And so they were.

This was, therefore, the Church's first Seminary, the household of Christ the Lord. Where in the world save there did Peter the Fisherman gain his strong and lofty faith, Thomas his burning desire to accompany his Lord to prison and to death, John, above all, the heavenly doctrine of love towards God and man, save from the daily companionship with the Incarnate Wisdom, whilst "He appeared upon earth and dwelt amongst men"? And, indeed, that Divine doctrine was not imparted with solemnity from the upraised doctor's chair, but was taught imperceptibly in familiar and daily intercourse. For thus whilst eating he gave them lessons; thus, never did sweeter or more beauteous words issue from the Divine mind than those celestial sayings He poured eloquently forth at His last supper, touching the love which He bore towards them and towards us.

And this His teaching He confined not to words but perfected by deeds, making them not so much His disciples and successors as His comrades and companions in His ministry. For as the eagle encourages its young to take wing, so did He send before Him His disciples, two and two, to every place He was Himself about to go, to preach the Word of God, and to heal the sick; so that under the very eyes of their Master they might prepare themselves for the still greater duties to be entrusted to them.

Here we have the most perfect specimen of a Seminary, in which the future guardians of the flock are taught by the Good Shepherd, and are prepared for the discharge of His office. Here we see the Prince of Pastors Himself, the Bishop and Founder of the whole Church, not disdaining to devote Himself to men without learning or even refinement; He is not ashamed, first of all to correct their ways, and then thoroughly to instil into them His own character and His own mind by living in constant intercourse with them. And thus at length prepared He sent them forth after a holy retreat into the whole world, gifted from on high with a new power, filled with the Holy Spirit, worthy preachers of His word, and sharers in His own perpetual priesthood. From this wondrous, yea divine, example, it was easy to foresee that immense advantage would accrue to the whole Church. Hardly, therefore, had she passed through the first three centuries, and laid aside her blood-stained robes, than men of wisdom and piety began to consider seriously the matter of the education of the clergy, and to make successful attempts thereat. And chief amongst these should be reckoned Saint Augustine, Bishop of Hippo, who gathered together into his own house and family, priests, deacons and subdeacons, all of whom led a truly apostolic life, faring alike in food, in goods, in dress. "I wished," he writes, "to have in this house a monastery of clerics!"[1] But the Second Council of Toledo provides us with the clearest evidence how accurately the foundation of Seminaries is described in the ancient Church, although they were not as yet known by this name. "As regards those whom the goodwill of their parents has in their earliest years destined for the clerical or monastic state, we likewise decree that as soon as they have received the tonsure, or have been associated with the work of the lectors, they are to be taught at the house attached to the Church under the eye and government of the Bishop. And when they have completed their eighteenth year, if, by God's inspiration, they choose a life of chastity, let them, as souls aspiring to the strictest way, be inured to the light yoke of the Lord; and, after trial of their profession, undertake, first of all, the duty of the sub-diaconate after arriving at

---

1. In Thomassinus, T. I., p. 623. Ed. 1688.

their twentieth year."[1] So also, in the Fourth Council of the same city, two kinds of societies are described as existing in the Bishop's palace, one of the priests dwelling with him, the other of the boys who, apart from them, were brought up and taught, with the view of the majority of them becoming in the course of time, candidates for the priesthood.[2]

But to come to times nearer unto our own, we cannot help rejoicing that the grace, or honour, as we might well call it, was given by our Lord to our own country to be the first to give to the Church both in name and reality a Seminary. For the most eminent and illustrious Cardinal, Reginald Pole, when making his visitation by apostolic authority, A.D. 1586, of the downtrodden and plundered Church in England, amongst the many remarkable decrees for the reformation of the realm which he drew up and issued, laid down this as the chief means of such reformation, viz., that every Cathedral Church should have a school attached to it, in which "should be instituted a nursery and, as it were a Seminary, of ministers." And this most able man goes on to describe and unfold so beautifully the whole subject, that he would seem to have provided the Sacred Synod of Trent not only with the idea but the very embodiment of the same in words. For all the wise provisions made in the Council of Trent in reference to the seelection and admission of youths, the course of studies, the providing for the support of the Seminary from benefices and other ecclesiastical resources, appear to be copied almost verbatim from Pole's decree.[3] And no greater honour could have been paid to anyone than this.

But far beyond any praise in our power to bestow, beyond every encomium of man, is that truly golden, truly Apostolic Decree, in which the Sacred Synod of Trent commanded that everywhere should Seminaries be founded and kept up. It is, indeed, a decree which, by reason of the wisdom and importance of its provisions, as well as the reverence due to every word, no lapse of time can make obsolete, no change of circumstances or variety of place can render impracticable or useless. For it lives by the vigour imparted to it by the unfailing Church of God, from whose fruitful womb proceeding, it grew unaided by the course of years, or by human industry, so as to produce straightway in all lands the richest of fruits.

Whilst this was going on, our own England languished, or rather lay prostrate and fallen, beaten down by violence and cruelty, so that she was unable to derive, for some time, any benefit therefrom. But our countrymen, though almost weary of their very lives, were not slow in following the plan which St. Charles was the first to carry out at Milan. Allen, a name worthy of all praise, soon founded the celebrated College of Douai, which for three centuries

---

1. II. Council of Toledo. Ibid. p. 629.
2. Ibid.
3. Conc. Collectio Regia, tom. X. p. 407.

sent forth as many confessors as priests. In England itself, however, it was impossible in those days to establish Seminaries.

But by God's mercy times have changed for the better; and, with the restoration of the Hierarchy, we can rebuild the temple, and give back to our holy places their ancient splendour. And now, like unto the blast of the priestly and Apostolic trumpet, sounds in our ears, full of authority, full of truth, the opening passage of that Decree. "Whereas the age of youth, unless it be properly trained, is prone to run after the pleasures of the world, and unless it be from the very beginning brought under the influence of piety and religion before habits of vice have taken possession of the whole man, it will never perfectly, nor at all without the utmost difficulty, and a well-nigh special grace from Almighty God, persevere in Ecclesiastical discipline; the Holy Synod ordains that all Cathedral, Metropolitan, and other Churches of higher rank shall be bound, each according to its means and the extent of the diocese, to maintain, educate religiously, and to train in Ecclesiastical discipline a certain number of youths of such city and diocese, or, if such are not to be met with therein, of the province, in a College to be selected by the Bishop for this purpose, near to the said Churches, or in some other suitable place."

So important was this Decree in the minds of those who heard it proposed, that it received the unanimous approbation of the Fathers; and thus, in the Acts of the Sacred Synod, is concluded the account of the Session. "All these points have met with unanimous approbation, indicated by the word "Placet," without any dissentient voice; and in this concord the congregation was dissolved, wherein verily had been present the Holy Spirit."

Obedient to the inspirations of the same Holy Spirit, or rather ever guided by the light sent forth by Him, the Chief Pontiffs of modern times have never hesitated whensoever the opportunity offered itself, again and again to inculcate and insist upon the completest observance of this Decree. Amongst them we must not omit to name, with the utmost reverence, Benedict XIII., a great restorer of Ecclesiastical discipline, seeing that addressing the Ordinaries of Italy in the Constitution, given in 1725, and beginning with the words, "Creditæ Nobis," he strictly enjoins them "that in those Cathedrals where a Seminary has not yet been established, they should strive for its foundation at once, and for its complete maintenance;" and not content with this Apostolic command, he appointed a congregation of Cardinals, under the style of the Congregation for Seminaries, and to it entrusted the charge of seeing to the foundation of Seminaries, and to the arrangement of their means of support provided from Benefices.

Scarcely could it have been possible for a Pontiff of such eminent ability and so great sacred learning as Benedict XIV., to

---

* Session xxiii., c. 18.

prove himself slothful in the matter of the education of the clergy. So far from it, hardly had he sat in the Apostolic chair, when he addressed an Encyclical Letter to all the Bishops of the Universal Church, which comes second in the list of writings of that most learned Pontiff, from which we have considered the following words alone need be quoted: "It should, therefore, be a subject dear to your hearts to establish a Seminary for Clerics as speedily as possible where there is not one, and to attend to its welfare wherever there is one."[1]

Finally, to come down to our own times, our Most Holy Lord and Chief Pontiff, who at present happily fills the illustrious chair of Peter, treading, as it were, in the footsteps of his renowned predecessor, Benedict XIV., in one of the first of his Encyclical Letters after his election, viz., in 1846, prescribes for Bishops, and inculcates upon them, the selfsame object of their solicitude, and in almost the same words; "wherefore nothing should be higher or more important in your eyes than, by every effort, activity and earnestness on your part, to found Seminaries for Clerics after the plan laid down by the Tridentine Fathers, where there are none, and to enlarge, if necessary, those that are already founded."[2] Nor need we speak of the way, in which the same most illustrious Pontiff exemplified in deed what he had taught by word. For there stands, and by God's helping grace, for ever will stand, that famous monument of this his desire, the "Seminarium Pium," instituted for the benefit of every diocese in the Papal Dominions, a work well worthy, indeed, of so great a name.

This voice, then, of the whole Church, heard at every period from her very beginning, and, indeed, from the day of Christ her Master, down to our own times, may truly be regarded as an Ecclesiastical tradition, of such a kind as to afford us an undoubted rule as to the means by which a body of clergy may be supplied to us, adorned with every kind of virtue, and in every way fit to work in the field of the Church. Not our ears alone, however, but our hearts has this voice of the spouse of Christ and our Mother penetrated, and it has aroused us in this Synod to gird up our loins for the further and more perfect building up of this house of God, in which the young olive branches may sit around our table—a heavenly table which abounds with bread.

Everyone of the Bishops proposes to apply himself carefully and earnestly at once to the task of founding a Seminary in his diocese in the best way he can. For as his is this spouse, to whom God Himself has bound him as by the tie of conjugal love; and as there is no more precious crown he can wear than the virtues of the Ecclesiastical state shining around him, no girdle more beauteous than a band of holy clerics surrounding him; so no more pleasing, or more welcome gift can each offer his spouse than a holy family of this kind, which gives joy now and hope in

---

1. Bullarium Romanum, Ben. XIV., num. 2. 2. Pii. ix., P.M., Acta, part 1, p. 19.

the future. May God, the giver of all graces, the implanter of good counsel, bless this determination, and thus make more than one of the Churches wedded to us, hitherto barren, dwell in a house the joyful mother of children. So be it! So be it!

Title II.

XIV. Colleges.

Although from what has been said it is sufficiently clear that the Bishops of England look forward confidently to have each his own Seminary in his diocese, nevertheless, nothing should be neglected which may as far as possible supply the want of one for the present.

The Secular Clergy of England are now trained at three Colleges, common to several dioceses. These are:—

1. The College of St. Edmund, in the Archdiocese, 24 miles from London, for two Dioceses.
2. The College of St. Cuthbert for four in full, and for a fifth in part.
3. The College of St. Mary for three, and partly for the one alluded to in the last number.

There remain three Dioceses—Newport, Clifton, and Plymouth—who, in this respect, are deprived of all help in England, and have no share in any of the said Colleges.

In reference to these Colleges generally, the Sacred Congregation of Propaganda, so far back as 1855, expressed its wish that in the next on-coming Provincial Synod, a careful inquiry should be set on foot, as will be better seen by the terms of the following letter.

Letter of His Eminence Cardinal Fransoni to the Cardinal Archbishop of Westminster.

My Most Eminent and Reverend Honoured Lord,

Although I am persuaded that your Eminence, in arranging the matters to be discussed at the Provincial Synod, has not overlooked the very important subject of Clerical Education, still you will allow me to recommend to you this object in a special manner, since upon it the progress of Religion greatly depends. On an occasion when the Bishops will be assembled together, it would be very opportune to take into consideration the method followed in the Colleges and Seminaries for giving young Ecclesiastics a thorough training in piety and learning, and to lay down at least the fundamental principles of the improvements to be introduced in order to obtain happier results. It is quite unnecessary to remind your

Eminence of the most wise Tridentine prescriptions on this matter, and of the regulations introduced by Holy Prelates, and recommended by a happy experience; it will belong to the discernment and enlightened zeal of your Eminence and your Colleagues, to make whatever regulations you may consider feasible and opportune, taking into account the state of the Ecclesiastical establishments in England, and other circumstances.

Meanwhile, with profound respect, I most humbly kiss your hand;

Your Eminence's most humble and devoted servant,

G. F. CARDINAL FRANSONI, Prefect.
AL. BARNABÒ, Secretary.

Rome, The Propaganda, June 27th 1855.

From this letter it is clear that the Provincial Synod has the duty and burthen imposed upon it, (I.) first of examining into the present state of these Colleges, and next (II.) of laying down certain principles by means of which greater and better results may be safely secured.

PART I.

On the Present State of the Colleges, and the Method followed therein for the Education of the Clergy.

And as we set ourselves to our task, the feeling implanted by nature in every generous soul takes possession of us, of love, that is, and gratitude towards those holy, and by us revered spots, where we all, after the first elements of faith and doctrine, received almost the whole of our Ecclesiastical education. There, not only as boys did we study literature, but either gained our Ecclesiastical vocation, or found it strengthened and, by God's grace, brought to maturity. There, taught by the bright example of our masters, by their eminent learning, and by their precepts of salvation, it was ours to imbibe into our souls doctrine ever sound and the teachings of piety.

Nor are those wanting among our number who, dedicated from early youth to the cloister, can testify in the same way to the zeal and devotion with which religious men strive earnestly to prepare young men for promoting Religion.

And unworthy as we feel ourselves of the honour of having such a burthen laid upon us, and not daring to imagine that we are endowed with the virtues proper to our state, yet, whatever in the discharge of our divine ministry has gained for us the favour of the Holy See, whatever of goodwill and zeal for religion the keen vision of the Chief Pastor has benignly beheld in us, verily every tittle of it we willingly bear testimony to having received from

P

these our Colleges. For these were the sources of our learning, whether sacred or profane: these were the foundation of the whole of our after progress. Wherefore, if we are now anxiously, and as it were with trembling hearts, about to treat of the education of clerics, and if the Holy See places in us such confidence as to command us to treat so important a matter, both this our own anxiety and that great condescension must be equally laid to the account of this our education. Moreover, the internal management of these Colleges, their course of studies, their scholastic discipline, have undergone little or no change as time went on; and hence upon all these points we can form a judgment from our own experience. And this much may at the outset be asserted, that if any change has in the course of years taken place, it has ever been for the better.

I. Thus, for instance, they have all been during the last few years either rebuilt from their foundations or been so enlarged as to be equal to new. In each a church of ample size has been built, and fitted with all the necessaries for carrying on the Ecclesiastical Offices in a worthy and proper manner.

Spacious libraries, well supplied with the best kind of works—notably those which concern theological teaching, such as the writings of the Holy Fathers, the Councils, and Commentaries upon Sacred Scripture—have been provided in two at least of them.

The buildings have not only increased to a great extent, but by their beauty and becoming ornamentation strike the eye even of non-Catholics and excite their admiration. Many things, likewise, which conduce to the study of the liberal arts, apparatus for the cultivation of the physical sciences, and such things as may easily recall the mind to God and to holy thoughts amidst worldly occupations, have been supplied in abundance.

All these things, indeed, pertain to what is outward, and as it were, material. Let us go on to matters of greater importance.

II. At the very outset it is necessary to notice that in all these Colleges boys destined, some to the lay, others to the clerical state, live and are educated together. Not, indeed, that this happens in the same proportion in all. The College of St. Mary has a greater number of lay than of clerical students: in that of St. Cuthbert the latter greatly prevail over the former; at the Metropolitan College but few, and those separately from the rest, are prepared for secular life.

And there are weighty reasons still for this mixed kind of training.

1. The poverty of the Colleges, which would not, in some cases at least, permit of a sufficient number of candidates for the ecclesiastical state being supported, unless aid came from the secular teaching. And so it can be asserted with truth, that up to the present time the best part of the support of the Colleges has consisted of the pensions of the secular boarders. Grave mischief

would, accordingly, accrue to two at least of the Colleges, if they were straightway deprived of this source of income.

2. The paucity of Colleges for the higher studies of lay youths. It must certainly be a matter of the greatest weight with the Bishops, that those youths in whose power it will one day be to protect the rights of the Church, and in every way to assist religion, should be educated in sound doctrine not only by Ecclesiastics, but under the very eye of the Bishops. And there are many heads of families who hold nothing more precious than that their sons should be educated with church students, so that they may share in the virtues peculiar to these, and even gain from God an ecclesiastical vocation.

3. Finally, the last-named hope becomes a motive for this method of education.

III. But although this is the case, by no means can it be said that the education is so arranged for lay boys that it is unfitted to form Ecclesiastics. This is clear enough from the fact already adverted to by us, that from these Colleges there have come not only some endowed with the Episcopal dignity but innumerable labourers remarkable for piety and zeal, to whose indefatigable labours the progress of the Catholic Faith amongst us is, after the increase granted by a merciful God, mainly owing.

The basis, therefore, of the whole system of education is almost that which is prescribed generally for purely Ecclesiastical Colleges and Seminaries. For the studies, the rules, the discipline, and pious exercises, are more or less the same as in that famous College of Douai, which all of ours regard as their Alma Mater, and which for so many years brought forth not so much priests as martyrs of the Church. And the students of our Colleges following closely in their footsteps have bravely given themselves not only to be speedily spent by labours but at any moment to meet death by attacks of pestilence. Hence we can truly say that if at any time lay boys are not any longer educated therein, no great changes would be necessary in the course of studies or the ordinary routine.

For (1); the students are well grounded in literature, having, as a matter of necessity, to make the study of the ancient languages the foundation of their whole course. For Protestants, against whom the battle has to be waged, spend almost the whole of their labour and time in gaining a knowledge of these, challenge reference to the original texts of the New Testament and of the Holy Fathers, and make much of this kind of learning.

To these our students add the knowledge of modern tongues (French and Italian in particular), and this conduces no little to the acquirement of sacred learning.

(2.) Likewise they are bound to attain to a knowledge of the elements at least of physical science and mathematics, seeing that from studies of this nature so many erroneous views are brought forward by moderns against the Faith. In these matters, as in sound moral philosophy, the education of all could be little if at all different. So that, if there is at any time anything to be done it is certainly not that anything should be taken away, but rather that some addition should be made.

IV. As to the religious instruction of the boys, if it is the same for all and adapted to the powers of all, it is certain that the greatest care is taken that it should be ample enough for both classes. For if in the one case it is to be the foundation only for the farther teaching that will be solidly added to it in the course of theology, it will form the whole of the lay boys' armoury, by the help of which they have to withstand and overcome the hostile attacks of error and vice. In this arena, as it may be called, they are trained in those virtues and sound principles by means of which they can combat the enticements of the world and the tendency of nature to evil. Nor can the Bishops say that they have been frustrated in this hope, when amongst the laity of their dioceses there are many young men, some even of the nobility, who have been educated at their Colleges, admirable for the firmness of their faith, for the exercise of charity, and for the splendour of their other virtues.

Hence, perhaps, it can be said, that the instruction in Catechism and in the rudimentary knowledge of faith and religion given to youths destined to the Ecclesiastical state is the more full and solid from the very fact that it covers the whole of the teaching imparted to lay boys. For it is of such a nature as not only to be a beginning and first taste of sacred study, but even to contain within itself the germs of theology and of controversy.

V. Finally, the spiritual exercises are such as perhaps might admit of diminution in a mere lay College. These are, with a few unimportant differences, the same as were in use with the approbation of the Holy See at the old College of Douai. To wit, daily meditation and presence at the Holy Sacrifice; the two visits to the most Holy Sacrament after meals; the daily practice of spiritual reading; two sets (even) of night prayers before going to bed; the recitation of the Rosary; the strictest observance of the Feasts of the Church; frequent Benediction of the Most Holy Sacrament; an exact and choral celebration of all the ecclesiastical offices, not only on Festivals, but in Holy Week and at other appointed times; frequent Communion for all, and for the ecclesiastical students several times in the week, after approaching the sacred tribunal of Penance; and spiritual exercises rigorously given and gone through. These are the points common to the lay and clerical students, from which, indeed, one might make some subtraction, but could nothing easily add.

PART II.

Suggestions for the Greater Efficiency of the Ecclesiastical Colleges.

It is easier to see and set down defects than to prescribe their remedy. All can do the former, few the latter. But if in what has gone before we have appeared to be composing an eulogy upon our Colleges rather than pointing out some of the faults, or at any rate blots, that attach to them, this must not be set down to mental blindness or to indifference. For what has been said merely implies that there are no faults which cannot be uprooted or completely removed. Defects, therefore, occur to us which must be made good, rather than evils which must be cured.

I. And, first of all, especially where the number of lay students is greatly in excess of that of the clerical, it is difficult to prevent a worldly spirit from getting by degrees, into the house and gaining an ascendancy over it. Experience has taught us that the vocations of many, although strong in the beginning, have become weakened and completely ruined by this kind of intercourse. And even by those who persevere there is sometimes imbibed an undue desire of the things of the world, which lessens the zeal for God and for souls, and draws them off from sacred pursuits to levities.

The sole remedy without doubt for this defect is the separation of the clerical from the lay students, as already, in our First Provincial Synod (xxii.,) it was fully and distinctly declared; and, indeed, in that chapter the whole matter seems to have been so thoroughly gone into, that it were better to refer to what was then decided than to make any new declaration. This alone may be added, that now the prospect seems brighter than when we thus wrote, of beholding Seminaries founded in each diocese. Then will each Bishop be able to watch over the education of his own subjects, and as it were infuse into them his own spirit. But, in the meantime, we inculcate afresh that those means be adopted which we there recapitulated for the education of youths aspiring to the priestly dignity.

For although solid instruction upon spiritual things is given to them together with the lay students, yet from their tenderest years their minds still bright with the purity of youth must be imbued and as it were animated with a more refined sense of things divine. Hence a stricter custody of the emotions and of the senses, a more intense application to study, a more exact observance of discipline, a more fervid piety in the Church, should at a glance distinguish from the rest those who have chosen the better part. Some special instruction should therefore be provided in every College for those who have devoted themselves to the ecclesiastical state, of such a kind as to lay the foundation for future progress. No general plan of such instruction can be minutely laid down, seeing that in each College the system of studies and the difference of inmates may be more adapted for one than another. Whether, for instance, this arduous duty should be laid on the ordinary confessors or entrusted to one spiritual director alone; whether altogether or a few at a time, the boys and young men should be exercised in this spiritual training; whether frequently or at long intervals; all these points, we think, should be left to the judgment and experience of those in whose charge is the College.

II. The want of priests, concurrently with the poverty of the Colleges, has made it necessary that theological students, whose whole mind should be devoted to study, are often appointed to duties connected with administration or discipline. And as the course of theology is never carried beyond the third year, and often not so far, it is impossible, save in the case of such as are gifted with more than ordinary capability, to acquire a complete and perfect knowledge of theology. Rarely can the Bishop allow time for a more extended course, and the College itself has neither sufficient means nor room for a body of professors. Nor, as in other countries, are our Colleges situated in cities, so that professors with other occupation in the churches can take upon themselves the duty of teaching for some portion of each day. They are in the country, and almost all that is requisite for the complete course of education in them must be within their walls. It is therefore not to be wondered at if the teaching body consists for the most part of those who are prosecuting their theological studies at the same time, or who put them off to teach literature. Of the two, these latter lose much less than the former, inasmuch as they are devoting themselves but to one occupation at a time. We commend, therefore, to the care and zeal of Superiors the foundation of chairs with a suitable endowment. But it is desirable that no cleric should spend less than four entire years in the study of theology, and that each should go through the whole of the course without any interruption.

III. Our Colleges are to be praised, that for teaching theology they have sought out and warmly received professors from foreign parts, whether Italian or German. This has taken place recently, and shews clearly that nothing is dearer to the Superiors than advancement in this study. But still it were, perhaps, to be wished that the number of theological chairs should be increased and filled by men of learning and even by graduates in honours. For then not only would the knowledge of sacred things be fuller and deeper, but very useful additions could be made to the branches now taught.

IV. For example, although the study of Sacred Scripture is not neglected, but rather considering the circumstances carefully cultivated, yet what is taught seems hardly sufficient for elucidating the questions which in these wretched times daily arise, or for the duty of preaching, or even for the ascetic and interior teaching of the soul. For it is difficult to describe how deep a **hatred there has grown up** in England in the minds of the enemies of religion against everything which is called or worshipped as God, especially His holy law. And objections of this kind are such that they can hardly be refuted without solid erudition.

V. For the acquirement of this an elementary knowledge, at least, of Hebrew would be doubtless a great assistance; so that all might sip of what a few with higher talents might perhaps follow up more extensively. And to have acquired even but a slight knowledge of it would be useless to no one.

VI. Since, now that the ecclesiastical hierachy has been happily restored in England, the administration of the dioceses must be carried on in accordance with law; and since important questions arise for discussion both in the provincial and diocesan synods, the solution of which depends upon the Canon Law, and is assigned to the study and counsel of priests; the necessity for setting to work at the study of Canon Law increases every day. All should go through the institutions at least of Canon Law, either in Devoti or some other approved author, and thus ground themselves upon sound principles.

VII. We particularly recommend the use of Latin in the study and teaching of theology, especially in maintaining scholastic disputes and public theses. For practice therein is for all ecclesiastics of the highest importance, particularly if they are promoted to any dignity or office, to enable them to draw up documents properly, and to write letters even with elegance in the Latin tongue.[1] But, in addition, dogmatic definition is always more accurate and the form of sound words more secure if the memory retains them, and they are quoted in discussion, in the language in which they have been handed down to us by the Church and her most eminent theologians. An end must, therefore we think be made of the neglect of this language of the Catholic Church, which may truly be styled the bond of orthodox unity and the medium of universal truth. Examinations in Theology should as far as possible be held in Latin.

VIII. "Faith comes from hearing, but hearing through the word of God. But how shall they hear without a preacher?" *(Rom. x. 15)*. It is, therefore, one of the sublimest of a Priest's duties to be the herald of God's word, not so much by eloquence of language as by fruitfulness in teaching sound doctrine. Nor of less weight must be judged other pastoral duties, such as explanation of the Catechism, direction of the faithful in the way of salvation, and many others which it would be superfluous to enumerate. It would doubtless be of very great service to those who are to become priests as well as to the flocks one day to be entrusted to them, if a short course at least of what is called pastoral theology could be added to the list of studies, even in conjunction with the study of asceticism. But if this cannot be done, it should at least be impressed upon the students that before proceeding to the

---

1. See Letter from Propaganda, p. 204.

exercise of their ministry, they should earnestly endeavour to gain some knowledge of these subjects. The mind of each one could in like manner be directed to the cultivation of liturgical and historical learning, "that he might be a perfect man of God prepared for every good work." (2 Tim. iv. 17).

IX. Finally, to come to an end of this matter: if we have shewn a wish that boys should from their earliest years be brought up and taught in piety and the ecclesiastical virtues, how much more do we desire to see those who are older and are advanced nourished no longer by milk but by the bread of the strong. They should now proceed from virtue to virtue, they should aim at higher things, by renewed endeavours they should draw nearer to God, that they may be found worthy of the heritage they have desired. Now should they be more and more indoctrinated in the ways of promoting in the Church, the glory of God and the salvation of souls, and spreading an ardent love for the most Divine Sacrament of the Eucharist, and a most tender devotion to Mary the Immaculate Mother of God, so that the minds of all may be inflamed with charity and zeal. And if at times the Bishop can himself preside over the conferences upon such subjects and add to them the force and grace of words of his own, nothing better or more suitable in our judgment can be imagined for training up in these our present Colleges a clergy full of the Spirit of God.

XV.—THE GOVERNMENT OF THE COLLEGE.

So far we have spoken of the internal discipline of the three Colleges. But seeing that it is of the highest moment that provision should be made for their right government, and that whatever rights pertain to the Bishops in whose Dioceses the Colleges are situated, as well as to those others who have an interest in them, should be fairly dealt with, the following scheme framed to meet the special circumstances of the three Colleges is laid down, provided leave of the Holy See be given. With the proviso, however, that this scheme is merely a provisional one made for a time and in force only until the Holy See abolishes it and provided that it does not interfere with or cause delay in erecting Seminaries after the mode prescribed by the Council of Trent as soon as possible in every Diocese.

1. Jurisdiction over and spiritual care of a College pertain only to the Ordinary of the Diocese in which it is situated.

2. The right and authority to determine and arrange as to material and temporal matters, the studies, government and discipline of a college belong to the board of Bishops who have an interest therein. To wit, to the Archbishop of Westminster and the Bishop of Southwark for the College of St. Edmund, situate in

the Diocese of Westminster; to the Bishops of **Hexham, Beverly, Salford, Liverpool** and **Shrewsbury** for the College of St. Cuthbert, situate in the Diocese of Hexham; and to the Bishops of **Birmingham, Nottingham** and **Northampton** for the College of St. Mary at Oscott, situate in the Diocese of Birmingham. We decide that the administration of the temporalities, both movable and immovable, of the Colleges shall be undivided, until the Holy See has passed judgment upon the several rights of each. But for this end, the Bishops having an interest in any one of the three Colleges shall nominate for that College one or three proper persons to draw up an accurate and conscientious account within one year and present it to the Holy See, of the property of every kind, sources of income and rights pertaining in any way to the said College, no matter where, with suitable observations as to the origin of each, its purpose, and present condition.

3. This Board should meet once a year on the day to be agreed upon by the Bishops interested at their first meeting. And this must be within one year of the date of approbation of this Synod.

4. If at any time the majority of the Bishops should desire it the Bishop who is the Ordinary must summon the Bishops who have a share in the matter to hold an extraordinary meeting.

5. The Ordinary of the place shall preside over every meeting; and when the votes are equal he shall have another and the casting vote. Where there are but two Dioceses, if the Bishops cannot come to an agreement, the question shall be laid before the Holy See for settlement.

6. That the vigilance and influence which come from a single and present superior may never be wanting, authority shall always be exercised by the Ordinary of the place, who is bound to adhere to the rules framed for his College and the decrees made by himself together with the other Bishops interested. The Ordinary, however, shall not have power to make any notable or extraordinary changes or to incur any notable or extraordinary expense without the consent of the majority of the aforementioned Bishops.

7. That the government of the College may be stable and firm, no essential changes as to the government and administration of the College shall be made unless it has been approved of by Decree at the annual meeting, and notice given of it at the meeting of the previous year.

8. Since the office of Rector is of such great importance and persons remarkable for their piety, wisdom and experience, should be chosen to fill it, the College shall be entrusted to one Rector or President, whom the assembled Bishops shall appoint by a majority of the votes.

9. The appointment of the Vice-Rector should be made by the Rector with the concurrence of the majority of the Bishops signified by the Ordinary.

10. The Professors of Theology and Philosophy shall be appointed by the Ordinary with the consent of the majority of the Bishops; the remaining Superiors and Professors by the Rector with the consent of the Ordinary.

11. The Procurator shall be chosen by the Ordinary with the advice of the other Bishops and the consent of the majority of them.

12. No ecclesiastical student can be received into a College without a document in which the Bishop whose Diocese he is for declares that he approves of him as a fit subject.

13. Unless the case be one of extreme urgency, the expulsion of an ecclesiastical student, even one not tonsured, shall not be determined upon by the Rector without the consent of the student's Bishop.

SEMINARIES.

IV. Westminster, Decree ix., p. 36.

1. Whilst our Lord lived upon earth for the salvation of the human race, He seems to have bestowed the utmost care in choosing Himself from amongst the people certain men to work with Him. And those whom He called from the world to Himself, He instructed sedulously with his own lips, He lived in their midst eating and drinking with them, ever preceding them in the way of the cross and He himself the first to accomplish before their eyes that which had to be done.

By words, therefore, and example He taught them, who were one day to rule the church in His name, that they should live amongst their disciples with the same intimacy and holy influence, fulfilling the precept: "Let him who is greater amongst you, become as the lesser; and him who is the master, as a servant."[1]

2. And we know that the Church religiously followed in these footsteps of our Saviour during those ages when it is undeniable that she shone with the splendour of perfection and enjoyed a full liberty.

In the Roman Church, from the time of Constantine until the thirteenth century the clergy were trained at the Lateran School under the eyes of the Pontiff. And as time went on, it was decreed at many Councils held in various parts of Europe that the clergy should be brought up near the Bishop or in his palace.

From the commencement, therefore, of the Church, it was altogether considered to be the right thing in reference to vocation to the priesthood, that the clergy should be educated apart from the laity. For those who are called to higher duties must be brought up under a higher kind of discipline.

3. And this distinction was as far as was possible, observed both in episcopal and monastic schools for the first twelve centuries. But when the episcopal schools had to a certain extent died out, owing to the establishment of universities in Europe, the

---

[1] St Luke xxii, 26.

church always took care that this distinction should be faithfully adhered to; and hence at these very universities, houses and colleges were set apart for clerical students to dwell in apart from others, that thus, to some extent at least, the evils which were apprehended as likely to beset the young levites from worldly intercourse might be avoided,

But as the evils which clerical students had to cope with in the universities by reason of the number and excessive freedom of the inmates became greater, divers remedies came to be suggested by different persons.

4. At length our own Cardinal Pole, Archbishop of Canterbury, published a constitution for the reformation of England, and in it he laid down the present system of Seminaries. This was three years subsequently highly praised and accepted at the Council of Trent.[1] And the word *Seminary*, by which Episcopal Schools established for the education of the clergy are now called throughout the Catholic world, this illustrious Cardinal was the first to make use of in the constitution for England quoted.

In the Tridentine decree it was not only enacted that diocesan Seminaries should be set up, but it was specially decided that those alone should be received therein whose "character and aspirations give promise that they will for ever devote themselves to the ecclesiastical ministry."[2]

5. Accordingly, since the Council of Trent, the acts of provincial synods, as well as the example and encyclical letters at all periods of the Chief Pontiffs, together with the terms of the concordats which the Holy See has in these modern times entered upon with several countries, plainly lay it down that according to the mind of the Church the Diocesan Seminary is under the power of the Bishop alone, and is essential to the completeness of a duly established diocese.

And if in several places the younger boys, both clerical and lay, are taught together—and this has been permitted owing to circumstances of place and time—yet the Church has never failed to urge that those aspiring to Sacred Orders, and who had arrived at a more advanced age, and especially those who are applying themselves to philosophical and theological pursuits, should live apart from the intercourse brought about by living in common with laics. In perfect accord with these wishes and prescriptions of the Church, the Bishops of England published the well-known Decree "Upon founding Seminaries" in the third Provincial Council of Westminster.[3]

6. Wherefore this Fourth Synod, having before its eyes the example of our Lord, as well as the practice of the Church and the needs of our time, decrees and determines:

---

1. Decree XI. Pro Reform. Anglic.
2. Council of Trent. Session XXIII. On Reformation, c. 18.
3. Decree XIII. See p. 218.

(1.) The Bishops shall, in their respective dioceses, exercise great care and caution in the selection of candidates for the Priesthood, either personally or by examiners appointed for this purpose. The Bishops shall, accordingly, use every endeavour to found and increase the number of burses, and encourage others to do so. The clergy shall do their part; and each in his own mission should carefully look out boys of a good disposition, and, in addition to literature, train them up in doctrine and virtue, so that they may be all the more fit to meet the approbation of the diocesan examiners, and to be admitted to the course of ecclesiastical studies. The Council of Trent "wishes that the children of the poor be chiefly taken, whilst, however, it does not exclude those of the rich, provided they are educated at their own expense, and keep before their eyes the aim of serving God and the Church."[1] Poverty which Jesus Himself consecrated shall be an impediment to no one who is superior in character and in talent.

(2.) The Bishops, each in his own diocese, shall leave no stone unturned that a Diocesan Seminary may be set up, in which the Church students may be taught their philosophy and theology apart from any intercourse with laics. But in cases where dioceses are so poor that they cannot singly provide Seminaries, it has been provided by the Council of Trent that the Bishops of several dioceses should form together by mutual arrangement a common Seminary.

7. It is greatly to be desired that, as Christ lived in the midst of His Apostles, so also should the rector of the Seminary, together with those to whom the teaching of the students is entrusted, live in common with the Seminarists, and both by word and example instruct, correct, and console them. And it would greatly add to the spiritual welfare of the students if a spiritual prefect were appointed in the Seminary by the Bishop.

Superiors should ever bear in mind that the special and chief end of the Seminary is that its inmates should learn to live for God alone in Christ. Therefore, the spirit of Jesus should penetrate and vivify the depths of the soul of each cleric, so that truly may he say what St. Paul proclaimed of himself: "To me to live is Christ;"[2] and elsewhere, "I live, now not I, but Christ liveth in me."[3] This should be his hope, this his meditation, this his primary exercise, to lead interiorly the life of Christ; a life shown outwardly by knowledge, by seriousness, by zeal for souls and piety.

8. They should oftentimes reflect how dangerous and unbecoming it is for one to be the means of bringing the grace of Christ to others who is not seen to be endowed with it beyond others.

The Seminarists should cultivate and cherish the most tender and ardent affection of piety towards Jesus the Lord and Master of

---

1. Council of Trent. Session XXIII. On Reformation, c. 18.
2. Philippians, i. 21.
3. Galatians, ii. 20.

Priests, dwelling ever most lovingly in the Most Holy Sacrament of the Eucharist in the midst of His disciples. They should bear in mind that in this mystery of His love exists their support during the struggle to come, the sustenance of their spiritual life, their strength in difficulties, their comfort in trials, their safeguard at the last hour. Hence, from the very commencement, they should refer everything to Jesus, adorable in the Sacrament of the Altar, as the Prince of Pastors, and humbly beg everything of Him as the source of all sanctification. And since the Lord Jesus has promised the vision of God to those who are clean of heart, all who are even at the first threshold of the Priesthood should cultivate a purity of body and soul free from the shadow even of uncleanness. And to arrive at this purity more easily and more surely, they should ever honour and imitate with a filial love and a most tender devotion our Immaculate Mother Mary, the Queen of Virgins, the Mother of God. They should also constantly cherish devotion to the protector of Virgins, Saint Joseph, the chief pattern of chastity.

9. In addition to other virtues characteristic of a Priest, this Synod considers that some should be specified which should be inculcated by the superiors of Seminaries with special earnestness, seeing that they are the particular antidotes and remedies for the deadly evils of our time.

The luxury, therefore, of this world—too lavish an expenditure upon food, clothing, and furniture, an effeminate life, delicate habits, too great a love of ease and rest: all of which things ever weaken one's powers and mind—should be subdued and overcome by a manly simplicity, by the love of the Cross, and by holy assiduity in labour. The Lord's servant in the Gospel is called to labour, not to repose. He should, therefore, learn to rejoice above all things in difficulties, in poverty, in contempt, in an humble and evangelical life. Never should he forget the precept of Jesus: "He who does not take up his cross and follow Me, is not worthy of Me."[2] "If any one will come after Me, let him deny himself, and take up his cross, and follow Me."[2]

10. It is of especial use to the young that from their early years they should keep method and order as strictly as possible both in their studies and other works. They should always bear in mind the example of our own Venerable Bede, of whom the historian says, that "he was never overcome by sloth, never rested from his occupation: was always reading, always writing, always teaching, always praying, knowing that the lover of healthy knowledge would easily overcome the vices of the flesh."[3]

Unless they shun sloth as a pestilence, and keep themselves manfully to work, they should be sure that hereafter they will neglect the vineyard of the Lord and by their laziness and inactivity prove the ruin of many souls.

---

1. Matthew, x. 39.   2. Matthew xvi. 28.   3 Roman Breviary.

11. The seminarist should be taught from his earliest years that avarice is the root of all evils, and he should conceive a deep affection for that poverty which our Lord chose as the inheritance of Himself and His Apostles; for He, as the Apostle tells us, "for you was made poor although He was rich, that by His poverty you might become rich."[1]

From his first entrance, therefore, to the seminary, the cleric should learn to love and reverence poverty as an evangelical counsel; and although he is not called upon to practise poverty by vow, yet he should become convinced that all must become poor in spirit, and that in this consists the likeness to Christ and to the saints. "Blessed are the poor in spirit, for theirs is the kingdom of heaven."[2]

The great model of the secular clergy, St. Charles Borromeo, did not expend his wealth upon himself nor hoard it in his coffers; but, living in strict poverty, he regarded the poor and the church as the real owners of his riches. And speaking to his priests he was wont to say: "You know how great is the perfection of poverty; what help it affords to those who are fishing for souls, and how amongst those first fishers the Apostles our Lord made it an essential requisite, seeing that he allowed them to possess neither bag, purse, nor scrip."[3]

12. Finally, this Synod considers that those to whom the education of clerics in ecclesiastical seminaries is entrusted, should be admonished to weigh well that the disturbance of human society and the everywhere prevalent seditions spring, as from a poisoned source, from an unrestrained lust for independence and unbridled liberty as well as from the spirit of criticism and the desire to carp.

This pestilent spirit is now working its way and being propagated very freely amongst men of every kind, especially by means of books, pamphlets and newspapers, in which everything sacred as well as profane is indiscriminately criticised and run down, and subjected, as is the wont of heresy, to the scrutiny and decision of each one's private judgement. Now nothing is more opposed to the ecclesiastical spirit or more contrary to the warnings of our Lord than this, for He has taught us by His word and by His life to be meek and humble of heart, and by His example to be obedient even unto death.

Wherefore it is necessary that the greatest possible reverence and deference towards the office and person of everyone in authority should be instilled into the minds of the young men whilst they are inmates of the Seminary; and this especially in reference to their own Bishop, who is the father and shepherd of his clergy. They should only speak of him with filial veneration, and willingly and without murmuring yield not only to his commands but to his wish and advice. They should learn betimes the

---

1. 2. Cor. viii. 9.   2. Matthew, v. 3.   3 Homily cxx. of St. Charles Barromeo.

lesson of respect and deference, since these should be shewn to all alike, as well the superiors of seminaries as the rectors of missions, together with those senior priests as fellow-workers with whom they will one day be sent forth. Hence the spirit of secretly condemning and all discontented murmuring should be carefully shunned, as extremely opposed to peace and to holiness. And whoever hears anything of the kind, should by word or at any rate by example put it down.

13. As education is now-a-days more widely diffused than heretofore, it is meet that the course of studies of priests should be extended and be attended to with greater care. It would, therefore, be desirable that the course of theology should comprise four years at the least. Theological studies must be attended to with the utmost earnestness, especially upon all points that are connected with dogma, morals, pastoral care, the spiritual and interior life, and the Sacred Liturgy. The students should likewise be taught the principles of common and canon law, the decrees and instructions of the Provincial Councils of Westminster, as well as sacred hermeneutics and ecclesiastical history. Moreover, since the clergy are trained to be the leaders and masters of souls, the false opinions of modern times should be treated of by the professors with especial attention, particularly those connected with points of philosophy, which are propagated in every kind of literature, and are constantly broached in ordinary society.

In teaching the seminarists, no other authors or works should be used but those that have been sanctioned beforehand by the ordinary.[1] From amongst those students who excel in talent and studies, some may be chosen at the will of the Bishop to go through a more complete course of theology at Rome or elsewhere, after they have happily finished their prescribed course.

14. Since preaching the word of God is one of the chief duties of a priest and the salvation and sanctification of souls depend much upon it, it is essential that the young men should be taught the holy practice of preaching whilst inmates of the Seminary. They should read attentively St. Augustine's books upon *Catechising the Ignorant* and upon *Christian Doctrine*, and St. Charles's instructions, to the end that earnestness may be imparted to them in acquiring a greater degree of piety as well as the spirit of prayer and a proficiency in learning, and each should weigh well what a herald of the Gospel should be if he would look for a happy result from his labour. The preacher of the Gospel should ever be mindful of the precepts of St. Charles: "He should not affect an over-refined kind of elocution; he should shun every kind of affectation . . . . he should make use of serious not pompous language . . . . he should consider himself as the fisher of men; and hence he should strain every nerve and fish in order to fill the evangelical net, to wit, to gain to Christ our Lord the souls of those who are perishing."

---

[1] Provincial Councils of Utretch, p. 313.

That students might be exercised and make progress in the practice of preaching, Pope Pius IX., in his Apostolical Letter *Cum Romani Pontificis*, ordained as follows for the Pius Seminary. "For practising preaching of the divine word we have decreed that several competent young students of theology shall be selected to explain the holy gospel from the pulpit during Mass." A competent ecclesiastic should be set aside "to instruct and prepare privately the students of his Seminary for this exercise and for sacred discourses by means of befitting rules and models."

And that they may more surely acquire the faculty of penetrating the minds of others and of propounding more lucidly the mysteries of faith with an eye to the capabilities of the many, all of which forms a chief part of the preacher's art, the Seminarists should be sedulously practised in catechising the poor. Let them, if possible, teach catechism in any schools not far from the Seminary, and immediately the work is done return to the Seminary.

15. It is part of a priests duty to direct and to lead consciences to perfection. Hence the Synod is wishful that in the Seminaries some time should be spent in Ascetic theology, and that suitable instructions upon this branch should be given, in order that the pious faithful may approach the pastors of their souls with confidence for spiritual direction.

16. Since the students will have to attend in the course of time to the management of missions and schools, they should study betimes and whilst in the Seminary the mode of keeping the registers, and keeping an account of income and expenditure, as prescribed in the Provincial Council of Westminster. They should likewise be practised in writing official letters, whether upon ecclesiastical or civil matters, politely and with due regard to persons in authority.

17. As to what pertains to the external and internal discipline of a diocesan Seminary, two remarks must be made. One is, that the discipline should be sufficiently strict, not only for the maintenance of order, without which common life cannot exist, but for completely ascertaining the docility of the candidates, their obedience, self-denial, piety and fitness for the ecclesiastical state; and no one should be promoted to sacred orders who has not shewn signs of real progress in these matters. The other, that as those who labour in the Lord's vineyard should, according to the Apostle, be all things to all men, great care should be taken that the Seminarists be taught to conduct themselves in such a way before the world as ever to combine priestly modesty and simplicity with politeness: "To no one giving offence, lest our ministry be blamed."[1] Always should the precept of the Council of Trent be borne in mind: "Thus it is becoming that clerics, called to have the Lord for their portion, ought so to regulate their whole life and conversation, that in their dress, comportment, gait, discourse and

---

1. 2. Cor. vi. 3.

everything else, nothing should appear but what is grave, regulated and marked by a religious tone; avoiding even slight faults, (which in them would be very great), so that their actions may impress all with veneration."[1]

18. Moreover, it must ever be apparent that rules from without in reference to progress in virtue are of little avail, unless they are willingly and cheerfully accepted and kept by the students, so that they serve not to the eye but please God from pure hearts. Beautiful is that maxim of St. Charles, laid down in the institution of his Seminary, to wit: "The acquirement of virtue depends mainly upon the earnestness and industry of each one, rather than upon the care of rectors and masters; so that the endeavours of others will avail little or nothing, unless one sets to work himself."[2]

But let no seminarist falsely persuade himself that a rule of life is unnecessary, seeing that, on the contrary, a secular priest, so called because he has to labour in the world, stands in greater need of a rule of life than others. But taught by his practice in keeping himself under restraint and living up to a rule of life, in the Seminary, he should easily come to understand how useful it will be for him, even upon the mission, to live in constant custody over self, and to conform his life to a rule adapted to his obligations and duties. "He who lives for rule, lives for God."[3]

19. Finally, since the seminarists are called to leave the conveniences and comforts of worldly life and to devote themselves wholly to God and the salvation of souls, they should shun contact with the world and not even at vacation time visit their relations without the Bishop's leave.

20. The proclamations as to those who are to be ordained should be made beforehand in the Seminary.

21. Lastly, since a Bishop according to the teaching of Benedict XIV., is bound to know his own candidates for the priesthood, and on his conscience rests their ordination, it will, therefore, be his duty to visit them frequently as their pastor and father, that he may know his own and be well known by them. Moreover, he will provide and require that he shall receive from every rector a distinct account at least once a year of the disposition, behaviour, progress in knowledge and in virtue, and perseverance in his vocation of each seminarist.

Benedict XIV. affectionately admonished the Bishops of the Catholic Church in reference to Seminaries as follows: "But it is essential that these colleges should be cherished by you with an especial devotion, manifested by oftentimes visiting them, examining into the life, disposition and progress of each young man, setting aside for their management fit masters and men imbued with the ecclesiastical spirit; honouring at times with your presence their literary exhibitions and ecclesiastical functions, and conferring rewards upon those who are foremost in shewing signs of ability

---

1. Session xxii. the Reformation. cl.   2. Part 3, c. 1.   3. St. Gregory the Great.

and have merited an extra degree of praise. For you will not repent of having bestowed nurture of this kind upon these plants in their youth; your labour will one day yield you a most joyous return in a rich abundance of good workmen. Often, indeed, have Bishops been wont to grieve that the harvest is great, but the labourers few; but, perchance, they ought also to grieve that they themselves have not bestowed the care that was due from them that labourers equal and fit for the harvest should be got ready. For good and earnest labourers are not born but made. And it belongs chiefly to the activity and care of the Bishops to see that they are made." [1]

---

1. Encyclical Letter Dec. 3. 1740.

CHAPTER THE TENTH.

THE LAITY.

EDUCATION OF THE LAITY.

IV. Westminster, Decree xvii., p. 69.

1. The teaching or education of those who have been "born again" is nothing but the conducting of man to God. For Christian education not only informs the intellect but directs and leads the will to God.

2. Those therefore, must not be considered to be educated, whose intellect alone has been cultivated, but, who in heart and soul are far from God by ignorance of the dogmas of faith, and, oftentimes, in consequence of this ignorance, by evil disposition and wickedness of life. Hence, justly has that insidious proposition been reprobated and condemned, that literature and science of every description should be studied apart from any religious teaching.[1] Likewise, must the modern growing idea be rejected, that the dogmas of christian faith can be expelled from the schools of a christian people. And to these errors must undoubtedly be added those long ago denounced by Pius IX., "The entire government of public schools in which the youth of any Christian state is educated, except, to a certain extent, in the case of Episcopal Seminaries, may and ought to appertain to the civil power, and belong to it so far that no other authority whatsoever, shall be recognized as having any right to interfere in the discipline of the schools, the arrangement of the studies, the conferring of degrees, the choice or approval of the teachers." "Moreover, even in Ecclesiastical Seminaries, the method of studies to be adopted is subject to the civil authority."[2]

---

[1]. Letter of Pius IX, to the Archbishop of Munich, Dec. 21st. 1863. For an account of this important letter see Dublin Review, 1864, p. 65, and the Home and Foreign Review, 1864, p. 697. The passage referred to is as follows : "Since all agree that progress in science and success in avoiding and refuting the error of the evil times in which we live, depend altogether upon that internal adhesion to those revealed truths which the Catholic Church teaches, they have recognized and professed that truth, which true Catholics devoted to the culture and futherance of science have ever held and handed down. And supported by this trust, these wise and true Catholics have been able to cultivate these sciences with safety, to unfold them, and to render them useful and stable. Now this cannot be done if the light of human reason, circumscribed as it is, does not, in searching even into those truths which it can read into by its own power and faculties, hold in especial veneration, as is but just, the infallible and uncreated light of Divine intellect, which wondrously shines forth on every side in the Christian revelation. For although these natural sciences depend upon principles cognizable to reason, yet Catholic students of them should keep Divine revelation as a guiding star before their eyes, that by its light they may avoid mistakes and errors when in their investigations and remarks they perceive that they may be led on, as oftimes happens, to give utterance to that which is more or less in opposition to the infallible truth of those things which God has revealed."

[2]. Syllabus Prop. 45, 46.

3. For to that cure of souls, conferred by our Lord Jesus Christ upon His Church belongs the education of every one baptized, of whatever condition,—rich or poor. This prerogative of supreme jurisdiction has been incontestably established by numberless decisions of Pontiffs and is still in full force, and calls back or keeps back all Christ's faithful from non-catholic schools.

Hence, at the First Provincial Council of Westminster, the Fathers deliberated most prudently upon this important matter, and earnestly exhorted all the faithful of England, as well rich as poor, carefully and dutifully to keep their children and wards from any kind of contact with non-catholic education. Conferring together immediately upon the restoration of the Hierarchy, they issued most weighty instructions to the clergy, in which priests on the mission were urged to erect and extend schools in each mission for the catholic education of the children of the poor. Moreover, the Fathers of the Council were desirous that other schools also should be carefully provided, in which children of a better class could receive their education. And they enjoined it upon all preachers and confessors, that from the pulpit and in the confessional they should use every means to admonish the faithful of the necessity of faith, of the duties of parents to their children, and of the account to be rendered to God, at His terrible judgment, if by their fault they are lost.[1]

4. Twenty years have now elapsed since these exhortations were issued by the Bishops of England in Synod assembled. And they are at this present time of even greater use, yea, of absolute necessity. For the laws lately enacted relative to elementary schools for the people, as they are called, clearly increase and aggravate all the dangers that beset catholic education. For instruction in the articles of faith is completely struck out of the *horarium* of instruction, and consigned to extra time. Aids and incentives to piety, which heretofore characterised and made holy the whole of the day, are for the future banished both from the books in use and from the lips of the teachers. The zeal and care of our earnest clergy must therefore be increased to the utmost, lest a single moment be useless or lost of that one hour, which is allowed for the instruction of the children in matters of faith and for the duties and practices of devotion. In reference to this dangerous mode of teaching and to the separation of religion from ordinary studies, our most holy Father, Pius IX, with pastoral solitude thus admonishes us. "But great as is the loss to men and to society by that most mischievous mode of teaching without reference to the Catholic faith and the power of the Church in the higher paths of literature and science and in the education provided in public schools and institutions, who does not see that much greater evils and losses ensue from this system if it is introduced into the schools of the people? For in these schools, beyond

---

1. I. Westminster Decree viii. 2, 5.

others, children of all classes of the people should from their earliest years be carefully taught the mysteries and precepts of our most holy religion, and skilfully fashioned to piety and morality as well as to religion and the way to conduct themselves in civil life. And in these schools religous instruction should so hold the chief place, and be of such importance in the course of studies and means of education, that the other subjects taught the children, should appear to be secondary. Hence the young are exposed to the greatest dangers unless their instruction in schools of this kind be intimately associated with religious doctrine. Indeed, in places and countries where this most pernicious plan for banishing the authority of the Church from schools was undertaken or carried out, not only straightway and without doubt ought the Church to make every endeavour with the utmost energy, and spare no pains that the children might have the requisite christian instruction and education, but she would be compelled to warn all the faithful and to declare to them that schools of this kind opposed to the Catholic Church cannot in conscience be attended."[1]

5. Wherefore, with all solicitude and in the very words of the Fathers we renew and decree what was determined at the First Council of Westminster: " Besides the teaching of the Catechism which goes on every day in the school, a catechetical instruction shall be given publicly in the Church every Sunday in which the mysteries of faith, the commandments of God and of the Church, and the Sacraments should be clearly and intelligibly explained. And the priest should strive that, whilst he lowers himself to the intelligence of the children, he should speak in a way to interest those who are instructed. In fact, by the style of his language and by illustrating his discourse with full and apt quotations from Sacred Scripture and examples from the lives of the Saints, he should bring his adult hearers to listen and to learn." [2]

Since the care of the young must be reckoned amongst the chief duties of a pastor, all to whom the charge of souls has been entrusted should be aware that it by no means suffices that the schools within the boundaries of the mission, whether public or private, be visited and managed by others, but that they themselves are strictly bound to watch over them and oftentimes go and see them. A catechetical instruction should be given either by the rector of the church himself or by his assistants, to the boys and girls of every mission on Sundays, in the presence if possible of the people, as well as at the schools at least once in the week. As to children in prisons, workhouses, and other abodes maintained at the public expense or by charity, missionary priests should have at their finger ends and keep before their eyes the civil laws relating thereto, that when occasion requires it, they may be able

---

[1]. Letter " Quam non sine" to the Archbishop of Friburg, July 14th, 1864.
[2]. I. Westminster Decree viii.

to handle the cause of the poor not only boldly but in a skilful and becoming manner, and to battle for and defend their religious rights, as well as establish for themselves the right to visit them at least at stated times.

6. In view of the daily increase of the class of family which can be regarded neither as rich nor poor, we make a similar decree for rectors of the larger missions to that most wisely passed at our First Provincial Council: that is, we recommend that as soon as possible schools should be set on foot, or even small colleges, in which children of the better class may be carefully taught subjects bearing upon the pursuits and business of life, in addition to the ordinary elements of education.

7. Finally, although the day so longed for by the Fathers of the First Council of Westminster, when a Catholic University should be established, has not yet dawned upon us, still, relying upon and encouraged by the authority and command of the Apostolic See, it is our intention to promote and set on foot a course of higher studies in literature and science. For the Sacred Congregation of Propaganda has long since by repeated letters admonished the Bishops of other countries that the foundation and management of a Catholic University belongs to the cure of souls and to the pastoral jurisdiction of the Hierarchy; and that accordingly to this same jurisdiction it belongs to get together and have ready everything that can conduce to the wished for end. By the truly wonderful providence of God, the Catholic Church in England, even during the direst straights of persecution and of poverty, has erected several Colleges, at this moment flourishing, which might be described as a beginning of a University properly so-called. Now to add to these foundations in due time their crown and completion would be a less difficult task for ourselves or our successors. For within the walls of these Colleges there are already a number of young men successfully pursuing a course of more advanced studies, who should be transferred to some other place, where, separated from mere boys and under a *régime* prudently adapted to their age and more manly habits, they could prepare themselves for the future trial of life, not by studies alone, but also by habits of discipline. And the dangerous changes lately effected in the Universities of England most clearly shew the need of such a work. For that catholic and christian glory with which Holy Mother Church enriched their very foundation has passed away; gone, too, is the old teaching of revealed truth, as well as that sacred study of literature and science by means of which the disciples of Jesus and children of God, illumined by the divine light, were once brought to the perfection of manhood. Beyond the pale of the Catholic and Roman Church is nowhere to be found the unsevered connection of all truths both natural and supernatural. And when this is wanting, human reason also becomes imperceptibly obscured, and the very nature of man losing its likeness to the Creator becomes lowered. Hence it is our duty, with the utmost

thoughtful determination, which can neither be broken by threats nor overcome by enticements, to preserve, defend and hand down inviolate to posterity that changeless method of Catholic teaching which we received from our fore-fathers. And to make this more certain and speedy, the Sacred Congregation which, in 1868, with the approval of the Chief Pontiff, had already invited the Bishops of England to take counsel together concerning the erection in due time of a Catholic University in England, at the beginning of this very year again warned us in the gravest manner that the glory of God and the welfare of souls at present demand that no stone be left unturned to overcome the obstacles in the way of founding a Catholic University.[1]

8. Wherefore, in obedience to this letter from the highest authority, we have determined to leave no means untried, with the co-operation of others, to establish colleges and form a body of Examiners, for making an annual inquiry into the progress made in the higher branches of study, for promoting the same, giving prizes according to merit, and conferring academical degrees, as well as for doing everything calculated to pave the way for a University properly so called.

On Mixed Education.
An Encyclical Letter of the Sacred Congregation of Propaganda.
(IV. Westminster, Appendix xi p. 157. Decree xvii.).

My Lord,

The establishment of Mixed Schools and Colleges for Catholics and heretics, which has unfortunately for some time become from day to day more common, has induced the Holy See, in its desire to provide for the sound teaching of the faithful, to recall to mind right principles on this subject, to make suitable regulations, and, either through the Holy Office or through the Sacred Congregation of Propaganda, to give all necessary advice in the cases that have been brought before it: and it has been thought fit to draw up a compendium of the same in the present Letter.

1. Although there is a difference between Protestant and schismatical schools, and although, generally speaking, greater evils perhaps are to be feared from the former, yet even the latter are very dangerous to Catholic youth. Wherefore the S. Congregation of Propaganda, by a circular letter of March 20, 1865, warned all the Eastern Bishops of the very grave danger to which young Catholics are exposed in attending schools directed by schismatics or Protestants, which are now being opened more numerously than ever in the chief cities of the East; and it urged them zealously, and, if necessary, with all the force of their ecclesiastical authority, to put a stop to such a practice. Bishops above all, and parish priests, are bound to use all possible care in making parents understand that the greatest evil they can inflict upon their offspring,

---

1. See Appendix xvii.; and on mixed Education and non-Catholic Universities, xv. and xvi.

upon their country, and upon our holy religion, is to expose their children to so manifest a danger, and that the danger is even increased when such schools are established for the direct purpose of making converts to heresy and schism. Everyone knows how great is the influence of the authority of teachers over the young minds of their pupils, and how strongly the pupils are thereby drawn to approve whatever their teachers say or do : whence it happens that, while receiving instruction in the above-named schools, they adopt almost unconsciously the errors of their teachers, and learn to despise the Catholic religion. Add to this the daily and familiar intercourse with young Protestants and schismatics, who by their habits, which often are corrupt, by their indocility, and by their satirical remarks upon our holy religion and the practices of the Church, pervert the minds and deprave the hearts of their Catholic companions. And let it not be thought that, amongst such schools, those that are established for elementary instruction, or in which only secular subjects are taught, are free from all danger ; for, besides the evils arising from association and intimacy with companions who have been brought up in heresy and schism, the teachers also are able to mislead the simple minds of their pupils by artifices which are the more effective from being less perceived. All this has been treated of in an instruction lately issued for Switzerland, by the Supreme Congregation of the Holy Office, on March 26, 1866.

2. So far we have spoken of Catholics attending Protestant and schismatical schools. To speak now of the attendance of schismatics and Protestants at Catholic schools, it is clear that in this second case there are not the same dangers for Catholic pupils as in the first : for, as the teacher, the instruction, and the books are Catholic, there is nothing to fear in this respect. The S. Congregation of Propaganda has, therefore, in times past tolerated, and even given leave for, the admission of the children of heretics into schools established in the Missions under the direction of the missionaries, and has allowed them to be instructed therein by the Catholic teachers. Nevertheless, the said Congregation was aware that even in such schools as these, Catholic as they are in their management and teaching, a great danger would still arise from the admission of schismatical and Protestant pupils, chiefly by reason of their daily contract with the children of Catholics ; and therefore, when allowing such admission, it was careful to prescribe certain precautions for preserving Catholic children from all danger of perversion, and non-Catholics from the danger of indifference to religion. Some of the resolutions passed in this matter by the S. Congregation may here be mentioned.

1°. At a special meeting, held December 18, 1742, it was decided that the Capuchin missionaries of Moscow, in addition to the instruction in foreign languages and secular sciences which they gave to the children of Catholics, might, in a separate room, give the same instruction to such non-Catholics as desired it. The use of a separate room entirely or almost removes the dangers above described, arising from the intercourse of Catholics and non-Catholics, in which the chief difficulty of the Mixed Schools consist ; if indeed schools can strictly be called *mixed*, in which a distinct and separate place is assigned to the non-Catholic pupils. But for want of space or of means, or through a scarcity of teachers in missionary countries, this separate system could not, without the greatest difficulty, be everywhere introduced.

2º Towards the end of the last century, the Reformed Missionary Fathers in Upper Egypt had opened Schools for Catholics in several stations of that Mission, which were also attended by the children of the Coptic schismatics. The General Congregation, held August 29, 1791, was of opinion that this might be tolerated, in order to dispose the Coptic heretics to Catholicity, and to avoid giving them offence ; but it added, " periculum perversionis per magistrorum diligentiam removeatur." In conformity with this resolution of the Sacred Congregation, the prefect of the aforesaid Mission was informed that there need not be any difficulty in allowing the children of heretics to go to the Catholic schools ; that, on the contrary, much good might be expected from their attendance, inasmuch as they might thus become acquainted with the solid principles of our true religion, and the influence of the teachers might gain them over to the Church ; but that, lest any one of the Catholic children should be perverted, the teachers must take care to exclude from the schools all heretical children of an immoral character.

3º Passing over other similar decisions, we may refer to the case of the Armenian Bishops of the ecclesiastical province of Constantinople, who, at a conference held in 1853, had enumerated among the means of converting the schismatics of their nation the allowing their children to attend Catholic schools. The General Congregation of Propaganda thereupon gave orders for a letter to be written to the Archbishop and Primate, saying that the proposed means was recognised as well adapted to effect the conversion of the schismatics ; but that great prudence was necessary to prevent any evil consequences. For, in the first place, the Catholic children might be in danger of perversion, if they were allowed to hold long conversations with the schismatical pupils ; inasmuch as there would be found among the schismatics shrewd and talented youths, who, by their training at home, had become deeply rooted in schism ; and among the Catholics there would be some of poor abilities, and of little religious feeling. Secondly, if the schismatics were obliged to attend the religious exercises of the Catholics, there would be danger of their becoming hypocrites by pretending to be Catholics, and of their thus becoming indifferent to all religion. The Archbishop was then reminded that there was no question of admitting them to the sacraments, as that must be preceded by a formal abjuration, and a sincere declaration of their return to the Catholic religion. Finally, in order to ward off the dangers above mentioned, in schools where Catholics and schismatics are mixed together, the Bishops of the province were advised to draw up in their next provincial council suitable regulations for these mixed schools, subject to the approbation of this Sacred Congregation.

3. We have lastly to speak of the admission of schismatics and Protestants into Catholic boarding-schools and colleges. It would be impossible to lay down a sure and adequate rule, applicable to every such house of education, without special and accurate knowledge of all the circumstances affecting them. Hence it would be necessary to know precisely the object of the institution, the social position and age of its pupils, the kind and extent of the education there given, and its rules of internal discipline, especially with regard to the intercourse permitted either in boys' or in girls' schools, between pupils of different religions : such as whether they may freely associate and speak with one another, or are forbidden to speak upon religious topics. It would also be necessary to know how then on-Catholics are directed in religious matters : namely,

whether they are educated in the Catholic religion, with, or without, the consent of their parents ; and, if they are not so educated, whether they are permitted, or even obliged, to be present, together with the Catholics, at holy Mass and other practices of piety ; whether they have always to abstain from receiving their own sacraments, or are allowed sometimes to receive them in their schismatical churches, and, if so, who goes with them. Again, it would be important to know the number of Protestants and schismatics in each institution, and in what proportion they are to the Catholics.

It would be necessary, therefore, that the superiors of the several Missions should obtain, if possible, the information above referred to, respecting the mixed boarding-schools (or colleges) under their jurisdiction ; and should send it to the S. Congregation, so as to be furnished in reply with instructions suitable to the peculiar circumstances of each case. In the meantime, however, it will be useful to make known a decision which the Holy Office has recently given in the case of a mixed boarding-school, of Catholic girls of the Latin Rite and schismatic of the Oriental Rite. But it will be well, before quoting it, to give some idea of the internal regulations of the school, in order that the decision may be better understood.

The establishment is under the direction of nuns, for the education of Catholic girls, together with schismatics of the Oriental Rite. The proportion between them has not always been the same. For the last five years the schismatics have formed about a third part of the school. They are instructed, not only in secular subjects, but also in the Catholic religion if their parents expressly desire it. Besides receiving Catholic instruction, the schismatical pupils have spiritual reading, make spiritual retreats, and are present daily at holy Mass, together with the Catholics. They used also to say their prayers together ; but now, by direction of the Ordinary, to avoid communicating *in divinis*, they pray apart from the Catholics of the Latin Rite, and in their own national language. If their parents ask it, the schismatical girls are taken once or twice a year to the schismatical church, under the care of trustworthy persons, to receive the sacraments; otherwise they do not receive the sacraments at all. The Ordinaries for the time being never, it must be observed, approved of this system ; but they tolerated it in the hope that these girls, having received a Catholic education, might, when they went home and became *sui juris*, embrace the Catholic faith, and so be the means of bringing their husbands and children to it : and in fact ten of them have abjured their schisms, and one has converted her husband. At all events the Prelates hoped that, even if all were not converted, their Catholic education would cause them to lay aside their prejudices against the Catholic Church, and their hatred and contempt of Catholics. On the other hand, as the present Ordinary asserts, on account of the dulness of their understanding, there is no fear of the girls who are *materially* schismatics ever becoming *formally* such ; and to this the superiors of the establishment bear witness. The school, besides, if it did not receive schismatical girls, would not have means sufficient for the support of the nuns who direct it, and for the admission of the Catholic boarders, who are generally poor, at a reduced pension.

In answer to this statement the Supreme Congregation of the Holy Office replied as follows:—

Friday, June 1st, 1866.

"Non-Catholic girls may be permitted to enter an establishment directed by Sisters, provided they are of a good disposition and are taught in the manner laid down, yet without being obliged to assist at the Sacrifice of the Mass and other ecclesiastical functions, which should be left to their own option; but they should be forbidden ever to dispute with the Catholic girls upon matters having reference to religion; to go to a non-Catholic place of worship for the purpose of receiving the sacrament from non-Catholic ministers (but if in any instance this can in no way be stopped, the Sisters should be merely passive in the matter); and also forbidden to be visited by friends and acquaintances, relations and guardians excepted, without the Bishop's permission. And upon all these points the relations or guardians of these girls should be clearly and explicity informed, and their consent given to them previous to the admission of the girls in question. And this should be stated in writing to the Most Reverend the Archbishop (Ordinary), with an admonition that he see to the fulfilment of all these matters and to the spiritual welfare of the girls, as far as possible, after they have left the establishment. And the Sisters should be instructed that, should any one of them seek to be reconciled to the Catholic faith, the case must be referred to the Archbishop himself, who will arrange some prudent course of action, according to the circumstances of each case. And he should be extremely cautious lest by the admission of non-Catholics the slightest danger should come to the Catholic girls of perversion or of indifference."

The sentiments of the above-named Sacred Congregation, and the precautions required by it, may be gathered from this decision. But the decree is not to be interpreted as a general rule, applicable to every other mixed boarding-school: and this, by reason of the variety of circumstances in each particular case; respecting which, as we have said, most exact information would be desirable, in order that suitable regulations and instructions might in each case be given.

4. On January 16, 1841, in a letter addressed to the Metropolitans of Ireland, to be communicated to their Suffragans, it was stated, in conformity with the aforesaid rules, that, as the result of the Irish National System of Education in the secondary schools or in the lower classes, which had been promoted by the English Government for children of every denomination of Christians, seemed not to have been, during the ten years that it had lasted, injurious to the Catholic religion, this Sacred Congregation had thought fit not to give any definite judgment on the subject, but rather to leave this mode of instruction to the prudence and conscience of the Bishops; for the success of the system depended necessarily upon the vigilance of the Pastors, the use of proper precautions, and the experience which the future should give. But the Sacred Congregation seriously impressed upon the Bishops of Ireland how necessary it was that all books injurious to faith or good morals should be excluded from the schools; and that the Government instructor of the Catholic teachers for the classes of religion, morality, and history, should be a Catholic, or else that there should be no such instructor at all. The plan, moreover, of giving [only] secular instruction in the mixed schools was considered safer than that of teaching briefly the so-called fundamental and common articles of the Christian Religion, and reserving special instruction for the different sects separately. ('Che sarebbe cosa

più sicura d'insegnare le belle lettere nelle sole scuole *promiscue* di quello che insegnare ristrettamente i così detti articoli fondamentali e comuni della religione Cristiana riserbando una speciale istruzione separatamente alle singole sette.') Finally, the Bishops and Parish Priests were exhorted to take every means for preventing the contamination of any of the Catholic children by this national system of education; and to use every effort to obtain a better system, and more equitable conditions from the Government. The Sacred Congregation further informed those Prelates that it was desirable that the sites occupied by the schools should remain the property of the Bishops or Parish Priests; and lastly that they were to discuss this grave matter in provincial Synod, and to inform the Holy See of any change that might afterwards take place.

5. When, in the year 1857, higher schools were about to be established in the cities of Ireland under the exclusive direction of the Council of National Education—a measure (as the Holy See was informed) full of danger, by reason of the Protestant character of the schools and of the intention ascribed to the Government of using them for the perversion of Catholics,—by a letter of February 20th of that same year the Bishops were exhorted, in the name of the Sacred Congregation, to defend their flocks with anxious zeal; to watch over them with a care and diligence proportioned to the danger with which the salvation of souls was threatened by the new system; and by suitable admonitions, sermons, and pastoral letters, to preserve the faith from the contagion of error.

6. In regard to the mixed University Schools and Colleges, established by the English Government on the same system for the scientific instruction of youth, this Sacred Congregation, in a letter of October 9, 1847, expressed to the Irish Bishops its fear that such Colleges would be dangerous to the Catholic faith and injurious to religion: and it admonished them to have nothing to do with such establishments; and exhorted them rather to improve the condition of the existing Catholic Colleges, and to endeavour to erect a Catholic Academy. To allay the fears which had arisen, the English Government made some modifications in the statutes of the aforesaid system; but this Sacred Congregation, on a subsequent examination of the question, and considering the great intrinsic dangers of the system, did not deem it right to change its resolution, as above given: and this was communicated to the Irish Bishops in a letter dated October 11, 1848.

7. Lastly, it will be well to add the reply which, after examining the rules, the Sacred Congregation, at its general meeting of August 31, 1863, made to the founder of the Institute of the Sisters of Notre Dame de Sion, established in France. Speaking of the girls educated in their schools, it said 'that it was the desire of the Sacred Congregation that, as a general rule, only Catholic girls should be received. That if it happened that, for some grave reason, girls of other religions were admitted, *to be brought up, however, as Catholics*, the Bishop of the diocese should be informed of it, so that he might, in concert with the Superioress, make such arrangements as should be necessary for removing all danger of perversion; and that one rule should be that, when the girls were visited by their relatives, a sister should always be present.'

I have thought it well to bring these points under your Lordship's notice, that you may be safely guided in a matter which is, in these days especially, of the greatest importance for the integrity of Catholic faith and morality. It only remains for me to pray that our Lord may have you in His holy keeping.

Your Lordship's affectionate Servant,
ALEXANDER CARD. BARNABÒ,
Prefect.

JOHN SIMEONI, *Secretary.*

Propaganda, April 25, 1868.

THE APPOINTMENT OF A BODY OF EXAMINERS, ETC.
(IV. Westminster, Appendix, p. 168. Decree. XVII., 8.)

MOST ILLUSTRIOUS AND REVEREND LORD,

The recent attempts upon the part of your government against catholic education and entirely to separate the teaching of youth in England from religion, abundantly show that nothing at this moment presses more upon the Bishops of your Realm than to take into efficacious consideration the erection of an institute for catholic young men. Wherefore, our most Holy Lord, in that parental solicitude for the eternal salvation of the faithful of England and especially of its youth for which he is so remarkable, at an audience of March 30th last, determined that a command in the Lord should be made, that in his name you should be recommended to arouse the vigilance and energy of the Bishops of your several dioceses at your next meeting, in order that some plan might be adopted to meet with efficacy the great evils which are so justly to be dreaded in this matter.

And on this occasion, I cannot omit to remind your Grace of what in January, 1868, this Holy Congregation with the approval of the Supreme Pontiff resolved relatively to entering upon a plan for erecting in due time a Catholic University in England. In other words, the Sacred Congregation expressed its opinion that, in conjunction with the Superiors of those Religious Orders which had colleges in the several Dioceses, action should be taken as to the appointment of a body of Examiners for conferring academical degrees and doing anything else that might pave the way for the foundation of a University properly so called. But as your Grace has not up to the present moment made known the upshot of the plan, I have not the least doubt that obstacles in the way of carrying it out have arisen. Now the glory of God and the salvation of souls require that every attempt shall be made to overcome these obstacles, and to the prudence and zeal of your Grace and to the Bishops of England it entirely belongs to do this. This being so, it will be your duty to make earnest exhortation to your fellow Bishops of the province both with regard to the promotion of scientific instruction to such an extent that no excuse shall be left for lay persons for sending their sons to non-Catholic Universities, and also the appointment of a body of examiners, as above; persuading those upon whom all this depends, that when it is a question of a people's eternal salvation, no sacrifice must be shrunk from. And I will not omit to notice that a plenary council of the Irish Bishops is in preparation for this year, chiefly for setting on foot efficacious plans in reference to catholic education. And upon this matter fitting instructions will shortly be sent to them from the Holy See. I therefore deem nothing more expedient than that the energies and pains of the Bishops of England and Ireland should be in union. For where the danger is a common one, justly should the means of defence be in common.

I pray God to preserve you long safe and well.

Rome at the office of the Sacred Congregation of Propaganda. April 2nd, 1873.

Your Grace's,
Most dutifully,
AL. CARD. BARNABÒ, Prefect.
JOHN SIMEONI, Secretary.

To the Right Reverend Henry Edward, Archbishop of Westminster.

ON NON-CATHOLIC UNIVERSITIES.
(IV. Westminster, Appendix xvi, p. 166. Decree xvii., 8).

MOST ILLUSTRIOUS AND REVEREND LORD,

In a letter of February 3rd, 1865, to their Right Rev. Lordships the Bishops of England, the Sacred Congregation of Propaganda intimated that it most willingly confirmed the decision unanimously agreed to by the above-named Bishops at a recent meeting held in London, that Colleges should not be founded at the Anglican Universities of Oxford and Cambridge, and that Catholic Parents should be on due occasion persuaded not to send their sons to these Universities, seeing that the said Sacred Congregation saw how completely this decision of the Bishops was in accord with the principles laid down by itself in accordance with the view expressed by the Supreme Pontiff, whenever it has been consulted in reference to the dangers of mixed schools. When, accordingly, the English Prelates had made known to the priests of their several Dioceses this decision, confirmed as it was by this Sacred Congregation, in an encyclical letter addressed to the clergy on March 24th, 1865, it was to have been hoped that catholic fathers of families would conform themselves thereto, in order in every way to keep their sons away from the danger of perversion. But certain things have recently occurred which abundantly shew that the declarations issued by the Holy See upon this matter together with the said encyclical of the Bishops to their priests were not sufficiently promulgated. Hence it seems necessary that pastorals should be published by each of the Prelates of England in which they should lay down a clear and determined course of action for the clergy as well as the faithful of their several Dioceses in reference to this most important matter, which is so intimately connected with the eternal welfare of souls. But in as much as all persons have not had the same opinion in respect to keeping away from non-Catholic Universities, and indeed there are some who think that catholic young men might be allowed to go to such institutions either by reason of the temporal advantages to be gained or because in their judgments the law absolutely forbidding it is not certain, I think it worth while that your Grace should clearly explain in your pastoral the doctrine concerning the avoidance of proximate occasions of grievous sin, to which no one can expose himself (without mortal sin) without grave and proportionate necessity, and without making use of the means by which the proximate occasion of sin is made remote. Now in the matter in question, seeing that by the Supreme Pontiff's declaration there is an intrinsic and most serious danger, not only in regard of morals but chiefly with respect to faith, which is altogether necessary for salvation, who does not recognize that the circumstances can rarely, if ever, occur in which Catholic Unversities can be attended without sin? The levity and instability natural to youth, the errors which in the said institutions are imbibed as it were with the air they breathe and without the antidote of solid instruction, the very great influence which human respect and the sneers of one's fellows have over the young, are both so present and so proximate a danger to young men of falling off, that generally speaking there cannot be imagined any reason of sufficient force to warrant their being sent to non-Catholic Universities. This being the case, you will in your wisdom put forward in your pastoral the grounds from authority and from reason in such a way that it will be abundantly clear to all, priests as well as faithful, what they ought to think and do in a matter of this weighty moment. And I will not omit to impress upon your Grace to arrange with the other Bishops of England, that the letter in question shall be identical for all and published uniformly by all.

I pray God long to preserve you safe and well.

Rome, at the Office of the Sacred Congregation of Propaganda, August 6th, 1867.

Your Grace's,
Most dutifully

AL. CARDINAL BARNABÒ, Prefect.
H. CAPALTI, Secretary.

To the Most Rev. Henry Edward, Archbishop of Westminster.

ON SECRET SOCIETIES.

AN ALLOCUTION OF OUR HOLY LORD POPE PIUS IX., IN

SECRET CONSISTORY. September 25th, 1865.

IV. Westminster, Appendix xix., p. 173.

VENERABLE BRETHREN,

Amongst the many machinations and devices by means of which the enemies of Christianity have dared to attack the Church of God, and to undermine and uproot it by their endeavours—fruitless as these are, that evil society, Venerable Brethren, must without doubt be included, which is commonly called Freemasonry,[1] and which formed at first in a secret and hidden manner has burst forth to the common ruin of religion and of human society. When our predecessors, the Roman Pontiffs, first discovered its dangers and wiles, mindful of their pastoral duty they considered there should be no delay in restraining by their authority this sect, eager for crime and bent on wicked measures against sacred and public rights; and with the sentence of condemnation as with a dart did they pierce and overthrow it. Clement XII., Our Predecessor, in his Apostolic Letter proscribed this same sect, reprobated it,

---

1. *Societas Massonica.* They are sometimes styled *Liberi Muratores.*

and forbade the faithful in any way to encourage or aid it, much less join it, under pain of excommunication to be incurred *ipso facto*, and reserved to the Roman Pontiff alone. And this just and proper sentence Benedict XIV. confirmed in a published Constitution, and did not fail to arouse the chief Catholic Sovereigns to do all they could to uproot so destructive a sect and to banish it from their midst. And would that these Sovereigns had but hearkened to the voice of our Predecessor! Would that in so important a matter they had not acted remissly! Never would they have had to deplore such uprisings of sedition as those within our own and our fathers' memory, never such flames of war as those with which the whole of Europe has blazed, never such a depth of iniquity as that which has afflicted and still afflicts the Church. And now when the fury of wicked men had in no way been set at rest, one of our immediate Predecessors, Pius VII., anathematized the sect of the *Carbonari*, which had arisen chiefly in Italy and had become spread far and wide. And Leo XII., inflamed with a like zeal for souls, condemned in an Apostolic Letter both the former secret societies we have enumerated, and all others under whatever name, which were conspiring against the church and the civil power, and forbade them to all the faithful under pain of excommunication. Yet these earnest endeavours of the Apostolic See hardly met with the success that was to be hoped for. For the sect of Freemasonry, upon which we are speaking, was never either overcome or held in restraint; but has been so far and widely spread that in these arduous times it everywhere holds up its head with impunity and grows bolder. And we think that this arises to a great extent from the false notion which has taken hold of many persons, in their ignorance perchance of the iniquitous designs conducted in these secret assemblages, that this kind of society is harmless, and has been set on foot solely for assisting people and relieving their wants, and that nothing, accordingly, is to be feared from it as regards the Church of God. But who is there that understands not how far this is from the truth? For what means that union of sects, irrespective of religion and faith? What mean those secret meetings, that the strictest of oaths made by those who are admitted, in fine, tends never to divulge anything relating thereto? Whither the unheard of atrocity of the penalties to which they agree to submit themselves should they ever fail in their oath? Impious, indeed without doubt, and wicked must that society be, which so dreads the light: for he who doth wickedly, saith the Apostle, hateth the light. And how far different from it are those pious Societies of the faithful which flourish in the Catholic Church? There is nothing in them kept back or concealed. The laws by which they are regulated are open to all; open are the deeds of charity which are carried on by them in accordance with the teaching of the Gospel. And not without grief do we see that Catholic Sodalities of this kind, so useful for encouraging piety and beneficial for the relief of the poor, are in some places attacked and indeed overthrown, whilst the dark Masonic Society, so opposed to the Church of God and so dangerous to the security of kingdoms, is encouraged or at least allowed? But this severely and sharply strikes Us, Venerable Brothers, that we see some of those remiss and as it were asleep in the matter of reprobating sects of this kind in accordance with the Constitutions of Our Predecessors, who in all reason should be most on the alert as to the duty entrusted to them and to their office in a matter so important. And if any persons are of opinion that the Apostolic Constitutions against secret sects, their members and supporters, binding as they are under pain of anathema, have no force in those countries where such sects are permitted by the civil power, undoubtedly they make a great mistake; and We, as you are aware, Venerable Brethren, have elsewhere reprobated the conclusion following from this evil interpretation, and again do We reprobate and condemn it. For does that supreme power of feeding and ruling the Lord's flock, which, in the person of most Blessed Peter, the Roman Pontiffs received from Christ our Lord, as well as that supreme *magisterium* which they must in consequence exercise over the church, depend upon the civil power, or can it be in any way restrained or fettered thereby? This being the case, we have determined, Venerable Brethren, to raise our Apostolic voice chiefly lest careless men and youths be led astray, but as well lest occasion be taken to uphold error through our silence. And here in this your assemblage we confirm the above-mentioned Constitutions of our Predecessors, and by our Apostolic authority reprobate and condemn that Masonic society and other societies of the same kind which differing only in unessentials are daily springing up, and which whether openly or in secret plot against the church or lawful power; and we wish them to be considered by all Christ's faithful of every condition and every place as proscribed and reprobated by Us, under the same penalties as are set down in the aforesaid Constitutions of Our Predecessors. It only remains now for us with all the earnestness of Our paternal soul to warn and arouse the faithful who perchance have entered their names with sects of this kind, to betake themselves to better counsels, to abandon those deplorable meetings and assemblages, lest they drift into the abyss of everlasting ruin. As to the rest of the faithful, in that anxious care which presses upon us for souls, we earnestly exhort them to take heed of the wily words of members of sects, who under the guise of acting legitimately, are led on by a violent hatred of the religion of Christ and of lawful governments, and look and work but for one end, to overthrow all rights as well divine as human. They should know that these broods of sects are like unto the wolves which clad in sheep's skin our Lord Jesus Christ foretold would come to devastate the flock. They should know that amongst them are those whose intercourse and companionship the Apostle has forbidden us, clearly commanding that we should not even greet them. May God, rich in mercies, moved by all our prayers, grant that the foolish may by His helping grace return to the heart, and the erring be brought back to the way of justice. May he grant that both the church and human society may be relieved from evils so numerous and so long standing, by restraining the madness of those abandoned men, who by means of the aforesaid unions contrive impious and nefarious things. And that all this may end as We desire, let us take as our mediatrix with the most merciful God the Most Holy Virgin, Mother of God Himself, Immaculate from her very origin, to whom it has been given to crush the enemies of the Church and the extravagances of error. Let Us also beg the patronage of the Blessed Apostles Peter and Paul, by whose glorious blood this our good City has been consecrated. By their aid and help, We trust that We shall more readily obtain what we crave from the divine goodness.

On Fenianism.

Decree of the Holy Office.

IV. Westminster. Appendix xx., p. 176.

Wednesday, January 12th, 1870.—Seeing that a doubt that arisen with some, as to whether the Fenian Society should be held to be included amongst those condemned in Pontifical Constitutions, our Most Holy Lord, by Divine Providence Pope, Pius IX., having taken the opinion of their Eminences the Cardinals Inquisitor-General against heresy throughout the whole Christian republic, lest the hearts of the faithful, the more simple among them especially, might be perverted to the evident danger of their souls, adhering to the Decrees upon similar matters elsewhere published by the Sacred Congregation of the Universal Inquisition, notably to the Decree of Wednesday, July 5th, 1865, has decreed and declared that the American or Irish Society styled Fenians, is included among the Societies forbidden and condemned in Constitutions of the Supreme Pontiffs, and particularly in the latest published by His same Holiness of September 27th, 1869, beginning *Apostolicæ Sedis*, in which, under number 4, those are declared to come under excommunication *latæ sententiæ*, and reserved to the Roman Pontiff, who "enter their names among the sect of either Freemasons or Carbonari, or other sects of the same character, which plot, whether openly or secretly, against the Church or lawful Governments, as well as those giving any kind of encouragement to the same sects, or not denouncing their secret heads or leaders, until they have so denounced them." And this is the reply He has ordered to be given to all the Bishops who have applied.

For D. ANGELO ARGENTI, Notary of the Holy Roman and Universal Inquisition.

L. ✠ S. GIACOMO VOGAGGINI, Substitute.

The following Rescripts have reference to the whole body of the faithful:—

On the Use of Lard upon Abstinence Days.

III. Westminster. Appendix iv., p. 84.

Most Holy Father,

I. In Formula 2,[1] which is sent to the Bishops of England, power is

---

[1] "It may be useful to mention, that the special powers over cases reserved by the Holy See, which are ordinarily granted to Bishops, are described in various lists, varying in the extent of the faculties given or in the conditions attached to them. These lists are called the *Formulæ*, and they are ten in number. Usually, the Bishops in Ireland receive the *Sixth Formula*, and the Bishops in England the *Second*; and according to the circumstances of each country, other *Formulæ* are granted. The expressions employed in them are sometimes transferred to the Papal concessions *in pari materia*, e.g., to a Bull granting a matrimonial dispensation; and hence you may have noticed that Moral Theologians, in discussing the clauses occurring in dispensations, generally quote the very same expressions as descriptive of such clauses.

"In addition to these *Formulæ*, which are sometimes called in Italian *Ordinarie*, because they are *generally* given, or *Stampate*, because they are in print, the Holy See grants other *Extraordinary* faculties to Bishops.

"*Sede Vacante*, the Sacred Congregation of Propaganda can renew the *Formulæ*, but (generally speaking), not the *Extraordinary Faculties*. The *Formulæ* are usually granted for six years, and thus the Vicars-Apostolic of England, named in 1840, applied for a renewal of F. II. during the Concave of 1846."—*Synods of Southwark*, p. 82.

given "to dispense, when they think fit, as to abstinence from meat, eggs, and things of a milky nature, on fasting days and during Lent." Now, the Bishops considering that oil is not a product of England, and hence cannot be used as a condiment, have, by virtue of this faculty, permitted the use of lard and of that melted fat (dripping) which, in England, is used for lard, in its stead. Seeing that its use was allowed in Lent, the faithful have for some years and in good faith been using it on abstinence days out of Lent.

The Fathers, therefore, of the Third Provincial Synod, humbly beg that your Holiness will deign, in your compassion for the wretchedness of the poor, and in consideration of the devotion with which they are wont to keep the laws of abstinence as well as of their good faith, to sanction the practice already commenced, and confirm the temporary Indult of the Bishops who have the Formula, in such a way that for the future use may be made of the said substances, that is, lard and dripping, as well in Lent as on the other fasting and abstinence days of the year.

2. For the same cause, namely, the want of oil, and because fish is scarce in many places, and other kinds of Lenten diet, such as fruit, salad, &c., cannot be had during the season of Lent, and inasmuch as a variety in the kinds of food allowed in Lent renders the observance of the fast more easy, they likewise beg that your Holiness will be pleased to grant that in the collation which is allowed amongst the strictly conscientious of the faithful, use may be made of milk and of butter, the which are already allowed in Scotland and in Belgium, and other northern parts, as well as of cheese, which is one of the principal condiments amongst the poor.

Wednesday, May 9th, 1860.

Our Most Holy Lord, by divine Providence, Pope Pius IX., at the accustomed audience, granted to the Reverend Father, the Assessor of the Holy Office, having heard the above-mentioned petition, together with the opinions of their Most Eminent and Reverend Lordships, the Cardinals of the Holy Roman Church, acting as Inquisitors General throughout the whole Christian Republic against the evils of heresy, as regards the first of the requests contained in the above-mentioned petition, graciously yielded thereto as asked for, with the exception of Good Friday, so long as the faculties granted in Form. 2 to the petitioning Bishops are in vigour. Whatsoever things to the contrary, notwithstanding. As to the second request, our Most Holy Father commanded the reply to be given that *it is non-expedient.*

L. ✠ S.   ANGELO ARGENTI, Notary of the Holy Roman and Universal Inquisition.

Rescript permitting the Use of Butter, &c.

Most Holy Father,

As Lent is drawing near, and the Bishop of Clifton is in Rome, he begs respectfully to lay before you, in the name of the other Bishops, that in England it is found necessary to dispense many persons from fasting by reason of their inability to provide themselves with the food allowed for the evening collation which is permitted by the Church to those who fast over and above the chief meal. It would not be necessary to dispense such persons from fasting if they could avail themselves of the permission which the Church gives to take a slight meal in the evening. But (1), oil, vinegar, salad, fruit, and such like things which are allowed as condiments, cannot be obtained in England except at a price beyond the means of the common people. (2), From the very fact that these kinds of food and condiment are not within the reach of the people, it follows that they do not make use of them, and hence cannot get into the custom of eating them. (3), A great number of these persons live with Protestants either in service or otherwise, and they, although not refusing to give them meagre diet on the days prescribed, are of course unwilling to procure them victuals and condiments which are not commonly used by the people. Hence confessors have no other resource than to dispense such persons altogether from fasting.

It is now asked if, instead of dispensing them from fasting, it would be lawful for confessors to keep them bound to the fast, but to tolerate the use of a little butter or cheese at the said collation by way of condiment, for these form the ordinary condiment or accompaniment of the people of England and other northern counties. Such permission exists in Scotland, Holland, Belgium, and the northern parts of France, countries adjacent to England; and if it existed in England also, the number of those who fast, which is ever on the decrease, would be greatly augmented.

Wednesday, March 18th, 1880.

Our Most Holy Lord, by Divine Providence, Pope Leo XIII., at the usual audience granted to the Reverend Father, the Assessor of the Holy Office, having heard the above petition and the opinions thereupon of the Most Eminent and Reverend the Cardinals Inquisitor-General, graciously granted that the Right Reverend Petitioners might permit the use of butter, cheese, and milk on fasting days at collation in accordance with the petition, provided that in other respects the fast be kept — Ash Wednesday and Good Friday excepted. All things whatsoever to the contrary notwithstanding.

J. PELAMI, Notary of the Holy Roman and Universal Inquisition.

DECLARATION OF THE SACRED PENITENTIARY IN REGARD TO THOSE WHO ARE DISPENSED FROM THE LAW OF FASTING ON ACCOUNT OF DELICATE HEALTH.

MOST EMINENT REVERENCE,

The Bishop of Salford humbly begs that your Most Eminent Reverence will deign to declare whether those who are dispensed from the laws of fasting by reason of ill health can eat meat more than once on days when meat is allowed?

The Sacred Penitentiary, having maturely and carefully considered the doubt raised, has decided that the answer should be, that the faithful who are lawfully exempted from the law of fasting, that is, taking only one meal, may eat meat at every meal on those days in Lent when the eating of meat is granted by Indult.

Given at Rome, at the Sacred Penitentiary, March 16th, 1882.

A. CARDINAL BILIO, P.M.,

Hip. Canûs. Palombi, S.P., Secretary.

The following Instruction has been issued by the Bishops.

The Laws of Fasting, and its Relaxations by Customs, Indults and Dispensations.

The following instruction of the Cardinal Archbishop and the Bishops of England has been addressed to the Clergy; and is to be kept in the Archives of each mission.

I. THE LAW OF FASTING, *when there is no relaxation,* is as follows :—

1. All persons who are seven years of age are commanded to abstain from meat on all fasting days; and from meat, eggs, milk, butter, and cheese, on all the days of Lent, Sundays included.

2. Those who are twenty-one, and have not yet reached their sixtieth year, and are not occupied in laborious work, besides abstaining as above, are commanded also to restrict themselves on fasting-days to one *full meal* a day, to be taken at any hour after mid-day. Besides the one full meal, however, a *collation* of not more than about eight ounces weight of food *(S. Alph., Lib. 4, Tract 6, n. 1025)* is permitted, which should also be taken any hour after mid-day. Meat or eggs may never be taken at collation; and of fish not more than two or three ounces *(S. Alph., ibid., n. 1028).* Milk, butter, and cheese are also excluded, when not specially allowed by Indult.

II. RELAXATIONS BY CUSTOMS.

1. A refection, of not more than two ounces in weight, is allowed by custom, in the morning, to those who fast.

2. The use of milk and butter is allowed in England, by custom, on all days in the year, at all times when a full meal is permitted by the general law.

III. RELAXATION BY INDULTS.

1. By the authority of the Holy See, the Bishops of England are accustomed to renew every year the following permissions, granted to the the faithful generally for the time of Lent.

i. They allow, at any time *when a full meal is permitted* by the general law :—

Meat on all days except Wednesdays and Fridays, Ember Saturdays, and the last four days of Holy Week. But when meat is taken, on any day in Lent, or any fasting-day throughout the year, fish is not permitted at the same meal.

Eggs on all days except Ash Wednesday and the last three days of Holy Week.

Cheese on all days except Ash Wednesday and Good Friday.

Dripping and *lard* (not *suet*) on all days except Good Friday.

ii. They allow at *collation,* to those who fast :

Milk, butter, and *cheese,* on all days except Ash Wednesday and Good Friday.

Dripping and *lard* on all days except Good Friday.

All these kinds of food may be taken in small quantities only, as a part of the collation and by way of condiment. Milk, in the Papal Rescript, is classed as food: and, therefore, like the other condiments, it may be taken only in small quantity. (*Note:* The Papal Rescript permits " in collatiuncula *esum* butyri, casei, et lactis *juxta preces*;" and the prayer was " to use at collation, as an addition to the bread, or as condiment, a little butter, or cheese.")

2. Besides the permissions of the Lenten Indults, the use of dripping and lard at dinner and collation—and of milk, butter, and cheese at collation—is permitted by the Holy See on all other fasting-days throughout the year.

The Profession of Faith and Absolution of Heretics.
(Decrees, &c., of Synod of Maynooth, 1875, 223.)

The question was raised by his Right Reverend Lordship the Bishop of Philadelphia as to the profession of faith and absolution of heretics on their confession, and on Wednesday, July 20th, 1859, their Most Eminent Lordship decreed that the following instructions should be issued:—

On the conversion of any heretic the first question to be asked is as to the validity of the heretical baptism. If, therefore, after diligent inquiry it is found that there was none at all or an invalid baptism, Baptism is to be administered unconditionally. But if, after inquiry, a probable doubt remains as to the validity of the baptism, then it should be repeated conditionally. But if it is clear that it was valid, in this case there must be the abjuration and profession of faith alone. Therefore in reconciling heretics the method is threefold.

1. If baptism is conferred unconditionally, neither abjuration nor absolution is requisite, inasmuch as the sacrament of regeneration cleanses completely.

2. If baptism is repeated conditionally, the course to be followed is this:—

(a.) The Abjuration or Profession of Faith.
(b.) The Conditional Baptism.
(c.) Sacramental Confession with Conditional Absolution.

3. When it is concluded that the baptism was valid, there is only the Abjuration or Profession of Faith, and this is followed by Absolution from Censures.

But it should be remarked that the Abjuration or Profession of Faith is different from that in the Bull of Pius IV. For the one which follows was prescribed by the Sacred Congregation of the Holy Office for heretics on their conversion, and this the petitioning Bishop will make use of together with the form of absolution which is coupled with it.

*　　*　　*　　*　　*　　*

The convert should remain kneeling whilst the Priest seated says the Psalm *Miserere*, &c., or the *De Profundis*, &c., with Gloria Patri at the end; at the end of which the Priest should say standing:

Kyrie eleison, Christe eleison, Kyrie eleison. Pater noster *(secreto)*.
℣. Et ne nos inducas in tentationem. ℟. Sed libera nos a malo.
℣. Salvum fac servum tuum *(vel* ancillam tuam*)*. ℟. Deus meus sperantem in te.
℣. Domine exaudi orationem meam. ℟. Et clamor meus ad te veniat.
℣. Dominus vobiscum. ℟. Et cum spiritu tuo.

Oremus.

Deus cui proprium est misereri semper et parcere: suscipe deprecationem nostram, ut hunc famulum tuum (hanc famulam tuam) quem (quam) excommunicationis catena constringit, miseratio tuæ pietatis clementer absolvat. Per Dominum, &c.

Then the priest seated, and turned towards the convert kneeling, absolves him from heresy, saying:

Auctoritate Apostolica, qua fungor in hac parte, absolvo te a vinculo excommunicationis quam[1] incurristi et restituo te Sacrosanctis Ecclesiæ Sacramentis, communioni, et unitati fidelium. In nomine Patris et Fi✠lii et Spiritus Sancti. ℞. Amen.

He should then give him some suitable Penance, for example, certain prayers, or visits to the Church, or something of that nature.

The Profession of Faith.

I,..............................(son or daughter), of.................., of the age of.........years, on my knees before you, the most Reverend Father..................., of the Order of Friars Preachers, Master in Holy Theology and Communion, General of the Holy Roman and Universal Inquisition, having before my eyes the Holy Gospels which I touch with my hands, and knowing that no one can be saved without that faith which the Holy Catholic Apostolic Catholic Church holds, believes and teaches, against which I grieve that I have greatly erred, born of parents who were out of the said Church, I have held and believed doctrines opposed to her teaching.

I now, with grief and contrition, profess that I believe the Holy Catholic Apostolic Roman Church to be the only and true Church established on earth by Jesus Christ, to which I submit myself with my whole heart. I believe all the articles that she proposes to my belief, and I reject and condemn all that she rejects and condemns, and I am ready to observe all that she commands me, and especially I profess that I believe:

The only God in Three Divine Persons, distinct from and equal to each other, that is to say, the Father, the Son, and the Holy Ghost.

The Catholic Doctrine of the Incarnation, Passion, Death, and Resurrection of our Lord Jesus Christ, and the Hypostatic Union of the two Natures, (the divine and the human); the Divine Maternity of the Most Holy Mary, together with her most spotless virginity.

The true, real, and substantial presence of the body, together with the soul and divinity, of our Lord Jesus Christ in the most holy Sacrament of the Eucharist.

The seven Sacraments instituted by Jesus Christ for the salvation of mankind, that is to say, Baptism, Confirmation, Eucharist, Penance, Extreme Unction, Order, Matrimony.

Purgatory, the Resurrection of the Dead, Life Everlasting.

The Primacy, not only of honour, but also of jurisdiction of the Roman Pontiff, successor of St. Peter, Prince of the Apostles, Vicar of Jesus Christ.

The Veneration of Saints and their Images.

The Authority of the Apostolic and Ecclesiastical Traditions, and of the Holy Scriptures, which we must interpret and understand only in the sense which our Holy Mother the Catholic Church has held and holds.

---

1. In serious or even small doubt as to whether the penitent has incurred excommunication by reason of professed heresy, the Priest should insert here the word *forsan*.

And everything else that has been defined and declared by the Sacred Canons and by the General Councils, especially by the Holy Council of Trent.

With a sincere heart, therefore, and with unfeigned belief, I detest and abjure every error, heresy, and sect opposed to the said Holy Catholic and Apostolic Roman Church. So help me God, and these His holy Gospels which I touch with my hands.

I,................................, as aforesaid, have with my hands signed this act of my sincere conversion and return into the bosom of the same Church, which I have recited word for word.

This...............day of......................

Letter from the Sacred Congregation of Propaganda upon the use of the Latin Language in Letters to be sent to the Apostolic See.

Most Illustrious and Right Reverend Lord,

It was an understood thing formerly that those who had to communicate with the Apostolic See in reference to matters ecclesiastical (those parties excepted who belonged to the Oriental rite), or to ask for favours, should make use of the Latin, or at any rate the Italian language. Nor indeed was this custom without important reasons, seeing that, amongst others, it could not be expected that the servants or officials of the Holy See, which receives letters or petitions from every nation upon the earth, should amid such a variety of tongues read and understand them all. Now, during the past few years, a practice has been growing of sending letters to this Sacred Congregation of Propaganda written promiscuously not only in French (which would create scarcely any difficulty), but English, German, Dutch, and other languages; and hence it often happens that the transaction of business of a sacred character suffers no little delay. This being the case, I cannot do otherwise than earnestly beg of your Most Illustrious Lordship to be sure to insist with even the laity, and particularly with your own clergy, that whenever they send any petition or any deeds having reference to ecclesiastical business to this Sacred Council, they shall be careful to make use, as far as possible, of the Latin or Italian language. And having mentioned Latin, it will not be out of place to direct attention to the fact that most serious evils have befallen the Church through the neglect of that language. For not only does communication between the Roman Church and the churches of other countries become more difficult, not only is lost that great advantage which Catholics when travelling of old enjoyed, to wit, of finding everywhere Christ's faithful-like brethren speaking the common tongue of their Roman fatherland; but also all the sources of science, as well sacred as profane, become gradually strange to our Christian people, and almost unintelligible, since, unless to those who know Greek, they can only be taught through the medium of Latin. Hence you will take care to see that the study of Latin is encouraged in your diocese, and a good opportunity of setting to work in this matter will be the reception of this letter in which I have judged that the subject should be brought under your notice.

I pray God long to preserve you safe and well.

Given at Rome, at the office of the Sacred Congregation of Propaganda, September 29th, 1868.

  Your Most Illustrious and Right Reverend Lordship's
    Most obedient,

      AL. CARDINAL BARNABÒ, Prefect.
      JOHN SIMEONI, Secretary.

SYNODAL LETTERS

OF THE ARCHBISHOP AND BISHOPS OF THE PROVINCE OF WESTMINSTER.

The following letters, of which the first four were published respectively after each of the Provincial Synods, are re-printed here, not only as containing much important instruction, but also as affording most interesting summaries of the work of the English Church, and of her solicitudes and aspirations, at different periods of her career.

FIRST SYNOD,

(July 17, 1852.)

A few months ago, we separately solicited your prayers, and we enjoined public supplications, to obtain for ourselves the light and guidance of God's Holy Spirit, in the Synod which had been convoked, and appointed to be held by us, on the sixth of July, at St. Mary's College. It is now our more pleasing duty, conjointly to address you, before separating; to announce to you, that Almighty God has graciously heard your prayers, and to claim from you a tribute of sincere and cordial thanksgiving to Him, for His many mercies bestowed upon us. For, although it would ill become us to speak with commendation of anything that we have done, and according to our divine Master's commands, we must needs say, at the conclusion of our work, that "we are only unprofitable servants [1]," yet we may not be silent, and withhold from you a share in that joy and gratitude which fill our own hearts: because God has dealt kindly with us in these days, which we have cheerfully devoted to our highest duties.

For to Him we attribute the peace and cheerfulness, the union and charity, which have made this our first Synod truly a meeting of Brethren dwelling in unity;[2] to Him we owe the edifying assiduity and exactness, with which all engaged in this holy work have discharged their allotted functions; to Him we refer the calm, the impartiality, and the prudence, which have distinguished the deliberations and conclusions of the theologians invited to assist us; and if it shall please Him, that there shall be found aught of wisdom, or usefulness in the decisions to which *we* have come, not to us, but to Him and to His holy name be given all the glory.[3] For on His promises we have relied, and to His light we have looked, and not to our own unworthiness, for being rightly led to conclude what might please Him best.

And surely, dearly beloved, it is no small token of the divine favour, that after many ages, during which the synodical action of our Holy Church has been here suspended, we should have been enabled, so naturally, and so easily, and with so much comfort and fruit, to re-assemble, and accurately perform whatever has been prescribed for such solemn occasions, and proceed in peace, and undisturbed calm, till we brought our undertaking to its joyful conclusion.

---

1. *Luke* xvii., 10.   2. Ps. cxxxii.   3. Ps. cxiii., 9.

Such mercies must not be passed by without their merited expression of gratitude; and we have therefore appointed the coming festival of the Assumption of the Blessed Virgin, Sunday the Fifteenth of August next, for a day of general and solemn thanksgiving. On it, this our joint Synodical Letter shall be read and published to our faithful people. In each church or chapel also there shall be performed an act of thanksgiving, either at the close of Mass, or at Benediction in the evening. The *Te Deum*, with its versicles and prayers will be sung (or recited where no music is ordinarily performed); and the Prayer for thanksgiving will be inserted in every Mass, under the same conclusion as the collect of the day.

We earnestly invite you all, dearly beloved, to join your hearts to ours, in the warm and hearty discharge of this duty of gratitude and love. For we feel assured that you will agree with us in the conviction, that through this Synod great and lasting blessings have been bestowed upon the Catholic Church in this country, so soon as the decrees and provisions, therein made, shall be published and put in force. You are not ignorant, that the Acts of a provincial Council have no authority, and therefore cannot be made public, nor can its decrees be enforced, until they shall have been submitted to the correction and judgment of the Holy Apostolic See, and so have received its confirmation. Until then, whatever has been enacted, necessarily remains suspended and secret; but we trust it will not be long before we may communicate it to you.

But in the meantime, we wish to impart to you such fruit of our deliberations as does not come within the limits of this stricter law; and to address you upon various topics possessing a religious interest, which we think it timely and profitable to urge on your serious attention. They will thus come before you with that weight and authority which the united voices of all your pastors can bestow.

1. The first, and paramount subject, on which we desire to speak to you, as fathers, conveying to their children the dearest wishes and interests of their hears, is—the EDUCATION OF THE POOR. On this topic you are yearly, and even more frequently, addressed by each of us; and it is difficult to add to the repeated and urgent appeals which are made to your consciences, and your sympathies. But the more the subject is considered, the more its importance increases, and the more we feel it our duty to awaken your minds and hearts to its pressing claims.

The education of the poor has always been considered as one of the most important duties confided to the Church. But while, in every age, she has faithfully discharged her obligation, it is clear that the manner of doing so will vary, with the circumstances of time and place. Where faith is undisturbed, and morality unassailed, where the war of life has to be with the inward passions more than with the outward world, then the training of the child in the way whereon he has to walk, is a simple task. The habit of divine faith gives a solid groundwork for the building which has to be raised; and simple instruction, line upon line, raises it up to the required measure, without hindrance, or opposition. The example of all around, the unanimity of their convictions, and the repetition of identical principles, co-operate with the early precepts, strengthen them, consolidate them, and help to keep unimpaired the foundation first laid. But where on every side aggression has to be encountered, where every stone that is added to the building is contested, and has to be defended, where not only counteracting, but destructive, influences have to be resisted, where not merely the superstructure, but the very foundation, must be secured, by endless precautions, and multiplied safeguards; the duty of attending to early education becomes complicated and difficult and requires more serious thought, more time, more agencies, and more vigilance, than at other times. And such is our case now. Except through a laborious education we cannot guarantee to our little ones a single sound principle, one saving truth. From the doctrine of the Blessed Trinity, to the smallest precept of the Church, they are exposed, even in childhood, to hear all dogma and all practice assailed, ridiculed, reasoned against, blasphemed. Systems of education, made as tempting as possible by promises of greater learning, or offers of present advantage, surround parents and their offspring; and too often the fatal bait is swallowed, and the religion of the child is sacrificed to an imaginary temporal welfare.

It is in the midst of this state that we have now to secure the education of our poor. If we wish to have a generation of catholics to succeed the present one, we must educate it: or others will snatch it up, before our eyes. If we determine to educate it, it must be with all the means and pains necessary to cope, first with the efforts made to defeat our purpose, and then with the dangers and temptations, that will beset those on whom we bestow this heavenly boon. In other words, our education must be up to the mark of modern demand, and yet it must be solid in faith and in piety.

The first necessity, therefore, is a sufficient provision of education, adequate to the wants of our poor. It must become universal. No congregation should be allowed to remain without its schools, one for each sex. Where the poverty of the people is extreme, we earnestly exhort you, beloved children, whom God has blessed with riches, especially you who, from position, are the natural patrons of those around you, to take upon yourselves lovingly this burthen, of providing, if possible, permanently, for the education of your destitute neighbours. Do not rest until you see this want supplied: prefer the establishment of good schools to every other work. Indeed, wherever there may seem to be an opening for a new mission, we should prefer the erection of a school, so arranged as to serve temporarily for a chapel, to that of a church without one. For the building raised of living and chosen stones,[1] the spiritual sanctuary of the Church, is of far greater importance than the temple made with hands. And it is the good school that secures the virtuous and edifying congregation.

2. We have said that our education must be up to the mark of modern demands: in other words, we must take advantage of the means afforded us, to render the *secular* part of our education as effective as that which others offer. The great bribe which the age holds out to our children, in exchange for the surrender of their faith, is a greater amount of worldly knowledge. This, it is true, is but a snare: such a one as deceived and ruined our first parents in Paradise;[2] and it is our duty ever to cry aloud, and warn foolish parents, that not all the wisdom of Solomon, even if it brought with it the wealth of the whole world, would compensate their children for the loss of their souls. But this will not suffice. We must remove the temptation as far as possible from human frailty: we must

---

1. 1 Petr. ii. 5.
2. ' You shall be as Gods knowing good and evil " (Gen. iii. 5).

not even leave an excuse to lukewarmness. Make your schools equal in every repect to those which are opened to allure away our children. Avail yourselves of every encouragement and every improvement which tends to raise the standard of your education ; and let there be no pretence tenable for sending Catholic children elsewhere.

In effecting these most useful purposes, and procuring means for encouraging a high order of education, as well as extensively diffusing its blessings, we consider that the institution established by us, and known as the *Poor School Committee*, has been eminently useful, and deserves our public approbation, and our joint recommendation. Composed as it is of priests and laymen, selected from all our Dioceses, it has attended to their several interests with fidelity and impartiality ; and it has been the instrument for obtaining assistance and means for education, which, without its co-operation, would not have reached us. Through it, the character of our poor school teaching has been signally raised ; and the erection of normal and training schools, which we now owe to its exertions and zeal, promises to secure, on a stable basis, the future enjoyment of this blessing. We, therefore, exhort and urge you to support this excellent Institution, by your liberal contributions, by your hearty co-operation, and by your friendly encouragement.

3. But while we thus wish to promote a secular instruction equal to what others offer, we consider sound faith, virtue, and piety by far the most important elements of education : and these, as we have already declared to you, we are the most anxious to secure, and to promote. We cannot, of course, conceal from ourselves, that the encouragement which the state, or the policy of the age, gives to education, has a tendency to increase the importance of worldly knowledge, if not to the disparagement, at least to the consequent depreciation, of religious learning. The inspection, the rewards, the honours, derived from the state, are strictly limited to proficiency in the former class of instruction ; and the youthful mind is easily led by its own ardour to pursue what obtains public approbation and reward, to the neglect of less prized, but far more important, acquirements. It is our duty to find a counterpoise for this undue preponderance : and, after mature deliberation, we have gladly adopted, for this purpose, the excellent suggestions made to us in Synod, by the Poor School Committee, through its worthy chairman. We propose, therefore, to appoint, in our respective dioceses, ecclesiastical inspectors of Schools, whose duty it will be to examine the scholars in the religious portion of their education, to grant certificates and award prizes for proficiency in it; and so give any one who aspires to be a teacher of Catholic children, the means of proving himself morally fitted for the office, and prevent the unworthy from obtaining so serious a trust. This plan, the utility of which must, at first sight, be obvious, will entail additional expense, and increase the demands on the funds of the Poor School Committee. But we rely on your sense of its vital importance, for redoubled exertions and augmented resources, to meet this new exigency.

4. While we thus turn our most serious thoughts towards the education, in sound faith and virtuous morals, of our poorest children, who are most exposed to the evil arts and temptations of enemies, we cannot overlook the wants of other classes, no less dear to us. Where there is a sufficient Catholic population to warrant it, we earnestly

recommend the establishment of a middle school, as it is called, in which a good commercial and general education shall be given to the children of families in a better worldly position. At present the youth of this class, aspiring to a higher standard of instruction, and for obvious reasons unable to attend the gratuitous, or poor, school, are generally sent to day-schools, where religious education is out of the question, and where often their faith is exposed to serious trials. The experiment of establishing such a school as we allude to, has succeeded in several towns: and we beg both clergy and laity to extend this great blessing, wherever they see a reasonable prospect of success.

5. We cannot leave the subject of education, without alluding to the effort that is being made by our venerable and beloved brethren, the bishops of Ireland, for the establishment of a catholic University. Acting under the directions, and with the approbation, of the Holy See, seconded by the co-operation of their clergy and their flocks, encouraged by the contributions of both hemispheres, these zealous prelates are aiming higher than we can dare—at the providing of an unmixed education of the very highest order. From our hearts we wish them success; and we are glad of this opportunity to testify to them our warmest sympathy. What we have hitherto done, we will continue to do— recommend the undertaking to the charity and liberality of our faithful people. Should such an institution grow up so near us, its advantages to us will be incalculable. We shall see open to future generations the means of a liberal, scientific and professional education, united with solid religious instruction, a blessing denied to the present; and we may see revived, what formed the pride of Ireland in early ages of christianity, multitudes, who loved heavenly, as well as earthly, wisdom, sailing to her from distant shores, to obtain the still undivided treasure at her hands.

6. You will see, by all that we have addressed to you, how solicitous we are about the preservation of the faith committed to our charge. It is no wonder that we should be so. While this is the groundwork of all piety and of our salvation, though without it we cannot possibly please God, [1] it has become less and less an object of care or of esteem to others. The innumerable contradictions of doctrine which have long prevailed in every system out of the catholic Church, fretting and clashing together, have worn themselves down into a smooth apathy; and the simplest hypothesis for getting rid of the scandal of contention about sublimest truths has been adopted—that they are matters of indifference. Hence, the attachment of the catholic to specific truths, and his jealousy of change in matters of religion, are derided as narrow-minded and illiberal; and the very characteristic which St. Leo gave to the worship of a Pagan Rome is now popularly attributed to genuine Christianity, that it is truly religious in proportion as it opens wider its arms, to embrace and comprehend more conflicting errors[2]. The age is one which rejects all strict dogmatism, and its spirit is the enemy of faith. It is difficult to be in contact with it, and not feel its influence. Its reasonings, its disdain, its jeers, its very blasphemies, become familiar, and cease to inspire horror; the sacredness of what is habitually assailed remains less vividly impressed on the mind; and many, who would die for their religion in general and its truth, do not feel so keenly about particular doctrines, each of which

---

1. *Hebr.* xi, 6.
2. Et magnam sibi videbatur assumpsisse religionem, quia nullam respuebat falsitatem. (In natali SS. Apostolorum.)

is absolutely necessary to form the whole faith of the Church, not one of which can be impugned, or given up, without destroying the entire structure of truth. Wherefore, dearly beloved, we earnestly exhort you, as the apostle found it necessary to do the first Christians, exposed as they were to the same dangers—"to watch, stand fast in the faith, do manfully and be strengthened."[1] "Let no man deceive you with vain," that is, specious "words."[2] Follow not your own opinions, nor those of other men; but remain steadfast in the teaching of God's Church, keeping the very form of sound words which she delivers to you,[3] and not reputing any thing light or unimportant which she communicates. Above all things prize the great blessing of unity, which is so distinguishing a mark of God's Church. Let there be no contentions, no dissensions found among you.[4] Hear the voice of your pastors, who in their turn are careful to preserve themselves in the unity of the spirit,[5] adhering closely to the Chair of Peter, wherein sits the inheritor of his jurisdiction and supremacy, holding the keys of Christ's kingdom, and the staff of pastoral jurisdiction over all the sheep of His one Fold.

7. But faith must be rooted in charity, and quickened by good works,[6] to be available unto salvation. And, therefore, we exhort you to all piety, and the faithful discharge of all your duties. For "godliness is profitable to all things, having promise of the life that now is, and of that which is to come."[7] In proportion as the times are evil, increase your own fidelity to the religious observances of the Church. He who frequently prays to God, who, if possible, daily attends at the adorable sacrifice, purges at short intervals his conscience from stains by the sacrament of penance, and often devoutly receives the source of life in the most blessed Eucharist, will not easily feel his faith weakened. Perform then these duties with cheerful fervour, "not with sadness or of necessity, for God loveth a cheerful giver."[8] Towards the most Holy Sacrament we warmly entreat you to entertain the most tender devotion; promote its honour, its solemn adoration, its silent worship, its frequent reception. In the ever Blessed and Immaculate Mother of God, we earnestly exhort you to feel a filial confidence, which is the fruit of love towards her Divine Son, and will make you have daily recourse to her patronage and intercession. Love the glory of God's house and the majesty of His worship; and minister to them generously, according to your means. Love the poor of Jesus Christ, His dearest disciples, and assist them charitably, especially by supporting such institutions as secure their spiritual, together with their temporal, welfare. Edify all around you by the blamelessness of your lives, the Christian order of your families, and the virtues suited to your conditions. "For the rest, brethren—whatsoever things are true, whatsoever modest, whatsoever just, whatsoever holy, whatsoever lovely, whatsoever of good fame, if there be any virtue, if any praise of discipline—think of these things."[9]

8. But you are exposed to trials of another sort, in which it is likewise our duty to direct you. Dearly beloved, we need not recal to your minds the many and various ways in which your faith, your morals, your pastors, your holiest institutions, your Church in fine, and your religion, have been lately assailed. We need not trace the progress

---

1. 1 Cor. xvi., 13.   2. Ephes. v., 6.   3. Jac. ii., 17.   4. 1 Tim. iv., 8.   5. 2 Cor. ix.,
6. Phil. iv., 8.   7. 2 Tim. i., 13.   8. Rom. xiii., 13.   9. Ephes. v., 2.

of injury from words to deeds, nor show the ripening of ill-judged expressions into destruction of property, shedding of blood, and desecration of what is most holy. And you know, too, that many persons around you would not hesitate to proceed to greater lengths, were it permitted them. Now, under these circumstances, your line of duty is clear, and we must not refuse to point it out to you.

First, then, we exhort you, not to be deterred by evil threats, nor by such injuries, from the free, the manly, and the Christian discharge of your duties, and the lawful defence of your rights, as citizens. Exercise the prerogatives which belong to you in an honourable and generous spirit. Shrink not from any obligation imposed upon you by your state of life. If in the senate, or among the representatives of the people, or a magistrate, or holding any office of trust or honour, or a simple citizen, remember that your rights are the same as those of other persons similarly situated; and allow no one to daunt you, or drive you from the fearless, peaceful, and dispassionate performance of the duties which ever accompany a privilege.

But, in the next place, we still more strongly exhort you to patience, to long-suffering, to meekness, to the uttering only of the blameless word, that "he who is on the contrary part may be afraid, having nothing evil to say of us."[1] Let nothing, however bitter that may be said, however unjust that may be threatened, rouse you to anger, or provoke intemperance of speech. Let no amount even of actual injury excite you to revenge, or to the desire of it. You particularly, among our poor children, who have felt more sorely than others the violence inflicted on yourselves or your neighbours, through religious animosity, we most earnestly and affectionately entreat, to put away all angry, unkind, and uncharitable thoughts. Be followers of him, who, "when he was reviled, did not revile; and when he suffered, threatened not."[1] "Be not overcome by evil, but overcome evil with good."[2] Look to the justice of the laws for protection from oppression and insults; and not to any unlawful combinations or exercise of your own strength. Remember, that even should justice be refused you here, God hath prepared a reward hereafter for the patient sufferer, that will amply compensate him for the light and momentary tribulations of this life.[3] Hear then, in this, as in higher things, the voices of your pastors and fathers in God, most lovingly reminding you, "that tribulation worketh patience, and patience trial, and trial hope; and hope confoundeth not."[4] Thus will your present trials only advance you in perfection, and through the Cross and Passion of our Blessed Lord unite you closer to him, and make you inheritors of his promises.

9. One and only one revenge can we permit you, that of praying for all who afflict, or persecute, or hate you. Beg of God to turn their hearts to charity and peace and bring them to the knowledge and love of his blessed truth. But not for them only must you pray, but for all who are not partakers of the same light and grace as have been vouchsafed to you. You have heard of the great charity with which God has inspired your brethren of other nations, of praying for the return of your beloved country to the unity of the faith. We surely will not be behind them in our zeal and love, where the motives, the interests and the rewards of

---

1. 1 Petr. ii. 25.   2. Rom. xii. 21.   3. Rom. viii. 18.   4. Rom. v. 3.
1. Titus ii., 1.

these virtues are so peculiarly our own. Pray then daily, though it be but by one short *Hail Mary*, for the return of your fellow-countrymen to the one Fold of Christ; that we may all be one, even as He and his Father are one.

And may the Father of mercies and God of all consolation pour out abundantly upon you every blessing; strengthening you to every good work, and perfecting you in all virtue and holiness, unto the day of our Lord Jesus Christ,[1] who with him, and the Holy Ghost, liveth and reigneth for ever and ever.

SECOND SYNOD.

(July 15th, 1855.)

It is now three years since we addressed to you our first Synodical Letter, at the conclusion of our first Provincial council. According to the provisions of ecclesiastical law, we at that time appointed the Tenth day of July, One Thousand Eight Hundred and Fifty-five, for the opening of our second Synod, if God would so mercifully permit it. It has pleased Him to allow us the enjoyment of our earnest desire; and hence on the appointed day, after due convocation, we met at St. Mary's College, Oscott, and under the Divine auspices commenced our second Provincial Synod. It was consoling indeed to us to meet again, with so small a change in our body; for in the interval only one of our Venerable Colleagues had been called away to the reward of his labours, the Right Reverend Dr. Burgess, Bishop of Clifton; for the repose of whose soul we duly offered up, in Synod, the adorable Victim of Propitiation.

I. As this solemn meeting, attended by three Archbishops, twelve Bishops, two Vicars Capitular, and one mitred Abbot, took place so soon after the dogmatical definition of the Immaculate Conception of the Blessed Virgin Mary, we feel it our first duty in addressing you, to turn your thoughts towards this great exercise of the power vested in the Chair of Peter. For, although indeed most of us have separately made known to you this important event, we deemed it right to record in the Acts of our Synod our gratitude to God, for having allowed the declaration of this glorious and consoling mystery to be made in our time, so that even many of our number were privileged to witness it. Still more do we now consider it becoming to communicate these feelings to you, who so willingly and so edifyingly take part in our sorrows and our joys.

We, therefore, most earnestly exhort you, dearly beloved in Christ, to increase your devotion, great as it has hitherto been, towards the Immaculate Mother of God. The history of saintliness in the Church, the observation of all engaged in directing souls, and the experience of every Catholic mind, prove that this devotion is the truest source of

---

1. Philip i. 6.

affection for our Blessed Lord, and for the mysteries of His life and passion. In exalting her, we exalt Him; in loving her, we love Him; in trusting in her, we trust in Him; in invoking her, we in truth invoke Him. For when she intercedes, He mediates; and so when she asks, she receives; when she seeks, she finds; when she knocks, the gate of mercy is ever opened. Devotion to her, is admiration of her virtues, and a desire to copy them. "The first incentive to learning," says St. Ambrose, "is the nobility of the master. What is nobler than the Mother of God?" (*De Virginibus*, lib. 1.) It is the inspirer of humility, the safeguard of purity, the nourisher of Divine Charity. It tempers our actions with meekness, it sweetens our prayers with confidence, it multiplies our devotions, it leads us to frequent oftener the holy Sacraments, and gain the Church's indulgences.

And now that this spouse of Christ, guided by Him, has formally added a fresh title to those already possessed by Mary to our veneration, confidence and love, it becomes us to use and apply it to her in our public and private devotions. Our oratories and churches, built under the invocation of it, will indeed attest to posterity how tenderly we cherished it; but our own warm-hearted piety, our own holy lives, and our own inflamed zeal, resulting from devotion to this endearing mystery, will be a still happier legacy to the generations that shall succeed us in perpetuating the Church of God.

II. Intimately connected with the solemn definition to which we have alluded, is the instruction given by the Holy Father to all his children, through the Bishops assembled on that great occasion. It may be doubted whether ever before the Chief Pastor saw gathered round him and addressed so many venerable prelates, collected from such various regions of the globe. When, therefore, he called them before him, and spoke to them words well pondered, and full of gravity, earnestness and wisdom, as the message which he would have them carry with them from him to their flocks, it was doubtless his intention that their import should be accurately conveyed to all who with docility listen to his words. Wherefore we, in Synod assembled, have thought it our duty to make known to you the authoritative instructions thus delivered, in the very words wherein they were expressed. We omit only such passages as relate to the Bishops themselves, and to the feelings of regard and affection which the Sovereign Pontiff entertains for them; or which refer to dangers or events in other parts of the world. These, therefore, are his words:—

"There are besides, Venerable Brethren, certain men, conspicuous for learning, who allow religion to be the most excellent gift God has given to men, yet, nevertheless, set so much store by human reason, and praise it to such an extent, as absurdly to place it on equality with religion itself. By following out their own silly conceit, they come at this rate to treat the systems of theology just like those of philosophy; through the former are based upon those dogmas of faith, than which there is nothing more certain and fixed; the latter are set forth and illustrated by that human reason, than which there is nothing less certain: for it varies with the various classes of intellects, and is liable to fallacies and beguilements that cannot be counted. Now, when the authority of the Church has been thus set aside, then the utmost scope has been furnished to questions most difficult and recondite; and human reason, though confidence in its own feeble strength, stepping forward with less restraint, has fallen into errors of the foulest kind, which we have neither space nor wish to recount, well known and sifted by you as they are—errors, which, both in regard to religion and the interests of the state, but especially in regard to the latter, have eventually shewn themselves to be signally mischievous. Hence to men of this stamp, who extol human reason beyond its due, we ought to shew that this is in direct opposition to that undeniable statement of the Doctor of the gentiles : 'If anybody think himself to be something, whereas he is nothing, he deceiveth himself.'[1] We must clearly point out to them what great arrogance it is to try to search to the bottom those mysteries which God, in His great mercy, has condescended to reveal to us ; or to dare to come up to the same and embrace them with the feeble and narrow powers of the human mind—far as they are beyond the strength of that intellect of ours, which, as the same Apostle saith, must be 'led captive to the obedience of faith.'[2]"

"But the followers, or rather the worshippers of this human reason, who put it before themselves as if it were a mistress they could depend upon, and promise themselves every success from its guidance, certainly have not borne in mind, how serious and keen a wound was inflicted upon man's nature through the guilt of our first parent,—a wound whereby at once both darkness was spread over the mind, and the will also rendered prone to evil. Hence it came to pass, that the most famous philosophers, from the remotest antiquity, though they wrote much which is admirable, yet spoiled their teaching with errors of the gravest dye : hence came also that continuous struggle which we feel within ourselves, and concerning which the Apostle says : 'I perceive in my members a law warring against the law of my mind.'[3] Now since it is clear that the light of reason has suffered loss from the original stain which has been propagated to the whole of Adam's posterity, and since the human race has fallen most deplorably from its pristine state of justice and innocence,—who is there that would esteem reason competent to ascertain the truth? Who that amid dangers so great, and powers so weakened, would say, that to prevent a ruinous fall, the assistance of a Divine religion and of heavenly grace was unnecessary for him to obtain salvation? And this assistance God gives most freely to those who with humble prayer ask for the same, as it is written,—'God resisteth the proud, but giveth grace to the humble.'[1] Hence it was that Christ our Lord, after turning Himself to the Father, asserted that secret truths of the highest nature were not laid open to the prudent and wise of this world, who are proud of their own talents and learning, and refuse to yield obedience to the faith, but, on the contrary, to humble and simple men, who stay themselves and find repose in the oracles of Divine faith.[2] This salutary teaching ought you to impress upon the minds of those, who exaggerate the powers of human reason to such a degree, as to presume that they can by its assistance fathom and explain even mysteries, than which nothing can be more misplaced, nothing more frantic. Use your efforts to call them back from this distortion of mind, by setting before them how that there is no greater boon granted by the Providence of God to mankind than the authority of Divine faith; that it is this which serves as a torch in the darkness; this which is the leader for

---

1. Gal. vi. 3.   2. 2 Cor. x. 5.   3. Rom. vii. 25.

us to follow unto life ; this that is absolutely necessary unto salvation ; inasmuch as 'without faith it is impossible to please God,' and 'he that believeth not shall be condemned.' "[3]

"There is another error, and that no less pernicious, which we find, not without grief, has invaded certain parts of the Catholic world, and has sunk into the minds of a great many Catholics, who fancy that we may well hope for the salvation of all those who are far from being within the true Church of Christ. This gets them into the habit of raising the question, what is to be the condition after death of those who have not yielded themselves up to the Catholic faith? And then they adduce reasons, of no manner of weight, and so forestal an answer favourable to this wrongful opinion. Far be it from us, Venerable Brethren, to dare to set boundaries to the Divine Mercy, which has no limits; far be it from us to wish to sound the secret counsels or judgments of God, which are a great abyss, and incapable of being penetrated by the thought of man. But, in pursuance of our Apostolic office, we would fain see both the anxiety and vigilance of you that are Bishops roused, that you may strain every nerve to drive away from men's minds the opinion, which is as heterodox as it is baneful, namely, —that in any kind of religion a man may please can be found the way of salvation. Let the ability and the learning you can command be used to point clearly out to the people entrusted to your care, that the dogmas of the Catholic faith are by no means at variance with the mercy and justice of God. For it must be held as of faith, that outside the Apostolic Roman Church no one can be saved; that this is the one only ark of salvation; that, into which he who does not enter will perish in the flood: but we must also hold it in like manner certain, that those who are under ignorance of the true religion, if that ignorance be invincible, are not themselves under any bane of guilt for the same before the eyes of the Lord. Still, who is there that would take so much upon himself, as to claim the power of marking out the limits of this kind of ignorance, viewed in its ever-varying ratios to so many nations, so many climates, so many talents, and so many other circumstances? It is true, indeed, that when we are set free from the chains of this body, and see God as He is, then we shall understand the close and beautiful tie which knits together the mercy and justice of God: but so long as we are upon this earth, bowed down with the weight of this mortal body, which bedims the soul's eye, let us cling firmly to the Catholic teaching, that there is one God, one Faith, one Baptism! To proceed any further than this in our enquiries is not given us. Yet, for all this, let us, as the demands of charity suggest, be ever pouring forth prayers, that all the nations around may be converted to Christ; and let us lend all the assistance in our power to the common salvation of mankind, inasmuch as the Lord's hand is not shortened, and the gift of Heavenly grace will be by no means wanting to those who, with single heart, desire and ask to be refreshed by this light. Truths of this kind must be planted as deeply as possible in the minds of the faithful, in order to prevent the possibility of their being corrupted by false doctrines, which have for their object the cherishing that indifference in religion, which, to the ruin of souls, we perceive is spreading far and wide, and gaining strength."

---

1. James v. 6.   . Luke x. 21.   3. Heb. x 6   Marc xvi. 16.

"Against the leading errors here set forth, whereby chief siege against the Church is laid at this day, make, Venerable Brethren, a valorous and persevering stand; and with a view to lash and destroy them utterly you must needs have in the work men of ecclesiastical spirit as companions and assistants. Undying indeed is the joy we feel that the Catholic Clergy leave nothing undone, and fly from no disagreeable toil necessary to the fullest discharge of their duty and of their office; that owing to this they are not kept back by the roughness or the length of any journey, or by the dread of inconveniences, from reaching countries severed by the vastest tracts of land and sea, in order to humanise the savage nations there by healthful instruction, and lead them to the discipline of the Christian law. Like joy, too, do we feel, that the Clergy themselves, amid the ravages of a most frightful pestilence, which threw so many towns and so many populous cities into mourning, have undertaken the duties of charity of every kind, and with such cheerfulness as to esteem it a privilege and an honour to themselves to be lavish of life for the salvation of their neighbours. This is an argument which will make it more evident still how in the Catholic Church, which is the only true Church, there burns that beauteous fire of charity, which Christ came to send upon the earth that it might be kindled. For we have seen religious of the other sex vieing with the Clergy in assisting the sick, and undismayed by the sight of death, which many of them with the greatest constancy underwent. Through this specimen of unexampled fortitude, those who dissent from the Catholic faith were struck with admiration and astonishment."

Such, dearly Beloved in Jesus Christ, are the instructions given us by the Father of the Faithful, and Vicar of Christ our Lord upon earth; to whose words, as affectionate children and dutiful disciples, you will ever listen with docility and cheerful readiness to obey.

III. Before descending from this higher sphere of authoritative teaching to which we have, in the first instance, led you, we must put before you another topic, on which the Holy Father has condescended to address us, and concerning which we have already issued a joint circular. The visit of so many prelates to Rome, on the occasion already referred to, has led to an increased desire on the part of many to see established there colleges for their different countries, or those enlarged which they already possessed. We have been more fortunate than the Catholics of other countries, in having long enjoyed this advantage. The English College has, for three hundred years, sent Missionaries to England, many of whom have shed their blood for the Faith.

But his Holiness Pius IX. seems to have anticipated the thoughts of others, by wishing to enlarge for our island the means of Ecclesiastical Education with which we were already blessed. He saw that our country required a still larger supply of clergy, and that Divine Providence was disposed kindly to grant it, by bestowing numerous vocations to the ecclesiastical state on converts to the faith. But however well furnished with human learning they might be, they and others, who were in maturer years on embracing that state, seemed to require some institution expressly planned for their benefit, in which to add theological to human science. For this purpose, the holy Father most generously established a new College, honoured by bearing his own name, which was soon filled with most promising candidates for the priesthood, whose conduct has proved most edifying, and whose assiduity and success in study give hope of much religious advantage. But the limits of this first foundation proved too straitened for its object; and it was resolved to take advantage of considerable unoccupied space in the English College, for the purpose of uniting under one roof, but with separate regulations, the two institutions. His Holiness, however, most justly considered that an arrangement intended to benefit the Catholics of England should receive their support, and that they should prove, by their zealous co-operation, their appreciation of what he had done for them. He has, therefore, under his own hand, by a special blessing, authorised the Rev. Dr. English, President of this new college, known as the Collegio Pio, to come to England, to collect the alms of the Faithful, both for the completion of the new buildings, and for the education of students. And further, as we have intimated, he has desired us to co-operate with him to the extent of our power, in this undertaking.

Having therefore maturely considered in what manner we can best second this expressed desire of him, whose wishes are to us commands, and prove to him our filial reverence and affection, we have resolved that a general collection be made in all the Churches and Chapels of our Dioceses, and have appointed the Sunday after the reading of this our Synodical Letter, namely, the Second Sunday in September, being the ninth day of the month, for this simultaneous collection; the proceeds whereof must be forwarded as early as possible to the Bishop or Vicar General of each Diocese. We earnestly exhort you, dear children in Christ, to gratify the paternal heart of our beloved Pontiff, which yearns with tenderest affection for your welfare, which desires most earnestly to see the strongest links of faithful attachment uniting us to him and his Apostolic See; and looks to us for some compensation for the undutifulness of other countries, once so Catholic, and some consolation for the injuries offered him by the enemies of our faith. Contribute generously to an object so dear to him, and thus increase the number of your zealous and devoted clergy, who are ready to give their lives for your salvation.

IV. For, dearly beloved, it is with feelings of exultation and spiritual joy that we give thanks to God, that what the Holy Father said, in his words already quoted, on the charity and intrepidity displayed by the clergy of the Catholic Church, under the visitations of cholera, can be fully applied to the zealous clergy over whom it is our consolation to preside. Never have they shrunk before the fiery scourge of pestilence, but they have faced sickness and death to succour the most destitute of their flock. But in addition to this general and daily-earned commendation, we rejoice to record thus solemnly the devotedness with which so many of them have abandoned the comforts of home, to carry consolation to our soldiers in the hospital, and even on the field of battle, with full consciousness of the perils that awaited them, derived from the experience that preceded them. For not a few of the number have "laid away their tabernacles,"[1] amidst the tents of those whom they had prepared for death, and given their dust to sanctify the soldier's unconsecrated cemetery. Nor must we refuse equal praise to those religious women, who have ventured to those distant regions, and by their tender assiduity in minis-

---

1. 2 Peter i. 14.

tering to the sick and wounded, have shut up the mouths of their ruthless persecutors at home, and turned enemies into friends.

Yet notwithstanding these beautiful evidences of religion, and these touching examples of virtue which war has produced, like flowers, the richer for springing from a grave, we cannot but consider it as one of the scourges of Divine justice, and the cause of much present and future misery. It is a calamity which we must ever beg the Almighty to remove, and to give us, in its place, the blessings of a just, an honourable, and a durable peace. Pray for this, dearly beloved Brethren and Children; pray also that God will inspire other labourers to go into that vineyard, or rather choice soldiers to step into the ranks of the fallen; for the number of our chaplains requires constant filling up. And show particular charity to the widows and orphans of the brave soldiers who have lost their lives in fighting the battles of our country.

V. There is another topic which cannot be omitted from our Synodical Letter; for it is one which we are bound to urge on you in season and out of season. Never must we be weary of pleading to you for the education of the poor. The necessity for it is ever new, ever more pressing. After much has been done, more comes up to be done. Its craving is insatiable, its demand unlimited, its claims uncompromising. Yet we must keep pace with them, and not be dismayed. We must proportion our efforts to the work, and not repine. Open freely your hands, and give abundantly to the little ones of Christ, that they may plead for you, together with their Angels, who ever see the face of their heavenly Father.

There is one particular form of this charity which is much required, and to which we rejoice to see your attention has been drawn,—the establishment of Reformatory Schools. The system adopted by the legislature makes it imperative on us to provide establishments, where youthful delinquents can be reformed without danger to their faith. Several, at least four, such establishments are in course of preparation in different parts of England; some under the efficient care of religious corporations. We earnestly exhort you, however, to multiply them, and extend them to the whole of England.

VI. Nor can we close this letter without reminding you, dearly beloved children, of another duty, not always sufficiently discharged; that of contributing to the adequate support of the clergy, who, removed from the gains of worldly life, labour exclusively for your spiritual welfare, "as having to render an account of your souls."[1] It is not merely as a claim of charity, but as an obligation of justice, that we inculcate this duty. St. Paul has clearly laid it down, on the same ground as that which gives to the labourer a right to his reward.[2] And again he writes, "Let him that is instructed in the word communicate to him that instructeth him in all good things."[3] If such be your duty, be not surprised, still less offended, if you be frequently reminded of it, by those who are bound to keep before your eyes the obligations imposed on you by God.

And now we call upon you all to return, with us, thanks to the Giver of all good gifts, for the happy completion of this second Synod; enjoining, that on the Sunday following the public reading of this letter, there shall be sung or recited the hymn *Te Deum*, with the usual versicles and

---

1. Heb. xiii. 17.   2. 1 Tim. i. 18.   3. Gal. vi. 6.

prayers, in every Church or Chapel under our jurisdiction, after Mass, and at Benediction.

Finally, we "commend you all to God and to the word of His grace, who is able to build up, and to give an inheritance among all the sanctified."[1] May He bless you, that you may the more abound in every good work, and in all faith, and grace, and charity; and "confirm you unto the end without crime, in the day of the coming of our Lord Jesus Christ."[2] to whom, with the Father and the Holy Ghost, be honour and glory, for ever and ever. Amen.

THIRD SYNOD.

(July 16, 1859.)

For the third time we have the consolation of addressing you in a joint synodical letter, We have supplied, through the divine blessing, the omission of our periodical Synod, to have been held, in due course, last year. But the delay, we humbly trust, will be for your profit, as it has given more time to mature our judgments, and our thoughts, on the important subjects which awaited our consideration.

So weighty, indeed, were many of these, that the period during which we sat was prolonged beyond that occupied by any previous Synod. We were, however, happy in this, that every Bishop composing our hierarchy was able personally to attend; and that with the exception of the late venerable Bishop of Liverpool, Dr. George Brown, we have to deplore no loss by death between the last and our present Synod.

A marked feature in this Meeting has been the great increase in the representatives of religious orders, ancient and recent; some present by virtue of office, others brought, as their theologians, by several Bishops. It has been pleasing to meet in the shady alleys of the grounds, or to see mingled with the robes of our Canons and other secular Priests, in our more solemn assemblies, the ancient habits of those venerable conventual bodies, which, though banished for centuries from our native land, have left their names indelibly impressed on the public places and thoroughfares of our cities. And scarcely less encouraging has it been to find established amongst us so many of those modern Congregations, which God inspired holy men to found, in order to meet special wants created by the changes in the social world.

The return of the first, and the establishment of the second class of monastic institutions, form a motive for great encouragement. For when the Divine goodness thus sends workmen to our vineyard, peculiarly qualified for the various works conducive to its perfect cultivation, we cannot but feel that this spontaneous mercy marks one of those hours in its providential care, when our heavenly Master goes forth into the very market-place of His better Jerusalem, to press into His service here whoever can be spared, or seeks more active occupation, even in a strange land.

---

1. Act. xxi. 22.   2. 1 Cor. i. 8.

Nor can we overlook, dearly beloved in Christ our Lord, that such a striking, and almost unexpected, aid from without does not, we humbly trust, come to us as a reproof, but rather as an approbation, and a support. For, although it may not become us to utter words of commendation which may seem to reflect back praise upon their source, it would be unjust in us, for fear of such an imputation, to hesitate one moment in expressing our hearty approbation, and even admiration of the devotedness to their duties of the Clergy of our province, of their disinterested zeal, their multiplied labours, their self-sought increase of toil, and their self-imposed burthens.

If you, the faithful children of the Church, enjoy increased facility for assisting at the celebration of the Divine sacrifice; if you witness not only on greater feasts, but on minor or local festivals, the Churches crowded, and the Altars approached by multitudes; if in towns you enjoy the blessing of devout evening services, with frequent benedictions, and expositions of the Most Blessed Sacrament; if you see the functions of the Church performed with a new splendour, and scrupulous exactness, with richness in every requisite for them, whether decoration, or vestments and plate; to whom do you owe all this but to your zealous Clergy, who have readily sacrificed their own time, honest recreation, and, we fear we must add, often health, to procure you the spiritual graces which these additional practices of devotion confer?

Again, if in every part of England new and beautiful Churches have arisen, with additional means for daily propitiation of God's wrath; if the old and wretched, though venerable, Chapels of our sires are being superseded by larger and more becoming edifices; if Schools have been enlarged and multiplied to more than double their former dimensions and number; if religious teachers are gradually becoming, in almost every town, the instructors of the future mothers of our flocks; whose has generally been the assiduity, the labour, the self-sacrifice, to do these great things for God, but the Missionary Priest, secular or regular, who, often nobly seconded by the generosity of the laity, has laboured for years, and spent himself before he has seen the first aspirations of his hopes crowned with complete success?

It was for a Clergy that worked thus that aid was needed; not to supply defects, but to add to our power. God looked mercifully from His high throne in heaven upon His servants, who had shrunk from no toil, and quailed before no danger, whose youth was often too early crushed or blighted for this world, or rather too early bloomed for the next, who had spared themselves in nothing, and in nothing sought themselves; and sent them His help from His holy place.

New wants in the spiritual life had sprung up, and God supplied them. How were our numerous Convents to meet the at least annual demand for a spiritual retreat, without bodies of men, ready for this new requirement? How even were they to be adequately provided with leisure to undertake the office? How were the Clergy of our multiplied Dioceses, almost at one and the same time, to enjoy the annual refreshment, now so valued by themselves and their congregations, of accurately conducted spiritual exercises, without learned and grave persons, trained by express study to their direction, and even extraneous to the class of ecclesiastics to whom they have to offer wise and pious counsel?

And further still, the time had manifestly come when masses of evil had to be driven into by combined force; when the accumulation of vice and indifference in our great cities had to be broken up piecemeal, dissolved, and washed away, so as to pollute no longer the streams in which they had collected and grown. Even in country places, the quiet course of sound old Catholic traditions had often become almost stagnant, with little influence, little progress, and little feeling. It had become obvious that the application of some new power was necessary for both. In the first especially, the combination of an almost rude strength, concerted operation, and often long continuance was necessary to drive a wedge into the resisting block of aggregated and hardened sin. And where could these conditions be fulfilled, except in a body of men trained up to the work on a uniform plan, free from other responsibilities, and able to raise their voice with a new energy in every place which they visited? Who does not remember the stirring and awakening results of the early labours of these missionaries—some of whom, like the good Fathers Dominic and Gentili, have now long departed to their only rest—when they first visited our congregations?

Thank God, then, that in all this His Holy Spirit has multiplied our power and our consolation, of which the fullest evidence was given us in this provincial Synod, by the truly cordial and brotherly co-operation of the two orders of clergy. But even this harmonious activity would be very insufficient if it were not well seconded and supported by you, our dearly beloved children, the Catholic Laity of England. At all times we have found you ready to come openly and boldly forward, to assert the principles of your religion and the claims of the Church. You have readily thrown into the scale, when needed, the weight of your rank, your ancient descent, your social position, and political influence; and, where Providence had not bestowed these, the weight of your numbers, and the unanimity of your voices. Much have we gained in this manner; not only in moments of crisis and emergency, when a resolute attitude was necessary to stay artificial agitation opposed to us, but in the more tranquil adjustment of our demands in favour of education for our poor. It has been by this support and unanimity of council and of action, that our Poor School Committee has succeeded in maturing and carrying measures which all now acknowledge to have procured most important advantages. It has been through the same combined activity that our separate reformatories have been obtained, on a footing of equality with those of others. And, finally, the zeal of all Catholics, and their earnest advocacy, have secured permanently to our soldiers, at home and abroad, the inestimable blessing of chaplains, honourably appointed, and treated as becomes their sacred office.

But we cannot pass over the most signal and public demonstration of our unanimity in truly Catholic efforts, so recently given, by one of the most numerous and distinguished meetings for any religious purpose ever held in the metropolis. When we consider what was the purpose of this assemblage,—in the eyes of God nothing less, in the sight of scoffers nothing more, than the eternal interests of the outcasts of society, whom crime has thrust into prisons, or wretchedness has swept into workhouses,—we thank the Almighty, in the sincerity of our hearts, that He hath given such a gift to you of compassionate charity and its courageous advocacy.

But, dearly beloved in Christ our Lord, let us earnestly remind you that our work, in this matter, is not yet complete. The just and salutary measures for which we have contended have not as yet been granted, still less carried out. They are three in number.

First,—the obtaining for our gallant and loyal Catholics serving in Her Majesty's Fleet, the same means and opportunities for receiving religious instruction, exhortation, and sacred ministration, as have been secured to our soldiers in the army; for surely there can be no difference of equitable claims between those who risk their lives on land, and those who doubly peril them at sea.

Secondly,—the placing of Catholic prisoners on the same footing as Protestants in all that regards religious assistance and consolation; for since, professedly, the prison is now regarded as a place of reformation rather than of expiation, and since no one can doubt that the root of faith once planted in the heart, and never totally destroyed by a career of vice, is the best, and often the only, hold which later calls to virtue can seize, it stands to reason that Catholic delinquents can be restored to a moral life by no one so well as by the priest, who alone knows their religious convictions, and can supply their spiritual wants.

Thirdly,—the attaining similar justice for the wretched inmates of the workhouse, whose only crime is often sad misfortune, and who are even more unfairly treated than professed and condemned criminals; for whereas the regulations of prisons are at least, in their respective classes, uniform, and prescribed by a public authority, the rules and usages of these receptacles of wretchedness are subject to the capricious enactments of local jurisdictions, sometimes, indeed,—especially in large towns,—just and liberal in their dealings with our poor, but often narrow-minded and bigoted to an almost incredible degree. Hence the visits of the priest to these afflicted and oppressed creatures of God are limited, hampered, and almost hindered, by troublesome and obstructive conditions, which require a strong hand to sweep them away, and substitute for them a generous and kind-hearted legislation.

Indeed, it ought not to be forgotten, that none of these classes of subjects of the Crown have forfeited, even by crime, their full right to religious toleration. It is no part of the sentence of the law upon any delinquent, that he shall be deprived of the means of practising his religion, or shall be compelled to submit to means directed to make him a Protestant. In this respect—that is, in what touches his soul—the jurisprudence of the land grants no authority, deprives men the most guilty of no single right. How much less should those who offer their lives to defend the honour and dominions of the Crown—how much less do those whom misery has struck down, lose by their position that freedom in believing in God, and in worshiping Him according to their consciences, which other members of the same state legally enjoy! Yet, practically they are treated, and theoretically their case is discussed, as if such a distinction did exist between them and others.

If we have entered into these details, it has been for the purpose of keeping your attention wakeful to the cause that our clergy and laity have so cheerfully undertaken, with a view and a determination that it shall be carried. Now, notwithstanding the energy displayed, and the prospect of success which seemed to await it, we must bear in mind that hitherto our hopes have not been realised, and no concessions have been definitely made. Our work, therefore, is not accomplished; and we must continue our unrelaxed efforts, and our happy co-operation, till we can congratulate, not ourselves, but our poor, that we have no more to solicit on their behalf.

While, however, we thus express our confidence in the faithful discharge of respective duties by every class of Catholics, to whom this our Synodical letter is addressed, there are several points of deep interest which have occupied our thoughts during this meeting, and which we consider worthy of being brought before your attention.

I. The first is, that ever new and ever engrossing topic—the education of our poor. Ever new, because ever true, is that divine word, that "the poor we have always with us." As a tide ever moving, and ever driving wave on the track of wave, each different, yet seemingly the same, so does the dull unvarying motion of time send forward a succession of young claimants to our tenderness and our charity. If you enter the school to-day which you visited six years ago, you seem to see the same objects before you, and feel tempted to exclaim, "Are we no more forward yet with this everlasting education?" "Yes," and "No," might be the honest reply. Yes! you contemplate before you what looks identical: the same eyes, the same casts of countenance, the same varieties of character, the same sprightliness and the same dulness,—perhaps the very same rags, and certainly the same squalidness and destitution. And you witness, too, the same patient, untiring round of teaching, of forbearing, of exhortation and mild reproof in the brother, or the sister, who has sat for years at the presiding desk, and will sit there, having ever the poor for companion and for charge, till death shall have transferred each to the companionship of guardian angels, whom both have imitated and helped.

And yet in the most essential respect, No! All that it profits to care for is different. These are all new immortal souls that have to be saved, and we must do for them what we have done for others. During the interval between our visits, more than one wave has passed over and away; and who will ever recover and rejoin the particles that composed it? Some have sunk into the sand, and are slumbering somewhere amidst children's graves; most have been washed out on the broad ocean of life, dispersed far and wide, even to the Antipodes; some float on nobly on the surface, while others, perhaps, are sinking. But you have done your duty generously to all, and to many who have succeeded them.

So now you are providing the same blessings for another generation; and another will follow this, and claim your succour, and you needs must grant it. This was not a temporary charity, that was to end in a few years. So long as God is not wearied with doing good, but goes on giving His world new souls to love Him and be saved, we must not tire of seconding, by our feeble efforts, His benevolent intentions. Nay, let us make up our minds that this is an heirloom that we have secured to our families—a legacy which we must leave to children and successors in our property. Never can the burthen be taken off any Catholic estate or possession, of educating the poor in the fear and love of God.

We need not, therefore, exhort you, as we have done in our previous Synodical Letter, to persevere in this important undertaking. We feel grieved every time that we notice a falling off in the returns of subscriptions collected for education; but never more than when we find this diminution affect the funds of our Poor School Committee, for every year adds another evidence to former proofs of the immense utility of this institution. In its exertions we can find no trace whatever of relaxation or fatigue; in its close adhesion to our episcopal policy, in its perfect coherence and unity in itself, and in its external activity as well as impartial administration, we detect no alteration or symptom of decline from first fervour. We feel happy in having at our side so faithful and so zealous a Council.

II. Connected with this subject is a special motive of grief to us. It is the great negligence,—perhaps a growing negligence,—of parents in sending their children to Catholic schools. Unfortunately, many Catholic poor, themselves not educated, allow themselves to be seduced by the advantages proposed, to allure their children to heretical schools, or to be carried away by the cry of "education," considered merely as a means of getting on in the world; and so do not either perceive the evils of an erroneous, or appreciate the blessings of a sound, education. Hence, even if anxious to give to their children the benefit of some intellectual training, they only think of its secular portion, caring but little for its religious, and really vital, element.

Let it, then, be the incessant endeavour of us all, to rouse the poor from this apathy. Let the pulpit, the confessional, the domestic visit, the tract, and the casual conversation, be brought to bear on this most grave and ruinous indifference. In inculcating the necessity of educating children, let such words and reasons be always employed as can be applicable to only one mode, only one principle, as can convince and persuade, that only an orthodox, sterling faith can form the solid basis of those virtues which alone can secure real happiness in this life, as well as salvation in the next: patience, meekness, purity, charity, piety, and unbounded reliance on God. In all missions or retreats given to the people, let this be a topic never omitted, and let the preacher fervently urge, among the matters on which conscience is to be examined, and if necessary, amendment be promised, the duty of not merely educating, but of educating as Catholics, all children whom parentage or guardianship enables or permits to do so; and let all who possess influence with the poor, as masters, as landlords, or as benefactors, insist upon care in this particular respect beyond any other. Hence we most warmly approve such pious associations as may exist for looking after the children of the poor systematically, where each member adopts, as a particular charge, a few families or children, frequently visited, or spoken to, for this special purpose.

By such multiplied solicitude, we may hope that parents will be brought to consider the education of their children in Catholic faith and observances, not so much as an advantage to their offspring, but as a duty of their own; not merely as a means of securing prosperity to those whom they shall leave after them, but, if in their reach, as a necessary condition of their own salvation: for let it be often urged upon such negligent parents—and if possible, inscribed on their very walls—that "If any man hath not care of his own, and especially of those of his house, he hath denied the faith, and is worse than an infidel." (1 Tim. v. 8.)

III. But there is another branch of education, no less important, which has greatly occupied our thoughts during the present Synod: it is that of clerical education. If you look back, dearly beloved, on the statistics of Catholicity in England, even within your memory, you will easily see how, year by year, the number of missions and of priests has increased, till both may be said to have been more than doubled in a generation. And this increase, while we sincerely thank God for it in the past, we humbly trust will yet grow a hundred fold.

It is evident that the means of supplying this exigent demand should keep just proportion with it; yet this is not the case. We have indeed excellent colleges at home; but though they have all been either rebuilt or considerably enlarged within a few years, their number has diminished. There were four ecclesiastical colleges when England was divided into four districts: there are but three now that it forms thirteen dioceses. There are undoubtedly excellent subsidiary colleges abroad. Rome, Lisbon, Douai, and Valladolid, contribute additional resources to our limited supply of priests; and more recently we have to thank the Divine goodness for having inspired a convert to the faith with those princely thoughts that, in old Catholic times, distinguished a Wykeham, a Chicheley, or a Wolsey, for the foundation of a college at Bruges, to educate additional clergy for England. Already the first house, prepared temporarily for the reception of students, has been exchanged for a larger and more commodious one; and even this is only held till ground can be found suitable for the erection of a new and complete edifice. With the kind concurrence of the learned and exemplary Bishop, the Very Rev. Canon Dessein has been appointed its first Rector; the Rev. Dr. Leadbitter, its Vice-Rector; and the Rev. Abbé Boone, its Procurator and Administrator; while the office of Professors is discharged by those of the Seminary, the schools of which are as yet frequented by the students.

While we yield to the modest reserve of the generous Founder, in not further alluding to his munificent undertaking, we not the less earnestly recommend him to your fervour and constant prayers, that God will give him length of days and vigorous health, to see it accomplished, and productive of solid and lasting benefit.

The Divine goodness has indeed manifested itself to us in this matter, so as to direct our particular attention to it. For example: in one diocese of France, an Archbishop has offered some free funds in his Seminary for the education of clerics for England. In another, a zealous priest, unbidden, has formed an association, and has collected funds through that charitable country, for the free education of English boys for our missions. The great Benedictine house of Subiaco has shown a signal interest in this holy work.

Yet all these means of providing a succession of apostolic labourers have not proved sufficient. Hence, we should be fearfully destitute of ecclesiastical ministers, were we not assisted by the zealous concourse of priests from many countries—from Italy, Belgium, France, and Germany. But still more heavily are we indebted to the episcopate and priesthood of neighbouring Ireland, for an efficient supply of excellent clergy, who fill up so many important missionary stations, which but for them would remain unoccupied, to the great detriment of religion. To all these ready fellow-labourers we owe indeed much gratitude; for they have so made England their home, that it would be difficult to discover that it is only their adopted country.

But while it is a great and signal blessing to any country thus to be able, by its overflow, to enrich others, it is no doubt a deficiency in any not to suffice for its own requirements. No church can be considered fully and satisfactorily established till it is self-supplying, and not dependent on the generosity and charity of foreign lands, or of separate hierarchies. It is our duty to labour, and not to spare ourselves, till we see our respective dioceses furnishing us with a steady and sufficient succession of missionaries, thoroughly trained under our own eyes, who begin their career where, through God's mercy, they intend to finish it; making the sacred ministry independent of circumstances or events, which may some day cut off, or seriously curtail, supplies from extraneous sources. For this we have determined to labour—for this, if it please God, to suffer—until we see accomplished the strong desire, or rather, fulfilled the wise injunctions of the holy Council of Trent, that each diocese should have its own Seminary, episcopal in name and in character, dear to the Bishop as the apple of his eye, and jealously reserved to his own superintendence and vigilant solicitude. (Sess. xxiii. cap. 18, De Reform.)

It is clear, however, that all this must be the work not so much of time, as of energetic and perseverant co-operation. The first and most important step to be taken is the collection of funds both for the present increase of ecclesiastical education, and for the foundation of diocesan seminaries; for it must be borne in mind that the want is present and urgent, as well as future and prospective. While our missions have increased immensely in number, the foundations for clerical education have not increased in anything like proportion; indeed, in many places there has been no increase at all. We are, therefore, most anxious to augment the number of clerical students in actual education at home and abroad; and for this we ask your charitable assistance. At the same time, we most earnestly recommend our nobler purpose of erecting local seminaries to your generous consideration. When you are looking around you for some truly excellent object for your charities; when you are weighing the value and importance of various institutions, to decide which shall be the recipient of your alms in life, the depository of your pious wishes and legacies after death; remember, we pray you, how immeasurably supreme are works of spiritual mercy; and how among these must be supereminent, that which includes them all—the furnishing to thousands, for an unlimited duration, of a holy and learned priesthood. Seldom, indeed, is this exalted application of disposable means taken to heart, or even brought under consideration. Perhaps some of us may have to reproach ourselves with this deficiency—because we have not clearly enough made it known, or urged its remedy. If so, we venture to hope that this united appeal, the result of much reflection and deliberation, aided, we humble trust, by the light of that Holy Spirit whom you all so fervently joined in invoking with us, will come now before you with a more efficacious pleading, than could have been the result of our separate and individual addresses.

Each bishop will, however, adopt those means for promoting these great purposes, which his own wisdom and experience may suggest to him, as most likely to prove successful in his own diocese.

IV. Since we last addressed you synodically, our country has added to its judicial institutions one concerning which we feel it our duty briefly to instruct you. A new court has been appointed with power to grant the dissolution of marriage, under the name of the Divorce Court. We need not remind you, our faithful and dearly beloved children, that such a tribunal can only have been established for those who hold marriage to be a worldly or temporal contract, dissoluble by the civil power; or who interpret Scripture on the subject, in a manner totally at variance with the sense ever held by the One, Holy, Catholic and Apostolic Church. But for you, who have always been taught, and believe, that the contract is based on the Divine declaration, that "what God hath joined together, let no man put asunder" (Mat. xix. 6); for you, who believe that matrimony is a sacrament, and a symbol of that indissoluble union, wherein Jesus Christ espoused His Church (Ephes. v. 32), such legislation is not, and cannot be. Never, therefore, can you have recourse to this tribunal, for purposes diametrically opposed to the doctrine of your holy Mother, the Church.

But even beyond this, almost superfluous, warning, we must sincerely deplore this innovation in our legislature, which we cannot but consider calculated to enervate great principles in the social and domestic life of our dear country, by creating facilities for dissolving bonds, the very sacredness of which administered a motive for their being respected, and being more easily preserved unbroken. Nay, it may be treated, by evil minds, as holding out temptations, if not inducements, to those preliminary acts which are requisite for obtaining relief from obligations that time or wicked passions have made distasteful. God grant that it be not so: and that a remedy may soon be applied to so serious a national calamity.

V. It is our duty to inform you, that having, in former Provincial Synods, appointed a Committee to revise the first Catechism, its labours, happily closed, have been laid before bishops appointed to examine them, and have received their approbation. The first publication of this revised and approved Catechism has been entrusted to Messrs. Richardson and Son, of Derby, and no other edition but theirs is to be considered as, at present, sanctioned for use in our Dioceses.

VI. We entered on the duties of this Synod amidst the distant, but harrowing details of war—of war between the two Catholic empires of Europe, of war upon the fair plains of Italy, of war sudden, rapid, and destructive of many lives. But what specially afflicted us was the intense pain and grief, which we knew affected the heart of our holy Father and Pontiff, whose peace was menaced, whose states were dismembered, and whose rights and character were rudely assailed by speech and by pen. It is true that the active and incessant occupation of our Synodical duties left us but little time to attend to other thoughts; yet we could not be indifferent to such subjects as these. But the more bright, as the more sudden, has come upon us the announcement of peace, or of its precursor, an armistice. We have thus been able to sing our united *Te Deum* in thanksgiving to the God of peace, as of battles, for so signal and so unexpected a blessing. And you have all joined with us, on the same day, through our different Dioceses.

Yet while we have thus justly rejoiced, our hearts are not entirely relieved of their load. We cannot but fear that the waters which have been stirred up by such a tempest, will long continue to heave and fret, and agitate with anxiety the tender heart of our supreme Pastor. We have, indeed, all heard with edification of the tranquillity and resignation which he has displayed, amidst the late trying occurrences; and how he devoted himself with unaltered countenance, and unruffled mind, to the arduous duties of his sublime office, while the tumults of war were almost within his frontiers, and the insults of insubordination almost within his gates. He had, indeed, been already a man of sorrow, one acquainted with grief; and we never feared his failing to preserve his soul in peace.

But such a new and unmerited return of trials that seemed ended, so unexpected an interruption of a prosperity that had crowned his unwearied assiduity in his temporal administration, may easily undermine the strength of the most vigorous and most serene temperament. The reign of our beloved Pontiff is too precious to the Church, and its lengthened duration is too important to all his and her children, not to demand our instant and unceasing prayer for his health, his tranquillity of mind, the peace of his dominions, and that of the Church. Continue, therefore, dearly beloved brethren and children in Christ, to offer up your earnest supplications to the Father of mercies, that He will look down with affectionate compassion upon His suffering kingdom on earth, and that he will preserve, prosper, and exalt her Head, and the Vicar of His beloved Son.

We trust that this expression of our filial and dutiful feeling, when placed at the feet of the Sovereign Pontiff, will be accepted by him, not only as our personal and united homage, but likewise as the tribute of that affectionate sympathy in which we are sure you join us.

To conclude, dearly beloved brethren and children in Christ, we entreat you to hold fast the doctrine of your holy Mother, the Church, in all simplicity of heart, without cavil, and without anxiety. Accept the truths of faith in the plain meaning in which they were taught you in your infancy, nor fear that the progress of human learning, or the discoveries of modern science, can shake the foundations of your everlasting belief. Keep ever "the form of sound words," which you have learnt, without innovation, without attempts to adapt it to any particular theory. Be content to remain docile children of the Church. It is true, thanks be to God, that her doctrines and practices are no longer objects of virulent attack, or blasphemous ridicule, as once they used to be, almost daily; but our dangers rather lie, on that account, deeper and less patent. It is by the attempts to draw away our middle classes, and even our poor, to unbelief in Christianity, that our religion is now most endangered. By lectures, by tracts, by periodical literature, by shallow science, by works of fiction,—by a thousand other means, the poison of infidelity is sedulously infused into the minds of many unprepared by preservatives, unfurnished with antidotes: and unfortunately, the havoc thus caused is perhaps greater than what sectarian attempts have ever effected, in seducing our dear children from the bosom of the Church.

Resist, all ye who can, these wicked efforts; exclude as much as possible from circulation among those whom you can influence, the pestilent works which bear infection into the Catholic home; provide, to the utmost, sound and counteracting knowledge, by the formation of such institutions, whether libraries, reading rooms, associations, lectures, or other means, as may help to direct the eager curiosity of the educated over safe and yet agreeable paths, nor suffer it to wander into the broad road of perdition.

Above all, encourage every practice of piety and approved devotion; for these are the great safeguards of faith—far more than intellectual discussion or abstruse investigations. Towards the most adorable Eucharist, and towards the Immaculate Mother of Our Lord, we exhort you to entertain the most tender, as the most solid devotion, and to promote it in all who depend on you, or look up to you, with singular earnestness and untiring fervour.

"Be nothing solicitous; but in everything, by prayer and supplication, with thanksgiving, let your petitions be made known to God.

"And the peace of God, which surpasseth all understanding, keep your hearts and minds in Christ Jesus.

"For the rest, brethren, whatsoever things are true, whatsoever modest, whatsoever just, whatsoever holy, whatsoever lovely, whatsoever of good fame,—if there be any virtue, if any praise of discipline, think on these things.

"And may God supply all your wants, according to his riches in glory, in Christ Jesus.

"Now to God and our Father be glory, world without end. Amen.

"The grace of our Lord Jesus Christ be with your spirit. Amen." (Philip. iv. 6 seqq.)·

FOURTH SYNOD.

(August 12, 1873.)

Fourteen years have now elapsed since the Third Provincial Council of Westminster was held. Nearly half a generation of men has passed away. Six of the thirteen Dioceses of England have carried to their last, it may be said their first rest, with noble testimonies of love and veneration, the laborious Pastors who in daily toil wore out their life for their flock. Westminster, and Beverley, and Hexham, Southwark, and Salford, and Liverpool, are represented in this our Fourth Council by other voices, bearing witness to the same faith and to the same authority. The Pastors come and go; the office and the fold remain the same for ever.

If it be asked why fourteen years should have been allowed to pass without our meeting in Synod, it may be truly said that, of many causes which justified the postponement of our assembling to legislate for the Church of England, the chief cause is to be found in the completeness of the Decrees of the three Provincial Councils already held. The first described and fixed the whole outline of the order, discipline, and worship, of the rising Church, which by the act of the Sovereign Pontiff had then come forth from its scattering and its inactivity; the Second treated of its temporal administration; the Third of its Ecclesiastical Seminaries, and the training of its Clergy. You may then ask, dearly beloved Brethren and Children in Jesus Christ, why we should again assemble; and what need of a Fourth Provincial Council. The law of the Church prescribes that such Synods be held every three years, unless by special permission of the Holy See this obligation be suspended. The Church does not wait till needs of new legislation shall force themselves upon us. It prescribes that we shall anticipate the pressure of necessity, and by constant vigilance prevent the abuses or disorders that demand correction. We give thanks to God that our meeting now is not for this need or purpose: there is another and more consoling reason for our assembling here. We meet now, not to reform or to correct, but to unfold and to expand, our former legislation. The supernatural growth of the Church in England during the last fourteen years demands that its internal discipline shall be enlarged and perfected. This visible growth, which is evident to all men—to some indeed a cause of unreasonable fear, to us of humility, thanksgiving, and increasing labour—can be ascribed to no other power than that of the Holy Spirit of God, who is sensibly breathing where He lists over all the face of the land; and to that also which is likewise His own work, the perfect order and action of the Church in its Pastoral Office, restored to us three-and-twenty years ago.

For three hundred years England had but one Pastor, afar off, and burdened with the charge of the universal Church. The Vicars Apostolic bore indeed his commission; and, as true fishers of men, they wrought works which we humbly desire at least to imitate, if we cannot equal. But their Vicariates reached from sea to sea; the Missions were few and isolated, with intervals of a day's journey from altar to altar. The creation of thirteen Episcopal Sees has opened thirteen sources of pastoral care; each of which again has thrown out a whole diocesan organization, and multiplied Churches, Missions, Clergy, Colleges, and Schools. The Hierarchy in its first nine years was as yet only gathering its strength to expand. In the last fourteen it has almost doubled its centres of action, and its resources of spiritual agency. Compare the state of the greater cities and towns of England before the year 1850 and at this time. The Missions have been divided and sub-divided into new districts, with resident Clergy in each; the number of Clergy in the larger Missions already existing has been steadily increased; the Schools and the children attending them are more than doubled; the devoted Religious who teach our children have multiplied in a still greater proportion; the works of charity and piety of every kind have sprung up and are springing up without ceasing; the means of Divine Worship, the popular devotions of the Most Holy Sacrament, and those also of our Blessed and Immaculate Mother, have spread everywhere, with so large an increase, that the whole face of England, especially in our large cities, begins to put on the aspect of Catholic lands, and to afford to the Faithful in most places a ready facility of daily devotion. In all this our beloved Clergy, Secular and Regular, have zealously and powerfully co-operated. But, as we have said, it is not to ourselves that we arrogate this supernatural work; but to the Spirit of God, and to the grace which attaches to the Pastoral care.

For two-and-twenty days the Church has held counsel in Synod; but we are not able as yet to make known the results of our deliberations. The decrees of the Council, until they have been approved by the Holy See, cannot be published. We have the happiness of announcing to you that this Synod, containing the whole Episcopate of England, two Mitred Abbots, the Cathedral Chapters by representation, the Provincials and Heads of Religious Orders in England, the Theologians and Officers of the Council, has for three weeks deliberated in the perfect unity of faith and charity, of heart and mind, of will and purpose, which is the heirloom of those alone who inherit from the Apostles. We now separate, to return to our several flocks and charges, in the full consciousness that it has been good for us to be here. The deliberations of the Council have been guided, from the opening to the end, with a mutual confidence and respect which will not only be long remembered, but will bind us all to each other when we are once more scattered to our distant fields of work. The Catholic Church from this Synod will have gained an incalculable increase in its solid unity, and in its vigour of action throughout the whole of England. For this grace of brotherly peace and concord we render our thanks to our Divine Master, who, according to His promise, has been in the midst of us, to help and to guide us.

We now address to you, dearly beloved Brethren and Children in Jesus Christ, a few words on some of the more urgent matters of our common duty.

1. And, first, we have to thank the Father of Lights and the Giver of all Grace for your fidelity and steadfastness in the faith in these days when some who were teachers among us have fallen away. The times in which we live are more dangerous than those of our forefathers. Persecution is a blunt weapon, which can but destroy the body: it gives strength and life to the soul. These days of subtil errors and poisonous refinement are far more perilous to the grace of faith, to rectitude of will, and to purity of heart: and when any one of these is infected, the fidelity of a Catholic is in peril. The whole atmosphere of this nineteenth century is charged with hostility to God and to His Church, to the doctrines of revelation, and even to the truths of the natural order. And this, which a century ago was confined to a higher class of over-cultivated minds, is now, by the unprecedented activity of the press, diffused through every class, reaching even to the skilled and the unskilled working population of all countries, above all of our own. From the highest to the lowest class, unbelief has its literature and its apostles. In the midst of all these perils you have to live and breathe, to listen, and to receive perhaps unconsciously a tone and a spirit adverse to piety, and maxims contrary to faith. Therefore, dearly beloved Children, we all the more rejoice over your constancy, firmly believing that the noble and inflexible fidelity we see in you is given you from above. While all religious belief around us from internal dissensions is crumbling away, your solidity in the faith is proved by your unity with one another and with us. We have indeed cause to thank God for you all, for you are "our joy and our crown."

2. We need hardly exhort you to take care that your children shall be like yourselves, perfect in Catholic faith, and in the instincts which protect the grace of faith from the spirits of error now assailing us on every side. "Our wrestling is not against flesh and blood: but against principalities and powers, against the rulers of the world of this darkness; against the spirits of wickedness in the high places."[1] But we need say no more. You are already roused to this duty. The work of our education in the last twenty years is sufficient proof. It has kept pace with the progress of which men are so loud. Burdened and hindered as we are with poverty, neither in quantity nor in quality is the education of the Catholic Church in England at a disadvantage. We might say more; but this is enough. The moral industry of our teachers, and the obedience of our children, has had its full effect even upon the intellectual development of our Colleges and Schools. We may confidently affirm that the

---

[1] Ephes. vi. 12.

most Christian, and most doctrinal schools in England, will be found, to say no more, not a whit behind any other schools in the standard of their secular instruction. You will, we are persuaded, labour together with us until every Catholic child of our poor shall be gathered into a Catholic School. You will deny yourselves that you may promote this vital work by your alms and contributions. Twenty years ago we had but one Poor School society. It may be truly said that now we have thirteen. Every Diocese is in itself the most efficient education society; and to this many give their aid readily and generously, as we already know. We need not repeat that, to the utmost of their power, all the faithful are bound to contribute, in the Diocese or Mission where they reside, to the education of the poor. These have a first claim upon you, as your nearest of kin in the household of faith. You will not fail to remember that the Poor School Committee, which was once, as we have said, our only society for education, is still our only society for the training of School Teachers, without whom all efforts to multiply our schools would be of little avail. The efficiency of a school depends upon the teacher. And the excellence of the teacher depends upon his training. Just in proportion as religion is banished from the school-time, the obligation to train a race of teachers, who for the love of God and of souls will make the religious education of our poor children their primary care, becomes graver and more urgent.

3. There is another part of our education system which now needs attention. Until the last quarter of a century a middle class hardly existed in the Catholic Church in England. There were indeed in parts of the country a few families of the yeomanry still faithful: but our flock was for the most part made up of a small number of venerable and honoured Catholic families, who represent the spiritual inheritance of our forefathers, and a multitude of the poorest in the land. At this time, partly by prosperity in the commerce and industries of our country, and partly by a large accession of educated families to the Faith, a numerous middle class has been formed, for which a corresponding education must be carefully provided.

4. And here, though it is not our intention to dwell upon it, we think it well to add that the Bishops of England fully recognize the duty which lies upon them, to mature and to provide a system of higher education, required by our youth from the age of 17 or 18 to 21 or 22 years. It has been our duty, under the supreme guidance of the Holy See, to warn all parents that they cannot send their sons to the national Universities without exposing them to the peril of losing either faith or morals, or perhaps both; and that no parent can so expose a son without incurring grave sin. This admonition, which we gave five years ago, we are now compelled to repeat with still graver warning. The late changes in the national Universities, by which all tests in religion have been abolished, caused us once more to seek the guidance of the Holy See. After reciting the decision of the Holy See, dated Feb. 3, 1865, the answer runs in these words: "The declaration then given was founded on the grave dangers which the said Universities presented: and the Catholics of England, both Clergy and Laity, complied with that declaration in the most edifying manner, although the state of the national Universities was far different then from what it has become since." "Not only does the Holy See perceive no reason why it should recede from the aforementioned decision of 1865; but, in proportion as the reasons which

called forth that decision have increased in gravity, so much the more necessary does it appear that that decision should be maintained."[1]

5. Charged, as we are, with the Pastoral care of the whole Flock in this land, we recognize our obligation to see that the education of every member of the Church shall be in accordance with the Faith out of which no one can be saved. We know that the education of the highest as well as the lowest of our people is a part of the cure of souls for which we must give account. Every baptized soul, whether of the rich or poor, has a right to Catholic education. Every Christian father and mother has a right to educate their children in the Faith. We are guardians of the rights of children who are born again in Christian baptism; and guardians also of the rights of parents, to whom God has given, both by the law of nature and of grace, an authority over their children higher than the authority of any human power. For this cause we recognize our duty to labour with all provident care that the higher studies of our Catholic Colleges shall be so raised and matured as to leave nothing wanting to a mature Catholic education; and though, at this time, we may not have the power to found a Catholic University, it is certain that those who come after us will be compelled to accomplish in some way this great and necessary work. We ought, therefore, in our day, to do all in our power which may prepare for such a completion of our Catholic and Christian education. While others are departing, further and further, from the traditions of the Christian world, and casting the revelation of God out of the range of human science and of intellectual culture, it is the duty of the Catholic Church, with a steadfast inflexibility, to preserve, and to transmit whole and inviolate to those who shall come after, not only the doctrines of Christian education and of science, but the principles and the method of Catholic science and of Christian culture. We have this precious deposit in trust, not for ourselves only, but for all posterity. Therefore, we cannot accept modern schemes of mixed education, or conform ourselves to them by the slightest deviation from the traditions of the Catholic Faith.

6. And this leads us to a last topic connected with the education of our youth, namely, the training of those who are destined to the Priesthood. Until a certain age they are educated in the same Colleges with boys or youths destined for the world. The early friendships formed in boyhood bind together the Laity and the Clergy through life. Their example may be mutually for good. Their path, as Christian and Catholic youths, is in common, until those who are to ascend the altar withdraw, for their last training in the life of interior perfection and of separation from the world. Four years, or even six, are a short time to set apart for the last formation of men who shall become the guides and pastors of souls. For this purpose it is necessary that the greater Dioceses, at least, should each possess a Theological Seminary. The lesser Dioceses may either combine together or unite with some one of the greater in a common Seminary. But to accomplish this we need your help. You can do no greater good than by training the Clergy of the future. You cannot more wisely apply, whether by gift while living or by bequest after your death, the means at your disposal than in the education of Pastors and Teachers for the work of souls. The need of such Seminaries is evident, for two reasons: first, because the multiplication of our people demands a multi-

---

[1] Letter of the Cardinal Prefect of Propaganda, Sept. 19, 1872.

plication of our Clergy; and, secondly, because the rising standard of intellectual culture, both in the Catholic and the non-Catholic population around us, demands a higher intellectual culture in our Priests. We would, therefore, earnestly exhort you to consider how you can promote the founding either of additional Seminaries, or of burses for the maintenance of Students in those that already exist. We would also specially exhort parents to remember that they can offer to the Lord no more precious gift than their sons to be His disciples. It is an exceeding honour and a signal grace to a house when a son is called to be a Priest. A vocation brings a benediction into the home, and sanctifies it by a special relation to the altar and to the presence of Jesus in the Holy Sacrament.

7. The change which has been introduced into the popular education of England demands of us all a redoubled effort to preserve the Christian formation and traditions of our people. Hitherto the whole education of our Poor Schools was pervaded with faith and piety. Even the books of secular instruction were so written or compiled as to form at one and the same time the intellect, the conscience, and the will. The secular instruction, without ceasing to be literary, or falling below the required standard of efficiency, was throughout Christian and religious. It is so no longer. Our national education has ceased not only to train Christian men, but even to form the character of citizens. Four hours of secular teaching, in which neither Christianity nor the religion of nature may be taught, will not form conscience, or will, or character in man. The office of shaping the character of men belongs to a higher power. God has placed it in the hands of parents and of those to whom they confide their children. It is one of the penalties of religious division, that, because men have lost the unity of Faith, the Faith is banished from the schools of a Christian people. The State has ceased to admit Christianity into schools, because the people is not agreed as to what Christianity is. In saying this, we do but recite and describe our position, that we may point out our duty for the future. All are bound, pastors and parents, and all the faithful according to their power, to labour, and, by all means they can devise, to maintain in the hearts and minds of Catholic children of every class the full doctrinal knowledge of the Faith, which throughout the four hours of the school time may no longer be taught. For this purpose no care on our part will be omitted, first, to provide catechetical formularies adapted to the several degrees of intelligence and culture in our youth; secondly, to maintain a constant and minute examination, year by year, of the religious knowledge in our schools by Inspectors in every Diocese; and lastly, to promote the diffusion of Catholic books, and, after the custom so widely spread in Catholic countries, of devotional objects, and of prints, and brief instructions of piety. We shall never know till the great harvest is gathered in, how much has sprung up from a diligent scattering of these unnoticed seeds of piety and faith. Happy are they who go through life casting the words of salvation along their path. "In the morning sow thy seed; and in the evening let not thy hand cease: for thou knowest not which may rather spring up, this or that; and if both together, it shall be the better."[1] This admonition we give above all to heads of families. Let

---

1. 1 Eccl. xi. 6.

your homes be schools of faith and piety. Gather your children and your servants together day by day in some common acts of prayer. Sanctify your households, that they may be worthy of the Apostolic salutation, "the Church which is in thy house."

8. We cannot leave this topic without urging on you, dear children in Jesus Christ, to ascertain carefully what is the character of the literature admitted into your homes. For the most part our English literature continues to be pure; and it is at least free from impiety. But there are recent books of fiction in prose and in poetry, and works professing to be history and philosophy, which ought not to be under your roof. You are not without advisers who can tell you the real nature of such works. Twenty years ago we were almost without a modern Catholic literature. We have now a literature growing up, partly original, partly translated from other languages, which for variety and excellence promises gradually to supply much of our need. In commending our modern works, we do not mean to give them precedence in solidity and truth of expression over our older books. In devotion indeed we should rather commend the writings of our Catholic forefathers, to whom the realities of persecution taught a deep and simple piety, such as men learn in suffering, and would desire to rest upon in the hour of death.

9. There yet remains one other subject on which we desire to speak: not indeed to instruct you; but to justify your fidelity, in cases which bring upon us much unreasonable and perverse censure from the world around you.

The Church has by its earliest discipline, and at all times, in language of great energy, condemned marriages of mixed religion. The reasons of this prohibition to you are self-evident; to the world they are, like the Catholic Faith itself, unintelligible. The Church has added to its prohibition the impediment whereby a mixed marriage without dispensation is unlawful. For grave causes, such a dispensation is granted by the Church. But it cannot be granted except upon the mutual and united promise of the two parties, Catholic and non-Catholic, made to the Bishop who grants the dispensation, that the Catholic party shall have perfect liberty to practise the Catholic religion, that all children born of such marriage shall be brought up in the Catholic Faith, and that the marriage shall be solemnized in the Catholic Church alone. Of these three conditions the first is so self-evidently right and necessary, that we need do no more than recite it. But on the two last much censure has been cast, and many things unreasonable and untrue have been said. We will therefore place in your hands a statement of the law of the Church, by which you will be able to satisfy all just minds, and to answer even those whose contentions are not just.

First, as to the education of the children in the Catholic Faith, it has been said, and thought, that the Church used to permit that the sons should be brought up in one religion and the daughters in another. The Church has never permitted such a thing; it could not permit it: because such a practice is intrinsically sinful. It would be not only the breach of a law, but it would also be a denial of the Catholic Faith. The Catholic Church knows of only one Faith in which we can be saved. To consent to, or to countenance, an agreement by which one soul shall be brought up out of that way of salvation would be a mortal sin, and a tacit denial of the one only way of salvation. This the Church has never done, nor has ever even implicitly countenanced. They who have done such things will answer at the judgment-seat for their own personal acts, which were not acts of the Church, nor sanctioned by the Church, but were in direct variance with its express commands and with the law of God. It is in the memory of living men that the Archbishop of Cologne endured imprisonment in vindication of this divine law. We are bound to walk in the one only way to life, and to allow no soul for whom we are responsible to be led away from it. The Catholic father or mother who, for interest or any worldly motive, consents that their offspring shall be educated out of the way of life in which they profess to desire to die, thereby denies in deed the Faith which they profess in words. Both by the natural and the revealed law of God, parents are bound to rear their children in the same grace of salvation in which they hope for eternal life. This condition, then, that all children of such marriage shall be brought up in the Catholic Faith, is not a new or an arbitrary rule. It is an intrinsic law, founded upon the revelation of God, old as the Church itself, and inseparable from the Faith. They who believe that all forms of Christianity are indifferent will perhaps not understand our words. They who believe that the Catholic is the only revealed way of salvation will need no further reasoning.

The other condition, that no Catholic shall solemnize marriage before any minister of religion other than the Priests of the Catholic Church, rests on principles equally plain. From the unity of the Faith springs the unity of Divine Worship. As it is unlawful to hold communion with any professions of faith out of the unity of Catholic truth, so it is unlawful to hold communion in any acts of religion out of the unity of Catholic worship. Matrimony is a Sacrament of the Church; and no Catholic can therefore hold communion with any marriage ceremony professing to be religious, or in the presence of any person professing to be a minister of religion, out of the unity of the Catholic Church.

So long as penal laws inflicted legal nullity upon all Catholic marriages unless they were solemnized before the ministers of the Established Church, Catholics were compelled to go before them to obtain the legal validity of their marriage and the legal security of their estates. But they went before the minister of the Established Church, not as a minister of religion, but as a civil authority, and for civil effects. Their Catholic marriage was the only marriage they recognized as perfect and valid before God and man; but, for its civil recognition and legal validity, they were compelled by penal laws to appear before the appointed civil officer, who was also a minister of the established religion. When, however, in the year 1836, this penal law was abolished, and the validity of Catholic marriages, with the presence of the Registrar, was legalized, the Registrar took the place of the Protestant clergyman, as the Protestant clergyman had until then discharged the office of the Registrar. From that moment the necessity of appearing before him ceased for all civil effects; and no other lawful motive for a Catholic to appear before him could exist. Thenceforward he could only be regarded as a minister of religion; and to go before him as such for any religious act, and especially for matrimony, which a Catholic knows to be a Sacrament, has ever been and ever must be forbidden, as an act intrinsically sinful. The highest authority in the Church declares such an act to be "unlawful and sacrilegious."

This, then, is no new or arbitrary law, recently enacted by us. It is as old as the Church, and directly, and by necessity, resulting from the unity of Catholic Faith.

We cannot but add another reason which ought to weigh with our fellow-countrymen, and to satisfy every just mind. The Catholic Church recognizes as perfect and valid the marriages of the people of England contracted before the law of the land, if there be no impediment which in itself annuls the contract. The Catholic Church does not re-marry those of the English people who are received into its unity. It regards them as already man and wife, and their children as legitimate. Therefore if any Catholic solemnize a mixed marriage before the Registrar, or before the Protestant Minister, the Catholic Church refuses to re-marry them. For two obvious reasons: first they are already married; and secondly, the Catholic party has committed a sacrilegious act. If the Catholic Church know before-hand that a Catholic intends, after his Catholic marriage, to commit that act of sacrilege, the law of the Church forbids the Catholic clergy to bless such a marriage. The intention to commit sacrilege excludes a Catholic from the Sacraments, and matrimony is a Sacrament. They who chose to forfeit the benediction of the Church chose their own lot. The Church is neither responsible for their act, nor severe in withholding a Sacrament which, if sacrilegiously received, would add sin to sin. But, beloved Brethren and Children in Jesus Christ, you know these things: and we are speaking rather to those who reproach you than to you.

10. And now, in drawing these words of affectionate counsel to an end, we would once more thank God for the graces which have visibly descended upon us since the first Councils of Westminster were held. They met in times when a momentary outburst of fear and of ill-will had revived what lingered and smouldered of the anti-Catholic spirit of England. We were then in the first beginnings of our restoration to order. The walls were raised; but the mortar was yet moist, and the structure had not hardened into solidity. We have now a system covering the whole land. The Church in England is now so rooted and so fruitful, that it needs only time to grow to its fulness. The malevolence which then threatened us has given way before a truer knowledge of what the Catholic Faith and Church really are. For three hundred years both have been studiously hidden from the intelligence of England by penal laws, and by controversial misrepresentation. Ever since the Church regained her liberty, this has become impossible. She is now seen, and heard and known. Englishmen have now for more than forty years, that is for nearly half a century, been with us in our Divine Worship: they have heard our preachers; they have seen our Colleges, Convents, and Schools; they have laid aside suspicions, fears, and hates, in the open light of day. These old superstitions are gone to the moles and to the bats. Educated Englishmen know us better. The poor in England have no animosities against the Faith of their fathers. Our people are mingled with them: they labour together and live together. They are accustomed to see with no wonder, and with good will, our Clergy and our Sisters visiting the sick and the dying in the same neighbourhood, in the same hospital, and even in the same house where they dwell. They have learned that the Catholic religion is the religion of charity, and that the Catholic Church is the Church of the poor. We

have heard them say more than this, but this is enough. There is at this hour spread over the breadth of England a benevolence towards the Catholic Church and the faith of our ancestors such as for three hundred years has never been. For this cause we have no alarms. If here and there violent and disappointed men attempt to rekindle old fires, or to imitate the despotism which is dooming ambitious statesmen to destroy their own works, it does not move us to fear. The world does not go back upon its path. The age of imperial religions is over. The civil powers of the world have separated themselves from God, and are making the experiment of standing by their own strength, and of ruling by their own wisdom. They have refused to learn from the Church of God that without God there is no society among men. They must learn it in the school they have chosen for themselves: that is, in the bitter experience of all who fall from God.

11. Pray then for the people of this land, for whose salvation we should gladly make any sacrifice, and if need be lay down our life. Pray for the Catholic Church in England, that in purity, and fervour, and charity, it may draw to itself the heart of those who are parted from us. Pray that the work of this our Fourth Provincial Council may be accomplished, in the sanctity of our Clergy and the fidelity of our Laity. Pray, above all, for the Vicar of our Lord, now bound for Christ's sake: that he may be shielded from all evil, and that his days may be prolonged to see the rights of justice for which he has stood steadfast through his long Pontificate, assailed by menace, treachery and violence, vindicated once more, and the Church once more in freedom under his paternal sway.

12. Finally, beloved Brethren and Children in Jesus Christ, the Fathers of the Council closed the deliberations of three weeks by an act full of consolation and of confidence. In the last days of the Synod, the Canons of the Cathedral Chapters, with a large number of Theologians and members of the Religious Orders, petitioned us that our proceedings might be closed by an Act of Consecration to the Sacred Heart of our Divine Lord. We joyfully acceded to this request, which morally represented the unanimous desire of the Council: and at the close of the last public Session, after the *Te Deum* had been sung, our last act was to offer up to the Sacred Heart of Jesus a thanksgiving for all the blessings bestowed upon us, upon our Clergy, upon our Flocks, upon the Church in England, and upon England itself; and to consecrate ourselves, and all that we are and have, with all the Acts of this Synod, to the Sacred Heart of our Divine Redeemer.

Synodal Letter on a College of Higher Studies.
(August 11th, 1874.)

The following letter was issued by the Bishops from Birmingham, and ordered to be read in all Churches on Sunday, August 30th, 1874.

Guided and encouraged by the words of our Holy Father Pius IX., we have undertaken the work of forming a College of higher studies for the Catholic youth of England. The Supreme Pontiff, by a special letter, under his own hand, has bestowed upon this work, and upon all who contribute in any way to its accomplishment, his Apostolic Benediction. We therefore proceed to lay before you an account of the nature of this undertaking, and of the reasons which moved us to enter upon it.

When the Catholic Church in England had received once more its perfect Hierarchical order, it had still to complete its internal organisation. The Vicars Apostolic, and the Faithful with them, had laboured in poverty and under penal laws, and despite of every kind of obstruction, to provide education for our Catholic youth. The ancient Universities, the Colleges, and Grammar Schools founded before Henry VIII., were lost to the Church. The impoverishment of the Catholics of England was in nothing more sensible than in the absolute privation of the means of culture. During the last hundred years, by self-denial, heroic constancy of purpose, and unyielding courage in the face of all difficulties, the Catholics of this country succeeded in laying the foundation of five Colleges, which at this day are our chief and noblest monuments of those times. The College of S. Edmund traces its existence back for a hundred years; S. Cuthbert's, at Ushaw, disputes priority with S. Edmund's. Both have passed their centenary. S. Mary's, Oscott, was founded about eighty years ago. The College of S. Peter and S. Paul at Prior Park was founded about the year 1829.

These four Colleges were the work of the Vicars Apostolic; and perhaps no nobler evidence is to be found in England of their wisdom, foresight, and faith. It was indeed an act of confidence, worthy to be not only admired but imitated, when a Bishop in literal poverty laid the first stone of S. Cuthbert's College on a bare hill overlooking the towers of Durham. It arose even then a work of no small proportions. It is now a pile of many quadrangles, exceeding in its magnitude many of our ancient Colleges.

The fifth great College existing among us is the work of the Society of Jesus. In magnitude and appointments the College at Stonyhurst would worthily rank with the foundations of our Catholic ancestors. After these five more ancient Colleges are to be enumerated many excellent foundations, such as Ampleforth and Downside of the Benedictines; S. Mary's, Rugby, of the Order of Charity; and more recently, again, other Colleges of the Society of Jesus and the like.

Such is at this time our provision for the higher education of Catholic youth.

A quarter of a century now has elapsed since the Hierarchy was restored in England. It finds itself possessed of its five great and excellent Colleges, and of a certain number of a lesser class which we forbear to enumerate. But as yet its Colleges are either schools for boys, or for boys and youths mixed together. It has not at this time any separate College for youths entering upon manhood, that is to say, after the ordinary College course is completed, or in other words, from seventeen to twenty-one or twenty-two years of age. It may indeed be said, and with truth, that at some of our greater Colleges courses of more advanced literature and science are provided, of which young men may, if they will, avail themselves. But it can hardly be said that to any great extent they do so, and it is obvious that such a course does not and cannot supply the need of a College in which young men alone are received without the admixture of boys, where more advanced studies can be made, under a discipline more fitted to the age of manhood.

It is therefore manifest that the Bishops of England at this day have need to take up and to carry to its completion the work so nobly begun by their predecessors. It may however be said that the Bishops have not been behindhand in the duty of education; but it is to be remembered that upon them has rested the cure of souls of the whole flock in England. They inherited from the Vicars Apostolic the five Colleges already mentioned, together with the Poor-School Committee, which was founded two years before the restoration of the Hierarchy: and from that date the chief pastoral care of the Bishops has been the Catholic education of their flocks. In the First Provincial Council of Westminster they issued a Pastoral Letter exhorting the Faithful in all their Dioceses to labour for the founding and maintaining of a pure Catholic education for the children of the poor. Even then in that same Pastoral they invited also the the Clergy and Laity to the work of providing for the education of the middle class. The Second Provincial Council was a supplement of the First. In the Third the Bishops dealt with the education of the Clergy in our existing Colleges and with the founding of Seminaries according to the Prescriptions of the Council of Trent. In the Fourth Provincial Council they proceeded to take up the only remaining part of the subject hitherto untouched, namely, the more advanced and higher studies of our youth after the ordinary College course shall have been completed. It may therefore be said that the subject of education, both of the Clergy and of the Laity in all its grades, has been among the chief cares of the Hierarchy from the moment of its foundation; and that the time is come when it must needs take up the work of providing a College of education for more advanced studies for the higher classes of the Laity. To this, as we said in the beginning, we have been invited and impelled in these last years by the Holy See. And in obeying this supreme injunction the Bishops resolved upon two things, the one to petition the Holy See to erect the Hierarchy in England into a Congregation of Studies, the other to proceed at once to the foundation of one College for youths after they shall have passed through our existing Colleges. It will be observed that we refrain from speaking of a Catholic University. In the present state of England, and with its present needs, we have more immediate and urgent works to do. An University in the mediæval sense, namely, an aggregation of Colleges within the circle of any one locality, as at Oxford and Cambridge, is a scheme which we do not, now at least, contemplate. The work of the Church has conformed itself to the needs of the time and of the Catholics of England. Our excellent Colleges are scattered over the surface of the country. They form centres of education to the North and to the South, to the West and to the Midland parts of England. Their action is thereby more diffused and beneficent than if they were transplanted to a common centre. Nevertheless, in framing the outline of this undertaking, care has been used so to frame it that all the Colleges in England may, if they will, stand in relation to a common centre, namely, the Bishops with the aid of a Senate in which two-thirds shall be laymen. In this Senate the Heads of Colleges, with the Heads of Religious Orders having Colleges, together with the Clergy and Laity chosen from all parts of England, have place. It has been so composed that any existing College, if it should so desire at any time, may stand in relation with it and find in it a representative. It is to be hoped that hereafter the means of encouraging and elevating our general intellectual culture by uniform action may thus be found. Every College in England might stand related to this central authority, without in any respect losing its own independence. Anything which should in any degree affect or interfere with the autonomy and inward administration of a College must gravely affect its efficiency. And from this, with the greatest watchfulness, we shall carefully guard whatsoever may be done hereafter. In taking as the model of their work the Congregation of Studies created by Leo XII. the Bishops were desirous of showing that every College would continue to possess intact and inviolate its own independence. In the constitution of that Congregation it is carefully provided that the Religious Orders shall enjoy undiminished the privileges and exemptions granted to them by the Holy See. Episcopal Seminaries are expressly exempted. This secures the independence of their Colleges from all interference on the part of any authority except the Holy See alone. In like manner the autonomy of our own Episcopal Colleges will be equally recognised and guaranteed. Having put this beyond the possibility of question or of doubt, we will go on to state what are the benefits to be acquired by all Colleges in union with a common centre.

First, it would be of great mutual advantage that all who are engaged in education should be able to interchange their experience and information. It is by comparison of methods and results that progress is to be made in all branches of knowledge. And inasmuch as education is in so great a degree a practical and empirical work, it is of especial use that all who are engaged in the formation of character and the communication of knowledge should be able to obtain the experience of others, and to test their own. The first great benefit would therefore obviously accrue to the Rectors, Professors, and Directors of our Colleges. Hitherto distance, constant labour at home, and the absence of any common centre, or stimulus to mutual communication, has caused and maintained an isolation from which it does not appear that any good can result.

Secondly, Premiums and Burses may be hereafter offered for proficiency in Literature, Science, and Art, which cannot fail to stimulate the industry of students, and therefore to raise their efficiency. Essays may be rewarded by prizes. A system of comparative examinations may be gradually created, and the results given in the form of class-lists.

Thirdly, a public interest and a spirit of co-operation, which, by reason of the isolation of our Colleges, has not and could not hitherto exist among them and among the Catholics of England at large, would be thereby created. The day may come when the Catholics of this country will look forward to the result of such comparative examinations with as much interest as may be seen at this time in other systems of education existing around us. And we may believe that the standard of culture and of efficiency in Literature and Science would be steadily raised and matured both in Professors and in Students throughout the Catholic Church in England. We refrain from entering at this time into the machinery whereby such a system may be carried into effect. All such details would be for the Central Council or Senate to suggest. We cannot leave this point without adding a few words on the present standard of efficiency of our existing education. In no country of the world was the Catholic Church more utterly stripped of the means of education than in England. A century ago it began once more, as we have said, in extreme penury of all resources, and what was harder, also in extreme privation of the means of intellectual culture, to form again on our own soil its Collegiate system. When we see what has been effected by others who possess the richest endowments, the traditional culture of the nation, the flower of its youth, a complete and wealthy provision of professional chairs, it is a matter of thankfulness and of wonder that in England we should both in Literature and in Science possess anything to compare with them. We do not indeed so far deceive ourselves as to believe that in the standard of efficiency attained and maintained by individuals in the great national seats of learning we can bear comparison, but in the equable and wide-spread cultivation of primary studies of a higher kind we believe that the average of our youth leave our Colleges with an extent and accuracy of information not inferior to the average of English youth.

But we must not be content with a comparison with a standard which is described by authorities who best know it as below what the means at their command and the demands of true intellectual cultivation require. The Catholic Church, as the "Mater Altrixque Scientiarum," has known how to press onward in raising the efficiency of its students and in promoting the habits of conscientious and industrious intellectual cultivation. What it has done it can still do; what it did once in England it can do again. It has no need to go out of its own field to seek for an impulse or a stimulus to higher aims. Moreover, it retains—and we sorrow for England when we say it—it alone retains the method of study which has created the Christian civilisation of the world. It retains, as a first axiom of truth, that all sciences, sacred and secular, flow from one source; and as a first principle of the highest education of man, that these sciences may never be put asunder. The Christian Philosophy which made the ancient Universities in vigour and solidity what they were has given place to a philosophy which claims as its perfection that it begins by destroying all belief. From this sceptical development of the national intellect, penal laws, social exile, exclusion from the public and national schools of learning, have saved us. We have our inheritance by a lineal descent, inviolate in all its principles, instincts, and spirit. What the Supreme Pontiff laid down as the true basis of scientific education we still possess as an heirloom from our forefathers. After declaring that Catholics are able, by adhering to the principle of the unity of all truth and the supremacy of revelation, to cultivate, to explain, and to render certain and useful all sciences, His Holiness adds, "which cannot be attained, if the light of human reason, bounded as it is even in the investigation of natural truths, attainable by its own powers and faculties, shall not venerate above all, as is due, the infallible and uncreated light of the Divine intelligence which shines forth everywhere in a wonderful way in the revelation of Christianity. For although the natural sciences depend on their own first principles, which are ascertained by reason, Catholic students ought to have before their eyes Divine revelation as a guiding star, to warn them by its light of quicksands and errors, where, in their studies and researches, they perceive that they may be led, as is often the case, to publish matters more or less contrary to the infallible truth revealed by God." *

The same also is declared by the Vatican Council in its definition of the relations of Reason and Faith:

---

* Apostolic Letter of Pope Pius IX., *Tuas libenter*, Dec. 21, 1863.

"For although faith is above reason, there can never be any real discrepancy between faith and reason, since the same God who reveals mysteries and infuses faith has bestowed the light of reason on the human mind; and God cannot deny Himself, nor can truth ever contradict truth. The false appearance of such a contradiction is mainly due either to the dogmas of faith not having been understood and expounded according to the mind of the Church, or to the inventions of opinion having been taken for the verdicts of reason. We define, therefore, that every assertion contrary to truth of enlightened faith is utterly false. Further, the Church, which, together with the Apostolic office of teaching, has received a charge to guard the deposit of faith, derives from God the right and the duty of proscribing false science, lest any should be deceived by philosophy and vain deceit. Therefore, all faithful Christians are not only forbidden to defend, as legitimate conclusions of science, such opinions as are known to be contrary to the doctrines of faith, especially if they have been condemned by the Church, but are altogether bound to account them as errors which put on the fallacious appearance of truth.

"And not only can faith and reason never be opposed to one another, but they are of mutual aid one to the other; for right reason demonstrates the foundations of faith, and enlightened by its light cultivates the science of things divine; while faith frees and guards reason from errors, and furnishes it with manifold knowledge. So far, therefore, is the Catholic Church from opposing the cultivation of human arts and sciences, that it in many ways helps and promotes it. For the Church neither ignores nor despises the benefits to human life which result from the arts and sciences, but confesses that as they came from God, the Lord of all science, so, if they be rightly used, they lead to God by the help of His grace. Nor does the Church forbid that each of these sciences in its sphere should make use of its own principles and its own method; but while recognising this just liberty, it stands watchfully on guard, lest sciences, setting themselves against the Divine teaching or transgressing their own limits, should invade and disturb the domain of faith.'" *

Adhering, then, to this unbroken tradition, and to this sacred method of intellectual cultivation, we have resolved to add to the existing Colleges of the Hierarchy a College of more advanced studies. The place selected for it is the Metropolitan Diocese, the ecclesiastical centre of the Catholic Church in England. This intention has been already made public, in a Circular sent by us to such of the Clergy and Laity as have consented to become members of the Council or Senate. We have thought it best to incorporate the same Circular in this Pastoral Letter, for the information of the Clergy and Laity at large. It runs as follows:

1. In the Synodal Letter addressed to the Clergy and the Faithful from the Fourth Provincial Council of Westminster, the Bishops have already made known that the growth of the middle and upper classes of our Laity, and the opening of the career of professional and public service, render it necessary to lay at least the foundations of a system of Higher Studies, such as are required by our youth from seventeen to twenty-one or twenty-two years of age. The development of such a system will, they trust, under God, be gradually made hereafter, as the growing needs of our Catholic Laity demand.

2. The Bishops have been both directed and encouraged to take this

---

* Dogmatic Constitution on the Catholic Faith, chap. iv.

step by the authority of the Holy See, and by the assurance that the powers necessary for its guidance and accomplishment will be granted.

3. They have, therefore, formed an Academical Council or Senate, composed of Clergy and Laity selected from the whole of England, as representing the experience and needs of the Catholics of the higher classes; and also to afford counsel derived from practical acquaintance with Literature, Science, and Art. The Lay Members of this Senate are to the Clerical Members in the proportion of two to one.

4. To this Senate will be committed the office of deliberating and advising on all subjects relating to study, examinations, rewards by prizes, purses, or otherwise; on the selection of lists of names to be proposed as Professors; and generally on all matters involving the welfare and progress of Higher Studies.

5. Inasmuch as the most pressing need felt at this moment is the want of some College wherein those who have passed through the ordinary college course, and are destined for our public service at home or abroad, for the Army, for the duties of public life which locally attach to our higher classes, and for various professions, may obtain, under the securities and guarantees of Catholic Professors and Catholic guidance, a more advanced study of Classics, Modern Languages, Modern History, Constitutional Law; of pure and applied Mathematics; of physical Science in application to certain professional employments; and, above all, a sound course of Mental Science and of the Philosophy of Religion, with a more complete and scientific treatment of the Faith; the Bishops have determined at once to proceed to the formation of one such College, with houses of residence, under the care of Tutors, attached to it : the first, as they hope, of many which, with the growth of our needs and means, may be founded hereafter in other parts of England, under the oversight of the Hierarchy, aided by the same Academical Senate, which has been for that purpose composed of Clergy and Laity selected from all parts of the country.

6. For various reasons, such as the greater number of Students already on the spot and requiring such a College, and the greater facility of obtaining a staff of good Professors and Lecturers, as well as the actual possession of a locality well adapted for such a beginning, the Bishops have decided to open a College at Kensington. They will be able by this commencement to test by experience the advantages of such a position as compared with the country.

7. The Bishops have invited the Right Rev. Monsignor Capel to undertake the formation of such a College. Monsignor Capel has expressed his willingness to do so, and to employ for the purpose the locality and the provision he has hitherto been making for the purpose of education.

8. The course of studies will be so ordered as to enable the students to present themselves for the Civil Service and other Examinations; and when required, to obtain such degrees as confer advantages in the practice of certain professions, and which, under the present state of legislation, can be obtained by Catholics at the London University only.

From what has been said in the above circular, it will be seen that the College we propose to found is not to be regarded as an University. It is strictly a College, and the first of this kind, placing itself in relation to the Council or Senate of advice. If at any future time other colleges existing in various parts of England should desire to confederate themselves together round the same centre, preserving their own independence inviolate if they be Colleges of the Hierarchy, and preserving all their exemptions and privileges intact if they be Colleges of Religious Orders, then an approximation would be made to the idea of an University not, as we have before said, to be congregated in one place, but dispersed throughout England, and yet confederated round one common centre. It is in hope that such a system of mutual sympathy, co-operation, and support may, under the providence of God, one day be formed, that the Senate contains among its members those who represent our existing Colleges. There would then be a system of education extending all over England, occupying its chief districts, and bringing education home to the most popular localities, and at the same time knit together so as to form one solid and compact organisation for the promotion of pure Catholic education in Literature and Science, and for the perpetuity of the methods and principles of study and of training which the Catholic Church has ever inviolably maintained.

Having thus fully explained to you, Reverend and dear Brethren, and dear Children in Jesus Christ, the outline and description of this undertaking, to which we very earnestly invite your sympathy and help, we will explicitly lay before you the way in which you can render assistance to our work.

The sum requested for the site and for the preparation of lecture-rooms, a theatre, and other lesser rooms in the house already standing on the property, may be put at about £25,000. Of this about one-half will be required by Christmas next; and a certain annual income for the first five years, the need of which would diminish as the number of students increases. These arrangments have been so made as to reduce to the utmost the cost of the first foundation, and to avoid all outlay in erecting new buildings whereby the College would be burdened with permanent debt. It is our desire to bring into existence first of all the living system of the College, its professors and Students, being convinced that, when its value is known and its benefits are seen, adequate means for future building and endowment will not be wanting. We begin again, as our forefathers began before, in poverty and patience and faith, confiding in the law of Divine Providence which never fails that when works needful for His Church are prudently begun, though much tried, and it may be for a long time tested by adversity, they never fail to root themselves, and in the end to prosper

We turn therefore to you, our Clergy and our Laity, to aid us in this vital, necessary, and arduous work. It is a work for the whole of England; and we appeal to you as the Pastors of the whole flock in England. We are responsible for the maintenance of the Catholic education of both Clergy and Laity; we are bound to hand it on as we have received it, pure and unchanged, without contact with modern and dangerous methods, untainted with the aberrations of science, falsely so called, and with Philosophy at a variance with faith. We remind you once more of the warnings of the Supreme Pontiff addressed to parents who expose their sons to the dangerous influence of systems contrary to the Faith. Unless our system of education be completed, as an arch is tied by its keystone, with a sound course of higher studies, the Catholic youth of England will, many of them at least, not only enter life and its professions without adequate formation, but will be compelled to seek their last studies from teachers and systems at least external to the unity of truth. We have before our eyes in France and in Germany the fatal consequences of higher education without the supremacy of faith and separate from the pastoral office of the Church. When the youth of a nation are formed in Universities and Colleges from which the traditions of Catholic culture and training are excluded a Laity grows up Catholic in name, but without Catholic insincts or a Catholic mind. The first effect of this must be that the Clergy and Laity, being diversely trained and formed, are first parted from each other in sympathy, and then opposed in spirit and in action. The internal Catholic unity is thereby perpetually disintegrating, until it is irremediably destroyed. The public opinion and legislation of such a people, as may be seen at this time in Germany, becomes not only uncatholic, but, anticatholic. The next effect in such a downward course is that the State shall claim to form the Clergy also to its own likeness. The whole Divine order is thus inverted, and the State endeavours to bring the Catholic faith under the administration of Government officials, or to prescribe it under penal laws. Such is the state of the law in Germany now at this time; such was the state of England once; such must be the state of Catholics in all countries if they do not preserve inviolate the traditions of Catholic education, its principles, method, and spirit. We appeal to you, therefore, not to give alms to educate the sons of the richer and upper classes—let no one so misconceive the breadth and importance of this work—we call on you to help us in completing a system which shall consolidate the Catholic education of England which shall draw to a centre its present widespread and noble efforts, and add one more College of a distinct and higher kind to those already founded by the Vicars Apostolic and by the Hierarchy since its restoration. It is not our purpose, therefore, to ask the offerings of the poor of our Flocks. They contribute year by year, and in their own homes all the year round, for their own children. But we earnestly ask of those who possess wealth, or even a sufficiency, that they help us in this undertaking. We especially ask of you to send your contribution, if you are able, in one sum at once, or to spread it over a number of years, or to leave it by Will to be applied hereafter. The amount needed for the first foundation of this College is a sum not so large as many spend in the gratification of some personal taste or some personal ambition. We would earnestly exhort you to do or to share in the doing of one such solid, lasting, and fruitful work, which shall hand your names down to the Catholic posterity of England as the many names of our forefathers which are still remembered day by day with benediction. It is not our voice only that speaks to you; the voice of the Vicar of our Lord has commended this work to your conscience and heart. Our Holy Father Pius the Ninth has bestowed his especial benediction upon all who help us. Lay this appeal to heart. Meditate upon it till you have measured its importance, and then give your offering as the greatness of this undertaking, as your fidelity to the faith of Catholic England, and as your desire for the greater glory of God shall prompt you.

APPENDIX.

Mode of Procedure in Ecclesiastical Trials.

The Bishops of England in their Low Week meeting of the year 1884, petitioned the Holy See to approve of certain additions to the decrees of the first and fourth Synods of Westminster, which treat of the conducting of causes against clerics. To approach those causes with the caution they deserve, and to lay before the Ecclesiastical authorities in Rome as accurately as possible all questions connected therewith, especially questions of fact, the Bishops deemed it desirable, after sentence had been passed, not to allow an appeal to be made to the Holy See straight from the Court of the Ordinary, as had been decreed; but first of all to bring the case before the Metropolitan. The following mode of procedure was therefore suggested by the Bishops:—

1. As often as any cleric, after trial by the Commission of Investigation, shall wish to lay an appeal against a sentence passed upon him by his Ordinary, this appeal shall be made, first of all, to the Metropolitan, who will submit to a second examination the process resulting from the first inquiry, and will examine afresh the cause according to the method prescribed for the Commissions of Investigation.

2. To constitute a Commission in the case of an appeal to the Metropolitan, three assessors will be chosen, to be selected from seven priests, nominated for this purpose by the Bishops every year in their meeting after Easter.

3. From the sentence of the Metropolitan it will always be lawful to appeal to the Holy See according to the decrees of the Sacred Canons.

4 In case of an appeal, the acts both of the first and second investigations are to be sent to Rome in writing.

5. If the first investigation should take place in the Metropolitan diocese, and the priest be therefore a subject of the Archbishop, the second investigation shall be made by the senior Suffragan, who will consult the Assessors of the Commission of Investigation of that diocese.

By a decree of the *Sacred Congregation of Propaganda*, dated the 28th of last June, 1884, the suggestions of the Bishops received the formal approval of the Holy See, and will, therefore, become for the future part of the Canon Law of this country.

Non-Catholic Universities.

The following Letter from the Sacred Congregation of Propaganda has been addressed to His Eminence Cardinal Manning:—

ROME, *January 30th, 1885.*

My Lord Cardinal,

I have received your Eminence's letter of the 20th of last month, and have learnt from it with pain that by some families little account is made of the admonitions of the Holy See as to sending their sons to the Protestant Universities. The letter points out that this arises, not so much from a want of good will as from their supposing that what they do is tolerated by the Holy See. To guard, therefore, the higher education of the Catholic youth of your country from this danger of perversion, I request that you will make known to the faithful that no change whatever has taken place in respect to the instructions upon this matter which were sent by my predecessor Cardinal Barnabò to the English Bishops on August 6th, 1867, and were afterwards inserted in the Provincial Synods of Westminster. For this purpose I should think it opportune to suggest to the Bishops of England to recall the said instructions to the remembrance of their flocks.

Your Eminence's humble and devoted Servant,

JOHN CARDINAL SIMEONI,
Prefect.

✠ D., Archbishop of Tyre,
Secretary.

His Eminence
The Cardinal Archbishop of Westminister.

✱✱✱ The instructions here referred are found at p. 254.

MASSES FOR DECEASED PRIESTS.

The "Pact."

The following Rescript, from the Sacred Congregation of Propaganda, is dated July 5, 1885.

Most Holy Father,

The Bishop of Clifton, prostrate at your Holiness's feet, humbly sets forth in his own name and that of the other Bishops of England, that on April 13, 1869, the Sovereign Pontiff Pius IX of happy memory, at the prayer of the Bishops of England, approved and confirmed a certain declaration in regard to Associations existing in England under the name of "Deceased Clergy Associations" (in which the members are bound to celebrate Mass for members deceased); a declaration in virtue of which no priest could enter the Association and so become entitled to the Masses after three years from the date of his entry into a diocese.

Now whereas it seems that the rule established by such declaration is neither altogether clear and certain—the declaration having actually been interpreted in more senses than one—nor always equal and fair in its operation, therefore the Petitioners (the Bishops aforesaid) humbly beg that in its stead your Holiness would establish the following new rule, viz.:—henceforth any priest whatever may at any time be enrolled in the above-named Associations, but that to become entitled to the Masses, he must have survived the date of his enrolment by one year. And as regards those who are enrolled in one of these Associations, and who shall remove into the other division of England, that these, on becoming enrolled afresh in the other Association, shall be entitled to the Masses at once without the year's delay. Wherefore, &c.

AT AN AUDIENCE OF HIS HOLINESS ON JULY 5, 1885

Our Most Holy Lord Leo XIII by Divine Providence Pope, on the report of me, the undersigned Substitute of the Sacred Congregation of Propaganda, was graciously pleased to grant the prayer of the foregoing petition given at Rome, at the Residence of the aforesaid Congregation, on the day and in the year already named.

PHILIP TORRONI,
Substitute,

L. ✠ S.

The following document, also from Propaganda, relates to the Missionary Oath :—

DECREE.

The Right Rev. the Bishop of Clifton in his own name and that of the other Bishops of England, has humbly implored of the Apostolic See, that the Oath taken by those who are ordained *titulo missionis* may bind them, not for one diocese only, as the custom has hitherto been, but for the whole ecclesiastical Province, so that priests thus ordained may, with the consent of both Ordinaries, be transferred from one diocese into another merely by the conferring of a fresh title, without the necessity of taking a fresh Oath. Moreover, he has petitioned that, as regards the past, missioners ordained *titulo missionis* for any diocese within the Province, may be transferred to another diocese within the Province by a new title and on taking a fresh Oath without recourse to the Apostolic See.

This petition having been presented to our Most Holy Lord Leo XIII, at an audience on June 28, 1885, His Holiness deigned to grant it in all particulars and ordered the present Decree to issue.

Given at Rome, at the house of the Sacred Congregation of Propaganda, August 18, 1885.

JOHN CARDINAL SIMEONI,
Prefect.

✠ D. Archbishop of Tyre,
Secretary.

Form of Petition for Dispensation from Publication of Banns.

MY LORD,

N. N. and N. N. *(here insert names)*, wishing to contract marriage, humbly beg for a dispensation from the triple publication of banns. The undersigned knows that no lawful impediment to such a marriage exists. The reasons for asking for this dispensation are...............

(To be signed by the priest who forwards the petition).

Dispensation for a Mixed Marriage.

MY LORD,

The undersigned applies for a dispensation, in order that A. B.,[1] a Catholic of the congregation of................., may marry C. D.,[1] a Protestant.

Both have promised that all the children, male and female, shall be baptized and brought up Catholics.

The Protestant party promises to allow A. B. the free exercise of the Catholic religion ;

And the Catholic undertakes to use every endeavour to induce the other party to adopt the true faith.

The undersigned believes that the dispensation may be granted, because..................

..............................*(Signature).*

For an ordinary Matrimonial Dispensation.

MY LORD,

Titus *(say whether Cath. or Prot.)* wishes to marry Bertha *(say whether Cath. or Prot.)*, notwithstanding an existing impediment of consanguinity (*or* affinity) in the............degree. Wherefore they humbly beg (*or* the Catholic party begs) that your Lordship will give the necessary dispensation to enable them validly and licitly to contract marriage.

I, N. N., priest, believe that such a dispensation may and ought to be given for the following reasons...............

N.B.—*In the above petition the real names of the parties are to be distinctly inserted where "Titius" and "Bertha" are put, unless there be a cognatio ex crimine.*

---

1. State real names.

INDEX.

A

ABSTINENCE. *See* Fasting.
ADVERTISEMENTS — of Singing, &c. 188
ALMS—Obligation of—to Church, Schools, Poor . . . 148
—— When to be considered Church Property . . 160
—— Collecting . . . 216
ARCHIVES—Diocesan . . 53
———— Of Missions . 172

B

BANNS—Of Marriage . . 147
—— Before Ordination . 241
BENCH RENTS . . 45, 161
BISHOPS. *See* References at p. 71

C

CANONS—Penitentiary and Theologian . . . 103, 112
CATECHISM—To be explained by Priest . . . 132, 153
———— Especially to *Confirmandi* . . . 137
———— And in the Confessional . . 142, 228, 231
———— Preparation for teaching . . . 239, 240
———— Revised Edition of 288
CEMETERIES—Catholic . 153
CHOIR — Attendance at, by Canons . . . 103, 7. 111
—— Dress . . . 101, 118
—— Dress of Regular Canons . 128
—— Women to be excluded from 141
COADJUTORS—Consultative Voice only in Provincial Synods 15
COMMISSION—of Inquiry . 53, 155
———— Procedure of 157, 184
———— Necessary in case of Deprivation of a Missioner . . . 183
———— in Appeals 309

COMMUNION—Paschal, . 140, 142
———— of Students . 228
CONFERENCES—Theological . 151
———— Regulars to attend . . . 202
CONFESSIONALS . . . 141
CONFRATERNITIES . . 65-8
———— of Christian Doctrine . . . 139, 153
CONVERTS—Irregularities on part of for Ordination . . 53
———— Confirmation of . 137
———— Confessions of 142, 262
———— Baptism of and Profession of Faith . . 262
———— Prayer for . . 273

D

DEANS—Rural . . . 52
—— should furnish Inventory to new Incumbents . 161
DIOCESE—Additional . . 8
———— Changes in limits of 8
———— Claim of Liverpool to Precedence . . . 13
———— Temporalities of . 52
———— Archives of . . 53
DOMICILE—for Marriage . 58, 77
DRESS—of Canons . 101,118
—— of Regular Canons . 128
—— of Priests . . 150, 177
—— the Beard . . . 178
—— of Regulars . . . 194
—— of Mendicant Brothers 217
—— of Church Students . 240
DUPLICATION . . 89, 140

E

EDUCATION—of Children . 172
———— of the Clergy 218, 239, 286
———— Clerical with Lay . . . 226, 235
———— Errors regarding 244
———— Higher 246, 270, 293, 299, 301
———— Mixed 247, 285, 306

EDUCATION—of the Poor 267, 284, 301
ELECTION—of Canons . . 103
——— of Bishops
104, 107, 108, 114
——— of Regular Canons 121
EXAMINERS—Diocesan . . 53, 56
——————— for Junior Clergy 152
——————— for Students 216, 236
——————— Board of, in place
of University . . . 253

F

FACULTIES—of Missionary
Rector and Junior Clergy
151, 175
——————— at Sea . . . 184
——————— of Regulars . 194, 213
——————— for Confessions of
Nuns 216
——————— of Students . . 230
——————— Formulæ of, for
Bishops 258
FAITH—Profession of . 47, 152
——— Orthodox . . . 130
——— Profession of, for Converts 262
——— Unity in, of English Catholics 292
——— and Reason . . 304
FASTING—in Lent . . 148
——————— use of Lard . . 258
——————— of Butter . . 259
——————— Dispensations . . 260
FONT 134-5

G

GIFTS. See Alms and Offerings.

H

HIERARCHY—Established
1, 98, 155, 231
HOLY SEE. See Rome.
HOUSE—of Priest . . 150, 174
——— Under Control of Incumbent 152
——— Funeral Rites at . 153
——— Common Table in Priests' 175
——— Religious, Foundation
of 104, 216
——— Privileges of Religious 200

L

LAW—Study of Canon . 231, 239
LEEDS—Diocese of, constituted 8

LETTERS—Dimissorial . . 42
——————— of ex-Corporation
("Exeats") . . 42, 154
——————— Commendatory 43, 154
——————— Testimonial, for Religious 214
——————— Use of Latin Language
in 264
——————— Synodal . . 266

M

MASS—Requiem . . . 67
——— Pro-populo . . 67, 203
——— Vestments, Chalice, etc.,
the Week-day and Sunday
M. 138
——— Rubrics and Singing . 141
——— on Holy Days . . 148
——— Anniversary . . 153
——— Prayers before and after 154
——— Retribution for . . 162
——— Requiem, for Priests . 167
——— Obligations . . 172-3
——— Fixed Times for . . 174
——— Low instead of High . 184
——— Roman Chant at . 187
——— not to be interrupted by
Music 188
——— Use of Organ at . . 192
MATRIMONY—Causes (in foro
externo) 57
. ——— Defender of . 58
——— Proofs requisite
previous to second Marriage 59
——— Mixed Marriages
61, 147, 296
——— before Non-Catholic
Ministers . . 62, 207
——— Dispensations 78, 147
——— Banns Confession,
Impediments . . . 147
——— Travellers and
Foreigners . . 58, 147
——— Divorce . . 287
MIDDLESBOROUGH—Diocese of,
constituted . . . 8
MISSION—New, Boundaries of,
etc. 155-6, 164, 204
——— Served by Regulars 160, 203
——— Support and Property
of . . . 148, 161, 165, 210
——— Accounts . . 163
——— Archives . . 172
MUSIC—Church Music . 185, *sqq*
——— Plain Chant . . 216

N

NEWPORT and MENEVIA—Benedictine Chapter, Statutes of . 119
——————————— constituted 122
NON-CATHOLIC—Schools . 131-2
———————— Children-Baptism of 134
———————— Doctors attending Sick 145
———————— Children in Catholic Schools and Convents 251
NUNS—Foundations, Visitation, Rules, Confessions, Dowries of 216
——— Work with the Sick . 277

O

OATH—Missionary 76, 159, 171, 183, and *App.*
OFFERINGS 161
————— Stole Fees . . 162
————— to Begging Clerics 163
————— to Bishops on Visitation 73
————— the Cathedraticum 165
————— to Missions of Regulars 210
ORDINATIONS . . . 53
————— Title to 55-7, 74, 146, 171
————— Knowledge of Subjects for 56
————— in Cathedral, etc. 145
————— Irregularities 55, 145
————— Examinations, Banns, Interstices, etc. . 146
————— Banns previous to 241
ORGAN—when and how to be played 191

P

PARISHES—Erection of, postponed for the present . 156
PERFECTION—in Bishops . 45
PONTIFICALS—Use of . 42, 83
PORTSMOUTH—Diocese of, constituted 9
PRECEDENCE—of Bishops and others . . . 13, 17
————— of the Vicar-Capitular 110
————— of the Vicar-General 111

PRESBYTERY. *See* House, Priests not to live out of . . 175
PROVOST— . . 103, 110, 112

R

RECREATION—Kinds of, to be shunned by Clerics, 149, 176
————— for People . . 177
RECTORS—Missionary, Irremoveable unless, etc. . 53, 155
————— Faculties of . 151
————— Appointment of . 154
————— quasi-Parish Priests 155
————— Decrees of Propaganda 156 175.
REGISTERS—Baptismal . 134
————— for Confirmation . 137
————— Marriage . . 147
————— Deaths . . 152
REGULARS—Canons of Newport and Menevia . . . 119
————— Removal of Missionaries 193
————— Temporalities 195, 209
————— Residence . . 196
————— Exemption of . 199
————— Attendance at Conference 201
————— with the Sick . 277
————— at the Third Synod 280
————— at Synods . . 202
————— Dividing of Missions 203
————— Elementary Schools 205
————— Colleges . . *Ib.*
————— New Foundations 207
RELIGION—Support of . . 148
RESIDENCE—on the part of Bishops . . . 47, 82
————— Priests 154, 164
RETREATS—for Clergy . . 151
————— for Laity . 154
ROME—Visits, *ad limina* 41, 84, 172
————— Decrees of Provincial Synods to be submitted to 291
RULES—Necessity of, for Clerics 241

S

SACRAMENT—Most Holy, in Domestic Chapels . . 64
————— Instructions concerning 137
————— Sodality of . 139
————— Benediction of 133. 159
————— Devotion to . 140

SACRAMENT—Viaticum 140, 153
────── Purifying Ciborium, Tabernacle, Altar Linen, etc. 153
────── Visits to, on part of Priests . . . 152
SACRAMENTS—Place for, Ceremonies, Vestments, Rubrics 133
────── Fees on occasion of 162
────── Hours for . . 174
SCHOOLS—Non-Catholic . 131-2
────── under supervision of Incumbent . . . 152
────── Day, Sunday, and Night 153
────── belong to places where erected 160
────── of Regulars . 195-6, 205
────── Poor, Ecclesiastical Inspection . . . 269
────── Middle . . . 270
────── Efficiency of Catholic, in England . . . 292
SOCIETIES—Secret and Forbidden . . . 255
────── Fenianism . . 258
SODALITY of Blessed Sacrament 139
SPONSORS—Baptism . . 134
────── Confirmation . 137
STATIONS of the Cross . . 66-8
STATUS ANIMARUM—by Bishops to the Holy See . 42, 50, 172
────── by Incumbents 152, 172
────── by nearest Priest . 164
STATUTES—Capitular . 109, 116
STUDY—Importance of, to Priests 151, 178
SYNODS—Diocesan annually . 42
────── Summary of Work of 290

SYNODS—Decrees of Provincial to be submitted to Holy See 42, 291
────── and published by Bishop in Diocesan . . . 42

V

VICAR—General . . . 52
────── Capitular . . 104, 114
VISITATION . . . 41, 44
────── Offerings at . 73
────── Churches of Regulars subject to, 193, 195, 209, 213
────── of Nuns . . 216

W

WESTMINSTER—First Provincial Synod of—Decrees approved 18, 22
────── Indiction . . 39
────── Mode of Life during 35
────── Second Synod, Approval of Decrees . . 243
────── Third Synod, Approval of Decrees . . 27
────── Fourth Synod, Indiction and Edict of . 32
WINE—Purity of Altar 64, 140
WOMEN—to be excluded from Choirs 141
────── Confessions of . . 141
────── Priests' Housekeepers 150
────── in Houses of Priests . 174
WORLD—Business of, forbidden to Clerics . . 151, 172
────── Wills . , . 153
────── Burthens on Missions . 154
────── Music, Savouring of, forbidden 188

www.ingramcontent.com/pod-product-compliance
Lightning Source LLC
Chambersburg PA
CBHW030739230426
43667CB00007B/769